UNDEAD SOUTHS

SOUTHERN LITERARY STUDIES

Scott Romine, Series Editor

THE GOTHIC AND BEYOND
IN SOUTHERN LITERATURE AND CULTURE

UNDEAD SOUTHS

Edited by
ERIC GARY ANDERSON, TAYLOR HAGOOD,
and **DANIEL CROSS TURNER**

Louisiana State University Press   Baton Rouge

Published by Louisiana State University Press
lsupress.org

Copyright © 2015 by Louisiana State University Press
All rights reserved. Except in the case of brief quotations used in articles or reviews, no part of this publication may be reproduced or transmitted in any format or by any means without written permission of Louisiana State University Press.

Louisiana Paperback Edition, 2022

Designer: Barbara Neely Bourgoyne
Typeface: Chaparral Pro

Cover image: *Broken Wing*, Melissa W. Miller, 1986. Oil on linen. 58 x 66 inches. Photo by Bill Kennedy. Courtesy of National Museum of Women in the Arts, Washington, D.C.

Library of Congress Cataloging-in-Publication Data

Undead souths : the gothic and beyond in southern literature and culture / edited by Eric Gary Anderson, Taylor Hagood, and Daniel Cross Turner.

   pages cm. — (Southern literary studies)
Includes bibliographical references and index.
  ISBN 978-0-8071-6107-4 (cloth : alk. paper) — ISBN 978-0-8071-6108-1 (pdf) — ISBN 978-0-8071-6109-8 (epub) — ISBN 978-0-8071-7858-4 (paperback)
   1. American literature—Southern States—History and criticism. 2. Gothic revival (Literature)—Southern States. 3. Literature and society—Southern States. 4. Southern States—In literature. 5. Southern States—In motion pictures. I. Anderson, Eric Gary, 1960– editor. II. Hagood, Taylor, 1975– editor. III. Turner, Daniel Cross, editor.
  PS261.U45 2015
  810.9′975—dc23

2015019975

CONTENTS

ACKNOWLEDGMENTS | ix

Introduction | 1
ERIC GARY ANDERSON, TAYLOR HAGOOD, and
DANIEL CROSS TURNER

1 Confederacies of Undead Imagination: Going South through Wastelands to *Jonestown* | 10
KEITH CARTWRIGHT

2 The Fall of the House of Po' Sandy: Poe, Chesnutt, and Southern Undeadness | 23
ERIC GARY ANDERSON

3 What Remains Where: Civil War Poetry and Photography across 150 Years | 36
ELIZABETH BRADFORD FRYE and COLEMAN HUTCHISON

4 Gray Ghosts: Remediating the Confederate Undead | 52
DANIEL CROSS TURNER

5 Melville's Zombies, North and South | 64
SASCHA MORRELL

6 Topographical Ghosts: The Archival Architecture of Old New Orleans | 76
SARAH HIRSCH

CONTENTS

7. Faulkner's Doom: The Undead Inhabitants of
   Yoknapatawpha | 88
   MELANIE BENSON TAYLOR

8. Faulkner's Deathways: The Race and Space of Mourning | 100
   ELIZABETH RODRIGUEZ FIELDER

9. Of Flesh and Bones: Incarnations of the Silenced Past in
   William Faulkner's and Erskine Caldwell's Early Southern
   Gothic Short Stories | 112
   ELSA CHARLÉTY

10. Monstrous Plantations: *White Zombie* and the Horrors
    of Whiteness | 124
    AMY CLUKEY

11. When Dead Men Talk: Emmett Till, Southern Pasts, and
    Present Demands | 136
    BRIAN NORMAN

12. Second Life: Salvage Operations in Cormac McCarthy's
    Undead South | 149
    SUSAN EDMUNDS

13. Last Roads Taken: Robert Frost, Cormac McCarthy, and
    Dying Worlds | 161
    BRYAN GIEMZA

14. Undead Genres/Living Locales: Gothic Legacies in *The True
    Meaning of Pictures* and *Winter's Bone* | 173
    LEIGH ANNE DUCK

15. Burying the (Un)Dead and Healing the Living: Choctaw Women's
    Power in LeAnne Howe's Novels | 187
    KIRSTIN L. SQUINT

16. The Indigenous Uncanny: Spectral Genealogies in LeAnne
    Howe's Fiction | 199
    ANNETTE TREFZER

CONTENTS

17. Crossin' the Log: Death, Regionality, and Race in Jeremy Love's *Bayou* | 211
    RAIN PRUD'HOMME C. GOMÉZ

18. "Life Refusing to End": The Transformative Gothic in Shani Mootoo's *Cereus Blooms at Night* | 224
    JAMEELA F. DALLIS

19. "More Dead Than Living": Randall Kenan's Monstrous Community | 236
    WADE NEWHOUSE

20. Going to Ground: The Undead in Contemporary Southern Popular Culture Media and Writing | 248
    TAYLOR HAGOOD

    Making Darkness Visible: An Afterword and an Appreciation | 261
    SUSAN V. DONALDSON

    WORKS CITED | 267
    CONTRIBUTORS | 293
    INDEX | 299

ACKNOWLEDGMENTS

The editors would like to take this opportunity to acknowledge some of this book's debts. We first want to thank the scholars who broke the ground of the "Southern Gothic" such as Louis D. Rubin and Elizabeth M. Kerr. Susan V. Donaldson, Anne Goodwyn Jones, and others furthered that work, and we are especially excited that Susan has written the afterword for this volume. She mentions in her afterword Patricia Yaeger, and we, too, want to acknowledge how much this book owes to her.

Many thanks to Margaret Lovecraft and Louisiana State University Press for taking on this project and for moving the collection forward so skillfully and efficiently. We appreciate crucial insights provided by the anonymous reviewer and by Southern Literary Studies series editor Scott Romine that strengthened the collection. Finally, we want to thank our contributors, who have made this project a realization; we have learned so much from you and have taken great pleasure in the ways you have expanded our original vision.

UNDEAD SOUTHS

INTRODUCTION

ERIC GARY ANDERSON, TAYLOR HAGOOD,
and DANIEL CROSS TURNER

When William Faulkner wrote, "The past is never dead. It's not even past," he probably wasn't thinking about zombies. But these sentences, which themselves rise up again and again, call to mind the pervading presence of diverse forms of undeadness—racial, ethnic, political, economic, historical—in "the South" as we understand it. *Undead Souths* considers literature, films, and other media that explore representations of death and deathways as well as figures returned from the grave. Undeadness describes a wide continuum of posthumous phenomena, from funerary rites and mourning practices to the shocking, overwhelming affect of terrifying spectacles and posttraumatic flashbacks, to figures from beyond death: ghosts, vampires, zombies, but also corpses unburied, decayed, desecrated, dismembered, yet still filled with life, or a kind of life, be it with the multitude of microorganisms drawing sustenance from decomposing bodies or the psychical afterlife of remembering the dead. This necrological impulse can also incarnate in metaphorical ways in texts that may not feature literal revenants but that present tropes of undeadness.

This collection engages such forms of southern haunting in a variety of historical and intercultural contexts that can be seen as being part of the South. Certain elements present themselves immediately in recognizably "southern" situations in conventional notions of the U.S. South. For example, zombification has been offered as a telling metaphor for the institution of race-based chattel slavery in the U.S. South, a legally encoded death-in-life existence expounded through Orlando Patterson's influential concept of "social death."[1] Even after slavery's abolishment, as Faulkner well understood, the "peculiar institution" remained a tragically powerful presence in the Jim Crow South. At the same time, the Confederacy's demise almost instantaneously gave birth to a Lost Cause ethos that suspiciously bears the marks of undeadness in its symbolic resurrection of fallen C.S.A. hero-saints. Indeed, the post-Appomattox, postemancipation, postplantation South was the site of numerous reburials of Confederate dead, physical resurrections that kept undead the searing memory of that nationalist insurrection against the U.S.A.[2] The essays herein discuss various revisitings of these familiar grounds, but they also explore the ways the tentacles of the U.S. South reach far and deep—into Haiti, which has its own "zombie" presence; into the soil of a Native South that preceded the construction of the South as the political-cultural imagined community it has been since the first decades of the nineteenth century; into the quasi-space of photographs, film, and the panels in comic books, where "southern" can be both enforced and reimagined in complex and radical ways. These kinds of spaces wash back onto already-held notions of the South, making it strange enough to be, at times, maybe even unrecognizable.

While we set out to reinvigorate important texts often classified under the aegis of *the* Southern Gothic (e.g., Poe, Faulkner, O'Connor, Cormac McCarthy), we also want to encourage closer attention to perhaps less obvious, but equally trenchant literature and media trafficking in southern undeadness. No longer satisfied with merely sitting up with the dead—that is, viewing the dead as hermetically sealed off from contemporaneous life, quarantined into the past—the essays in *Undead Souths* show how the dead contain cultural vibrancy in the present: if we let them in on the critical conversation, the still-living dead will speak volumes. The included essays offer new ideas and language to account for the various forms of haunting and horror associated with the U.S. South—not merely sameness masquerading as difference. This is accomplished not only by the integration of new critical schemata, but also by the sheer spectrum of topics, which span from original perspectives on the aforementioned southern literary giants; to various new mediations of the Confederate undead; to occluded crossings between Native and black displacements in Charles W. Chesnutt's fiction; to southeastern Choctaw

INTRODUCTION

funeral rituals and ghostly genealogies; to "hillbilly" horror flicks set in the "mountain South"; to the spectral architectonics of old New Orleans; to Civil War daguerreotypes and the poetic rejoinders of the current U.S. poet laureate, Natasha Trethewey; to posthumous political articulations of Emmett Till's fate; to rhizomorphic global South iterations, including Haitian zombie mythology in Herman Melville's depiction of chattel and wage slaveries, transregional reroutings and rerootings between T. S. Eliot's *The Waste Land* and Wilson Harris's *Jonestown*, circum-Caribbean emanations in the "plantation horror" genre of classic U.S. cinema, as well as diasporic transplantations in the surreal fiction of the Irish-born, Trinidadian author Shani Mootoo; and to considerations of undeadness as a figure for southern figuration itself across an array of media, including cinema (*White Zombie* and *Two Thousand Maniacs!*), television (*True Blood* and *The Walking Dead*), and comics (*Bayou* and *The Goon*)—and many, many undead things in between.

While proposing arguments that push past or at least navigate confining essentialist and exceptionalist definitions of the region, *Undead Souths* examines the continuing importance of the local as a prime space of political, economic, and social interactions that deeply influence and are influenced by national and global issues. Even amid this fluid, transnational, transcultural backdrop, figures of the southern undead abound and remain very much grounded in the southern cultural landscape. *How* and *why* is the South so undead? *How* and *why* do the remains of the South's always mixed, often vexed histories keep rising again? Just as the undead figures bodied forth in the texts under scrutiny pass through boundaries, so *Undead Souths* aims to cross established intellectual thresholds, summoning multiethnic, transnational influences within and without the traditional geographic and conceptual bounds of the U.S. South. The essays in *Undead Souths* cover a great deal of ground, spanning the collection of spaces and places identifiable as southern from the Appalachians southward to the Caribbean and stretching into the U.S. West.

This book thus casts a wide net, including essays by both established and emerging scholars on both canonical and less familiar texts in a variety of forms, from many historical periods, and driven by diverse critical and theoretical approaches. Rather than insist on common, consensual definitions of "the South" and "southernness," we gather together multiple, nuanced arguments about the meanings and the viability of these terms. The essays explore a broad spectrum of ways in which the South has been and, indeed, remains undead. Individual essays, like the volume as a whole, take into account changes that have been wrought in southern studies over the past decade, and our book helps map as well as redefine the field. At the same time, the essays herein engage various linked fields, such as African American studies, Native American studies, gender and sexuality studies, and film/new media studies. Naturally, we are also interested in advancing evolving work on horror and the gothic, popular genres that have taken on new life (pun intended) in television and other productions—for example, *True Blood* and *The Walking Dead*—set in the contemporary South.

The primary aim of *Undead Souths*, then, is to make sense of the multitude of undead figures and figurations proliferating in southern culture over the past two centuries, and to do so in original ways by driving critical discussion beyond the now-threadbare tropes of "*the* Southern Gothic"—singular and capitalized—as if both the region ("Southern") and the genre ("Gothic") are readily identifiable, monolithic entities. Indeed, in some traditional readings, "Southern" and "Gothic" become nearly synonymous. There is the standard checklist of gothic motifs: "haunted houses, evil villains, ghosts, gloomy landscapes, madness, terror, suspense, horror" (Goddu 5) as well as "tangled genealogies, subterranean flights, incest, doubles, supernatural incursions, and, of course, hauntings" (Bailey 4). The essays in *Undead Souths* diversify and expand this myopic view, pluralizing regional and generic identifications into multiple, even contradictory forms of what counts as "southern" and as "gothic"—all the while unsettling settled ideas of connections between the two. Old tropes of *the* Southern Gothic are themselves now decayed, long-standing images and ideas mummified and cracking into dust. While these essays acknowledge the continuing presence of this older idea of the gothic, they primarily work to think beyond that often-bounded term.

The work herein, moreover, explores fear and form in ways that resist the political acquiescence and escapist overtones often connected with the gothic and horror genres. On the contrary, these essays mark out the undead South as a crucial space for intellectual, emotional, and political commitments that shed light on why so much southern literature/media has been—and continues to be—so dark. *Undead Souths* looks to make the darkness visible, not as an escape into an alternate reality or fantasy world, but as an unruly means of political and social confrontation. To see dead people is to face the past and its many cultural irruptions in the present. In analyzing diverse images of southern necrologies, we unveil how these eerie figures record, critique, and/or invent convulsive, disruptive constructions of the South. In so doing, they force us to reimagine an already imaginary South. Southbound specters become holograms of an otherwise inarticulate, often distressing past. Vampires below the Mason-Dixon puncture and punctuate the region's bloodthirsty histories and bring them back to life. Dixie-fied zombies feed on cultural mindlessness and brainless devotion to rote codes of value. These supposedly unreal undead forms become all-too-real, counteracting the derealization of the southern past and present. The southern undead haunt the region's status as "a consumption-based economy—the South of the museum, the reenactment, the themed space, the tourist destination" (Romine, *The Real South* 5). The ephemeral reproductions of clichéd southernness that Scott Romine sharply exposes in *The Real South* (2008) seem to be aiding and abetting a kind of cultural zombiism. It is this submission to empty repetition of past cultural modes, a will-less recitation of past citations of what signifies southernism, that *Undead Souths* aims to address and redress.

With these things in mind, we have focused on "undeadness" as a new term both more flexible and more precise, able to encompass older concepts of the Southern Gothic while allowing room for additional modes of theorization. For both the editors and the contributors, "undead" is a metaphor, a receptacle, a mode. These essays endow undeadness with a dense theoretical texture, and identify ways in which southern undeadness comes in and out of contact with other manifestations of southernness. While "gothic" is often constricted by the weight of both generic and regionalist expectations, "undeadness" is rooted in and routed through a surprisingly dynamic physicality. Undeadness also intensifies the frequency and range of encounters between inextricably amalgamated human and nonhuman forms, from the makeup of the human corpus to the structures of natural and built environments. The material insistence of undeadness broaches the grotesque (often considered a subcategory of the gothic) in exposing the physical underpinnings of human subjectivity as transformations in and of the body spark and shadow mutations in and of consciousness. Yet undeadness also expands to illuminate more subtle interchanges between the animate and inanimate, worrying the very lines between the two and challenging an anthropocentric conception of ecology, which should be no longer viewed as mechanistic, inert, something to be mastered by humanity. Such imbrications with the nonhuman surround, which show how extensively and intensively "inanimate" bodies and things express agency within, and beyond, cultural systems, gesture toward Monique Allewaert's account of the "parahuman" in *Ariel's Ecology* (2013), according to which humans, nonhuman animals, and the environs coalesce into a "more than human collectivity . . . not grounded on human exceptionalism" (113). In a turn particularly pointed for figurations of southern undeadness, the parahuman acts acutely in concert with the black diaspora across the U.S. South, for whom "the brutal colonial circumstance of dismemberment and bodily disaggregation" generated models of personhood "that registered a deep skepticism about the desirability of the category of the human" (86).

Crosshatching current developments in physics and biology (the latent vibrancy of all matter that reflects levels of agency beyond human choice) as well as philosophy (the turn to posthumanist thought), undeadness speaks to a new understanding of human bodies as always contingent, transformative assemblages of human and nonhuman, living and dead materials. The textualities interpreted throughout *Undead Souths* envision bodies, living/dying/dead/undead, as "vibrant matter," per Jane Bennett: biological-cultural-environmental congregations that counter the long-held notion of "an intrinsically inanimate matter" while revealing "the material agency or effectivity of nonhuman or not-quite-human things" (ix). Just as, through the lens of undeadness, we see more clearly the constructed nature of the individual body and therefore of subjectivity, we also note how extrahuman materials and forces infuse and influence cultural and political bodies, as traditions and other institutional practices take on a life of their own—though at times such forms outlive their efficacy, the structures ossify, undergoing the endless recyclings of cultural zombification.

This idea of undeadness links to recent notions of object-oriented ontology founded in intricate mergings, even on a subatomic level, between human and nonhuman matter. Drawing on quantum mechanics and posthumanist philosophy, object theory describes how purportedly "animate" and "inanimate" materials interface inside and alongside the human body, calling attention to the thingness of humans and the agency of the nonhuman surround.[3] Undeadness, thus understood, is further entwined with

INTRODUCTION

concepts of disease, infection, and contamination and therefore consonates with recent anxieties over global pandemics and how these threaten to corrupt masses of individual human bodies as well as the projected consistency and soundness of bodies politic, regional and national. Undead art forms can help bring to the surface the politics behind how we attempt to quarantine not simply the infectious contagions themselves but also the potential social menace surrounding the emergence and spread of such diseases. Several of the visions of undeadness analyzed in *Undead Souths* represent what Priscilla Wald terms "outbreak narratives": medical, media, and literary/cinematic accounts that seek to explain and contain the ill effects of the sociopolitical threats brought on by mass contagion. Exploring the "epidemiology of belonging," Wald notes the interspersion of medical and cultural-ideological conceptions of purity, infestation, and containment in outbreak narratives that often display a faith in herd mentality espoused by a discrete population alongside a desire to scapegoat the outlier as potential carrier of infestation into the group. Such tensions—commingling narratological, medical, and sociological strands—may well put us in mind of how the undead rarely mind their own business but work hard to unsettle the livings' business-as-usual. Consider, for instance, how the Louisianan vampires of *True Blood* infect their human others with life-changing, identity-shifting blood-borne pathogens in a manner that bites back against the ghettoization of HIV patients in outbreak narratives encircling the AIDS epidemic in the 1980s and 1990s. Or think of the endless throngs of sick and sickening zombies peopling the pages/screen of *The Walking Dead* who stumble forth tirelessly in the thin rags of civilization, appearing always in bad taste and bad health, yet unfazed by our containment strategies. Ranging from rural Kentucky to downtown Atlanta, these zombies embody equally ripe contagion-carriers that disable the working order of the "healthy" humanoid herd while debasing our social and economic codes of value. The infected, infectious zombified masses induce widespread panic as they broadcast (quite literally through the AMC television remediation of Robert Kirkman's graphic narrative) a highly communicable dis-ease with the instabilities of contemporary U.S. and southern political economies, our *lack* of immunity to internal and external modes of catastrophe.[4]

By incorporating new, constructive critical frames rising out of undeadness, *Undead Souths* more vigilantly and more vigorously traces the "eerie life of the dead in an age without ghosts, that is, the matter that escapes the concept that ought to master it by making it thinkable" (Horowitz 97). The volume more effectively historicizes horror by considering the U.S. South, not in isolation, but in connection with other cultures and places. The aesthetics of undeadness are given cultural and geographic specificity by interleaving these images with emerging scholarship in southern studies, including critiques of essentialist and exceptionalist definitions of the South associated with the New Southern Studies; work on critical race theory and depictions of the Native South as well as convergences between southern and Caribbean cultures; new conceptions of horror and haunting that unbury underlying economic and sociological drives; and redefinitions of affect that move past the fatalistic cycle of trauma, personal and cultural, as a chronic condition with no hope for improvement. The essays in *Undead Souths* reveal how the region cannot be spirited away into political obsolescence and cultural oblivion. To invert the famous words from Flannery O'Connor's Hazel Motes, the South is a cultural space where what's dead *doesn't* stay that way, with major impacts on the region's present and future.

NOTES

1. Describing the cultural ways in which slaves are marked as social aliens who have no rightful place in the master's community, Patterson asserts that "the definition of the slave as an outsider, as the enemy within who is socially dead, allows for solidarity between master and nonslave as honorable members of their community vis-à-vis the dishonored slave" (34). The structure of cultural practices and symbolic rituals that conferred authority onto the master relied on an "overwhelming concentration on the profound natal alienation of the slave" (38): "The slave is violently uprooted from his milieu. He is desocialized and depersonalized. This process of social negation constitutes the first, essentially external, phase of enslavement. The next phase involves the introduction of the slave into the community of his master, but it involves the paradox of introducing him as a nonbeing. This explains the importance of law, custom, and ideology in the representation of the slave relation" (38).

2. For more on the exhumation and reburial of dead Confederates, see Drew Gilpin Faust's *This Republic of Suffering: Death and the American Civil War* (2008) and William Blair's *Cities of the Dead: Contesting the Memory of the Civil War in the South, 1865–1914* (2004).

3. Key expositions of object-oriented ontology include Karen Barad's *Meeting the Universe Halfway: Quantum Physics and the Entanglements of Matter and Meaning* (2007), Graham Harmon's *Towards Speculative Realism* (2010), Jane Bennett's *Vibrant Matter: A Political Ecology of Things* (2010), and Timothy Morton's *Hyperobjects: Philosophy and Ecology after the End of the World* (2013).

4. This deep cross-hatching between medical and social forms of contagion has long held association with southern culture, as Melissa Stein contends in her assessment of the role of scientific discourse in bolstering Jim Crow down South: "[W]hite supremacists both within and outside medical science often used disease and contagion as rhetorical devices to frame their discussions of post-Emancipation race relations more generally, particularly the place of the black race in America's body politic. These medical metaphors resonated for a broad audience in the United States during this period, which saw a sharp increase in public health education and disease consciousness" (126).

1

CONFEDERACIES OF UNDEAD IMAGINATION
Going South through Wastelands to *Jonestown*

KEITH CARTWRIGHT

In calling out to the specter we encounter a new kind of nightmare: not the gothic terror of being haunted by the dead, but the greater terror of not being haunted, of ceasing to feel the weight of past generations in one's bones.

—PATRICIA YAEGER, "Consuming Trauma; or,
The Pleasure of Merely Circulating"

The sense of eternity gives a perspective on things and events which makes for a refreshing clarity. I don't care how many rabbits jump over my grave, they don't make me shiver. But I always speak courteously to them when we meet. In mythology the rabbit is the great African hero, as the monkey is in China. From my father's childhood to mine the stories of Bre'r Rabbit and Bre'r Fox were widespread . . . [and] instilled into a child's mind the lost resemblances between man and beast.

—ANDREW LYTLE, *A Wake for the Living*

Going South, during my West Kentucky "dry-county" high school years, meant driving to a strip just across the Tennessee line (The Cotton Club, The Big Apple, The 641 Club), a space fabulous and gothic, wet with spirits and musication, all tempered now by the white crosses planted on both sides of Highway 641. Marking a zone below temperate borders, and lodging what "should" be past or unaccredited and illicit but won't stay out of circulation, the South serves as an underworld crucial to drier normative spaces. In *Turning South Again* (2001), Houston Baker directed readers to Patricia Yaeger's invocation of the Homeric *nekuia* (Odysseus's summoning of the dead) and to Yaeger's reminder that the dead "must be fed on the life blood, the figures of the present, if they are to speak" (31). Here, turning south again may allow for blood-wetted revision—a hosting of both the historically specific *and* the spectral "sense of eternity" described by Andrew Lytle as lost ecologies of communion: "If we dismiss the past as dead and not as a country of the living which our eyes are unable to see, as we cannot see a foreign country but know it is there, then we are likely to become servile" (4). Even though southern time-spaces harbor a more numbing sweep of servility than Lytle (or Baker at first take) dared acknowledge, our Souths remain riddled with rabbit holes into alternative potentialities, thick with briar-patch matrices of relation to "foreign country" and causes we otherwise might configure as alien or lost to us.

No matter how much an "old" southern studies may be lambasted for what Jon Smith has called its obsession with "folklore, orality, the presence of the past, the sense of place, and the sense of community" (*Finding Purple America* 30), powerful southern countercultures of performance (and rememory, reemplacement, restoration of community) remain in need of proper respects. The new won't disentangle from the old, or come generationally clean. And we in the humanities need to nurture a *hippikat* (Wolof "open-eyed") poetics if we are to begin to respond—in any real way—to the question that opens Smith's recent book: "What does it mean to be hip in the twenty-first century?" (1). A truly open-eyed hipness calls us back to contact zones: to greet witch-rabbits, drink detoxifying cassina (and vomit up much of what we think we know), pour spirits at place settings for the dead, and tend our gardens for the sustainable perspective of clarity they make upon eternity. We may not need a New Southern Studies, just a deeper (more holistically conservative) one, hospitable to comings and goings beyond accustomed borders, beyond generational periodicities invented by professors and journalists, and beyond English.

Whenever we remark on the pervasiveness of the past in southern spaces, we should recognize that wonderment over such a thing may be born of a peculiarly smug Anglo-Protestant gaze upon creolized cross-cultural space.

The very notion of the undead attests to a presence that won't stay in its grave, without the agency even of an All Saints' Day. "Death" translates more imprecisely than we often realize, as my introduction to the Senegalese poet Birago Diop (whose animal fables were assigned in a required third-year Sewanee French class) clarified in the poet's insistence that "Those who are dead are not ever gone," and his call to

> Listen more often
> To things than to Beings
> Hear the voice of fire,
> Hear the voice of water.
> Listen in the wind to
> The bush that is sobbing:
> This is the ancestors breathing.
> Each day they renew ancient bonds,
> Ancient bonds that hold fast
> Binding our lot to their law,
> To the will of the spirits stronger than we
> To the spell of our dead who are not really dead (153–54)

Diop's poem (swung beautifully southward by Sweet Honey in the Rock) moves us closer to a Brer Rabbit–informed sense of eternity and to Homeric obligations of the *nekuia*. Technological advances hardly free us from these demands to greet and listen. Indeed, the repertory is only augmented as the dead find voicings beyond the hold they already have on our dance steps, cooking, and speech—as West Kentucky poet Joe Bolton recognized with his own spin on how "The old and the new songs of heartbreak sound the same. / It's only when the needle grinds in the grooves / That a sadness greater than your own comes on, / And the dead begin to live again, in you" (5).

The stakes of listening to the dead and of garnering a groove-sense of eternity have never been higher than in our digitized moment of climatic change. Who are the dead whose voices will be archived and anthologized, accredited and fed, whose word we hail (or will hail us) as bond? Who are these (un)dead of Miami or Tallahassee? Of Louisiana's Angola Prison or the grooves of our Cotton Clubs? English departments do not help us enough with these questions, and have played a vexing role in compounding certain illiteracies of the imagination. Our abandonment of grounding in Homeric, Ovidian, and biblical metamorphoses—coupled with an ignorance of translocal African, Indigenous, and creole contact knowledges—has left us trafficking in a stale daily bread of medieval England and Massachusetts Bay unleavened by a shallow multiculturalism that challenges neither our base structures of communion nor our deference to Puritan/Anglican patrimony. Nowhere in the United States are the stakes more charged than within southern institutions of education facing postplantation needs for full integration of our racialized corporate body and corpus, our cornbread-fed ancestors who defy the trickle-down machineries of a zombie-proliferating "voodoo economy." Without a more holistic embodiment of the past in our bones, whatever we do within "English" will remain ripe for the disparagement that Bradford Keeney, president of the Louisiana Association for Marriage and Family Therapy (and accomplished researcher/author), lays on the mental health professions: "The profession is iatrogenic—causes more harm than cure—and its foundation sits on collapsing sand dunes. Therapists too easily ignore the solid bedrock of the global wisdom traditions. Our mental health professionals are simply doing the bidding of the drug companies and the academics who try to get research grants for their non-inspiring form of number-crunching masochism. We must act now, before pharmacology and psychiatry turn the world into zombies" (265).

Bestiaries of Southern Wilds: Slipping beyond Vampiric Zombifications

The global wisdom tradition of the African rabbit may not have been taught to Andrew Lytle and William Faulkner at school, but Rabbit's pedagogy traveled in the performances of an apartheid-traversing cross-cultural community. Nowadays we hardly respond to Rabbit's taunting "What's up, Doc?" Still, fabulous models of tricksterly instruction circulate around us. Doe-women that hunters thought had been skinned and consumed manage to show up with unaborted offspring in the hunting camps of Seminole and Creek narratives, as well as in the Yoknapatawpha of "Delta Autumn." Similar tales of ruminant erotics challenge hunters in the Georgia woods, Louisiana's bayous, across the Caribbean, and from the deep bush visited by West African divination narratives. Peoples in touch with their shape-shifting relations with otherness carry the capacity of becoming birds (William Gilmore Simms's "The Lazy Crow," Morrison's *Song of Solomon*). Careful reading of the beasts of southern wilds in frontier texts by Birago Diop and

Joel Chandler Harris, Ben Okri, Lydia Cabrera, Erna Brodber, and Zora Neale Hurston may provide reappraisal of a fabulosity that resisted plantation zombifications to open a wider terrain of authority in service of "our dead who are not really dead."

The soucouyant, prevalent throughout Franco-creole plantation zones, is a vampire-like succubus carrying shape-shifting capacities for preying upon sleeping victims. Soucouyants inhabit the Guadeloupe of Simone Schwarz-Bart, the Martinique of Patrick Chamoiseau, the Dominica of Jean Rhys, and the Trinidad of David Chariandy's Canadian fiction, and they slip through the keyholes of southern memory as "the hag that rides you" in Sapelo Island (Georgia) resident Cornelia Bailey's description of the figure associated with sleep paralysis (211–12). The hag rides canonical American fiction as well, and links the text of *Huckleberry Finn*—through the body and narration of Jim—to a world of hoodoo, ghosts, divinatory hairballs, and undead aspirations for freedom. Her racialized erotics resurface in James Weldon Johnson's "The White Witch" and in the murderous Lula of Amiri Baraka's *Dutchman*.

The counterpart of the soucouyant is "the perfect Gentleman," whose tales circulate throughout the circumatlantic . . . often as a marriage to the Devil. In Amos Tutuola's *The Palm-Wine Drinkard*, a young Nigerian woman meets "a beautiful 'complete' gentleman . . . dressed with the finest and most costly clothes" in the market (201), but as readers follow the couple into the bush, the gentleman's every hired part is returned until "they reached where he hired the skin and flesh which covered the head," and he was thus "reduced to a 'SKULL'" (204). The tale finds reassembly in Edgar Allan Poe's "The Man Who Was Used Up," wherein we meet a hero of the Seminole wars whose every flawless attribute—from chest, to hands, calves, feet, teeth, eyes, and voice—turns out to have been purchased from a variety of well-branded craftsmen's shops. Our perfect gentleman is finally reduced to a squeaky-voiced blob dependent upon his slave Pompey for his prosthetic assembly. Poe's genius comes across most fully when read from an Afro-creole narrative legacy against the grain of a used-up "discipline."

At the crossroads of American literature, southern studies, and wider Atlantic/hemispheric routings lies a body of cross-cultural narrative assembled outside our accrediting institutions of knowledge. This undead corpus has always circulated among a folk-intelligentsia wary of broadcasting it in open air (as in "High Walker and Bloody Bones" from Hurston's *Mules and Men*). In the face of historic segregations, southern institutions of learning bear a responsibility to reassemble and integrate more fully our bodies of knowledge and disciplinary means of knowing. Rabbit's and Turtle's tales lead the way. My own recent book, *Sacral Grooves, Limbo Gateways* (2013), examines how Turtle's (or Tortoise's) powers of shell-shaking reassembly unite a body of literature discernible in Chinua Achebe's *Things Fall Apart*, Lydia Cabrera's *Afro-Cuban Tales*, and Earnest Gouge's *New Fire*, as well as in performances from Puerto Rico, Brazil, Creole Louisiana, and various Southeastern Indian nations. Beaten to pieces by women affronted by his efforts to peer up their skirts for a powerful vision, Turtle manages to shake mutilated parts together in a dance familiar to readers of Joy Harjo, Linda Hogan, and especially LeAnne Howe's *Shell Shaker*. Turtle reveals that our bodies of knowledge can (and probably should) have a stick taken to them, and that we can find therein the medicine-capacity to do an integral dance of reassembly via a reanimation (of panther-people, porcupine-women, and "life everlasting") that can help us slip past the vampiric blood-suckings of *osano* (horsefly-creatures) and *Inkilish okla* (English people), and remain supple in the face of consumer capitalism's Midas touch.

"A Heap of Broken Images": Old Possum's Wastelands

T. S. Eliot, one of English's/*Inkilish's* major spirits whom we may think we have outgrown, famously insisted in "Tradition and the Individual Talent" on the poet's need "to write not merely with his own generation in his bones" but also with an "appreciation of his relation to the dead poets and artists" (31). Eliot directs the would-be poet into "the whole of the literature of Europe from Homer" as well as "the whole of the literature of his own country" (31), immersions that render "the past . . . altered by the present as much as the present is directed by the past" (32). As Eliot put it, the artist "must be aware that the mind of Europe—the mind of his own country— . . . is a mind which changes, and that this change is a development which abandons nothing *en route*, which does not superannuate either Shakespeare, or Homer, or the rock drawing of the Magdalenian draughtsmen" (32–33). Clearly, post-plantation artists and curricula have yet to channel the full-mindedness of our schizophrenic/shape-shifting Souths. For Eliot, "the progress of an artist [or of a scholar or curriculum] is a continual self-sacrifice" (34), moving toward a vision "of poetry as a living whole of all the poetry that has ever been written" (34), a single gulf-matrix of performance akin to Édouard Glissant's notion of creolization as "unstoppable conjunction . . . like a tumultuous and boundless Mississippi" (30). Choosing to become a British subject, Eliot was hardly up for the task of channeling all the material washed by his native Big River—from Henry Dumas's "Ark of Bones" to Joy Harjo's encounter with Hernando de Soto's bones in "New Orleans." Perhaps it's simply a matter of economy—too many rams to kill, too many Tiresias-thirsts to assuage. But Eliot intuited the enormity of the challenge and left us to build a structure within "English" set up like a giant Day of the Dead table through which every single body, tale, song, and medicine-dance that has ever been on the Mississippi (or Apalachicola or St. Johns) may reemerge in the initiation of *The Sacred Wood*'s model poet: "a more finely perfected medium . . . at liberty to enter into new combinations" (34).

Born and raised in St. Louis (of New England parentage), Eliot experienced his own marginal southernness as an inescapable contagion. For Eliot, something akin to creolization marked both his power and his self-perceived taint, portrayed, as David Chinitz has pointed out, in letters to his English friend Mary Hutchinson (1919), as a fear "I may simply prove to be a savage" in English society (21). Invited, apparently, to bring his emblematic troubadour's lute to one of Hutchison's soirees, Eliot replied, "it is a jazz-banjorine that I should bring, not a lute" (21). He feared he was more minstrel than troubadour, a self-described "southern boy with a nigger drawl" whose adoption of the persona of "Old Possum" (in correspondence with Ezra Pound) camouflaged tricksterish strengths as weaknesses (23). Whatever else he was or would become, Old Possum Eliot was a southerner, marked—if only in his own mind—by that supposedly uncivil drawl and by a Big River feel for the jazz banjorine.

Our sacrificial descent into Eliot's *The Waste Land* (1922) reveals that "the living whole" of Western humanities has come to its zombifying dead end. Like Homer, Virgil, and Dante before him, Eliot goes to the underworld of the dead and undertakes a pilgrimage familiar to the tales of Chaucer or King Arthur. The hyacinth girl offers a first recognition: "I was neither / Living nor dead, and I knew nothing" (136). Madame Sosostris, the reader of the table's Tarot deck, shows early-twentieth-century Anglo-modernity to be a set of circles in Dante's hell: "I see crowds of people, walking round in a ring" (136). Although its ring-walking hardly offers the medicine of the counterclockwise ring shout or shell-shaking stomp-dance, *The Waste Land* does diagnose a zombifying condition wherein "you know only / A heap of broken images" (135). In this "Unreal city" the cards of the Tarot deck, like the sybil's leaves, scatter without holistic, reanimating readings, and we come to a suppressed knowledge of zombie outbreaks: "I had not thought death had undone so many" (136). The poem's insistent demand to "speak" and especially to "think" conjures a stop-time silence (in breaks between sections, stanzas, and lines) and a carnivalesque skeleton-krewe:

> 'Are you alive, or not? Is there nothing in your head?'
> But
> O O O O that Shakespeherian Rag—
> It's so elegant
> So intelligent (138)

Eliot's inability to unincorporate his muse's drawl and ragtime marks the very possibility of *The Waste Land*'s patchwork modernity ... based on sampling techniques, mosaic remix, and the impact of radio and phonograph sound technology, as Jay Watson recently noted in drawing on Juan Suarez's reading of the poem (87–107). Although Eliot has become the emblematic straw man of the Eurocentric high canon, we must reassess how the southern dead's creolizing irruptions into modernity worked as a driving force behind his attempted escape into an always already contaminated *Inkilish*-ness.

The Waste Land can help English departments to recognize their Lost Cause investments: academic enshrinement of a heap of broken images (anthologized chronologies and periodizations of one damned thing after another) that betray a disciplinary illegitimacy (useless save for a dwindling but key traditional role in legitimizing university degrees in business, nursing, criminal justice, and other professional studies). "English" configures itself around British and American literary nationalisms: nation-tables set for pantheons of the foundational (and recently canonized) authorial undead. In Eliot's great modernist poem, we follow Tiresias, who has "walked among the lowest of the dead" (141) and come to recognize that anything short of recreative vision keeps us in a "dry sterile thunder without rain" (144), a world of immanent climate change where "there is no water" (144), only "voices singing out of empty cisterns and exhausted wells" (145). *The Waste Land*'s parting image of a wounded Fisher King "upon the shore / Fishing, with an arid plain behind me" (146) aligns with the closing lines of another great modernist poem—Aimé Césaire's *Notebook of a Return to the Native Land:* "the great black hole where a moon ago I wanted to drown it is here I will now fish the malevolent tongue of the night in its motionless veerition!" (85). We might think too of the Big River world of Huck and Jim fishing on (fellow Missourian) Twain's Jackson Island before they enter the fog that will cause them to miss Cairo. Neither Twain nor Eliot could see a way through to tables set for all our creole ancestors. *The Waste Land* does, however, put creole poetics into play in its very structure—in the breaks, assemblage aesthetics, and polyphony of the poem's exposure of the humanities as undead Lost Cause.

"This Ghost of a Chance You Fishing For": Wilson Harris's *Jonestown*

If we were to name the most vital living heir to Eliot, we could hardly do better than look to another marginal, Big River southerner, long settled in England: the Guyanese author Sir Wilson Harris. In "Tradition and the West Indian Novel," Harris directed Caribbean artists across racial and linguistic borders in pursuit "of wider possibilities and relationships" (150). In calling the Caribbean novel beyond realist conventions and beyond a politics of victimization, Harris invoked Eliot's unlikely mentorship, asking, "[H]ow is it that figures such as these [Eliot and Pound], described in some quarters as conservative, remain 'explosive' while many a fashionable rebel grows to be superficial and opportunistic?" (150). Harris's body of work, from *Palace of the Peacock* (launched under Eliot's approval for publication with Faber and Faber, 1960) through *Jonestown* (1996) and more, has made it clear that Eliot's mosaic reconfigurations of tradition helped fuel an "explosive" cross-cultural response from waters so dread that one of Harris's characters asks another (and the reader) as they head into Guyana's interior, "You think you really want this ghost of a chance you fishing for?" (*Palace* 41).

Rising from gulfs of consciousness inherent to *The Waste Land*'s colonial-era project, Harris's "hosting of history," as Samuel Durrant describes the Guyanese novelist's Eucharistic-Homeric-shamanistic project , would have us consume a ritual morsel of the other in order to become possessed of all of the unappeased, unsubstantiated specters dispossessed by global modernity's conquistadorial designs. Harris continually references "waste land" and "wastelands" as late capitalism's environmental and cultural legacy. It is only through dialogue with specters of waste and loss that we may slip through "predatory coherence" (*Jonestown* 8), to cultivate "a form shorn of violence in its intercourse with reality," one that "comes to us in its brokenness to activate . . . a reach of the Imagination beyond all cults, or closures, or frames" (8).

No novel provides a more compelling engagement with our wasteland challenges and inheritances than does Harris's *Jonestown*, wherein the legacies of Columbian conquest meet with the Indigenous ritual violence of ancient Mayan cities and with Guyanese racial antagonisms leading up to (and distillate from) independence, all narrated within the frame of Jonah (Jim) Jones's orchestration of mass murder–suicide via cyanide-laced Coca-Cola (rather than Kool-Aid here). The retraversing task in the "Dream-book" of narrator Francisco Bone's account of Jonestown's Day of the Dead is to avert scriptings of progressive catastrophe, "to unlock closure" as "one becomes . . . a vessel . . . imbued with many voices . . . a multitude" (5) of "the broken communities, the apparently lost cultures from which I [or creolized readers] have sprung" (6). Francisco Bone's Guyana narrative provides a model for sustaining undead literacies of the imagination. And its communions of brokenness point to ways in which southern studies may function as gifthorse or tar baby inside the walls of a Wasteland humanities.

Francisco Bone's Jonestown Dream-book recalls how "[t]he Caribs ate a morsel of enemy flesh when the Spanish priests and conquistadors invaded their lands. They sought to know and digest the secrets of the enemy in that morsel. They hollowed the bone from which the morsel had come into a flute that is said to inhabit all species that sing" (16). This "morsel, a flute, a fury," allows a musical retraversal of "frames in which conquistadorial priests of old sought to conscript the Imagination" (16). We reenter these frames of missionary conscription of the imagination to "see how tribal are pacts or institutions founded on coercion and conquest," and the glance we gain into "this abhorrent tribalism" calls for "different weddings and marriages to reality" (25). *Jonestown*'s shell-shaking need to "Break the mould if you are to live and grow" (31) goes beyond multicultural addendum and becomes an epistemological challenge that southern institutions have dodged in the unfinished work of the civil rights movement. Harris is adamant about the unfinished nature of this challenge: "Equality . . . is only possible when originality is seen to be native as much to the powerless as to the powerful" (32). Underutilized resources of "shamans and seers and magi in the Americas" (32) are key here to revivifying the possibility of matriculation within/from "the state of embalmed institutions" (72). This model helps us see that without this "undying originality" and its "resistance to the predatory coherence of fact that masquerades as eternity," our "art is dead" (46).

Such composite origin-ality accesses remains of imaginative literacy from global Souths too long positioned as raw resource providers to the knowledge production industry. Insisting that "[e]ducators . . . need to be re-educated" (123), Harris would turn global/southern curricula and accrediting agencies to a far more flexible limbo-reinvestigation of what has been dismissed or occluded as folklore, as censored spectacle or deviltry. *Jonestown*'s readerly/writerly avatar Francisco Bone rises from the novel's composite Day of the Dead altar and from "the sick-bed of the humanities" (214) charged with altering destinies scripted of "misconceived beginnings, misconceived empires": "Write upon the walls of rotting, colonial institutions, test every fabric of a biased humanities, break the Void by sifting the fabric of ruin for living doorways into an open universe" (216). What *Jonestown* calls for is nothing less than a new corpus and subjectivity reconfigured by "the Carib, cannibal morsel which one must digest and transform in oneself within the cellular organs of a new body" (219). Only in becoming an assemblage bound up in what we would see as otherness may the humanities (and perhaps humanity itself) find the ghost of a chance.

Coda: "The Stones and Other Things . . . Have Virtue"

If we are to transform departments of English through creolizing conduits, then this third ancestral table (set apart from American lit, apart from British) will include and consume the other two. This table for the southern dead will be built to accommodate mosaic structures of interpenetration and polyrhythm, alternative handlings of time and space, ecologically attuned sensibilities, and will delve into that which has been rendered immaterial and spectral but which remains tenaciously present. This third spirit-table will vibrate between the flows of what we used to call "world" or even "postcolonial" literature and the locally specific/globally inclusive formations of each particular space around which we may be gathered. It will hail us from beyond English and through other registries of *Inkilish*—in a gulf-assemblage built of a thousand separatisms, un-American yet American, not-English yet familiar in its homegrown semiotics and notlanguage.

If we aim to fashion and play a Carib bone flute (for its musical appeasement and knowledge of the other), we may learn from the Arawak-Taíno providers of the morsel of flesh and bone for Carib flutes. The Taíno, who had migrated from rain forests of the Amazon, and the Guyanas, across the Caribbean archipelago, were the first "Indians" Columbus encountered. The language of this contact shaped subsequent accounts of the Indies. For example, Cabeza de Vaca (1542) describes meeting a *canoa*, or "canoe" (5) on the Florida coast—where other Taíno words were applied to Gulf Coast reality: *bohios* ("thatched houses," 8), *caciques* ("chiefs," 17), *maize* (19) and *areitos* (religious dances of healing and purifying invigoration, 35). During one season of *areitos*, Cabeza de Vaca and comrades found themselves turned into "physicians without giving us any examinations or asking for any diplomas, because they heal diseases by blowing on the patient, and with that puff of breath and their hands they drive the illness out of him" (35). The Indians withheld food from the Spaniards until they consented to performing healing rites first attributed to Taíno *behiques* (shamans): "[A]n Indian told me that I did not know what I was saying when I said that what he knew was useless, because the stones and other things that grow in the countryside have virtue" (35). Finally, the captive Spaniards and their African grew hungry enough to begin the *behique* work that gave them economic-social "use" over their long sojourn, treating the sick "by making the sign of the cross over them, and breathing on them, and reciting a Pater Noster and an Ave Maria" (35). Cabeza de Vaca notes a smoke that "they get drunk on," and describes a central rite of communion across the region: the drinking of cassina accompanied by purgative vomiting (59–60). Although Cabeza de Vaca could not afford to use the word "*behique*" for the ritual activities he had engaged, his textual authority draws from deep immersion in the Indigenous Gulf South. Caribbean Taíno vocabulary does the translation work between Spain and the vast new terrain of Florida. Indeed, when we think of our use of words like "barbeque, canoe, hammock, hurricane, and tobacco," we see that southern hospitalities draw from a profoundly Taíno-mediated host (Alegría 18).

This Taíno/Arawak continuum connecting the Orinoco basin of South America to the islands of the Caribbean and Bahamas also reached the Florida coast via the Gulf Stream. Florida's Timucuan peoples were the first to encounter conquistadors such as Ponce de León, Narváez, and Menéndez. The Timucuan language, recorded by Father Francisco Pareja, appears to have an Amazonian ancestry, linking Timucuans (despite their Muscogean acculturations) to Arawakan/Waroid/Tucanoan migrations from the Amazon and Orinoco basins (Granberry 14–60). In the bone flutes of shamans and writers from the Peruvian Amazon and the Guyanas, the *areitos* of Boricuan memory in Puerto Rico and its diasporas, the stomp dances and Plains-style powwows of Muscogee peoples who absorbed remnant Timucuans (and perhaps with the *behiques'* ayahuasca, cohiba, or cassina in our bellies and bloodstream), we may break into a sweat and vomit up our accredited knowledge. "English" could help us do this, help account for the losses, gulfs, and Midas-obsessions that (dis)connect us—if its gated communities were broken down to help us hear the ancestral grooves of Senegalese banjo-cats and Taíno *behiques* in the Grateful Dead or Rolling Stones. Around this altar of the Indigenous and creole dead—with its barbeque served in hoecakes and its tipplings of chicha on Mother Earth—we may begin to step to Turtle's Gulf-rhythms of reintegration charted by Lydia Cabrera in Havana and Miami: "Tiny sounds began to multiply, the sounds of body parts that had been mutilated, killed, and spread far and wide beginning to seek each other out, to piece themselves together and come back to life!" (148).

2

THE FALL OF THE HOUSE OF PO' SANDY
Poe, Chesnutt, and Southern Undeadness

ERIC GARY ANDERSON

Though sometimes taught together, the grotesques and arabesques of Edgar Allan Poe and the conjure tales of Charles Chesnutt are almost never conjoined in scholarly writing on any of the wide range of topics, questions, and issues relevant to the study of either Poe or Chesnutt. In this essay, I make a shape to begin to fill this lack, concentrating on two eerily compatible stories from two distinct yet affiliated segments of nineteenth-century American literary and cultural history: Poe's "The Fall of the House of Usher" (1839) and Chesnutt's "Po' Sandy" (1888). Clearly, Usher's house is not Po' Sandy's, or Julius's, or John and Annie's. Chesnutt's "post-bellum–pre-Harlem" color line differs from Poe's antebellum race consciousness; Poe's checkered relationship to the South differs from Chesnutt's. But like Addie Bundren's disembodied yet disturbingly visceral articulations of shapes and lacks, presences and absences, the haunted voices and spaces in "Usher" and "Po' Sandy" vault beyond the gothic and into a more expansive, more permeable, less easily defined or contained undeadness. Bringing Poe and Chesnutt together, and looking briefly at a Lumbee ghost story, I argue that this undeadness surfaces most often in the form of spaces riddled with spectral presences and absences, crosshatched by deep intercultural histories, and propelled by the departures and returns of specters, memories, and stories. Both stories make a space for—pointedly and purposefully *entertain*—horrors and hauntings; both stories also cast undeadness as entertain*ing*, or at the very least absorbing, a good story worth performing and (especially) worth retelling, the better to fuel and sustain the haunt and destabilize if not destroy any vestiges of the homely (*heimlich*).[1] Put another way, both Poe and Chesnutt place readers in the intimate company of a carefully structured architectural uncanny which paradoxically embodies the disembodied, reanimating the undead in or as an ancestral mansion, planks of lumber, and a story told and retold.[2]

In moving beyond the gothic, Poe and Chesnutt also stretch beyond the southern, both in their lives and in their art. Each was born in the antebellum U.S. North, Poe in Boston in 1809 and Chesnutt in Cleveland in 1858, and each moved to the South while still very young. Each also felt the South's gravitational pull, though in very different ways, after leaving it, and for each this gravitational pull was one part of a literary life each writer saw as national, even though neither wrote short fiction explicitly about "America" anywhere near as much as he wrote about actual neighborhoods and regions (Chesnutt) and unnamed though specifically described, topographically and architecturally distinctive places (Poe). While Chesnutt's conjure stories can be mapped, as Sarah Ingle has recently demonstrated, Poe almost never turns to an identifiable South in his writing, just as he rarely turns to any other mappable, actual places. That said, Poe, the less regional writer of the two, has been claimed by the South in ways that Chesnutt, who moved to Fayetteville, North Carolina, with his freeborn parents the year after the Civil War ended and lived there for seventeen years, has not. The long-running debate about Poe's "southernness" has taken up his residency in Richmond, Charlottesville, Charleston, South Carolina, and Baltimore; his association with the *Southern Literary Messenger* from 1835 to 1837; his stories "The Gold-Bug" and "A Tale of the Ragged Mountains"; his literary representations of, and other pronouncements about, and silences about race; and concomitantly his indeterminate views on slavery. Poe is included in the *Norton Literature of the American South* as well as in other southern literature anthologies, though, Scott Peeples points out, "his place in the canon of Southern writers remains marginal" (20). But this was less so in the late nineteenth century, as James Hutchisson asserts: "After Reconstruction, the South claimed Poe as a product of its culture, easily seeing his work as part of its project of memorialization, especially so since Poe's life story was a saga of a lost cause" (14). As Peeples observes, "Poe never seemed more Southern than he did during the decades following Reconstruction" (20).³

The *idea* of Poe as a southern writer was flourishing in the South as Chesnutt was publishing his conjure stories, which he begins to do in 1887 after leaving southeastern North Carolina for Cleveland. Chesnutt seems to have had little if anything to say about Poe, but he turned south again and again, in his novels as well as his short stories, long after settling in Cleveland for good. Like Poe, however, Chesnutt typically does not cast himself as a regionalist or southern writer. But, in his late essay "Post-bellum—Pre-Harlem" (1931) and elsewhere, Chesnutt retrospectively reflects on his achievements as an African American writer who takes up African American subjects and whose literary purview includes other African American writers as well as white writers whose literary methods and concerns he shares. Scholars began recovering Chesnutt in the 1960s and 1970s; by the early 1990s, Poe studies had also evolved to the point where, as Peeples writes, "[n]ot only is race crucial to our understanding of Poe, but Poe is crucial to our understanding of race in American literature and history" (100). But much still seems to be hidden in plain sight, especially given Toni Morrison's often-quoted valuation that "no early American writer is more important to the concept of American Africanism than Poe" (32). This might seem a pretty broad hint to make connections between Poe and Chesnutt; it also opens a pathway toward undeadness. Acknowledging the paradoxical American "dependency" on Africanism, the ways in which "Africanism" is the subject and "American" the modifier, Morrison redefines Melville's "power of blackness," contending that "[t]his black population was available for meditations on terror—the terror of European outcasts, their dread of failure, powerlessness, Nature without limits, natal loneliness, internal aggression, evil, sin, greed" (37–38). Though himself a black writer, Chesnutt comes near to tapping the powerful "fabricated brew of darkness, otherness, alarm, and desire" (38) that comprises American Africanism, signifying on it via both John and Julius and even "playing in the dark" a little as he walks over, around, and alongside the color line in the conjure tales.

More broadly, Morrison explores the nature and the staying power of racially inflected undeadness. But undeadness also channels the gothic, which has proven one of the sturdiest conduits for talking about the workings of race and cultural power in American—and, notably, in southern literature. Like Morrison, Poe and Chesnutt do not disregard the gothic. But neither do they settle for it. Instead, they stretch beyond it to embrace the extranormal; both are haunted not only by undead bodies and supernatural transformations, by conjure roots and family roots, but also by histories of settler colonialism and interracial violence that originate in various places and connect, at times very specifically and at times very elusively, to the U.S. South. As Teresa Goddu has argued: "[T]he American gothic is most recognizable as a regional form. Identified with gothic doom and gloom, the American South serves as the nation's 'other,' becoming the repository for everything from which the nation wants to disassociate itself. The benighted South is able to support the irrational impulses of the gothic that the nation as a whole, born of Enlightenment ideals, cannot" (3). In this reading, the South serves as the nation's psychic and cultural dumping ground. (As Goddu suggests elsewhere in her book, the South's status as gothic repository is hard to reconcile with the region and nation's traumatic history of Indian removal.) Goddu argues further that "[b]y so closely associating the gothic with the South, the American literary tradition neutralizes the gothic's threat to national identity. As merely a regional strategy, the gothic's horrifying hauntings, especially those dealing with race, can be contained" (76). But such acts of literary containment are themselves fantasies, or (at best) hard to pull off and ill-advised.[4] After all, southern writers are part of "the American literary tradition" rather than separate from it; and why would southern writers be party to containing such unruly, sometimes dangerous circumstances and impulses inside their own region? Undeniably, "southern" and "gothic" have been snugly fused, but these fusions all too often lock the gothic and the South alike into generic and regionalist predictability that runs counter to what is most uncanny and disturbing about the various subterranea and other currents that feed into and cycle through the gothic. What if the gothic cannot be neutralized? As Morrison and others contend, ghosts and demons are not so easily managed, let alone exorcised. Or, as María del Pilar Blanco argues, what if the gothic is already too neutral and neutralizing—so locked into its generic habits that it comes to seem predictable and even ubiquitous rather than truly unsettling? Like Blanco, I "want to give primacy to haunting as a diversified experience of space, more than as a certain category of literature" (18). Undeadness offers a better lens through which to look at haunted spaces, including but not limited to southern haunted spaces, from both within and without, to see and think about absent *and* present Souths, some more Indigenous than others, in part by describing transatlantic, Caribbean, circum-Mississippian, multiracial networks that convey and propel the undead in and out of the South. In other words, undeadness pervades the South and southern literature without being exclusive to either, without contributing to narrower definitions of either, and without placing region and nation in opposition.

Both "The Fall of the House of Usher" and "Po' Sandy" are horror stories that evoke and exemplify undeadness. Both the ancestral mansion in "Usher" and the more recently built schoolhouse in "Po' Sandy" enclose dead, dying, and/or undead people who haunt from very deep within the structure itself. In both stories, built structures take on eerie, person-like characteristics, and these buildings also illustrate, in very different ways, what William Gleason calls the architecture of segregation. The house of Usher is socially and geographically remote to the extent that it is nearly beyond society, while the houses and outbuildings in "Po' Sandy" reflect and to some extent perpetuate antebellum southern racial and cultural hierarchies. Further, as Anthony Vidler explains, the bodily analogy in architecture also helps turn a house into a haunt. From at least the fifteenth century, theorists believed that buildings, like people, could fall ill and die: "But beginning in the eighteenth century, there emerged a second and more extended form of bodily projection in architecture, initially defined by the aesthetics of the sublime. Here, the building no longer simply represented a part or whole of the body but was rather seen as objectifying the various states of the body, physical and mental" (71–72). In tandem, Gleason's architecture of segregation and Vidler's architectural uncanny raise unsettling questions about how and why "home" transmutes into built manifestations of racial and cultural (and gender and class) separation, violence, and undeadness. Both Poe and Chesnutt use the loaded metaphor of the haunted house to capture social and cultural anxieties about blood mixing, racial embodiment, class visibility, the solidity of the union, and various other forms of possession and dispossession.

In both stories, departure/return, both a narrative structure and a metaphor, suggests that undeadness flares up in the forms of various kinds of comings and goings: false death/premature burial and return from the grave, or escape from plantation and return to bondage, for example, or ways in which white and black characters in the conjure tales temporarily depart from their own racial identities (or do they?) only to return to them later, seemingly more unchanged than changed as a result of their ventriloquist performances. Departure/return stories also signify on the uncanny, itself a departure/return story about the evacuation and recovery of the repressed.

As such, it's not surprising that Usher's house feels so little like home. The narrator makes himself at home in this house only to the extent that he joins its inhabitants in experiencing its unhomely dangers and powers—but he also arrives at and departs from Usher's house as a man who is, or who might as well be, without a home of his own. Strikingly, he never offers up a contrasting picture of a happier home, or, indeed, of a home of any sort, the address on Usher's letter to him and the place he presumably returns to after Usher's house falls. Where is his home? What does it look and feel like? Who does he live with? Who are his neighbors? John and Annie are less mysterious; though John describes their northern home scantily, he provides many details about the new and, they hope, profitable "home" they make in the Reconstruction South. Julius, Sarah Ingle argues, works hard at making a home that bears African American historical weight; he "attempts to enshrine the memory of slavery in the swamps, creekbeds, marshes, trees, vineyards, sawmills, abandoned buildings, and other landmarks of his rural community" (156) and "functions as a commemorator every time one of his stories inscribes the life of a slave into a particular landmark" (156). Put another way, he claims the former plantation as home, and claims it for African American history, often against John's claims of possession and attempts to control and overwrite history.[5] John, Ingle argues, "remains unaware of his proprietary struggles with Julius and with the ghosts of the dead that recur throughout the stories" (158). But Julius's rich awareness of undeadness also entangles him in a home place that is (*a*) deeply haunted and (*b*) an undead plantation replete with undead slaves and slave masters. In both "Usher" and the conjure tales, the idea of home cannot easily be uncoupled from a lived experience of—or a stubborn imperviousness to—undeadness.

Roderick Usher certainly seems undead to the narrator, with his "cadaverousness of complexion," "very pallid" lips (401), and a "character of phantasm" (408). His "chief delight" as a reader is the *Vigiliae Mortuorum* (409). At one telling moment, as the narrator catches his only glimpse of the apparitional Madeline, Roderick Usher performs an undead act of self-burial that perhaps anticipates the premature burial of his sister; he "buried his face in his hands, and I could only perceive that a far more than ordinary wanness had overspread the emaciated fingers through which trickled many passionate tears" (404). Not long after Usher and the narrator entomb Madeline, "the pallor of his countenance had assumed, if possible, a more ghastly hue" (410); on his final night, "[h]is countenance was, as usual, cadaverously wan" and, as if in sympathetic undeadness, storm clouds flew with "life-like velocity" (412). Meanwhile, Madeline shows signs of incipient vampiric power; the mere sight of her afflicts the narrator with feelings of stupor, oppression, astonishment, and dread, and, "dead," she sports "the mockery of a faint blush . . . and that suspiciously lingering smile upon the lip which is so terrible in death" (410). In an eerie anticipation of early-twenty-first-century object theory, which investigates the wide-ranging influence of "inanimate" bodies on social spaces as well as the ways these "things" appear to express forms of agency, Usher places belief in another form of undeadness: "the sentience of all vegetable things." In "Usher," things have sentience and houses and people feed on each other and influence each other reciprocally. (In "Po' Sandy," the creeping vine that covers the haunted schoolhouse is merely "ambitious but futile" [14].) Poe's story posits a closed circulatory system replete with dangerous reciprocities, submerged histories, and loose ends. What happens to Usher's servants? to the narrator's horse? And what about the peasantry? The narrator reports that "the 'House of Usher' [is] an appellation which seemed to include, in the minds of the peasantry who used it, both the family and the family mansion." Who, and where, are these people, and what is *their* take on the collapse of house and House into the swampy tarn?

While one of Usher's problems is that he doesn't get out enough—in fact, "for many years" running, he does not get out at all (403)—Po' Sandy's problem is that he gets out too much, passed around as he is from one of his master's children to another, and to other kinfolk as well. Sandy yearns for the stability of "home," even though "home" for him is the plantation on which he is a slave: "[H]it's Sandy dis en Sandy dat, en Sandy yer and Sandy dere, tel it 'pears to me I ain't got no home, ner no marster, ner no mistiss, ner no nuffin. . . . I wisht I wuz a tree, er a stump er a rock, er sump'n w'at could stay on de plantation fer a w'ile" (17). His second wife, Tenie, a fellow slave, reveals that she is an out-of-practice conjure woman, and the couple decides to transform Sandy into a tree, after which he loses his mouth and ears but seems to maintain sentience, consciousness, and the capacity to suffer. Then, still in the form of a tree, he is cut down and run through the mill saw. In succession, Sandy is turned into a tree, then into lumber, then into a kitchen, then into a schoolhouse. Along the way, he turns into a haunt, an undead and also, quite literally, a house of Sandy.

Though the white transplants from the North are obviously not slaveholders, the war is over, and the plantation South is crumbling, the story of Sandy suggests that undeadness reanimates the history of plantation slavery in the South, and even more particularly a history in which a slave can be both homesick for his master's plantation and run through a sawmill by the same master's orders, conscious, while his wife is forced to watch. For Sandy, neither self-transformation nor remaining as he is turns out to be a good, viable option; he becomes an undead avatar of the plantation slavery system that cuts him down and chops him up and forces him to remain aware of his own unending undeadness. Retelling the story of Po' Sandy, Julius rehearses this horror, thereby commemorating and preserving Sandy's undead state. For Tenie, as for Sandy, conjure works but does not help. And what of John and Annie? Julius practices narrative conjure on them; a highly skilled rhetorician, he matches stories to situations and often ends up getting or preserving what he wants. But why does Julius invite Sandy and Tenie in particular to haunt John and Annie in particular? Richard Brodhead floats the idea that John and Annie suffer from "experiential deprivation"—that they seek "a life richer in *life*" and are, in this sense, themselves undead or at risk of undeadness (11–12). The story of Po' Sandy cautions them neither to remain the same nor to change—but to do what, instead? Leave an old schoolhouse untouched so that Julius's group of secessionist churchgoers can use it? Tear it down so that they can reconstruct it as an old-style southern plantation kitchen? Either way, some form or strain of social undeath lingers. Sandy presumably remains undead until the last piece of the last plank of him crumbles to dust. The undead status of the house and House of Usher is somewhat less clear; "rushing asunder," the house implodes into fragments and falls into the tarn that provided it with a mirror image of itself—but then it rises up from beneath the surface, again and again, with each retelling of its undead story.

Indeed, for Poe and Chesnutt as for the narrator of "Usher" and Chesnutt's various narrators, the impulse to retell—to transcribe, transmit—the story is of paramount importance. This repeatability—retelling, reading, rereading—enables undeadness. Burying the Ushers and their house in the tarn, the narrator and Poe and his readers unbury them again and again; embedding and embodying Sandy's haunt in planks of timber, Julius and John and Chesnutt and their readers unembed and reembody him as the slave Sandy and the tree Sandy again and again. Reanimating the dead, these stories and their writers, tellers, and readers confer undeadness on them. Why do they do this? Chesnutt's readers pretty frequently ask after Julius's motives as a storyteller, but why does John retell Julius's stories? And why does the narrator of "Usher" tell this story? The latter never clarifies who he understands his audience to be, and he never reflects explicitly on his need or desire to tell what happened. If he tells the story to expel his terror, then he also reactivates that terror—as his at times nervous, even hysterical tone and style indicate—and he concludes the story without finding let alone offering much respite. Likewise, John does not say much about why he transcribes and transmits "Po' Sandy" or others of Julius's stories. Clearly, John does various other things for leisure, and he also expends a significant amount of time working at his business venture. John and Annie obviously enjoy listening to Julius's stories, but John does not *need* to transcribe them, whether for money, literary or ethnographic ambition, or personal satisfaction. Further, writing these stories down requires him to reproduce black dialect—to ventriloquize cross-racially—and to look bad on occasion. Perhaps Julius's motives in telling conjure tales to John and Annie have to do with the ways the stories and their tellers cross the color line: Julius voices slaveholders and other white people as well as black people in black dialect and then passes the story on to John, who transcribes and in a sense "speaks" in black dialect. The "frame tale," seen in this light, works by misdirection; its uncanny narrative architecture helps transmit and reanimate stories that are in large part about haunted, haunting, frame-splintering boundary crossings.

In "Usher" and "Po' Sandy," as in other Poe and Chesnutt stories, storytelling, and particularly story*re*telling, sets in motion an eerily undercover strain of undeadness. In both stories, "dead" figures come back to "life," "past" histories recur and remain present, inanimate structures awaken and keep reanimating, and the storytellers' decisions to build yet another structure—the story itself—suggests that an obsessive impulse to build and rebuild, to tell and retell, cedes power to forms of undeadness that haunt beyond the gothic. Here, both Chesnutt and Poe activate a strain of the uncanny that Freud finds in "The Sand-Man": "[W]e have particularly favorable conditions for generating feelings of the uncanny if intellectual uncertainty is aroused as to whether something is animate or inanimate, and whether the lifeless bears an excessive likeness to the living" (Freud 2003, 140–41). But, more than Freud, Poe and Chesnutt evoke the particular, embedded nature of uncanny repetition. In their narratives, undeadness operates in both unreconstructed and ever-reconstructed space and time; it is at once an outcome, a conduit, and something to be anticipated. By virtue of frequent retelling, it may also come to seem an inevitability or, at least, a force difficult to arrest. And, as I have begun to suggest by connecting Poe's undead House of Usher to Chesnutt's undead House of Sandy, undeadness is a flexible and capacious thing—a point which comes clearer and extends farther when I bring in a third text: a Lumbee ghost story.

As Renée Bergland has argued, spectral Indians remind U.S. citizens of the destructive violence of colonial invasion and dispossession. These ghosts stand as evidence that non-Native settler colonists got a great deal of what they wanted, at great cost; but at the same time Native ghosts challenge this assumption of victorious, over-and-done-with Americanization. They keep things unsettled. But Bergland also points out that Indian ghosts, though prevalent, are not ubiquitous; for example, in her study they haunt the North far more than they do the South. Even so, the absence of Indigenous people, living or dead or undead, is striking in both Poe and Chesnutt—and perhaps most particularly in Chesnutt, who lived, worked, and grounded his conjure tales in Cumberland County, North Carolina, which adjoins Robeson County, home of the Lumbee Tribe and the historically Native American University of North Carolina at Pembroke, which opened in 1887, the year Chesnutt published his first conjure story, "The Goophered Grapevine," and the year before he published "Po' Sandy." As Lumbee historian Malinda Maynor Lowery explains, Lumbees in the 1880s were hard at work "creating a [statewide] presence as a 'tribe'" (*Lumbee Indians* 147). Poe and Chesnutt—one writing in the contexts of slavery, sectional crises, and Indian removal, and the other

THE FALL OF THE HOUSE OF PO' SANDY

writing in the contexts of Reconstruction, Jim Crow, the Dawes Allotment Act, and state legislation that, in 1885, recognized the Lumbees as "Croatan" and established a separate school system for them—share something more troubling than undeadness: an erasure of American Indian histories and cultures, and a refusal to write Indians into their stories *even as* ghosts. Taken together, Poe and Chesnutt thus help map some of the hot spots as well as some of the limits of nineteenth-century southern undeadness. As I have argued, the specters that haunt and trouble "Usher" and "Po' Sandy" and many of their other stories are house-bound, but they are also traveling creatures, reflections of the complex historical and intercultural dynamics that contribute to the construction of Uncle Julius's (and Po' Sandy's) schoolhouse and John and Annie's plantation house in North Carolina as well as the shape and isolation of the House of Usher. But the story of undead Souths is about more than just where the bodies are buried and when and where they rise up; it is also about the bodies that are missing, the differences between absent presences and just plain absences.

Consider, for example, a representative Lumbee ghost story:

> Lumbee land in Robeson County is so particularly valued because it has been inhabited by Lumbee ancestors for centuries. For hundreds of years Lumbees have struggled to maintain ownership of their homes and property. . . . Through all of this, their homeland has[,] in a way, become an extension of Lumbees themselves. Lumbee ghost stories are often place specific and involve features of the land which are important to the people. By passing down stories with an emphasis on place and land, the importance and connection to land is maintained through generations. An example of one such story is a well known tale about Henry Berry Lowrie. There are many variations of this story, but one version states that every night Henry comes up from the swamps in order to visit the grave of his wife Rhoda. This story is important not only for its historical significance, but also for its subtle emphasis on land features. It is important to notice that Henry comes from the swamp to visit Rhoda. The swamp is a land feature which is extremely prevalent in Robeson County. Throughout the history of the Lumbee the swamps have served as a place of safety and protection from the outside world. Rather than having Henry come from an unmarked grave, or merely appear at Rhoda's tombstone he seems to be a permanent resident of the swamp. This serves as a perpetual reminder of the crucial role that the swamps played in the life of Henry Berry Lowrie. It also places a kind of honor on the swamps. Just as Henry Berry was

and is a distinctively Lumbee man, the swamps are a distinctively Lumbee land feature. (Lowery, "Ghost Stories")

Like "Usher" and "Po' Sandy," this is a departure/return story about the undead, set in an uncanny home alongside a swamp. Strikingly less horrifying and more pedagogically minded than either the Poe or the Chesnutt story, the Lumbee story presents the ghost, the swamp, and the graveyard as teachings, first and foremost. Its lesson is encapsulated in three words in the final quoted sentence: "was and is."

Every time somebody rereads or retells "The Fall of the House of Usher," or a Chesnutt conjure story, or a Lumbee ghost story, Madeline Usher and the House of Usher and Po' Sandy and the house of Sandy and Henry Berry Lowrie rise up again only to return to the strangely swamp-like tarn (Usher), the edge of the swamp (Sandy as tree), or the Robeson County swamp. Reanimated, these characters and the stories about them reenact various kinds of undeadness. Blanco writes that "haunting can indicate how American authors write spaces that are in the process of being transformed, rather than simply describe locations where the past has been interred" (16). To think about undeadness is to move beyond the gothic and toward not only haunted houses, not only dead bodies in houses, not only houses as undead bodies, not only a slave's homesickness for the plantation where his tree body is run through a sawmill while his wife is forced to watch, but also Lumbee ghosts who reaffirm that we are still here, that here remains ours, that we, too, are undead.

NOTES

1. Freud observes, in "The Uncanny," that "German usage allows the familiar (*das Heimliche*, the 'homely') to switch to its opposite, the uncanny (*das Unheimliche*, the 'unhomely') . . . for this uncanny element is actually nothing new or strange, but something that was long familiar to the psyche and was estranged from it only through being repressed" (Freud 2003, 148).

2. In *The Architectural Uncanny*, Anthony Vidler explains that "[a]rchitecture has been intimately linked to the notion of the uncanny since the end of the eighteenth century. At one level, the house has provided a site for endless representations of haunting, doubling, dismembering, and other terrors in literature and art" (ix).

3. Peeples notes, for example, that in an 1889 piece for *Lippincott's Magazine*, Thomas Nelson Page claims that Poe "is the one really great writer of purely literary work that the South produced under its old conditions" (qtd. in Peeples 23). This leads Peeples to observe, "Not only

was Poe a far better writer than, say, Henry Timrod or William Gilmore Simms, but he did not carry overt Confederate baggage as those writers did" (23).

4. See also the powerful treatments of this theme in Leigh Anne Duck, *The Nation's Region: Southern Modernism, Segregation, and U.S. Nationalism;* and in Jennifer Rae Greeson, *Our South: Geographic Fantasy and the Rise of National Literature.*

5. Eric Sundquist notes a further complication: "Chesnutt's own evocation of . . . 'de ole times,' like that of [Joel Chandler] Harris, employed an analogous superimposition of historical time frames that allowed him to explore both the resurgence of plantation typology in post-Reconstruction history and the countering origins of modern African American culture in the 'ole times' of slavery, the middle passage, and Africa" (357–58).

3

WHAT REMAINS WHERE
Civil War Poetry and Photography across 150 Years

ELIZABETH BRADFORD FRYE and COLEMAN HUTCHISON

The American Civil War was a conflict captured as much by the camera as the pen. While it was indeed a "poetry-fueled war," the memory of those tumultuous years was also conditioned by photographic images of battles, leaders, and ruins (Barrett 3). As Timothy Sweet argues in his pioneering study *Traces of War: Poetry, Photography, and the Crisis of the Union*, poetic and photographic representations of the war were sympathetically invested in the "transformation of wounds into ideology during and after the Civil War" (2).[1] Such a twinning of poetry and photography should come as little surprise. After all, both were ascendant media in the immediate antebellum period; during the war, the explosion of periodical print culture meant that both northerners and southerners had unprecedented access to poems and images of their shared world at war.

This essay considers the connections among poetry, photography, and the physical traces of the American Civil War through a *longue durée* frame. The following pages read four disparate texts in relation to one another: a poem from Natasha Trethewey's collection *Native Guard* (2006), an image from Sally Mann's art book *What Remains* (2003), a poem from William Gilmore Simms's anthology *War Poetry of the South* (1866), and an image from Alexander Gardner's *Photographic Sketch Book of the Civil War* (1866). By emphasizing common elements of poetic and photographic representation across 150 years, we identify a heretofore overlooked Civil War memorial tradition.

Despite their generic and historical differences, these four texts share, we argue, a macabre site specificity, in which the living and the dead, the past and the present, are brought into increasingly close physical proximity. These poets and photographers render the memory of the American Civil War as an emplaced experience, a phenomenon "ineluctably place-bound" (Casey 19).

Although separated by a century and a half, these text pairs are, we offer, in intimate conversation, particularly around issues of race and representation. They also take place all over the South. We begin in Vicksburg, Mississippi, a place where, according to Trethewey, "the living come to mingle / with the dead, brush against their cold shoulders." By locating past, present, living, and dead in the same space, Trethewey draws on a long southern literary tradition, one that may have reached its apex in the elegiac poems collected by William Gilmore Simms (among others) in the immediate aftermath of the Civil War. Simms's own "Morris Island" (ca. 1863) is an excellent example of the genre, since it, too, emphasizes the purportedly physical coexistence of the dead and the undead. Both of these poems emplace Civil War memory in specific sites; moreover, both cast said sites in a peculiar, ghastly light.

A similar dynamic is at work in Sally Mann's dark, muddy images of Civil War battlefields (ca. 2003). Her haunting photographs of twenty-first-century Antietam assume a prior knowledge of Civil War–era photographic history and raise the question, What remains of the war today? Needless to say, Mann is not the first photographer to have asked such a question. Alexander Gardner's famous image "A Burial Party, Cold Harbor, Va., April, 1865" shows recently emancipated African Americans collecting human remains. While Mann and Gardner use the play of presence and absence quite differently in their photographs, both tout the fundamental interpenetration of place and memory, and both emphasize the morbidity of their respective sites. Taken together, these four texts speak to the deathly relations of Civil War poetry and photography and their strange traffic in the undead.

"Come to Mingle with the Dead"

It is a critical commonplace that Natasha Trethewey's poetry is wary of any easy remembrance of things past. Haunted by the South's dark histories and scenes of violence, Trethewey often employs photography as a central metaphor to question the workings of personal and public memory. As

Katherine Henninger has noted, Trethewey's use of photography offers "a highly contemporary, sophisticated model for how we might reread the 'evidence' of southern history for the unheard and unseen, and how once acknowledged, this evidence leads to new mappings of the past and future South" (170). Because her poems require the reader to consider what is beyond the scope of her framing, Trethewey's work blurs the lines between word and image, black folks and white, the quick and the dead.

Even poems not explicitly about photography are informed by this macabre photographic sensibility. In "Pilgrimage," we join the speaker in Vicksburg, Mississippi, for the annual commemoration of one of the most important sieges of the American Civil War. Significantly, the poem precedes those in the collection that excavate the little-known history of the Louisiana Native Guard, one of the first regiments of black Union soldiers, whom Trethewey resurrects through dramatis personae. But before she speaks from beyond the grave, Trethewey offers "Pilgrimage" as a contemporary meditation on selective public memory. The poem also serves as a bridge back to Trethewey's depiction of her own past; it immediately follows the book's opening section in which the poet draws from personal recollection and family lore.

"Pilgrimage" unfolds across a series of landscapes and vignettes that stress the physical presence of the dead, as well as its living speaker's struggle with their forms. Amid these memento mori, Trethewey touts the complexity of Vicksburg's site-specific representation of the Civil War. As the poem's title suggests, these yearly events—which include tours of antebellum homes and the Vicksburg National Military Park—align roughly with both the anniversary of the Siege of Vicksburg (May to July 1863) and the celebration of Easter. For its participants, then, this "pilgrimage" takes on the status of religious rite, and the Mississippi becomes not unlike the River Jordan. These pilgrims (such as they are) seek sanctification via an encounter with holy ghosts. Accordingly, Trethewey's account of the spectacle highlights the city's desire for a reunion with its Confederate dead:

> Every spring—
> *Pilgrimage*—the living come to mingle
> with the dead, brush against their cold shoulders
> in the long hallways, listen all night
> to their silence and indifference, relive
> their dying on the green battlefield. (19–20)

Trethewey's speaker, however, does not share her hosts' enthusiasm for calling back the spirits of the dead, their names inscribed in stone and steel by the Daughters of the Confederacy.

Indeed, "Pilgrimage" begins not with hulking memorials but with a menacing panorama of the Mississippi River. The speaker's initial observations assume a solemn, dark cast: "Here, the Mississippi carved / its mud-dark path, a graveyard / for skeletons of sunken riverboats" (19). In addition to this array of bones, Trethewey's speaker senses something ominous in the water. "Here," she writes, "the river changed its course, / turning away from the city / as one turns, forgetting from the past" (19). This sense of historical amnesia, manifested in a river that "forgets" the events of its own "life," is coupled with an overwhelming sense of decay. The landscape itself seems unsettled and unsettling: "the abandoned bluffs, land sloping up / above the river's bend—where now / the Yazoo fills the Mississippi's empty bed" (19). In these initial lines, Trethewey perverts the pastoral, making the reader immediately aware of something rotten in the state of Mississippi—despite the poem's "southland in the springtime" setting. Furthermore, Trethewey's repetition of the deictic marker "here" draws that reader into the city's morbid tableaux.

The city's ghostly figures then confront the speaker in strikingly physical terms: "Here, the dead stand up in stone, white / marble, on Confederate Avenue" (19). After these dead "stand up," Trethewey concludes the line with a hard enjambment, causing the reader to focus on the whiteness of the monuments. This deft rhetorical move also subtly gestures back to the collection's titular Native Guard, who are nowhere to be found in this "grave" place. Here in Vicksburg—a black majority city—the conjured, reanimate dead seem exclusively "white" and "Confederate" (Census Bureau).

In keeping with the collection's themes, Trethewey's speaker is thus figured as an outsider; even the dead seem strange and far away to her: "At the museum, we marvel at their clothes— / preserved under glass—so much smaller / than our own, as if those who wore them / were only children." But these lines also betray a tenderness, an attempt at recognizing the humanity of those who are simultaneously long-gone and ever-present. Indeed, Trethewey's speaker momentarily puts herself in the place of one of the Siege's female diarists: "I can see her / listening to the shells explode, writing herself / into history, asking *what is to become / of all of the living things in this place?"* This is a surprising scene of sympathy between strange bedfellows. Like the anonymous Confederate woman, Trethewey is writing herself into history. After their respective close encounters with death, both women feel as though they are living things in a world of ghosts. Given the poem's insistent rhetoric of location, *"this place"* renders Civil War–era Vicksburg and contemporary Vicksburg proximate, even intimate.

It is at this moment that the poem declares, "This whole city is a grave." Yet, what ultimately disturbs Trethewey's speaker is not that she is surrounded by the nonliving but that her black ancestors are nowhere to be found. Despite the beauty of the poem's springtime setting—a pleasing view of "the old mansions hunkered on the bluffs, draped / in flowers—funereal—a blur / of petals against the river's gray" (20)—the living are threatened by a myopic and eventually racist view of the past. When a representative black figure finally emerges in the poem, she takes the form of a familiar character from Margaret Mitchell's *Gone with the Wind*: "The brochure in my room calls this / *living history*. The brass plate on the door reads / *Prissy's Room* [. . .]" (20). Here is another nonliving being with which the speaker must contend. Just as the Confederate dead are reanimated as *"living history,"* Trethewey's speaker finds herself relegated to *"Prissy's Room"* and thus asked to recognize herself in a much-maligned depiction of black womanhood. Living briefly in *"Prissy's Room"* proves to be the most disturbing kind of forgetting, a retreat into a fictionalized past.

Thadious M. Davis has recently argued that Trethewey's poetry relies on an "apertural space" (58) through which the poet locates herself and views the world. Davis's observation that this space is "primarily gendered and connected to a woman's body" is particularly instructive in interpreting "Pilgrimage's" conclusion. In the poem's last stanzas, Vicksburg is shrouded in gloom; as night descends, the Mississippi is revealed to be not the River Jordan but the River Lethe. The poem concludes with the speaker's chilling sense of her own imperiled black body: "[. . .] A window frames / the river's crawl toward the Gulf. In my dream, / the ghost of history lies down beside me, / rolls over, pins me beneath a heavy arm" (20). In this arresting final image, Trethewey's speaker once again gazes out at the river full of skeletons. But now, in a revision of the "Mississippi's empty bed" (19), she shares quarters with an unwanted intimate: the burdensome and suffocating specter of southern history. In closing the poem with "the river's slow crawl toward the Gulf" (20), Trethewey revisits and revises the poem's initial image of a natural world marked by decay. But now the speaker is framed in a scene of potential violence, as this place and its history threaten to pull her into a river of skeletons. At last, Vicksburg's troublesome version of the past threatens to become her grave, her cave, her catacomb.

"Exuberant with Seed"

A similar sense of menacing seduction attends Sally Mann's murky images of Antietam, which were included in her 2003 series *What Remains*. Like Trethewey's treatment of Vicksburg, Mann's photographs of the notorious Civil War battlefield envision nineteenth-century mass death and destruction from a twenty-first-century perspective. Yet, while Trethewey's ghosts prove frightening reminders of large-scale historical inaccuracies and distortion, Mann's images make alluring the process of earthly decomposition. The fragility of human life is a driving force in all of Mann's work, and the Antietam images are no exception. Mann's book couches images of the battlefield between a series of "portraits" of anonymous corpses rotting in the woods of the University of Tennessee's "body farm" and blurry renderings of the faces of Mann's own children. Thus, Mann places her representations of Antietam between the visages of her most beloved intimates and the likenesses of putrid, dead strangers. However, no human bodies—dead or alive—appear in Mann's battlefield scenes. These shadowy prints stun the viewer with their vacancy: a field shows only a tree bending gently in the wind, the horizon darkens ominously, and night draws nigh.[2] Ultimately, the images raise the question, what remains of the war today?

A clue may lie in Mann's technique. The photographer used glass plates smeared with silver nitrate and a vintage 8x10 view camera to create *What Remains*. Because this process emulates those of her nineteenth-century predecessors, Mann deftly populates her images with the spirit of theirs. Yet, as she notes in the documentary film *What Remains*, Mann's Antietam images constitute an even more deliberate response to Civil War photographers like Alexander Gardner, who worked as an assistant to Mathew Brady (Cantor 38:01). Not surprisingly, Antietam was the first battle depicted by Gardner. Gardner's images of the battle became some of the most famous and most heavily reproduced of the American Civil War (Lee and Young 38–43). Mann

FIGURE 1. Alexander Gardner, [Antietam, Md. Bodies of Confederate dead gathered for burial]. Library of Congress, Prints & Photographs Division, LOT 4168.

pays quiet tribute to Gardner by literally following in his footsteps, traveling to Antietam and reimagining the landscapes that he made famous.

This is not to say that Mann's images are completely derivative—on the contrary. In looking at Mann's photographs, we hold Gardner's piled bodies in our minds, so much so that the former's images seem a negative of the latter's (figure 1). This sense of inversion is crucial to understanding Mann's interplay of past and present, presence and absence, dead and undead. While nineteenth-century photographers hoped for clean, focused images, Mann deliberately imbued her landscapes with haziness and spots by waving her hand in front of the lens. Several of her images are marred by dark shadows or nearly eaten by the chemicals of their composition. Whereas Gardner et al. used the most recent and readily available technology to depict Civil War casualties, Mann's manipulations of similar equipment place front and center the contrivances of her macabre aesthetic.[3]

Critics have frequently commented on Mann's deft oscillation between the realism and romance of decay. Her apposition of the pastoral and the mechanical—an apposition she may well have cribbed from Gardner—has received less attention. In a 2013 talk given at the Smithsonian, Mann described her trip to the battlefield in highly lyrical terms:

> Just past dawn, I pulled my rolling darkroom into a far corner of the field by the Burnside bridge. The grasses were pendulous with dew, and it took a hot spring sun to lighten then into an airy undulation. I watched it happen. The fields began to ripple like satin cloth flapping in slow motion as each stalk, exuberant with seed, swayed in easy unison with its neighbors. I looked across those oblivious fields sculpted by death and thought the Bible is right: surely, the people is grass. (Cantor 13:56)

As her language reveals, Mann at first appears intent on perpetuating the relationship between photography, nature, and mass death that had its roots in Civil War–era photography. Indeed, Mann's choice to represent Antietam as "oblivious fields sculpted by death"—as mere landscape—seems to draw "a recuperative pastoral frame" around the conflict's great casualties (Sweet 8). As Sweet cautions, such pastoralism is not without political consequence, since it "usually implies that death resulting from war is somehow as natural as any other death" (8–9). But in this series, it is Mann's deathly images of the present—not the distant, Civil War past—that promote a naturalized, dust-to-dust aesthetic. In *What Remains,* the body farm's recent dead emerge from piles of leaves, Mann's dear greyhound withers to a stack of bones, and a faint sickliness tints the faces of her children, as if to say, these, too, shall pass. The dead at Antietam are long since gone; they are now the very stuff beneath Mann's feet.

In a series obsessed with past, present, and impending fatality, Mann refuses to render the Civil War dead as fully dead. Instead, like Trethewey, she reveals the grisly truth about this pastoral setting: This garden is in fact a graveyard. In turn, while Mann's words suggest pastoral comfort, the images themselves overwhelmingly call attention to the technology that made them. In doing so, Mann's battlefield photographs ask viewers to attend to the decidedly unnatural causes of Civil War deaths, all those machines of war that produced twenty-three thousand bodies at Antietam alone. After all, her "rolling darkroom" is foregrounded in Mann's description of "those oblivious fields, sculpted by death." Ironically, then, her bucolic scenes help to unearth a bloody past.

"To Decay Unnoticed Where They Fell"

When it came time for Alexander Gardner to cull images for his extraordinary *Photographic Sketch Book of the War*, that bloody past was not even past yet. By the summer of 1865, Gardner was able to draw on a diverse if geographically limited set of more than three thousand negatives that he and his team of assistants had produced throughout the war. The resulting *Sketch Book* is among the most unusual and important fine press books of the nineteenth century. Limited to an edition of two hundred copies, the book was comprised of two volumes of fifty albumen print photographs. Each print was hand-pasted onto the boards alongside letterpress-printed descriptive captions. Despite its prohibitive initial cost—$150 for a set—several images from the book are now iconic representations of the American Civil War. The *Sketch Book* has also become "a foundational volume in the history of American photography, the first book to rely so heavily on pictures for its meanings" (Lee and Young 1).

Said meanings are, however, inchoate at best. The book offers a disjointed or desultory Civil War narrative that focuses almost exclusively on the movements of the Army of the Potomac. More to the point, the *Sketch Book* lavishes most of its attention on unexpected photographic subjects: camp life, panoramas, and the material culture of war. Although "A Harvest of Death, Gettysburg, July, 1863" (36) may be the collection's most familiar image, it is far from representative. Actual bodies—human or animal—appear in only a handful of Gardner's plates, and all but one of those gruesome photographs come from the Battle of Gettysburg (36–38, 40–42, 44). Instead, Gardner offers image after image of military fortifications, bridges, and ruins. To Gardner's mind, these are the traces of war worthy of photographic preservation.

The collection's most arresting image is also its most macabre. "A Burial Party, Cold Harbor, Va., April, 1865" appears late in the chronologically arranged *Sketch Book* and features five African American men collecting the heavily decayed remains of Union and Confederate soldiers (figure 2). The image's background shows three of the five men using shovels to disinter

FIGURE 2. Alexander Gardner, "A Burial Party, Cold Harbor, Va., April, 1865." *Gardner's Photographic Sketch Book of the War* (Washington, D.C.: Philp & Solomons, 1866), 94.

bodies or parts of bodies, while a fourth reaches down to grasp something, perhaps a skull. This ghastly labor takes place on uneven, patchy ground, with a distant tree line rising ominously above the scene. As with Mann's images, we are forced to think about what lies beneath this "oblivious field." But Gardner's photograph (made from a negative by John Reekie) leaves little to the viewer's imagination.

Crucially, all of the men in the background look down at the ground and their grim work. This is in sharp contrast with the man who sits in the foreground, next to a stretcher teeming with human remains, including no fewer than five skulls and one prominently displayed severed leg. The dark-skinned man looks directly at the camera; the bleached white skull beside him does the same. If the former's proximity to the latter gives him pause, then his expression betrays no emotion. In this heavily staged photograph, both the living and the dead meet the viewer's gaze without hesitation.

"A Burial Party, Cold Harbor, Va., April, 1865" has occasioned no small amount of commentary. And with good reason. This "Party" picture begs to be read in aggressive ways. Critics and historians have various interpreted it as: the apogee of Gardner's pastoralism; a racial allegory; a dramatic rendering of the causes and effects of the American Civil War in a single, powerful frame; and a "gothic relay among dismembered body parts and between words and images" (Lee and Young 90).[4] But few commentators have noted how resolutely Gardner places this "georgic of the aftermath" in a specific location at a specific moment in time (Sweet 135). The plate's characteristically dilatory caption notes that this burial party was collecting remains produced by two battles, not one: the Battle of Gaines' Mill in 1862 and the Battle of Cold Harbor in 1864. Since Hanover County, Virginia, remained fiercely contested in the nearly two years between the battles, burial parties were unable to properly collect the dead from the field. The plate's revolting centerpiece captures the welter of the deceased and the dismembered that accrued over time.

Gardner's accompanying purple prose lays the blame for this "sad scene" on southerners who had not done their duty: "It speaks ill of the residents of that part of Virginia, that they allowed even the remains of those they considered enemies, to decay unnoticed where they fell. The soldiers, to whom commonly falls the task of burying the dead, may possibly have been called away before the task was completed. At such times the native dwellers of the neighborhood would usually come forward and provide sepulture for such as had been left uncovered." Although Gardner goes on to acknowledge that such scenes were not uncommon during the war—in both the South and the North—his disparagement of the "native dwellers of the neighborhood" stings. This was, finally, a failure of southern hospitality. Thus, Gardner's unnerving memento mori circulated both with a painstaking sense of place and as a subtle indictment of the South. Scenes like this were, Gardner argues, the result of southern neglect, if not outright southern malevolence. Such an indictment is especially urgent given the context of this image. The Battle of Cold Harbor was a resounding Confederate victory. It was also an immensely bloody affair for the Union, which suffered nearly thirteen thousand casualties. Gardner ensured that the unceremonious decay of their bodies and body parts did not go "unnoticed." In doing so, he also ensured that the gothicism of this scene would be remembered as a specifically southern gothicism.

"Each Rampart Proves a Grave"

At the same time Alexander Gardner was culling images for his *Sketch Book*, William Gilmore Simms, the leading light of southern letters, began sifting through an immense archive of Confederate poetry in order to produce a "creditable" anthology. Perhaps because the war had all but ruined Simms—both personally and professionally—the aging literary lion gave nearly a year of his late life to the project, which he called *War Poetry of the South* (1866). In addition to being one of the largest and most diverse contemporary anthologies of the poetry of the Civil War South, it is also, by a significant margin, the most important. Simms drew poetry from all of the Confederate States, as well as several Border States; he also included a good deal of his own verse. Not surprisingly, then, the 205 poems in the collection vary greatly in tone, topic, and literary quality. The result is a generous and more or less representative sampling of Confederate literary culture.[5]

In his remarkable prose preface, Simms assured readers that he had excluded a "large proportion of pieces [...] of elegiac character," lest the volume strike too dour a tone or seem in any way defeatist (vii). But, despite his better editorial intentions, *War Poetry of the South* reads like the poetic equivalent of Gardner's stretcher: the volume teems with dreary imagery and dirges, lost love and laments. Death is everywhere on these pages. Paul Hamilton Hayne's oft-reprinted "Our Martyrs" is indicative of the anthology's mood:

> I AM sitting lone and weary
>   On the hearth of my darkened room,
> And the low wind's *miserere*
>   Makes sadder the midnight gloom;
> There's a terror that's nameless nigh me
>   There's a phantom spell in the air,
> And methinks that the dead glide by me,
>   And the breath of the grave's in my hair! (277)

But it is Simms's own poem "Morris Island" that offers a macabre site specificity sympathetic to that of Gardner, Mann, and especially Trethewey.

First published as an unsigned poem in the *Charleston Mercury* on October 5, 1863, Simms reprinted "Morris Island" three-quarters of the way through *War Poetry of the South*. Breaking from tradition, Simms's irregular ode does not address an event, an ideal, or a person but instead a locality. This is an ode to a place—and an unattractive place, at that. Morris Island is located at the mouth of Charleston Harbor; because of this plum position, it was a hugely important strategic asset during the Civil War. The Confederates heavily fortified positions across the 800-plus-acre island, and, as the main theater of action for the Siege of Charleston Harbor (July 18–September 7, 1863), it witnessed a great deal of bloodshed. Most famously, it was the setting for the Second Battle of Fort Wagner, which decimated the Fifty-Fourth Massachusetts Voluntary Infantry, a regiment of black soldiers led by the Boston blueblood Robert Gould Shaw. By the end of that battle, on July 18, 1863, the Fifty-Fourth had suffered some 272 casualties, including Colonel Shaw. Abandoned in September 1863 by Confederate troops, the Union took control of the island, including Batteries Wagner and Greg. Simms would sing the island's praises just a few weeks later.[6]

The ode opens with no small amount of patriotic gore:

> OH! from the deeds well done, the blood well shed
> In a good cause springs up to crown the land
> With ever-during verdure, memory fed,
> Wherever freedom rears one fearless band,
> The genius, which makes sacred time and place,
> Shaping the grand memorials of a race ! (327)

Although the nationalist sentiment expressed here is more or less unremarkable—in truth, much Confederate verse trumpeted the cause of "freedom" and heralded a new "race" (Hutchison, *Apples and Ashes* 4–14, 99–143)—Simms's sanguinity warrants some comment. The image of "blood well shed" bubbling up from the ground and nourishing the "ever-during verdure" is as grotesque as it is compelling. As with Trethewey's Vicksburg, Simms's whole island is a grave, but the living and the dead mingle here in less intimate ways. What lies beneath this now sanctified ground is a gory fount of national memory. Lest one miss the point, Simms quickly moves to connect blood, dirt, and poetry: "The barren rock becomes a monument, / The sea-shore sands a shrine ; / And each brave life, in desperate conflict spent, / Grows to a memory which prolongs a line !" Once again, the "well shed" blood of southerners feeds growth and expansion—poetic and otherwise.

As these lines suggest, Simms does not idealize his titular subject. In an unusual apostrophe, the speaker catalogues the island's unattractive features: "Oh ! barren isle oh ! fruitless shore, / Oh ! realm devoid of beauty" (327). Morris Island is worthy of an ode only because its rough, uninhabitable terrain proved the site of such sacrifice and loss. To this end, the poem pulls no punches about the hopes for a Confederate victory in Charleston Harbor. Indeed, the immortality of the island seems predicated on Confederate defeat, not Confederate victory. Simms imagines a future in which "the grandshires at the ingle-blaze" teach southern children about the struggle to maintain the batteries on Morris Island:

> Watching the endurance of the free and brave,
> > Through the protracted struggle and close fight,
> Contending for the lands they may not save,
> > Against the felon and innumerous foe ;
> Still struggling, though each rampart proves a grave,
> > For home, and all that's dear to man below ! (328)

Thus it is the grandchildren of Confederates—twentieth-century southerners, perhaps—who will listen to this tale. Yet Simms's insistent use of the present tense and contingent rhetoric (e.g., "Contending for the lands they may not save") confuses the temporality of the poem. It bears repeating: Simms wrote and published his poem after the Confederate abandonment of the island. As such, and à la Sally Mann, past and present, dead and undead seem to occupy the same frame here. The poem stages Morris Island as a meeting place for souls both departed and to come.

As he is wont to do, Simms then ties his contemporary moment to a historical precedent. The poem's final stanza hails the "undaunted" efforts and "martyr's might" by which "They make for man a new Thermopyl ; / And, perishing for freedom, still go free !" (328). Simms is no doubt thinking of the Battle of Thermopylae (480 BCE), and suggesting that Confederates draw inspiration from the relatively small number of Greeks who, gravely outnumbered, gave their lives to defend their homeland against a Persian invasion. Such Spartan sacrifice helps to explain the seeming paradox of someone "perishing for freedom" but somehow still going "free." In death, the martyrs of Thermopylae achieved eternal life. Simms wants the same for the martyrs of Morris Island—the Confederate martyrs of Morris Island, that is. Their blood can feed the "ever-during verdure" of southern memory; their ghosts can help to shape subsequent myths about the South and its purportedly "good cause."[7]

Conclusion: What Remains Where

Simms's "Morris Island" can be drawn into easy, close conversation with a number of twentieth-century poems about the American Civil War, including both Allen Tate's "Ode to the Confederate Dead" (1928) and Robert Lowell's "For the Union Dead" (1960). Both of those poems, in turn, clearly influenced Natasha Trethewey's *Native Guard*. And so we return to where we began, having traversed four southern states, numerous Civil War battle sites, and more than 150 years. The four disparate texts discussed above suggest that the memory of the American Civil War is indeed an emplaced experience. Despite their radically different representational politics, Trethewey, Mann, Gardner, and Simms all insist on the importance of place—of showing what remains where—to the ways the war is remembered and revised over time.

This is particularly the case in the U.S. South. After all, most of the American Civil War was fought on southern ground. That fighting produced, in turn, a staggering number of deaths—whites and blacks, southerners and northerners alike. As Drew Gilpin Faust and Mark S. Schantz have argued, the war forever changed America's "culture of death." In addition to producing at least 620,000 bodies, the conflict fundamentally changed how Americans remembered those dearly departed. These four poems and photographs speak resoundingly to such a shift. More to the point, they also argue that locality helps to shape Civil War memory in profound ways. Returning to the same ground again and again, these poets and photographers traffic in the undead and unearth a vital Civil War memorial tradition.

NOTES

1. See also Rosenheim, who argues that the camera "defined and perhaps even helped unify the nation through an unrehearsed and unscripted act of collective memory-making" (1).

2. See Mann, *What Remains*, 95. The image is also available in the "Battlefields" section of Mann's website: http://sallymann.com/selected-works/battlefields.

3. Of course Civil War–era photographs were themselves heavily manipulated. Gardner famous staged several of his Gettysburg images. Frassanito has gone so far as to suggest that Gardner may have dragged the body in plate 40 some forty yards in order to create plate 41 (see Frassanito 186–92).

4. The best of such readings are, respectively, those of Sweet (135–36), Lee (43–51, in Lee and Young), and Young (87–94, in Lee and Young).

5. It is no surprise that William Gilmore Simms deemed an anthology of southern war poetry worthy of both publication and his time. After all, Simms was a lifelong advocate for a

distinct and distinctive southern literature. He also thought of himself first and foremost as a poet (see Hutchison, "Surplus Patriotism").

6. The island was also home to the short-lived but much-dreaded "Swamp Angel," a 200-pound Union Parrott rifle artillery that pounded the city of Charleston in August 1863. In 1864 the Union Army relocated six hundred captured Confederate officers—"The Immortal 600," as they came to be known in southern lore—to Morris Island, where they served as human shields against Confederate bombardment.

7. As J. V. Ridgely argued, Simms was, at base, "a maker of myths about the South's past, present, and future during the most important period when the area was seeking its identity" (20–21). On other gothic poems by Simms based in South Carolina, see Fisher.

4

GRAY GHOSTS
Remediating the Confederate Undead

DANIEL CROSS TURNER

> From the inexhaustible bodies that are not
> Dead, but feed the grass, row after rich row
> —ALLEN TATE, "Ode to the Confederate Dead" (1927)

A century and a half after Appomattox, imagery of the Confederate States of America—including, perhaps most visibly, the Confederate "battle" flag—still catalyzes regional and racial tensions, evoking at once nostalgia and trauma, heritage and hate. This essay surveys a spectrum of spectral remediations of the Confederacy, concentrating on the Rise (again) of the Confederacy over the past few decades. Why is Confederate iconography *still* so undead in contemporary media, from print (literature and folklore) to audiovisual dimensions (film, television, popular music, graphic narratives)? Taking as a departure point that these gray ghosts—some purely invented, some "real"—serve as uncanny reflections of cathected social and political tensions,[1] I treat these Confederate undead as murky figures—simultaneously transparent and opaque—of cultural *desires* as much as *fears*, Žižekian stains of the real.

Much of the posthumous recrudescence of dead Confederates shades into the posthuman. At times these ghost-gray soldiers come back abstract and intact, translucent figures stolen from silent reels of *The Birth of a Nation*, mute and will-less avatars undergoing some cosmic serial looping, aloof and estranged from the color timing of the present. But many undead return fouled, bloodied, and broken-bodied, cyborg Confederates. Their forms are hybridized by the processes of injury, decay, and/or remediation, something lost in translation. Their creepy corporeality suggests the *dis*integration of the human—the fact that, even while alive, the body is an ad hoc assemblage of living and dead matters, continuously in process of growth and rot. The disaggregated human subject incessantly incorporates materials from other living and nonliving things into our corpus, an intercourse that only quickens and spreads postmortem. Smashed and spoiled figures in tattered butternut question the efficacy of human agency on individual and collective levels, signaling that human behaviors are conditioned heavily by nonhuman actants.[2]

Undead Johnny Rebs, then, point to existential matters of life and death (philosophically speaking), but also to sociopolitical and economic assemblages (culturally speaking). Like the tiny bulbous skulls atop the grain stalks that a zombified Jefferson Davis harvests in the weird—and weirdly prophetic—illustration from the October 26, 1861, *Harper's Weekly*, deathliness crops up everywhere in the field of contemporary southern and U.S. media. If the original illustration prophesied myriad deaths, North and South, approaching on the battlefield, as well as the cultural demise of agrarianism (once enslaved Africans are fled, Jeff Davis will be left alone to reap the crop) and the potential dissolution of two political bodies (U.S.A. and C.S.A. are both imperiled), it also scatters the seeds for multifarious remediations of the war and its divisions in future: those multiplying little death's heads metastasize like so many tumors in the gray matter of U.S. national consciousness to come.[3] In fact, to pay due homage to the unfulfilled yet not fully undone nation and its head dead Confederate, in 1893 Davis's body would be dug up from its initial resting place in Louisiana and reburied in Hollywood Cemetery in Richmond, Virginia.[4] The contemporary undeadness of the Confederacy reawakens the notion that all nations are "fantasmatic objects knotted together by ambivalent forces of desire, identification, memory, and forgetting, even as they simultaneously move within, across, and beyond a series of spatial and temporal borders" (Cooppan xvii).

Ghosts simulate a paraleptical doubling, where two realities superimpose in time and space, like a photographic double exposure. This marked interpenetration of past and present bears especial weight in the context of the U.S.

South, a culture often imagined as peculiarly time-bound.[5] The South has long been figured as a "belated" region chained to its past, or at least the bullet points of its large-schemed history, especially "The War" and its foreshadows as well as continuing afterlives: forced dissemination of Africans through the Middle Passage; chattel slavery underpinning a plantation economy; the Cult of the Lost Cause;[6] postplantation apartheid and spectacle lynching. As Stephanie McCurry's *Confederate Reckoning* (2010) asserts, the creation of the Confederate States of America was a seminal event since it marked the founding of "a proslavery and antidemocratic nation-state dedicated to the proposition that all men were not created equal" (1). The ghosts of the Confederacy reflect, as through a glass darkly, lasting shards of this political economy, unique even among slaveholding states in the hemisphere at the time. These absent presences and present absences take shape at times as mournful histories (traumas suffered on the battlefield or through racial violence), at times as nostalgic respites under the pastoral atmospherics of the Old South.

I will concentrate on manifestations of Confederate undeadness that betray "postsouthern" impulses, arising at a historical moment when the South's "familiar way of making and maintaining meaning, its orthodoxy or consensus, had ceased functioning, as it were, on involuntary muscles and had become a kind of willed habit" (Kreyling, "Fee, Fie, Faux Faulkner" 1). The metaphor here intimates the habitual redundancies of the undead, encore performances of the same acts, as ghosts keep repeating themselves ad infinitum. Physically compromised C.S.A. spirits, in their hyperreal maimed forms, represent the Deleuzian "Body without Organs" par excellence. Their condition rhymes seamlessly with postsouthern ponderings on the relative realness of "the South," the deconstructive freeplay between the region's conceptual and geopolitical groundings. Texts that body forth the Confederate undead in postsouthern fashion automatically allegorize the death of the author, if not of authenticity: every PoSo writer is a ghostwriter, while film and sound recordings become very like the condition of a ghost, the demands of these media enabling serial reiterations that go on and on well after the performers are long gone. Suspended over the void of virtual southernness, often clad in rags of parody and pastiche, these C.S.A. wraiths become ghosts of ghosts, spectral simulacra.

Yet, as Scott Romine contends, the impulse toward multiplying, overtly "inauthentic" versions of southernness should not be seen as reflecting cultural lack (the pained loss of a once "real," *deep* South), but should be taken as multivalent—not broken—signals of the desire for local identifications in an increasingly deterritorialized world. Indeed, roughly six hundred thousand lost their lives in the U.S. Civil War, and, judging by the immense reams of ghostlore dedicated to the conflict, it seems at least six hundred thousand ghosts have since emerged—this denotes excess, not lack. There is a naughtiness, a transgressive pleasure, in invoking the Confederate undead. Reviving dead Confederates is a cultural no-no partly because it hints at disloyalty to the winning nation, splicing cacophonous chants of "C.S.A.! C.S.A.!" into the national applause sound track ("U.S.A.! U.S.A.!"). The recalcitrance of Confederate undeadness infects the national body politic, casting a pall over U.S. narratives of redemption and progress. Confederate *revenants* make us see the painstaking, contingent process of nation-(re)building through narrative, graphic, and audiovisual remediations of this Lincolnesque Romantic-nationalistic ethos, where honor, above all, means to die for one's country.[7]

The divisive racial politics imbricated with Confederate imagery gives this transgressive impetus a darker turn. The PoSo mode can be a screen for projecting culturally messy matters, but eventually we see through the transparency of its figures into contemporaneous pressures, the gritty conflicts of our everyday environs. There are diverse sociopolitical payoffs for particular materializations of the Confederate undead, depending on their historical situatedness. Some gray ghosts puncture the inflated hero-saints of the Lost Cause, sending their looming forms zipping into the abyss like pierced parade balloons, to show that the grandiose C.S.A. past, often *wasn't*. Other medial geists unbury dead Confederates to reboot frames of regional and national identifications, challenging the "regressive" position of the former Confederacy and current southeastern United States. These ghostly figures draw connections, sometimes unpleasant, to the complexities and complicities of the South vis-à-vis the "modern" nation.

The mythopoetic impetus of the Lost Cause elevates Robert E. Lee, Stonewall Jackson, and J. E. B. Stuart to secular sainthood, while obscuring the central role of chattel slavery as a driving factor behind the Civil War. Stonewall Jackson's death, in particular, inspired much Lost Cause mythology, yet his afterlife is bound up in less luminous fictions. L. B. Taylor records the legend of what's become of the general's arm, which has transformed into a *phantom* pain. Taylor's account begins by addressing the fact that many of Jackson's troops, seeing the general continually at prayer, "imagined that angelic spirits were his companions and counselors" and began already to think him supernatural (71), while historian E. A. Pollard notes that a "colonel came to Richmond with the report that Jackson had gone mad; that his mania was that a *familiar spirit* had taken possession of a portion of his body" (71). When Jackson was wounded by friendly fire at Chancellorsville, his corps surgeon, Dr. Hunter McGuire, amputated the general's left arm on May 2, 1863. Jackson did not recover, and pneumonia claimed him by May 10. While most of Jackson's corpse is buried in Lexington, Virginia, Jackson's chaplain discovered the amputated arm at the field hospital and had it buried separately at the nearby J. Horace Lacy estate. Rumors hold that Dr. McGuire, fiercely loyal to his lost patient, haunts the grounds in full dress uniform, toting the amputated arm, longing to return the limb to its rightful owner. The physical dismemberment of Jackson's corpse carries over its division into the spiritual displacements of the afterworld, the general's lack of bodily integrity allegorized in the bloody stump, ruined relic, questioning his psychic integrity as Lost Cause martyr.

J. E. B. Stuart, the spirited Confederate cavalier with his high-plumed hat, has also undergone postmortem operations of late. As Taylor notes: "If Robert E. Lee exemplified the dignity and integrity of 'The Cause,' [Stuart] typified the flair and savoir faire. [. . .] He was the Sir Lancelot of the Civil War" (26). "Dashing" and "daring" are words that get used a lot when invoking Stuart. Taylor relates a ghostly reenactment one hundred years to the day of Stuart's crossing of the Chickahominy Creek in Virginia, after leading a dashing, daring charge to harass Union General Joseph Johnston's troops. The modern witness to this ghost-ride felt as if he had "somehow stumbled into some sort of historic time warp" (33), as he hears the sounds of the spectral forces building a makeshift bridge, then chats with an amiable C.S.A. officer adorned, as was Stuart's wont, in "thigh-length black leather boots, yellow sash, and a hat with a brilliant feather" (34). A real-life historical reenactment had been planned for that day, but *apparently* was canceled because a U.S. military convoy was scheduled to move through the area. Perhaps the reenactors, rebelling against the military injunction, remediated the crossing anyhow, so the observer mistook *real* fake Confederates for undead ones, a live performance for an unliving one. We might well ask what either set of redubbed gray soldiers has at stake in reliving the past. For the living, is it a means of rekindling childhood nostalgia for playing war? Or is it that special ethos of refashioning (literally) oneself as a rebel with a cause (or Cause), the desire whetted by a mild case of thanatos syndrome via the aura of defeat? And for the dead, are these gray ghosts actually trying to *unlose* the war in an alternate history? What spoils, then, to the victors (already spoiled)?

Stuart gets redrawn in DC Comics *G. I. Combat*, which included an offshoot series called "The Haunted Tank." In the July 1975 edition, "The Saints Go Riding On," Stuart's namesake and descendant commands a U.S. Army tank—yes, a *Sherman* tank, in a wry PoSo wink, sporting a Confederate flag—against the Nazis during World War II. Stuart receives sound military strategy from the ghostly guardian presence of his cavalry general forefather. The men under Jeb's command can't see or hear ghostly J. E. B. so naturally feel their leader has gone batshit. They can't, however, argue with results, so they keep doing whatever the living Jeb tells them the undead J. E. B. has told him to tell them to do. The strip begins with two nuns praying for protection to statues of St. Anthony, St. Francis, St. Sebastian, and St. Paul in a country church in war-ravaged Italy. The church, predictably, gets dive-bombed by a German Stuka. J. E. B., astride his ghost-white horse, directs his humanly counterpart, "Hurry, Jeb—or you will be too late to save those trapped inside the church—who will later be the instruments of saving *you!*" (2). The tank gets there in time to save Mother Superior, who insists the men salvage the saintly statues by storing them inside the tank. Mother Superior makes explicit the connection between Catholic and Confederate icons by assuring the younger Stuart that she, too, can see posthuman J. E. B., for "Faith gives us the vision to see things which cannot be explained!" (12). In between, she proves herself a crack shot as a gunner, and when their tank gets "mired in marshy ground" while pursued by Nazis, she cleverly uses the saint statues as decoys for the four soldiers, who appear to have abandoned their tank and taken cover in the underbrush; the Nazi tank riddles the icons to bits.

From the illustrations, it's tough to say whether the soldiers are stuck in the swampy South or the marshy junglescapes of Vietnam, rather than the Italian countryside—a telling confusion that overlays the setting of a seemingly just war (World War II) with two questionable ones (the U.S. Civil War and the U.S. War in Vietnam). "The Haunted Tank" exploits C.S.A. iconography to enact the possibility of redemption for the American military in the throes of Vietnam. The men in Stuart's tank act alone: their loyalties project vertically (to one another, to the noncombatant victims of war) rather than horizontally (to military hierarchy or larger combat objectives). The series also suggests through the palatable, if hooey figure of Ghost J. E. B. the ascendency of military intelligence (J. E. B. always knows best what's coming, the ultimate reconnaissance man) and technology (as his tank gets K-BLANG'ed! to smithereens, the German commander exclaims, "How could an *abandoned* tank [. . .] *destroy* [. . .] us? [11]) to displace the human at the center of military ops and place the posthuman in charge. "Haunted Tank" thus offers an eerie precursor to the video-game-like precision bomb-strikes of the 1990s Gulf Wars and the automated drone attacks of the current wars in the Middle East. The comic summons the fantasy of bloodless combat, the ultimate in modern technowar, a facet signified in the outsized gallantry of the spectral Stuart on horseback seamlessly lassoing the tank and easing it right out of the quagmire.

The *still* walking wounded of the Confederacy includes the Headless Torso at the Battery Carriage House Inn in Charleston, South Carolina. Like Dr. McGuire hefting Stonewall Jackson's phantom limb, this gray ghost reflects trauma in its literal meaning of "wound," debunking the organic intactness of the human body as the basis for individual subjectivity. Likely a casualty of the Siege of Charleston Harbor in 1863, his corporeal wholeness is severed severely. The decapitated form appears to guests in Room 8:

> The visitor saw the torso of a man floating in the area between his bed and the wall. The apparition, broad-shouldered and with a large chest, was just inches away from him and seemed to make a deep gasping sound—as if he were having difficulty breathing. The man later said the ghost was so close that he could make out details of his long overcoat. [. . .] But as soon as he made contact with the specter, it began to emit a low-pitched, loud, unearthly sound, something like a cross between a growl and a howl. (Coleman 204)

The Headless Torso sounds the depths of inarticulate history, of corrosions hidden beneath the sheen of the Lost Cause. He is at once a posthuman reminder of the visceral spoils of the war and a grim admonition about the facile conversion of wartime trauma into cultural tourism: gray ghosts as tourist trappings, as spectral place-markers of regional distinctiveness— mirroring Paul Grainge's understanding of nostalgia as less an emotional than an economic mode. The website for the Battery Carriage House Inn contains a link called "Ghost Sightings," using the thrumming growl-howl of the Headless Torso to drum up dollars, to tap the region's status as "a consumption-based economy—the South of the museum, the reenactment, the themed space, the tourist destination" (Romine, *The Real South* 5). Yet his ungainly, gasping presence dims in some measure the brisk, bright aura of antebellum Charlestonianness branded and repackaged.

Herschell Gordon Lewis's *Two Thousand Maniacs!* (1964), a ghostly gorefest which hardly merits "B-movie" rating, places southern clichés—voice, place, rurality, backwardness, The War—in an added set of quotation marks through the decidedly déclassé splatter-film ethos. The Confederate dead rise again as carnal, cannibalistic ghosts, who return from the grave in 1964, one hundred years after Union troops massacred the inhabitants of their small Georgia town. These neo-Confederates lure unsuspecting Yankee tourists to their ghost town to help them "celebrate" the centennial, inventing cruel and unusual punishments to avenge the past. The vengeful, corporeal ghosts feast on their Yankee visitors in a gory smorgasbord, bodies and souls, turning the human corpus to dead meat. Cannibalism here caricatures the South's image as a heightened repository of savage carnality, a nexus of primitive violence set against national progression. Lewis's Confederate flesh-eaters are a send-up of regional exceptionalism at the height of the civil rights movement, parodically shaking loose the substructures of the Lost Cause at writ's end.

George Saunders's *CivilWarLand in Bad Decline* (1996) also plays up PoSo ghosts at a bad Civil War theme park, a space of hokey reenactment and redressing the war in period costumes, which, like Baudrillard's Disneyland, worries the lines between the "real" and the simulacrum. These ghosts in the machine of late capital summon the question, in Martyn Bone's formulation, "Is there a danger that the parodic poetics of postsouthernism are neutered, even co-opted, by a socioeconomic system that has derealized the foundational sense of place more than hyperreal fiction ever could?" (46). Such fluidity of placelessness, of aregionality, could lead to formlessness, to a sense of never belonging, except as a consumer-citizen. The park features the spectral echoes of the McKinnon family, whose patriarch has gone mad from posttraumatic stress in the war and hacked his wife and girls to death with a scythe, then blown out his brains. When the scene is done, it suffers post-posttraumatic repetitions, many unhappy returns: "Then he gets up and starts over. It goes on and on, through five cycles" (24). He blames this on "hatred and the war," and, as a CivilWarLand employee buries a visitor's severed hand in an on-site swamp (long story), Mr. McKinnon recalls "a boy he once saw sitting in a creek slapping the water with his own severed arm" (19), a further humiliation of the human, the corpse becoming just like any other failed machine with bad or missing parts. In a commingling of the comic and the grotesque à la Barry Hannah, somehow this is funny—so much so that Ben Stiller bought the film rights to the story. The ghosts who occupy CivilWarLand are as real as anything, no more, no less. When the park features holograms of famous Civil War figures, the ghosts don't know the difference: "It's always a confusing time for the McKinnons. Last year the Mr. got in a head-to-head with the image of Jefferson Davis" (20). Lampooning grimly the South's mournful and never-ending re-remembrances of the war, the McKinnons don't know that CivilWarLand and its employees are "chronically slumming" (12). There is total interpenetration of present and past, since both are a matter of endless reconstruction, constant anachrony: the McKinnons live on, accepting as presents—and *the* present—Rubik's Cubes, copies of *Playboy,* plastic lighters.

Ron Rash's "Dead Confederates" (2010) fulfills its titular promise. A couple of DOT workers plan to turn an extra dollar from relics retrieved after late-night exhumations of C.S.A. corpses. Wesley Davidson, the brains behind this unburial detail, has "always been big into that Confederate stuff, wearing a CSA belt buckle, rebel flag tattoo on his arm. He wears a gray CSA cap too, wears it on the job. There's no black guys on our crew, only a handful in the whole county, but you're still not supposed to wear that kind of thing" (46). The Lost Cause emerges as a financially viable mode of traffic in/with the dead, a form of posthumous cultural tourism through the Civil War antiques trade, where remnants of the expired nation outrank those of the extant, for "them that buys this stuff pay double if it's Confederate" (50). The old-timey aura of defeat proffers an imaginary out from the bloated demographics and messy political currencies of the U.S.A. Inside the cemetery, the narrator feels pressures of the dead irrupting into the present, the bony scaffolding of the set-aside everywhere underfoot and undergirding the now: "But it's too quiet, in a spooky kind of way. Because you know folks are here, hundreds of them, and not a one will say ever a word more on this earth" (53).

The pair unbury a Confederate lieutenant, deep-sixed in full regalia some twenty-five years post Appomattox, a notably nonredemptive resurrection as the corpse is animated now only by the slow, smokeless burning of decay: "There's a silk shirt you can tell even now was white and a belt and its buckle and some moldy old shoes, but what once filled the shoes and shirt looks to be little more than the wind that blusters a shirt on a clothesline" (56). Fierce nostalgia for the Confederacy transmogrifies into "some dust and bones the color of dried bamboo [that] spill out" (57)—the bamboo faintly echoing failed U.S. military incursions into Southeast Asian geopolitics. When the two are apprehended at their dirty work, Wesley tries to convince the old gravekeeper that the things of the dead are being brought back into circulation, not for money, but on account of sentiment for "all them that fought for a noble cause" (62). Rash gives the lie to such grandstanding on the Lost Cause, exposing its blustery rhetoric as *nec*romanticism, even having a dry joke at Wesley's expense: "Soon as we get [the coffin lid] off, Wesley puts his left hand on his shoulder, and I'm thinking it's some kind of salute or something, but then he starts rubbing his arm and shoulder like it's gone numb on him" (66). Highfalutin salute turns into fatal stroke: Wesley enters into a confederacy with the dead. He's dug his own grave, since the narrator and the old man decide to let Wesley's corpse share coffin space with the dead Confederate, past and present commingling inextricably henceforth. The narrator keeps the C.S.A. loot, including a sword and scabbard in mint condition, which fetches $5,200 at "a big CSA convention where a whole auditorium is full of buyers and sellers" (73), and he uses this windfall for his mother's health-care bills, comforting himself with the thought that "both them graves had big fancy tombstones of cut marble, meaning those dead Confederates hadn't known much wanting of money in their lives" (74). Yet he's haunted by hypnagogic hallucinations, where the undead past returns in all its terrifying literality: "The only bad thing is I keep having a dream where that old man has shot me and I'm buried in the hole with Wesley" (74). If the past is never dead, not even past, Rash's tale doesn't bog down in any solipsistic pathos, but returns to deal plainly with the living: "There's always a price to be paid for anything you get. I wish it weren't so, for it's a fearsome dream, but if it's the worst to come of all that happened I can live with it" (74).

In an expanded version of this chapter, one might well wish to shift gears from PoSo to GloSo—that is, to consider more fully the transouthern, transnational or global South implications of current recastings of the Confederate undead. Take, for instance, how the HBO series *True Blood* (2008–present) revamps old C.S.A. ghosts into Confederate vet/vampire Bill Compton. Tara McPherson provides an excellent account of global capital at work in *True Blood*'s Louisiana, where "southernness" is an economic mode, becoming a brand that reproduces "the logics of niche marketing and mass personalization" (336) while exploiting labor imbalances and tax breaks between Hollywood and the *other* LA. We note the tropes of an as-yet undead "Southern Gothic" amid Compton and his posthumous/posthuman compatriots. But we also see him fighting his own gray ghosts, "struggling to come to terms with his history, with what he is and has done"—a parable, perhaps, for "how a guilty whiteness might seek redemption" (341). Compton's melancholia works as "an affective wedge," hampering his transition into "a transformed subject who can feel southern in new ways" (341). Such exorcisms aren't easy, and the promise of "a postidentity sociability" (348) may wind up abetting the tricky alliances forged by global media, both on—and *behind*—the screen. Yet McPherson's idea of "expansive relationality" presents a new approach to the Confederate undead, pressing beyond group-based modes of difference (regional, racial, sexual identifications) and offering some respite from the incessant working conditions of global capital.

Ghosts often speak in parables, if at all; like the events they summon, if darkly, they are beyond words, flickering holograms of inarticulate history. Yet, under closer scrutiny, these ghosts of the Confederacy materialize material conditions that drive and disrupt ideas of the American South on regional, national, and transnational levels: the blight of antebellum plantation economics fractionalized and rebranded into cultural tourism; fever-pitched Anglo-Saxonism beset by multiethnic striations from within and without the region; sectionalism and regional exceptionalism haunted by the ghostlier demarcations of transregional influences, passing through old borders of what counts as "southern." Like viruses (computer or physiological), the Confederate undead keep massing in the current southern and American body politics. One might rightly ask why a war that lasted only four years continues to hold captive our regional and national attentions. Why does the Confederacy rise again and again—unfulfilled—in ghostly forms? Does their ghostliness mask or unveil deeper cultural fault lines, confirm or deny official historiographies of the war and its continuing aftermaths? Beyond the mythos of the Lost Cause and unabashed neo-Confederate stances, these and other ghost (hi)stories of the Confederacy confirm that the afterlives of the Civil War continue to proliferate in multiple, even contradictory ways, gesturing toward deeper impulses of modernity and a more comprehensive understanding of regional definition. There are more things in heaven and earth than are dreamt of in our philosophies. Not reckoning these subalternate histories, unheeding the undead, is, as Ovid said, building a cenotaph, with offerings to the ghost that is no ghost.

NOTES

1. For culturally informed theories of ghostliness, see Avery Gordon, Renée Bergland, and Kathleen Brogan.
2. For more on vibrant materialism, see Bruno Latour, Jane Bennett, and Claire Colebrook.
3. Coleman Hutchison's study of Confederate literature's connection to nationalist identity helps contextualize current manifestations of the Lost Cause.
4. Abraham Lincoln underwent a similar brush with undead transition as the target of an 1876 plot by a counterfeiting ring to abscond with his remains at Oak Ridge Cemetery in Springfield, Illinois. They planned to rebury the dead president's corpse among the dunes of Lake Michigan and ransom the body in exchange for the release of their "coney" cohort, master engraver Benjamin Boyd, who was imprisoned in the Illinois State Penitentiary. The inchoate U.S. Secret Service was tipped off and foiled the attempt, but not before the wannabe body snatchers broke into the marble sarcophagus and began their exertions to remove Lincoln's lead-lined coffin.
5. Leigh Anne Duck critiques the illusion of the South's backwardness as just that: an illusion, albeit a powerfully imprinted one, buttressed by literary and other media artifacts that construed the region against the "progressive" nation.
6. Alan Nolan outlines Lost Cause claims: slavery was not the sectional issue, and the South would have given up slavery voluntarily; slaves were essentially happy with their condition; and the Civil War resulted from burgeoning southern nationalism. Gaines Foster details the pivotal function of Lost Cause ideology to the postwar South; he argues, however, that the mythos lost power in the early twentieth century, which makes the contemporary resurrections of the Confederate undead all the more curious and trenchant. Caroline Janney offers a gendered perspective on the Lost Cause, while William Blair contends it was "one of the tools of a powerful elite, with invented traditions helping to fend off challenges to the rule of former Confederates" (3).
7. Stephen Berry criticizes how the brute untidiness of death gets airbrushed out of histories of the war. Even when recounting stories of hog-eaten corpses at Gettysburg, "no one doubts that, as a country, we passed the trial and took the right turn at the crossroads" (1). For a balanced vantage, we should reconstruct the historian as "death investigator" (176).

5

MELVILLE'S ZOMBIES, NORTH AND SOUTH

SASCHA MORRELL

Among what C. L. R. James famously dubbed the "mariners, renegades and castaways" of Melville's fiction are numerous figures of living death. While they resist the imposition of single meanings, they are recurrently associated with the dehumanizing effects of labor exploitation, with overtones of racial domination. In this, Melville's undead anticipate the idea of the zombie that crossed into mainstream U.S. culture during the United States' military occupation of Haiti (1915–34). Distinct from the predatory zombie of contemporary horror film, this Haitian-American zombie was effectively a walking corpse, raised from the dead or deadened in life, and made to work for a zombie master. From African religious roots, the zombie had evolved in Haiti into the pure embodiment of alienated labor power, and the ultimate symbol of enslavement as "negation" (Dayan 37–38).[1] There were other versions of the zombie figure in Haitian mythology but, as Kordas notes, it was this version that seized U.S. imaginations, perhaps because it resonated so powerfully with long-standing and intensifying anxieties about labor exploitation in the United States itself, and about the exploitative character of the United States' neocolonial projects (16–17).[2]

Such resonance is certainly evident in the text generally credited with popularizing the term "zombie" in the United States, William Seabrook's best-selling 1929 travelogue *The Magic Island*. Seabrook reports hearing of zombies working for "low wages" for the Haitian-American Sugar Company, a corporation that is (as Seabrook points out) the epitome of modern U.S. big business

(94–95). Similarly, the toil of the blank-eyed Haitian zombies working in the sugar mill sequence of Victor Halperin's film *White Zombie* (1932) evokes mindless repetitive labor on the factory assembly line (Murphy 53; Inglis 43; Bishop 75–76). The zombie, emissary from an exoticized Caribbean, found itself at home in the United States, and if the slavery connection meant it found particular resonance with southern writers, as other essays in this volume have shown, it was no less relevant in northern industrial settings.

This was not least because when the Haitian zombie entered mainstream U.S. culture, it entered a terrain where figures of living death had already been performing similar functions in relation to both slavery and wage-labor exploitation. Explicit invocations of the Haitian zombie by U.S. writers and filmmakers were inevitably colored by established traditions, the Frankenstein myth being one.[3] As early as 1829, the African American activist David Walker had framed the degraded position of American blacks as an undead condition, asking white Americans, "What is the use of living, when in fact I am dead?" (75). But the figure was by no means exclusively associated with southern slavery. This essay uses Herman Melville's fiction as a case study that exemplifies just how richly developed was the nineteenth-century discourse linking the undead to the dehumanizing effects of labor exploitation and racial oppression. Often working in tandem with metaphors of man as machine, Melville's living dead serve as part of an economic gothic that extends beyond the southern plantation into maritime settings and northern industrial contexts. Like later appropriations of the Haitian zombie, they are figures that facilitate the transference of labor anxiety between the scenes of plantation slavery and industrial wage labor.

In considering how Melville's representations of labor dependency anticipate early uses of the zombie in U.S. fiction and film, it is worth remembering that Melville himself was being brought back from the dead in the 1920s and 1930s in the so-called "Melville revival."[4] Melville's literary resurrection coincided with the advent of the zombie-as-such in U.S. culture, and some of the developments that made Melville's work seem so relevant for the times (intensified industrial production, the increased division of labor, stark racial division, immigration, imperial expansion) were the same that made the zombie pertinent. On the other hand, this essay will highlight instances where Melville's living dead perform very different symbolic work to that associated with the Haitian zombie. In particular, the figure of Queequeg in

Moby-Dick offers an alternative, more redemptive version of the living dead body not as empty or negated but as a figure that resolves the conventional division between material and spiritual realms, enabling access to the deeper mysteries of existence.

Mariners, Renegades, and Zombies

Melville's most explicit representations of slavery as living death occur in his satirical travelogue *Mardi* (1849), with the American South evoked through a fictionalized South Pacific. Slave labor first comes under scrutiny on the island of Odo, where the higher classes live in "elevated" comfort while "condemn[ing] their drudges to *a life of deaths*." These drudges are "helots" who toil in trenches that are likened to "graves" to produce "nutritious Taro" for their overlords. One visitor, Babbalanja, remarks that toil is natural, but not this kind of alienated labor "when man toils and *slays himself* for masters who withhold *the life he gives to them*" (853–54, emphases added). Another island, Vivenza, more specifically allegorizes the United States, and the plantations in its "extreme South" are worked by slaves from Hamora, representing Africa. The slaves seem dead or inhuman, but a dialectical ambiguity arises as to who is ultimately deadened in such exploitative relations, as the master's life ultimately derives from the slave's living death:

> "Who eat these plants thus nourished?" cried Yoomy. "Are these men?" asked Babbalanja.
> "Which mean you?" said Mohi.

Quizzed by the travelers, the slave driver Nulli denies that the slaves have souls. But when they speak to one of the slaves directly, he says "[u]nder the lash, I believe my masters, and account myself a brute; but in my dreams, bethink myself an angel" (1188–90). Meanwhile, the slave driver Nulli is described as "a cadaverous, ghost-like man," and his very name suggests "nullification" (through the Latin *nullus*, none). As in Hegel's master-slave dialectic, in which the master's dependence on the slave's labor negates the master's ostensible dominance, it is the exploiter rather than the slave who is ultimately negated or "Nulli[fied]."[5] Melville very possibly had Hegel in mind; Melville's 1849 journal of his European travels records that he discussed the philosopher's ideas at length with the Germanophile intellectuals George

Adler and Franklin Taylor during the sea voyage.[6] In any case, we see Melville using the figure of a living-dead laborer to work through the dialectical complexity of master-slave relationships, with haunting implications for the United States' dependence on plantation slavery.

Melville's concern with the dehumanizing effects of labor exploitation extends beyond the slave plantation in *Moby-Dick* (1851), in which Ishmael calls attention to the ethnic diversity of the laborers "supplying the muscles" for white American "brains" in numerous industries (131), and Captain Ahab denies his multiethnic crew any independent consciousness, viewing them as mere "tools" to his overbearing purpose (230). The relationship between Ahab and his "swart" servant Fedallah (236) warrants special attention, as Ishmael describes it in quasi-Hegelian terms which introduce the same dialectical ambiguity seen in *Mardi* as to who is ultimately deadened: "Ahab seemed an independent lord; the Parsee but his slave. Still both seemed yoked together, an unseen tyrant driving them" (584). The master's seeming "independence" is implicitly illusory, since bondage "yokes" and "tyrannizes" both master and slave. Ishmael earlier described Fedallah standing in Ahab's shadow so that "if [Fedallah's] shadow was there at all it seemed only to blend with, and lengthen Ahab's" (358). As in the first stage of Hegel's master-slave dialectic, and as with the logic of zombification, the servant seems to lack any independent being.[7] But Fedallah will achieve a final ascendancy over his former master, and it is precisely as an uncanny "undead" figure that the servant negates his negation: when Fedallah is drowned in the chase for Moby Dick, he resurfaces as a "half-torn body" with "his distended eyes turned full upon old Ahab" (618).

Specific allusions to southern slavery surround the "poor little negro" Pip, who becomes an undead figure when he is temporarily abandoned in the open water after leaping in terror from a whaleboat during a chase. Pip afterward continually speaks of himself as having died, as when he proposes that his "drowned bones now show white, for all the blackness of his living skin" (580), and his haunting presence unnerves his shipmates. Ishmael explains that "the sea had jeeringly kept his finite body up, but drowned the infinite of his soul" (453). Pip is not literally a slave, but the boy's understanding of himself as a soulless corpse is connected with the reduction of black people to mere objects in chattel slavery for, before Pip went overboard, the second mate Stubb had warned him, "I won't pick you up if you jump [. . .]

a whale would sell for thirty times what you would, Pip, in Alabama" (452). This threat seems fulfilled when Pip is indeed left behind; as the black boy experiences the heartless immensity of the ocean, he is also experiencing Stubb's negation of his being. When Ahab later encounters Pip, he marvels, "I see not my reflection in the vacant pupils of thy eyes," fearing that he will therefore "sieve through" the boy, and no sooner has Ahab spoken than Pip begins advertising himself as a runaway slave: "Reward for Pip! One hundred pounds of clay—five feet high [. . .]!" (567). Pip's living-dead condition resonates with the idea of the Haitian zombie as "the ultimate sign of loss and dispossession" (Dayan 37–38).

But as the slave driver Nulli seemed at least as dead as his slaves, Ahab, too, has been associated with a kind of living death: he no longer sleeps, finds that "smoking no longer soothes" (141), and lives "shut up in the caved trunk of his body" (166). Since the vitality of each on his own is impaired, the curious rapport that develops between Ahab and Pip suggests a reciprocal need, with Ahab admitting, "Thou touchest my inmost centre, boy" (567). Having once allowed Pip's touch, however, Ahab finds Pip "follow[ing]" him everywhere as his inescapable shadow. When Ahab tries to repudiate the connection, the black boy pleads: "Ye have not a whole body, sir, do ye but use poor me for your one lost leg; only tread upon me sir; I ask no more, so I remain a part of ye" (580). Although Ahab and Pip are not literally slave and slave master, the image of Pip as the "lost leg" without which Ahab "ha[s] not a whole body" affords a powerful image of the structural dependence of white on black.

As Ahab's living-dead "lost leg," Pip has a counterpart in the ship's automaton-like carpenter, upon whom Ahab literally depends "for a bone to stand on." As the carpenter fashions his new leg, Ahab curses "that mortal inter-indebtedness that will not do away with ledgers" (514). Whereas Pip is associated with African slavery when he offers to "complete" Ahab's body, the carpenter (although a skilled artisan) is described in terms echoing contemporaneous critiques of the deadening effects of factory labor: he has been reduced by repetitive toil to a "mere machine of an automaton" or "Sheffield pocketknife" whose "soul" is an "unreasoning wheel" (509–10).[8] In casting the vacant-eyed Pip and the automaton carpenter as twin props on whom Ahab depends, Melville hints at the United States' dependence on the deadening regimes of slavery and wage labor. Long before the imported figure of the Haitian zombie "linked the history of chattel slavery [. . .] to modern wage slavery" for American audiences (Zieger 740), Melville had configured that linkage through tropes of living death.

On the other hand, the figure of Queequeg in *Moby-Dick* offers a version of living death that operates within very different parameters, and ultimately has more positive connotations. Queequeg proves to be a figure of great warmth and vitality, yet on his first appearance at the Spouter Inn, Queequeg superficially resembles a walking corpse: Ishmael dwells on the islander's "dark, purplish yellow face," his "bald purplish head [that] now looked for all the world like a mildewed skull" (24), and Queequeg actually peddles embalmed heads. For all Queequeg's morbid associations, however, Ishmael is "redeemed" from a cold, atomized existence through his friendship with this "soothing savage" (57). It is striking that the Spouter Inn's proprietor is called "Peter Coffin" (26), for Queequeg's coffin will provide Ishmael's life-buoy in the final wreck, serving as a kind of undead double for Queequeg's body (625). The coffin is made of "dark planks" of "heathenish" lumber from "aboriginal" islands, onto which Queequeg has copied the tattoos from the "living parchment" of his own skin (521, 524). The double survives the original to save Ishmael, and while Fruscione suggests this can be read as a final image of white racial dependency (22–23), it also keeps alive the loving bond of bosom friendship between Queequeg and Ishmael.

Queequeg's undead associations are deepened by the strange circumstances surrounding the coffin's construction. Queequeg commissions the coffin from the ship's carpenter when he falls morbidly ill in chapter 110 ("Queequeg in His Coffin"), before entering a deathly trance. Suggestively, this near-death state is said to be the direct result of his excessive labors, which Ishmael describes in terms of live burial: harpooneers endure "harder [. . .] toil" than ordinary crewmen, and it was down "in the gloom of the hold" while "bitterly sweating all day in that subterranean confinement" that Queequeg caught his fever. That fever takes him "close to the very sill of the door of death"; Ishmael describes how Queequeg "wasted and wasted away in those few long-lingering days, till there seemed but little left of him but his frame and tattooing." When he is "lifted into his final bed," Queequeg assumes the attitude of death: "crossing his arms on his breast [. . .] there lay Queequeg in his coffin" (519–20).

Since Queequeg has been toiling in service to Ahab's overbearing purpose, this might suggest the deadening effects of alienated labor, as seen in *Mardi*.

But, unlike the blank eyes of the later Hollywood zombie, the cadaverous Queequeg's eyes "seemed growing fuller and fuller [. . .] rounding and rounding, like the rings of Eternity" as "a wondrous testimony to that immortal health in him which could not die, or be weakened." Taking on an intensified vitality, he sees the coffin itself as a "canoe" bound for the afterlife (520). Here, Melville offers a version of the living dead as a shaman-like figure, bridging the divide between physical and spiritual worlds and in contact with otherwise inaccessible realms of understanding. This allows Melville to stage a curious encounter between one version of living death and another, as Pip approaches Queequeg in his coffin. While Queequeg lies with eyes closed, Pip asks whether he is bound "to those sweet Antilles where the beaches are only beat with water-lilies" and, if so, whether he will "do one little errand for me? Seek out one Pip, who's now been missing long: I think he's in those far Antilles." The impaired Pip imagines that Queequeg has the power to restore him to wholeness. Mysteriously, Pip's absence from himself is related here to his supposed presence in the Antilles and—given the association of Pip's living-dead condition with Stubb's threat to sell him—this inevitably evokes West Indian slavery, even as Pip's imagined Antilles are perversely associated with "sweet" refuge rather than toil.[9] Still, as Pip recalls himself "dying" as a "coward," he instructs Queequeg to "tell all the Antilles [Pip's] a runaway. [. . .] Tell them he jumped from a whale-boat!" (520). Since Pip did not literally jump overboard in the Antilles, which the *Pequod*'s course has not touched, Mackenthun suggests Pip's words may be expressing a larger "collective memory" of Africans transported across the Atlantic (189, 197).[10]

Immediately after reading Pip's address, we are told Queequeg "suddenly rallied," explaining that "he had just recalled a little duty ashore, which he was leaving undone" (520). Could this "little duty" have something to do with the "little errand" Pip asked for in the Antilles? In which case, are the undead Pip's overtures somehow responsible for Queequeg's return to the living? Are their respective ethnicities relevant? The text offers no definite answers, only riddles. What is certainly striking, given that Queequeg's death was brought on by excessive labor, is that what recalls him to life is a "duty" of his own, apparently independent from his service to Ahab, which is not unlike the Hegelian idea that "the slave recovers his humanity [. . .] through *work*" (Fukuyama 194 quoting Hegel).

Living death in *Moby-Dick* is complex and manifold, for if Pip's vacancy affords clear parallels with Haitian zombie mythology, his association of the undead Queequeg with spiritual depth and healing is clearly at odds with that tradition. Whereas the Haitian zombie was antithetical to the stereotypes of primitive vitality that white commentators habitually sought for in Afro-Caribbean cultures (Zieger 740), Queequeg presents a version of living death that is entirely consistent with *Moby-Dick*'s more general association of "primitive" or "savage" others with spiritual plenitude and vitality, as an alternative to the sterility of white Western being.

Cadaverous Triumph

In Melville's short fiction of the 1850s, the connection between labor exploitation and a living-dead or mechanical existence persists, with a stronger focus on the living dead as a potential figure of resistance and retribution, and with more specific attention to northern wage-labor settings.

In her 1938 account of her travels in Haiti and Jamaica, *Tell My Horse*, Zora Neale Hurston wrote: "Here in the shadow of the Empire State Building, death and the graveyard are final. [. . .] But in Haiti there is the quick, the dead, and then there are Zombies" (179). However, it is precisely in New York City that Melville had located the living dead in his celebrated magazine tale "Bartleby, the Scrivener: A Story of Wall Street" (1853). In one of its interpretive dimensions, "Bartleby" evokes the haunting of American capitalism by the perpetual specter of class dependency, embodied in a living-dead employee who once hired cannot be dismissed.[11]

Engaged in the deadening repetitive labor of copying legal documents, Bartleby is described alternately as automaton-like and "cadaverous." His pallid figure anticipates Melville's depiction of wage-labor slavery in the sketch "The Tartarus of Maids" (1855), in which deathly white women toil silently in a New England paper mill (the locus classicus of wage slavery in the "Deep North") with a zombie-like vacancy: "rows of blanklooking girls, with blank, white folders in their blank hands, all blankly folding blank paper" (328–29). These wage workers are at least as cadaverous as the plantation slaves of *Mardi*. Unlike those drudges, however, Bartleby converts his negation into a "cadaverous triumph" when he commences a "passive resistance," putting off his employer's demands with the famous demurral, "I would prefer not to" (649).

In their "Zombie Manifesto" (2008), Lauro and Embry theorize the zombie as a figure that "disrupts the entire system" but whose own "subject position is nullified" (94–95), and this is equally fitting as a description of Bartleby. The narrator's efforts at "getting rid of Bartleby" (664) prove futile, and his living-dead body becomes associated with the very architecture of the law office: frequently observing Bartleby in "dead-wall reveries" or looking on "dead brick wall[s]" (658–59, 662, 668), the narrator even imagines having to "mason up his remains in the wall" (670). When the narrator imagines "all Broadway" involved in his case, remarking how the "scrivener's pale form appeared to me laid out, among uncaring strangers," he seems to intuit that Bartleby's "innate and incurable disorder" is linked to an "excessive and organic ill" infecting society as a whole (658–59).

When Bartleby dies a more final death in the prison called "the Tombs" (677), the narrator hears "that Bartleby had been a subordinate clerk in the Dead Letter Office at Washington." Exclaiming, "Dead letters! does it not sound like dead men?," the narrator imagines Bartleby having toiled among mail that never reached those who "died despairing [. . .] died stifled" (677–78). Melville installs this specter of living death not only at the center of American finance (Wall Street) and general society ("all Broadway") but at the center of American politics (Washington, D.C.). Melville's undead are by no means confined to the South.

On the other hand, it is in a specifically Haitian setting that Melville revived the idea of cadaverous triumph in his story "Benito Cereno" (1855). It is unlikely that Melville was drawing on Haitian zombie mythology for this tale of slave revolt, but he was certainly alluding to the Haitian Revolution.[12] In adapting the story of a slave-ship mutiny from Amasa Delano's travel memoirs, Melville changed the ship's name to *San Dominick* (evoking Saint Domingue, later Haiti) and pulled the action back from 1805 to 1799 to coincide with the height of the Haitian conflict (see Beecher 43–58). In this context, Melville offers versions of living death that resonate with the Haitian zombie as a figure of enslavement as negation but maintains the idea that it is ultimately the master who is deadened in such exploitative relations, and that the slave retains the power of revolutionary escape.

Failing to perceive that the Spanish slave-ship captain Benito Cereno is being forced to conceal a slave mutiny, Melville's Captain Delano believes that "negroes" are "unaspiring," possessing "a limited mind" (724). The African rebel Babo satirizes the negation of racial slavery when Cereno praises him to Delano, protesting disingenuously, "Ah, master [. . .] don't speak of me; Babo is nothing" (177). Befitting the idea of slavery as living death, the slave ship in "Benito Cereno" is compared to "a vault," with "dead-lights" closed "like coppered eyes of the coffined," and its hull "purple-black, tarred-over," suggesting a putrefied corpse (761, 713).[13] But its appearance also recalls the valley of dry bones in Ezekiel 37:1–14, in which skeletons start up from their graves (683–84), and the resurrection imagery furnishes a fitting emblem of slave uprising. When the mutiny is belatedly revealed, a shroud flies from the prow to reveal that "a skeleton" has "been substituted for the ship's proper figurehead, the image of Christopher [Columbus]" (752). Since Columbus first landed in Hispaniola, this strengthens the Haiti connection (Sundquist 183). As the skeleton swings into view, it "cast[s] a giant ribbed shadow upon the water," so that when "one extended arm" seems "beckoning the whites to avenge it," we must also imagine its shadowed arm beckoning to the blacks (745).

Appropriately, the tropes of living death in "Benito Cereno" are ultimately applicable less to the enslaved African than to the white exploiter. Deprived of will and puppeted by Babo, the traumatized Cereno is continually described as pale and corpselike, marked by his "cadaverous sulleness," "ague of coldness," and "morbid" manner (736–77). In contrast, the slave's living death becomes a triumph. Although Babo is captured and executed, the "unabashed" gaze of his severed head suggests an undiminished vitality (762–63), recalling the challenging gaze Fedallah leveled on Ahab in *Moby-Dick*'s conclusion. The threat of slave resistance survives the particular agent. In contrast, the moribund Cereno "would not, or could not" look on Babo in court, and in the tale's conclusion he draws his mantle about himself "like a pall," silenced by a "shadow" he calls "the negro" (762). Whether in the clerkly environs of the New York law office or in association with slave revolt in Haiti, Melville's living-dead workers retain the capacity to literally or metaphorically deaden their masters.

Conclusion

How did the entry of the Haitian zombie into Anglo-American letters infuse and transform existing traditions of the living dead? How did those traditions transform the zombie itself, or influence its subsequent migrations? These are large questions; this essay has shown that Herman Melville's work will be an especially rich resource for exploring them further.

I earlier noted the coincidence of the Melville revival with the Haitian zombie's advent in U.S. culture. One text that shows their combined influence is *Babouk* (1934), Guy Endore's neglected and meticulously researched novel of the Haitian Revolution, which expressly uses the zombie as a symbol of enslavement but also recalls "Benito Cereno" through its hero, the rebel slave Babouk, whose name unmistakably alludes to Melville's rebel slave Babo, and who likewise becomes a figure of deathless power when, like Babo's, his severed head is set on display and continues to exert a defiant gaze (cf. Wald 17). As this example suggests, the afterlife of Melville's undead in twentieth-century representations of the zombie will merit further investigation.

Melville's living dead transgress regional and national borders, appearing in both North and South, and in both onshore and offshore settings. Melville's fiction can help us to understand why the Haitian zombie, born of the history of plantation slavery, would be equally at home in the modern American factory. His fiction reminds us that nineteenth-century writers were already using the undead to explore some of the anxieties to which the word "zombie" later became attached; in a sense, the zombie's entry gave existing tropes of living death new life. The Haitian-American zombie as it appeared in such texts and film-texts as Seabrook's *Magic Island* and Halperin's *White Zombie* was an overdetermined figure, and its entry was a moment of continuity more than rupture. Indeed, rather than allowing U.S. writers to articulate what they could not articulate before, the entry of the zombie so-called can be seen to have enabled the displacement onto an othered Haitian space of a figure that was previously too close to home.

NOTES

1. On the differing accounts of the zombie's origins and etymology, see Rushton and Moreman 2; and Ackermann and Gauthier 466–94.

2. For distinguishing labor exploitation from other motives for zombification in Haitian tradition, see Ackermann and Gauthier 474–75.

3. Numerous critics have recognized how the nightmare of Shelley's *Frankenstein* was bound up from the first with British anxieties about West Indian slavery and have explored how Shelley's novel influenced representations of American race relations in the nineteenth century

(see Young, esp. 77–78). On the other hand, an industry boss in Mark Twain's *No. 44* conceives of a scheme to reanimate dead bodies to deploy them as cheap factory labor. Considering nineteenth-century influences on twentieth-century zombie films, see Bishop 73, 97–98.

4. Spark (2006) examines the revival's extent and politics.

5. Hegel writes, "[J]ust where the master has effectively achieved lordship," he finds he has achieved "not an independent, but rather a dependent consciousness" (236–37).

6. See Pochmann 436–40. If we accept Susan Buck-Morss's influential claim that the Haitian Revolution influenced Hegel's master-slave dialectic, it would follow that the revolution indirectly influenced Melville's dialectics of living death (see Buck-Morss 14–20).

7. See Kordas 16; Bishop 69–70; and Lauro and Embry 87.

8. On comparable critiques of factory labor, see Rice 2–3, 23–34; and Beatty 17.

9. This floral sweetness may be comparable in its irony to the "paradox of peaceful greenery and crimson flowers and sugar cane" envisioned in Haiti in William Faulkner's 1936 novel *Absalom, Absalom!* (202).

10. Mackenthun compares the collective memory associated with the baby ghost in Toni Morrison's *Beloved* (1987). The eavesdropping Starbuck's comparison of Pip to one who speaks in "ancient tongues" from "forgotten childhood" seems relevant here (520).

11. On the guilt associated with labor exploitation in "Bartleby," see Kuebrich 395–404.

12. If the zombie-as-walking-corpse mythology had yet developed in Haiti, it had not yet entered Anglophone letters (see Kordas 16–17). It is not impossible that Melville encountered other African or Afro-Caribbean accounts of living death, however; on how "Benito Cereno" evinces Melville's interest in African cultures, see Stuckey 63–80.

13. Melville's *Redburn* expresses how "the suffocated and dead were [. . .] weeded out from the living every morning" during "the middle passage" (67).

6

TOPOGRAPHICAL GHOSTS
The Archival Architecture of Old New Orleans

SARAH HIRSCH

In *Cities of the Dead* (1996), Joseph Roach observes that New Orleans is a place "where the dead remain more gregariously present to the living, materially, and spiritually, than they do anywhere else" (xii). No one understood this more than George Washington Cable, who invoked the city's haunting past in his fiction and nonfiction alike. Serving as an archivist and cultural historian, Cable utilizes detailed accounts of New Orleans's topography and architecture in his narratives to articulate the secrets of what he calls the "semi-submerged" city (*Grandissimes* 269). Cable's attention to detail in describing the scenes and the settings of old New Orleans is meticulous. He pays close attention to the topographical multiplicity of the city and its unique architecture—the textures of its swamps and wetlands, the greenery and tropical flowers that spill over verandas and old porticos. In Cable's descriptions he introduces two distinct attributes of the city. New Orleans, with its pervading aqueous landscape, is described as "dream like" with a "profound stillness," but it is a dream that transforms itself into something vaguely haunting and potentially sinister: "A land hung in mourning, darkened by gigantic cypresses, submerged; a land of reptiles, silence, shadow, decay" (9). Cable's New Orleans is a land "populated with phantoms" (15).

Cable uses a materiality of haunting by transcribing the structural residues left behind. The "old family fortunes and colonial architecture already in stages of decay" serve to define Cable's narratives of old New Orleans seen in his collection of short stories *Old Creole Days* (1879), which subsequently influenced his novel *The Grandissimes* (1880) and his nonfiction anthology, *Strange True Stories of Louisiana* (1889) (Roach 179). Though these texts vary in form and delivery, all are in essence ghost stories. They invoke the presence of the past—of buildings vacated or long gone, their inhabitants vanished; of roads no longer traveled; of customs buried and unearthed like the tombs that hold New Orleans's dead above ground. Cable's narratives engage in a "palimpsestic cultural geography."[1] The excavations of the city's structures and streets serve to reveal the secrets of his characters. His material melodramas and their gothic tenor is not necessarily southern, but Louisianan, specific to Louisiana's imperial and colonial histories which echo among its structures.

Building off Jennifer Rae Greeson's assertion that the South is "a term of the imagination" and that Cable's work tends to trade in the cultural rather than the material, my aim is to remove the veils of the gothic to reveal Cable's tangible documentary approach, in a sense, exploring the material aspects of Cable's narratives to redefine the gothic as a mode of seeing (1).[2] New Orleans is a place for hidden things to resurrect themselves, and for Cable they resurrect themselves in narrative. The real-life places Cable documents convey the history of the characters in his fiction as well as in his recordings of the city's most pervasive and notorious legends. In the manuscripts, the figures of the infamous Madame Lalaurie, her haunted house on Royal Street, the tragic character of Bras-Coupé in the *The Grandissimes,* and the haunting features of the town pariah Jean-ah Poquelin and his ghostly leprous brother, Jacques, in *Old Creole Days* are all brought to life. What these characters and their corresponding stories have in common is that they are all are connected to New Orleans's history of slavery. In Louisiana, place is undead; thus the gothic works to illuminate rather than conceal. Cable's fiction and nonfiction accounts rely on the moment of revelation, which is made possible through the textured artifacts of the archive and the stories they carry.

The Mississippi River and the Haunted House

In the rendering of old New Orleans, Cable painstakingly re-creates the geographical landscape of the old city, with its gunwale sidewalks, crooked streets, and antiquated architecture. This landscape precedes the disappearance of the "self-styled aristocracy" of the nineteenth-century Creoles who "continued to speak French and to cling to the props of the Ancien Régime way of life: the box at the opera, the mansion on Esplanade, the black servants" (Benfey 14).[3] The strategic placement of the city at the mouth of the Mississippi and its watery topography of swamps and bayous set the stage for the eerie undertow that permeates Cable's narratives of local color. In describing the river's hold on the Louisianan imagination, geographer Craig Colten introduces the river in the following way:

> The Mississippi's delta is otherworldly, so interminably flat that one scholar says "nine-tenths of [it] is sky." It is a place of seemingly endless, interconnected marshes, swamps, and bayous, with little solid land anywhere in sight. Cattails, irises, mangroves, and a wide variety of grasses thrive in the delta's soggy environment. Muskrats, otters, minks, raccoons, and of course alligators all inhabit this watery world, while crawfish, or "mudbugs," as locals call them, burrow in a constantly replenished supply of muck. Much of the delta remains a wetland wilderness—a great place for a fish, or perhaps even a fishing trip, but a forbidding location to build a city. (4)

The Mississippi's prohibitive landscape marks New Orleans as an intractable, uninhabitable environment not meant for a colonial outpost, much less a metropolis. It is "otherworldly," a place that is forbidden, full of potential dangers, a slippery mass of wild, sodden foliage that is at once menacing and beautiful. Ultimately it is the Mississippi River that makes New Orleans and its complex histories legendary, a phenomenon that gets transcribed into the text. For Cable, the environmental topography of southern Louisiana makes the inclusion of the river's capricious if not duplicitous personality necessary in authenticating the New Orleans narrative. The watery panorama where the "sky and the marsh meet in the east, the north and the west" is described as "solemn," "flat," and "repellent," but Cable, a true local, contends that this is not always so: "There were long openings, now and then, to right and left, of emerald-green savannah, with the dazzling blue of the Gulf far beyond, waving a thousand white handed good-byes as the funeral swamps slowly shut out again the horizon" (*Grandissimes* 8–9). It is a somber if not haunting landscape, but one that can be punctuated with revelation and glimpses of what lies beyond the dense and shady surroundings of the swamp.

The landscape does not stay rooted in Cable's stories. It becomes dynamic, a part of the city's architecture that is integral to the stories themselves. This is illustrated in the detailed description of Jean-ah Poquelin's house in *Old Creole Days*:

> The house was of heavy cypress, lifted up on pillars, grim, solid, and spiritless, its massive build a reminder of days still earlier, when every man had been his own peace officer and the insurrection of blacks a daily contingency. Its dark weather-beaten roof and sides were hoisted up above the jungly plain in a distracted way, like a gigantic ammunition-wagon stuck in the mud and abandoned by some retreating army. Around it was a dense growth of water willows, with half a hundred sorts of thorny or fetid bushes, savage strangers alike to the "language of flowers" and to the botanist Greek. They were hung with countless strands of discolored and prickly smilax, and the impassable mud below bristled with *chevaux de frise* of the dwarf palmetto. Two lone forest-trees, dead cypresses, stood in the centre of the marsh, dotted with roosting vultures. The shallow strips of water were hid by myriads of aquatic plants, under whose coarse and spiritless flowers, could one have seen it, was a harbor of reptiles, great and small, to make one shudder to the end of his days. (179–80)

We are introduced to Jean-ah through the description of his overgrown, decaying plantation house. His personality is defined by his connection and commitment to his house and its secret: his diseased half brother Jacques, who comes down with leprosy after accompanying Jean-ah on an ill-fated journey to Guinea in order to profit from the slave trade. If the purpose of the gothic is to repress that which cannot be admitted to or named, Cable's fiction and the details of the landscape and the architecture unearth the unspeakable and repressed truths of slavery, mixed-race genealogies, and the consequences of the illegal smuggling of human flesh. As Cable writes, "The man and his house were alike shunned" (183). Jacques's "disappearance" and Jean-ah's rejection of New Orleans society and that society's rejection of him are ascribed to the house itself: "Among both blacks and whites the house was the object of a thousand superstitions" (183–84). The story of Jean-ah hinges on what happens to his "haunted mansion" and the coveted canal behind it that hides the lurking dangers that swim underneath (185).

For Cable the real stories and their secrets are hidden among the buildings, the streets, and their surroundings (the swamps and bayous and slow creeping canals). As critic Christopher Benfey tells us, "For Cable, New Orleans is a haunted city; and its secret tales of the past are coaxed from particular buildings and streets" (114). This is why in Cable's stories so much detail is paid to the description of the architecture and placement of the buildings—what streets they reside on and what the natural environment and passage of time has wrested upon them. It is important for us to know that the canal next to Jean-ah Poquelin's dilapidated house does not run but "crawls" and is filled with "big ravening fish and alligators" (180). It is important for us to know that the adjoining fourth-floor door that connects to the main house of Madame Lalaurie's mansion has "*two* pairs of full length batten shutters" held by 18-inch iron hooks (*Strange* 196). These details add to the lore of the story and to the legendary status "The 'Haunted' House in Royal Street" has in New Orleans. It is one of those narratives that is "told and retold with the causal disregard to historical accuracy that affects many New Orleans memories" (Benfey 4). Madame Lalaurie is long gone, but the mansion remains.

Cable asks us to dig around in buildings in order to recognize the palimpsest. He asks us to find the remnants of what is hidden underneath the ground or within the walls. Benfey notes how Cable implores his readers to look precisely toward that which occludes entry and is meant to avert disclosure:

> [Cable] guided his readers into the narrow streets of the French Quarter, with their dilapidated buildings, wrought-iron balconies, and secluded courtyards harboring the secrets of the inhabitants. He invited his readers to peek "through a chink between some pair of heavy batten window-shutters, opened with almost reptile wariness," or to look "through the unlatched wicket in some *porte-cochère*—red painted brick pavement, foliage of dark palm or pale banana, marble or granite masonry and blooming parterres." (112)

Cable's readers are privy to the various "gossips" that always invade his texts to articulate the rumors that surround the characters and the buildings with which they are associated: Jean-ah and his broken-down plantation house, Madame Lalaurie and her ghostly mansion, and the Grandisimmes' decaying Esplanade estate. That which is battened down and precludes any openness, the insulated Creole courtyard, is exactly where one should look. The details relay the clues to the secrets of the building and its inhabitants.

As Avery Gordon explains, "[T]he ghostly haunt gives notice that something is missing—that what appears to be invisible or in the shadows is announcing itself" (15). Cable's stories that are hidden in the closed-off buildings are disclosed by the recognition of the concealment itself. The acknowledgment of the unintelligible is the first step to deciphering what it is.

For Cable, buildings do talk, and the Old Absinthe House in the French Quarter is a building that suggests this. The faded wooden plaque applied to the historic tavern's aging brick edifice reads: "A tradition in the french quarters. This is the bar known to travelers the world over. From it came the famous absinthe drip. The bar where Jean and Pierre LaFitte, Andrew Jackson, Mark Twain and other celebrities were served. If it could talk what stories the bar would tell of a thousand and one nights crowded into history."[4] The signage on the Old Absinthe House is indicative of what the buildings provide Cable; they invoke a narrative and particular history. Madame Lalaurie's haunted house talks: "You hear the walls and the floors saying those soft nothings to one another that they so often say when left to themselves. While you are looking straight at one of the large doors that lead into the hall its lock gives a whispered click and the door slowly swings open" (Cable, *Strange* 195).

In Cable there is something always going on underneath the surface, beyond the shutter, the garden gate, or the door. Even the idyllic place of the Café de Exiles that figures in the short stories of *Old Creole Days* is closed down, blemished by jealousy, murder, and intrigue. The broken-down relics of the once-grand homes and spaces still resonate with a past that is eternally fixed and relevant to the understanding of the city. New Orleans is a city whose past ever informs its present. As our narrator tells us at the end of "Café de Exiles" the boisterous character Major Shaughnessy "knows the history of every old house in the French Quarter; or, if he happens not to know the true one, he can make one up as he goes along" (117). Even if the story is partly fabricated, every house nonetheless has one.

It is noted that the "house is the most persistent site, object, structural analogue, and trope of American gothic's allegorical turn" (Savoy 9). But in Cable's narratives, the house is not merely a symbol or representation of abstract qualities or an overused trope. It is the material vehicle through which the story is told. It is the conduit for the "hints, allusions, faint unspoken admissions, ill-concealed antipathies, unfinished speeches, mistaken identities and whisperings of hidden strife" that are revealed in the narrative excavation of New Orleans and its secrets (*Grandissimes* 96). New Orleans's history is partly a history of its ghosts, and Cable unearths these specters through his stories, which focus on the remnants of where these ghosts still remain. The buildings themselves become the living dead.

The Grandissimes and the Materiality of Cultural Memory

The Grandissimes is a novel built on secrets—secret identities, secret loves, and secret alliances that all come crashing down within the historical and cultural framework Cable provides. As such, the surface value of the novel is not the real value. Things are not what they seem in this "semi-submerged" city. The palimpsest, what lies beneath, is used both literally and figuratively in Cable's novel of hidden identity. The numerous subplots that proliferate at a dizzying pace in the novel serve to disguise the initial discussion, topic, or theme. The story taken up in the narrative is just a veneer that sets the stage for the disclosure of more complex relationships and discoveries. The excavations of the shadowy and ominous landscape is used to employ the melodramatic mode, to "pierce [the] surface [and] interrogate appearances" (Brooks 2). Cable moves "beyond the immediate context of the narrative" by providing an omniscient narrator that takes the reader on a range of historical odysseys (Brooks 2). It is an overt application of drama's "narrative voice, with its grandiose questions and hypotheses [that] leads us in a movement through and beyond the surface of things to what lies behind" (Brooks 2).

The narrator's intense detailing of the material presence of the architecture and the landscape ultimately transcribes a haunting of the ruins. In Cable's narrative, buildings are not only haunted by ghosts but are ghosts themselves. These structural specters "produce material effects" as they embody the undead (Gordon 17). "To impute a kind of objectivity to ghosts," Gordon explains, "implies that, from certain standpoints, the dialectics of visibility and invisibility involve a constant negotiation between what can be seen and what is in the shadows" (17). Cable carefully traverses this delicate relationship by playing with the temporal framing of the novel. After all, the spatial is informed by the passage of time. The Grandisimme family's broken-down mansion still displays the architectural features that tie it to an "irrevocable past" in much the same way that Madame Lalaurie's infamous haunted house remains as much a part of the cultural memory as it does the cultural landscape (*Grandissimes* 157). It is from the architecture and streets of New Orleans, its histories and cultures that Cable's stories are formulated. Using the architecture as an archive, the residual ruins provide the story.

Cable spends a lot of time in his narratives evoking the pathos of the city through its architectural and topographical changes, blending the new with vestiges of the old to remind the reader that the landscape of New Orleans contains a multitude of stories. For example, in *Strange True Stories of Louisiana*, Cable recounts the story of the haunted house of Royal Street and the infamous slave owner Madame Lalaurie. It is said that Madame Lalaurie practiced grotesque atrocities upon her slaves in utter secrecy. When this was discovered, she was run out of town by an angry mob. Her mansion was subsequently turned into a school and then, off and on, into private residences, but no matter its facility, those who inhabited the space came to an untimely demise or spoke of its haunted qualities. During one of its many renovations, bones were rumored to be found within the walls. Though in this work Cable implores his readers to take note of New Orleans's present, he immediately calls upon the past, stating: "New Orleans belongs to the present. [. . .] And yet I want the first morning walk that you take together and alone to be in the old French Quarter. Go down Royal Street" (192). Hence we descend into another world as Cable takes us through the door of this decaying mansion, hinting at the legend before us: "[I]t was through this doorway that the ghosts—figuratively speaking, of course, for we are dealing with plain fact and history—got into the house" (196). But it is not just the house that we are introduced to but the view from its belvedere windows that Cable narrates in full detail. As in all his stories, the landscape serves to tell bits and pieces of New Orleans's history: the dynamic centrality of its port and the city's proximity to the river, its years as a Spanish colony and the layout of its old districts. The view is partly of "new" New Orleans, but the past always creeps in as we are only privy to this panorama from the attic of a house situated in the Vieux Carré.

In the rendering of his narratives it is not sufficient for Cable to simply map the landscape. For him it must be brought to life by the people who frequent these houses, streets, and spaces in order for the reader to comprehend New Orleans's transformations and the residues left behind. So when Madame Lalaurie is forced to flee the city, the historical trajectory of the road she travels is meticulously detailed—so much so that it has a story all its own that is just as fascinating as the haunted house on rue Royale:

> The old Bayou Road saw a strange sight that afternoon [the time of M. Lalaurie's escape]. Down at its farther end lay a little settlement of fishermen and Spanish moss gatherers, pot-hunters, and shrimpers, around a custom-house station, a lighthouse and a little fort. There the people who drove out in carriages were in the habit of alighting and taking the cool air of the lake, and sipping lemonades, wines, and ices before they returned homeward again along the crowded way that they had come. In after years the place fell into utter neglect. The customs station was removed, the fort was dismantled, the gay carriage people drove on the "New Shell Road" and its tributaries, Bienville and Canal streets, Washington and Carrollton avenues and sipped and smoked in the twilights and starlights of Carrollton Gardens and the "New Lake End." The older haunt, once so bright with the fashionable pleasure-making, was left to the sole illumination of "St. John Light" and the mongrel life of a bunch of cabins branded Crabtown, and became, in popular superstition at least, the yearly rendezvous of the voodoos. Then all at once in latter days it bloomed out in electrical, horticultural, festal, pyrotechnical splendor as "Spanish Fort," and the carriages came rolling back. (*Strange* 213)

Bayou Road and its constantly evolving cultural significance offer Cable the chance to examine how the histories of the city can be experienced through the narration of its architectural and topographical genealogies. In essence, Cable's writing is cultural geography at work. This is why he deems it necessary to identify for the reader the historical arc of the city's past as it echoes along old Bayou Road, the Spanish Fort, and Bayou St. John.

By documenting the changes in the old Bayou Road, Cable unearths New Orleans's past and archives it within the haunted house narrative. This tactical writing practice of inserting stories within a story is also utilized in *The Grandissimes*, particularly in the story of Bras-Coupé, which is based on a true story of a one-armed slave who, after attacking his master, fled into the swamps to avoid detection. This account was widely reported in many New Orleans newspapers at the time and was well known by Cable and his contemporaries.[5] The complete account of the legendary tale is placed in the middle of *The Grandissimes*. This move speaks to the story's importance and Cable's commitment to it as an earlier version, entitled "Bibi," had been rejected by *Scribner's* magazine due to its violent content. The intersplicing of Bras-Coupé's story into *The Grandissimes* does not come as a complete surprise to the reader as Cable repeatedly goes back in time in order to provide context for the present conditions of his characters. The format of the novel invokes the temporal essence of the city it represents, as the past reverberates and reincarnates itself among the present. The flashback form of the novel, its ability to move back and forth in time, is what makes the inclusion of Bras-Coupé's story not only necessary, but possible, as it further illustrates the deep-seated bitterness and multilayered circumstances that fuel the feud between the two families. Bras-Coupé's story takes up just two chapters, but it resonates throughout the entire novel. He continues to haunt the novel as he repeatedly returns as a specter of slavery and insurrection.

In his review of *The Grandissimes*, writer Lafcadio Hearn, himself a documenter of New Orleans, described the novel as "the most remarkable work of fiction in the South, [a] dream which is not at all a dream, a tale which is but half a tale, a series of pictures which, although in a certain sense created by a pencil of an Impressionist, wear a terrible resemblance to terrible realities" (qtd. in Cleman 79). Cable often based his narratives on real-life accounts. The result is that the dreams and the tales that make up Cable's stories ultimately give way to the realities that inform them; and those realities, as the story of Bras-Coupé shows, can be dark. As Greeson attests, Cable was recognized by his contemporaries as "the master over the enchanted, semi-tropical realm, beautiful with flowers, yet marked by the trail of the serpent," and there definitely is an "Edenic" quality in his representations of New Orleans ("Expropriating" 130). Within the picturesque representations of the city (the French market at sunrise, the ferrying of the numerous tugboats, the promenading public on the levee) there is an underlying darkness, a silhouette of something sinister lurking about in the narrative picture.

In essence, Cable is trying to negotiate a sense of nostalgia in *The Grandissimes* that is both tinged with the qualities of nightmare and with hints of the bizarre; the peculiarity of a city that lies between the "funeral swamps" and the raging mouth of the Mississippi River (9). As historian Pierce Lewis asks: "What other city had such an illogical and dangerous site, but insouciantly went about its mixed business of commerce and fun in defiance of threats from pestilence, flood and hurricane? Above all, what other city was so extravagantly charming?" (10). The threat and promise of New Orleans is in its contradictory mythology. Its Mediterranean-style ease and Old World mélange are tempered by the threat of being "sold down the river" and the terror of slavery as witnessed in the story of the haunted house and Bras-Coupé. It is in this sense that New Orleans exhibits her gothic tenor. The gothic and melodrama influence one another: melodrama aims to puncture the surface, and the gothic is "fascinated with what lies hidden in the dungeon and the sepulcher," what lies in the depths of the tomb (Brooks 19). The palimpsestic essence of New Orleans maintains that its secrets will eventually be excised from the tombs and brought out into the open, for the city holds many incisive clues of its original forms. To utilize the words of Peter Brooks, in *The Grandissimes* the "description of the surfaces of the modern metropolis pierces through to a mythological realm where the imagination can find a habitat for its play with large moral entities" (5). The haunting of New Orleans lends itself to melodrama as melodrama is the aesthetic of excess, and New Orleans is all about this kind of extravagance. In his descriptions of the city, Cable displays an element of melodrama's overindulgence. Beneath the "gilded surface" of the Place d'Armes, the vibrant levee populated with its pleasure-seeking elite, is a "revelation of sin"—of slavery, of the broken specter of Bras-Coupé and of Madame Lalaurie fleeing her legacy of violence and the vengeance of the mob (Brooks 6).

Ultimately, the shadow that casts the largest pall on the city of New Orleans *is* the shadow of slavery. It is this nefarious thing to which the city's architecture—its large dormer windows, breezy belvederes, and Spanish-tiled rooftops, gas lamps, shuttered porticos, and wrought-iron verandas—openly gives refuge. Slavery is the thing that "old" New Orleans harbors and that "new" New Orleans—Cable's New Orleans, as it is imagined in narrative and actually lived—reels from.[6] It is what links *Old Creole Days*, *The Grandissimes*, and *Strange True Stories of Louisiana* together; as Gordon informs us, "that which appears absent can indeed be a seething presence" (17). Madame Lalaurie's rue Royale retains its haunting capacity within the novel that nevertheless grants New Orleans its strange and unsettling gothic charm. As one of the main characters in *The Grandissimes* walks down the infamous street, our narrator reveals to us: "Upon every side there seemed to start away from his turning glance the multiplied shadows, of something wrong" (96).

NOTES

1. Cultural geography is a subset of the hemispheric approach toward American studies outlined by Caroline Levander and Robert Levine in *Hemispheric American Studies*. This reframing of the national takes into account the "extra-national": transnational dialogues comprised of complex interlocking international histories and cultures brought on by diasporic movements and encounters (2–3).

2. In *Our South*, Greeson explores this idea more fully, stating that Cable "soft-pedals the new (and not too flattering) role into which he casts U.S. readers by bringing cultural expropriation, rather than material expropriation, to the fore in his stories" (264).

3. The definition of Creole is a much-contested and ever-changing term. When I use the term "Creole," I am referencing the old definition, which applied to the descendents of Spanish and French colonials.

4. I saw this on my visit to the tavern in 2009.

5. The character in *The Grandissimes* does not have a missing arm; rather his lack of personal subjectivity is metaphorically implied in his name, Bras-Coupé: cut arm.

6. Cleman notes that in *The Grandissimes*, "Cable identifies slavery and racial caste as the central problems of Southern life, the guilt of the past encumbering the present" (63).

7

FAULKNER'S DOOM
The Undead Inhabitants of Yoknapatawpha

MELANIE BENSON TAYLOR

> "The South," Shreve said. "The South. Jesus. No wonder you folks all outlive yourselves by years and years and years."
>
> —WILLIAM FAULKNER, *Absalom, Absalom!* (1936)

To return to the quip that begins the introduction to this collection, when Faulkner penned his now-famous quote "The past is never dead. It isn't even past," he probably wasn't thinking about ghosts or zombies. What he *was* describing was an anxiously modernizing New South, a temporal and geographic space where the burdens of history nourished the soil and suffused a man's character, and where the possibilities of regeneration were ceaselessly thwarted by the aftershocks of a harrowing past. While we generally regard Faulkner's famous remark as a lamentation, albeit a self-critical one, its persistence in even contemporary cultural discourse persuades us to see it also as a harbinger. What exactly did Faulkner and the modern South know about the living dead, and why does this notion continue to be both so relevant and somehow still so revelatory?

Fortunately, Faulkner's fictional visions are, if not prophetic, at least a snapshot of crises not simply local or ephemeral or aberrant but, rather, symptomatic of national pathologies we continuously labor to deny or conceal. None of this is news to practitioners of the New Southern Studies, which has already gone a long way toward removing the facade from the "exceptional" South and the United States all at once.[1] But what I'm concerned with tuning into here are the *effects* of that protracted repudiation: what happens to a culture locked in obstinate, perpetual denial? Perhaps things like zombies happen—at least figuratively—within a cultural imaginary anxious to pathologize and thus defang its demons. Faulkner's undead inhabitants may not be remarkable to contemporary zombiephiles; but prior to their twenty-first-century guises and Hollywood makeup, his reanimated corpses are prescient precursors to today's shuffling, disease-ridden manifestations of our imperfectly buried national crimes and crises.[2]

The zombie is primarily a racialized figure with roots in Afro-Caribbean slavery. As early as the eighteenth century, we have reports from colonial Saint Domingue of slaves whose souls, and often their bodies, would labor for eternity. According to Afro-Caribbean scholar Elizabeth McAlister, "the zombie was born (so to speak) in what Michael Taussig (1987) terms the colonial 'space of death' and is inextricable from the 'culture of terror' of the plantation" (461). The trope would have continued and striking relevance for the modern world that issued from the plantation complex, situated at "the nexus of capitalism, race, and religion" (McAlister 461). Indeed, as Deleuze and Guattari argue in *The Anti-Oedipus*, "the only modern myth is the myth of zombies" (335). One of the first appearances of the zombie in American culture came with the 1932 film *White Zombie* starring Bela Lugosi.[3] The racial themes in the movie are explicit, as its title suggests, but the plot hinges ostensibly on a love story: a wealthy Haitian plantation owner hires a witch doctor to put an amorous spell on the woman he covets, but instead she is transformed into the eponymous "White Zombie" slave ready to "perform his every desire!" Predictably, the racial elision of this white maiden-turned-slave is too sorrowful for the master to accept, and so he tries in vain to have his prize returned to purity. For southerners in the 1930s, such a narrative might seem like a supernatural perversion of a *Birth of a Nation* plotline, and an expression of the seductive yet repellent intimacy with which racial "Others" may enter and occupy our lives—and, finally, be regulated. "[I]n each context," both Haitian and U.S., McAlister explains, "race is the pivot on which these dynamics articulate themselves" (458–59).

In films like *White Zombie*, the zombie slave shifts from policing racial distinctions to regulating feminine desires and agency in ways sure to resonate with white southern masculinity on the brink of a vexed new order. Likewise, another popular film of the era, *I Walked with a Zombie* (1943), also takes place on a plantation in the West Indies, and it, too, employs the zombie curse as a method for controlling not just slaves but women and their errant desires.[4] It is tempting to find in such films parallels to *Absalom, Absalom!*, with its Haitian shadow narrative imported to Mississippi along with a tribe of (zombie?) slaves "from a much older country than Virginia or Carolina but [not] a quiet one" (11). Under Thomas Sutpen's thrall, his wife, Ellen, quickly becomes zombielike, a "preserved woman [. . .] unimpeded by weight of stomach and all the heavy organs of suffering and experience" (54–55). Their daughter Judith, too, "slept waking in some suspension so completely physical as to resemble the state before birth [. . . in] complete detachment and imperviousness to actuality almost like physical deafness" (55). Finally, there is Rosa, next in line for Sutpen's spell, a feathery corpse of arrested girlhood in a lace collar, her dangling feet and tinny voice a signifier for a life and sexuality interrupted. She narrates the Sutpen saga to Quentin Compson "preparing for Harvard in the South, the Deep South dead since 1865 and peopled with garrulous outraged baffled ghosts, listening, having to listen, to one of the ghosts which refused to lie still even longer than most had, telling him about old ghost-times" (4). The second "ghost" is, of course, Rosa herself, who is denied the chance to live fully by the "demon" master Sutpen, but also by the apocalyptic "South" itself.

Such imaginative monstrosities insinuate themselves into American culture by way of these conveniently remote but uncannily intimate plantation geographies. Exploding onto the American pop-cultural scene in the modern era, these films echo the persistent nostalgia of the Southern Literary Renaissance: back-looking, ambivalent, anxious refractions and desires activated by the pressures of modernity. The zombie motif thus becomes a repository for domestic anxieties held at a fantastical remove; once imported, these servile wraiths begin to collect additional anxieties about gender, history, and nationalism. In Faulkner's imagination, the dispossessed South is quite clearly a landscape of ghosts in ways that hardly need to be stated. What makes many of his wraiths more rife with implication, however, is the curiously retrograde aspect of their dehumanization. In the above examples, all retreat into some "state before birth," before "suffering and experience," arrested and "preserved" in the ether of memory. Further, these ghosts are often women who infect others, like Quentin, with their knowledge; they are vessels of history's primal outrages, yet they somehow transcend its trauma. As Mr. Compson baldly puts it: "They lead beautiful lives—women. Lives not only divorced from, but irrevocably excommunicated from, all reality" (156).

I don't intend to aver or explore Faulkner's own filtered misogyny here; rather, my point is that his characters approach their ghosts and zombies with ambivalence, a discomfiting mixture of both revulsion and desire. Whether female or black, the Other that imperils white masculinity in Faulkner's cosmos threatens to devour it. Such specters prove not just horrifying but bizarrely reassuring in the face of social upheaval. Rosa, in fact, hurls herself into it, "at full blind tilt into something monstrous and immobile," only to stop short when she collides with Clytie's black body: "Because there is something in the touch of flesh with flesh which abrogates, cuts sharp and straight across the devious intricate channels of decorous ordering [. . .] the liquorish and ungirdled mind is anyone's to take in any darkened hallway of this earthly tenement. But let flesh touch with flesh, and watch the fall of all eggshell shibboleth of caste and color, too. Yes, I stopped dead" (111–12). She both craves and fears contamination by the "thing" that excites her innermost desires and anxieties. Through her, we intuit an ambient fear in Faulkner's work that once "ungirdled" by social order, we might be swallowed whole—and the only way to avoid it all is to "stop dead."

While the overt revulsion here is certainly racial and sexual, "caste" also operates as a fragile container easily breached. Indeed, underlying the symptomatic twitches of racism and sexism is a consternating economic illness—and its etiology begins but doesn't end in the perversions of slavery. Contemporary zombies, in fact, are rarely considered racialized figures (most, in fact, are now emphatically white) and are instead construed as capitalism's grotesque progeny.[5] Yet the genealogy of such a critique was palpable in both Haitian folklore and early U.S. films: as McAlister notes, the pop-cultural zombie emerged in modern culture as an index of capitalism's proliferative effects, embodying "the excessive extremes of capitalism, the overlap of capitalism and cannibalism, and the interplay between capitalism and race in the history of the Americas" (462).[6] Sutpen is described by Rosa as just this kind of malevolence incarnate, the ultimate zombie master and incarnator: "the evil's source and head, which had outlasted all its victims—

who had created two children not only to destroy one another and his own line, but my line as well" (12). The contagion spreads, rendering Sutpen's victims gray, shadowy shells, smiling dolls, paranoid killers, or howling idiots. Sutpen's design was born in the plantation South but then nourished during his apprenticeship in Haiti. By making him return a devil with the capacity to infect and propagate a society of zombies, Faulkner engages in the same ambivalent dance of recognition and disavowal that typifies the American relationship to its founding fictions and colonial crimes. To fall victim to that fever is to be infested by a mobile, immortal lust for power, place, and prosperity, one that in Faulkner's modernizing world rises up through both the past and the archipelagos of plantation history, rooting in a modern landscape infused with opportunity but condemned to the same petty longings and dehumanizing logic.

Importantly, then, the zombie archetype continues to haunt Faulkner's characters, who move further away, conceptually and temporally, from those infectious plantation parables. For Charlotte Rittenmeyer in *The Wild Palms* (1939),[7] her romantic flight from the strictures of marriage ends in a fatal abortion performed by her hapless lover Harry. Once a vibrant, harsh, passionate woman, she becomes merely

> a face whose skin was drawn thin over prominent cheekbones and a heavy jaw [. . .] just sitting there in that complete immobility which the doctor [. . .] did not need the corroboration of the drawn quality of the skin and the blank inverted fixity of the apparently unseeing eyes to recognize at once—that complete immobile abstraction from which even pain and terror are absent, in which a living creature seems to listen to and even watch some one of its own flagging organs, the heart say, the secret irreparable seeping of blood. (5)

But how did she get here, to such a state? Like so many of Faulkner's characters, Charlotte and Harry lurch forward into a fate that demands not just the laboring body but the "heart," estranged here beyond recovery. The couple literally cannot survive in this world simply because they lack the financial resources to do so. They slip into the world of expectations and appearances, and find themselves stripped of love: "We were too busy." Harry explains: "[W]e had to rent and support a room for two robots to live in" (109). They become the New South's white zombies, slaves to work and survival at the expense of love; and as artists, their fate is not simply typical, but resonant of Faulkner's own fear that his creative passion would become a robotic exercise in subsistence. Harry and Charlotte become "thrall and slave" to the system (113), and so their only hope of recapturing freedom and love is to escape society altogether—but of course, there is nowhere they can go where the corrosive calculations of American capitalism don't follow them because there is no cure or deliverance for the disease that has ruined them: "this was worse than death or division even: it was the mausoleum of love, it was the stinking catafalque of the dead corpse borne between the olfactoryless walking shapes of the immortal unsentient demanding ancient meat" (118). Faulkner's language here imagines a putrid modern marketplace with no place for love or humanity, and with no avenue of surrender—only the lumbering corpses of memory and desire, the "demanding ancient meat."

Nonetheless, "freedom" for Harry and Charlotte means fleeing the shackles of money and propriety, a dream flagrantly demolished when Charlotte's body "produces" the embodiment of their audacity in an unplanned pregnancy. We must then read the bungled abortion, and the subsequent death of Charlotte herself, as a perverse act of erotic love. Later, Harry masturbates in his jail cell, thinking, "there was just memory, forever and inescapable, so long as there was flesh to titillate. . . . *Because if memory exists outside of the flesh it wont be memory because it wont know what it remembers so when she became not then half of memory became not and I become not then all of remembering will cease to be.*—Yes he thought *Between grief and nothing I will take grief*" (273). His masturbatory memorializing thus becomes the consummate expression of contemporary "production," both economic and romantic. Worse, Faulkner intimates here what much of his work bears out: as long as we are imprisoned in our flesh, we will be consumed by memories—by "suffering and experience." The zombielike escape achieved by so many of Faulkner's women seems increasingly preferable to the grief of living in "reality."

A similar message adheres in the novel's companion narrative, "The Old Man," though the tale seemingly works oppositely: a baby is born on an Indian mound rising out of the Great Flood, in striking contradistinction to Charlotte's fatal abortion. When the tall convict finds his momentary "freedom" threatened by the woman he must usher to safety, along with the unborn child she carries—a signifier of desire's immanence—he comes suddenly upon an Indian mound in the middle of a raging flood: the convict grasps at it, "plunging at the muddy slope, slipping back, the woman struggling in his muddy hands [. . .] as if his own failed and spent flesh were attempting to carry out his furious unflagging will for severance at any price, even that of drowning, from the burden with which, unwitting and without choice, he had been doomed" (148). It is, typically, unclear whether Faulkner means to show the convict's "will" inclined toward rescue or release, and thus, whether the Indian mound will aid or abet his true desire. What *is* clear is that the tall convict construes freedom in purely mercenary terms: outside of the fences of Parchman prison, he finds himself coming back to life, reanimated by hope and desire: "*I had done forgot how good making money was. Being let to make it*" (219). The convict's dream is no less fruitless than Harry's, though, as Faulkner steadily unveils a world where "freedom" is not simply the opposite of "slavery" but its uncanny twin, its tantalizing refraction. The tall convict, of course, ends up back in prison by the end of the narrative, not because he couldn't have escaped logistically, but because he literally does not know how to be free in this world.

The tall convict dramatizes what we see so persistently throughout Faulkner's career: a discomfort with the messy perforations of modernity, the tangle of opportunity and foreclosure that routinely stymie his characters' attempts to flourish. Unlike that of many of his peers, though, Faulkner's back-looking nostalgia reverts not to plantation idylls but to an epoch more "ancient" and primordial—a yearning he unveils by allowing his characters to draw close to aboriginal antidotes, like the Indian mound that appears briefly to save the convict and issue forth new life. In this instructive universe of alterity and romance, solid ground is regained; spiritual and emotional wisdom and values are recalibrated. Importantly, though, the moment's typically thick ambivalence hints at the vexed complexity of such salvation, an awareness perhaps of historical continuity rather than rupture or crisis. In other words, he causes us to question whether the seeds of human doom are inherent or historical, metaphysical or material. The tall convict does successfully use the mound to deliver a baby, but is "doomed" to carry that burden "unwitting and without choice." Indeed, "doom" is a prevalent word in Faulkner's world—and it appears perhaps most importantly in his Indian stories. Primarily, it serves as moniker for old Ikkemotubbe, who called himself "The Man," a mistranslation into French as "du Homme," elided as "Doom." None too subtly, Faulkner sketches these early Choctaw chiefs as ambitious, corrupt, and foolish: in their aspirations to be "The Man," they invite doom upon their own people, just as catastrophically as Sutpen does. Ultimately, Native Americans are rendered no more immune to the seductions of power and acquisition than their white successors; in fact, they may have aggravated such lusts, as Ike McCaslin intimates in his lamentation that the Indians sold what wasn't theirs to sell, setting in motion a multigenerational nightmare of land exchanges and exploitation that would ravage the countryside and its people: "on the instant when Ikkemotubbe discovered, realized, that he could sell it for money, on that instant it ceased ever to have been his forever, father to father to father, and the man who bought it bought nothing" (240).

Inserted between indictment of the Indians' corruption and a lament for the vacancy of modern possession is Faulkner's reminder that what will be passed down "father to father to father" is a heritage of rapacity and self-interest with no yield, a terrible birthright haunting the genealogy of the "cursed" South. The Indian example is so disappointing, Faulkner implies, because their potential to resist was so great but, finally, so vulnerable to the "discovery" of profit and its seductions. They epitomize the weakness of man before the temptations of capitalism, the "doom" that corrodes man's relationship to his chattel and his women; worse, their memory lives on to delude and infect those who come after. Whenever Indian analogues in Faulkner's work appear, they tend to embody the frustrated hopes for ancient alterity, so tangible in the landscape and imagination of the South, but so dramatically undermined by the terrible forces of upheaval assaulting its inhabitants. Those undead hosts are rife in Faulkner's work, uncannily resurgent, alive as traces in the bodies and environments of the South's black and white heirs.

Indigenous traces and parables abound in Faulkner's fiction in ways that demand further attention. Perhaps the most bizarre, and certainly the least discussed, comes in his 1931 story "Idyll in the Desert," published initially by Random House and later anthologized in *The Uncollected Stories*. It is recognizably an early version of Harry and Charlotte's illicit love story in "The Wild Palms," related to an unnamed narrator by a mail carrier named Lucas Crump.[8] The tale is set in the Southwest, at a camp for tuberculosis patients. A man arrives there to convalesce and is soon joined by his lover—a married woman. She nurses him back to health, and then he promptly leaves her.

Thinking that he will surely be back, she waits there for eight subsequent years while slowly dying from the disease he infected her with. Her cuckolded husband sends money periodically, and Crump agrees to trick her into believing that the cash comes from her missing lover. Upon each delivery, the woman tosses away the money but savors the suggestion of her lover's care. Moreover, she is never seen eating: she is sustained not by worldly goods or even food but solely by the prospect of love—and, importantly, by the nurture of an "Injun" woman whom Crump commissions to care for her. Fittingly, the Indian nurse is part of her apparatus of survival beyond the boundaries of civilization, propriety, and money. But the story ends badly: she dies, and neither her remarried lover nor her husband recognizes her wasted body in the end.

Like the later Charlotte Rittenmeyer, the woman rejects the world of money and propriety, but not before it expels and refuses to acknowledge her. She is left without place, identity, love, or recognition—a sober commentary on the grave returns of her audacity in escaping the geography and economics of the South and modern American society all at once. As he relates the sad story, Crump the mail carrier habitually gets off track, explaining that it is because he "talks so seldom." When he finally finishes telling his colorful tale, the narrator asks,

> "Have you got any Indian blood?"
> "Indian blood?"
> "You talk so little. So seldom."
> "Oh, sure. I have some Indian blood. My name used to be Sitting Bull."
> "Used to be?"
> "Sure. I got killed one day a while back. Didn't you read it in the paper?" (411)

The levity of the moment (he is almost certainly joking) is disturbingly out of joint with the narrative he tells; moreover, Crump's claim to be the reincarnated spirit of Sitting Bull makes no immediate sense. But when we consider the frame narrative as the real story here, the device that structures our understanding of the emotional turmoil and negotiations he oversees, it becomes obvious that Faulkner-as-Crump (author of both this embedded tale and the later "Wild Palms" narrative it predicts) offers a subtle commentary on the defeated soul of modern America. The mail carrier watches people arrive at the consumptive camp and drop out of the world and its codes, yet he observes that for most, "the hardest habit of all to break [is] [o]wning things," even on their deathbeds: "They could live in a house on earth with it for years without even knowing where it was, but just try to get them to start to heaven without taking it along" (403). The relationships he witnesses function in much the same way, structured as they are by cash, subterfuge, and a dogged fixation on immaterial certainties that never materialize. Crump thus becomes an assuaging influence, a ghostly emissary from a tradition of resistance and trauma, doling out cash only for necessaries like food or a buffalo robe.

In the end, then, the story's odd frame allows us to see the specter of the undead Indian as a nutritive antidote, as palliative care for those dying (literally) of *consumption*—that infectious disease of not just the lungs but the economy rampant in the modern material world. As the story's title announces, such sufferers might find an "idyll" in the southwestern desert, away from commerce, away from the South, away even from marriage, peopled by Indians like the Sitting Bull wraith or the "Injun" nurse "who couldn't talk enough of any language" to give away the hoax (409). Yet this "idyll," like the memory of the plantation coveted earnestly by so many of Faulkner's southern peers, fails to deliver on its promise of salvation. While the Injun nurse and Crump/Sitting Bull don't *seem* to speak the language of modern capitalism very well, in the end, they apparently do. Ironically, it is the mail carrier who maintains the vital link between the outside world and this cocoon of fantasy: he delivers the deadly illusions that can sustain the ailing woman only briefly. As Sitting Bull—a role he adopts seemingly at whim, and with a discernible bite of sarcasm—he is not just a martyr of colonial resistance but rather a conniving spirit of the modern world, just another maladjusted zombie feeding on the weakness of others. Prior to the closing revelation of his "Indian blood," and presumably prompting it, the narrator asks, "You must still have had some of the money the husband sent you to fool her with." The Mail Rider equivocates; he "spat carefully, wiped his sleeve across his mouth." The narrator's subsequent query—"Do you have any Indian blood?"—can thus be read only cynically, as a tacit suggestion that his *Indian* blood is what makes him deceptive, greedy, doomed, abject—and dangerous. It is, perhaps, an infection that affects all Americans, a reminder of colonial trauma and capitalist transcendence, an evil that will be ceaselessly reborn not just in Mississippi but in the broader national body. The marked irony of the reticence he claims is loudly proclaimed in the end: such narratives *do* speak, filtered through absurd characters and futile Indigenous proxies, if only we might pay attention to the deeper narratives beneath the headlines of the national "papers."

In the end, Faulkner's most unsettling zombie archetypes lie somewhere in an uncanny, infectious trinity of alterity: Indians, African Americans, and women all threaten to poison and drain the nation's white men of their capacity to resist, to rise above, to repudiate the corrosive influence of colonial-capitalism and all of its mobile, infectious doom. They are thrall and slave to a system that offers freedom with one hand and retracts it with the other. He might have predicted that we would find ourselves here, in 2015, battered by economic disaster, environmental apocalypse, and humanitarian crises—and projecting these new terrors on the very ancient form of the tropological zombie. Faulkner's grim visions warn us against creating false distance—this is not "just" pop-cultural hysteria—and he cautions especially against false hope. The mystical, romantic Indian trope, for instance, is just a screen for a loss we cannot abide, and a scapegoat of the disaster that we cannot own. As Comanche critic Paul Chaat Smith puts it, white and Indian culture are "locked in an endless embrace of love and hate and narcissism. [. . .] We are the country, and the country is us" (6). We are endlessly fascinated with ghosts, zombies, and Indians alike because they are all culturally manufactured tropes, all mutations of anxieties that embody our deepest fears and desires.

Seeing our own cataclysmic cultural moment in the context of Faulkner's should jolt us into a similarly probing, if unnerving, sense of continuity and urge us to, as Rosa Coldfield urges herself: "wake up, Rosa; wake up—not from what was, what used to be, but from what had not, could not have ever, been; wake, Rosa—not to what should, what might have been, but what to cannot, what must not, be; wake, Rosa, from the hoping [. . .] there was nothing there to save [. . .] only that dream-state in which you run without moving from a terror in which you can not believe, toward a safety in which you have no faith. [. . .] I stopped in running's midstride again though my body, blind unsentient barrow of deluded clay and breath, still advanced" (113–14). The question remains: Is the forward march of modernity simply a shuffling, zombie-filled race into "nothing," or can we cultivate hope in something yet unseen and unfathomably alive on the horizon?

NOTES

1. See, for instance, Leigh Anne Duck, *The Nation's Region;* and Jennifer Greeson, *Our South*.

2. While I am arguing here for an early, subtle variation on the zombie motif in Faulkner's modern South, the trope has had continued contemporary relevance within the region. In literature, texts like Alden Bell's 2010 novel *The Reapers Are the Angels* have been widely categorized as Southern Gothic: Bell's effort was touted by author Michael Gruber as "an astonishing twist on the southern gothic: like Flannery O'Connor with zombies." Not incidentally, Bell's protagonist is named Temple, perhaps as an allusion to Faulkner's Temple Drake in *Sanctuary*. On the screen, zombie-themed television shows like *The Walking Dead* are set explicitly in the contemporary South.

3. It is unknown whether Faulkner had seen or heard of the film, though his repeated forays to Hollywood would seem to increase the likelihood that he was aware of this proliferating genre.

4. In this case, the mistress of the plantation is falling in love with another man, so her mother-in-law has her turned into a zombie and thus preserves the marriage.

5. The notion of the zombie as a capitalist phenomenon has even infiltrated economic theory itself. See, for instance, Chris Harman's *Zombie Capitalism;* and Satyajit Das, "Dead Hand of Economics."

6. See also Mimi Sheller, *Consuming the Caribbean: From Arawaks to Zombies* (2003).

7. This is the title of the original work published in 1939, which contained the intertwined novellas of "The Wild Palms" and "Old Man." The work was reissued in 1990 by Noel Polk under Faulkner's intended title, which had been rejected by the publisher: *If I Forget Thee, Jerusalem*. In what follows, I will refer to the title of individual stories.

8. Lucas Crump seems a phonetic cousin to Lucas Beauchamp (pronounced Bee-chum), which suggests an irresistible link to the later mixed-race character who goes digging obsessively for gold in an Indian mound in *Go Down, Moses*. The intertextual importance of the Indian mound is worth exploring here, especially in a novel that prominently features Sam Fathers and Indigeneity.

8

FAULKNER'S DEATHWAYS
The Race and Space of Mourning

ELIZABETH RODRIGUEZ FIELDER

Beyond the decaying plantation house of Sutpen's Hundred and the grotesque eccentricities of Rosa Coldfield and Emily Grierson, there is another, unlikely gothic space in Faulkner's fiction: the jail. In *Requiem for Nun* (1951), lawyer Gavin Stevens proclaims the fate of African American prisoner Nancy Mannigoe, who has been recently sentenced to death for the murder of Temple Stevens's baby: "In the eyes of the law, she is already dead" (*RN* 72). This state of being "already dead" while still living marks a version of haunting in Faulkner's oeuvre: one where imprisoned black bodies are suspended between life and death. The jail raises questions about the processes by which life and death are determined by larger forces: the legal system becomes conflated with religious belief, just as Nancy's sentencing is titled a requiem—a religious ritual of mourning. In this essay, I focus on two moments where Nancy's life is subject to ritual—her possession in "That Evening Sun" (1931) (TES) and her sentencing in *Requiem*—in order to show the connection between the power of religious ritual and the ritualistic nature of state power. In both cases, ritual performance acts as a means of cultural expression as well as an important element of identity formation.

In Faulkner's dark vision of these processes, identity continues to be determined by the legacies of slavery and other forms of racialized oppression. As such, *Requiem* demands to be read with reference to, in Jay Ellis's words, "the history of slavery [that] remains so close to the dark provenance of Southern Gothic" ("On Southern Gothic Literature" xx). However, even as Faulkner's representation of ritual practices in "That Evening Sun" and *Requiem* should be placed within the highly local, visible, and disciplinary space of the jail, it also extends to unlikely places beyond the borders of both the U.S. South and the United States through the mystery of circum-Atlantic ritual. This conflation of U.S. southern and circum-Atlantic spaces allows for what Justin D. Edwards sees as a connection between gothic discourse and Freud's notion of the uncanny that Edwards summarizes as a "sense of strangeness when the unfamiliar appears at the center of the familiar." If we consider the jail alongside the home as sites of "developing selfhood" for a community, then "the breakdown of those sites through the recognition of something familiar will trouble the smooth surface of identity" (xxv). In "That Evening Sun" and *Requiem*, Faulkner's gothic discourse challenges the notion of social progress as the jail becomes a site for the continuous repetition of dehumanization and racial oppression.

Just as a requiem is a performed ritual, *Requiem* is a performed novel; its hybrid form between novel and play draws attention to the characters' *actions* in relation to text. My critical approach draws from performance theory that discusses how social identities depend on participation in ritual practices ranging from theatrical performances, to rites-of-passage ceremonies, to everyday routines of social functioning. As Richard Schechner has argued, engaging in performance ritual allows for a temporary suspension of social boundaries in order to create a "restored behavior" once the ritual/performance has been completed.[1] In *Theater, Sacrifice, Ritual: Exploring Forms of Political Theater*, theater historian Erika Fischer-Lichte connects drama to forms of sacrificial ritual that "turns a religious group into a social and political community" (32); in doing so, Fischer-Lichte reads the political potential of the performing body to define social boundaries. Faulkner's ambiguous prose draws attention to the bodily actions of his characters in a way that corresponds with Joseph Roach's notion of "orature," in which the motions and actions of the characters convey what cannot be communicated directly through text.[2] This means of expression is necessary to marginalized groups dependent on "messages that are coded and encrypted; to indirect, nonverbal, and extralinguistic modes of communication where subversive meanings and utopian yearnings can be sheltered and shielded from surveillance" (Conquergood 36). By focusing on bodies in action in

"That Evening Sun" and *Requiem,* even within prose, we are required to read beyond Faulkner's text in order to grasp cultural expression existing outside the epistemologies of a white, male-dominant society.

Given my emphasis on performance, it would be remiss not to consider Faulkner's own interests in theater, which date back to his beginnings as a playwright and drama critic for the university newspaper, the *Mississippian.* In a 1922 article, Faulkner claims that the "wealth of natural dramatic material in this country" relies on language, what he defines as the "earthy strength" of American English ("American Drama: Eugene O'Neill"). Strikingly, Faulkner grounds dramatic language within ethnic cultural expression:

> Our wealth of language and our inarticulateness (inability to derive any benefit from the language) are due to the same cause: our racial chaos and our instinctive quickness to realize our simpler needs, and to supply them from any source. As a nation we are a people of action [. . .]; even our language is action rather than communication between minds. [. . .] [A] mass of subtleties for the reason that it is employed only as a means of relief, when physical action is impossible or unpleasant, by all classes, ranging from the Harvard professor, through the garneniaed aloof young liberal, to the lowliest pop vendor at the ball park. ("American Drama: Inhibitions," pt. 2)

Faulkner envisions the dramatic dialogue as action and thus positions orature as a means to express the "dynamic chaos of a hodgepodge of nationalities" ("American Drama: Inhibitions," pt. 1). Perhaps this is why, even though Faulkner was not a playwright, Albert Camus insisted, "He is in my opinion, the only true tragic dramatist of our time" (Foote 168).

Faulkner explores social performance through the medium of dramatic dialogue in *Requiem,* yet his oratorical style of writing describing performed ritual was already evident in some of his best gothic fiction, including "Pantaloon in Black," which first appeared in *Harper's Magazine* in 1940, and the earlier "That Evening Sun," which was first published in 1931. In both of these stories, haunting and possession suggest alternate locations rooted in a circum-Atlantic culture existing outside of white-dominant society. Through literary clues suggesting vodou practices, the rituals enacted on the bodies of Rider and Nancy are described through action and cryptic dialogue that exemplify how "performative language can play a crucial role in the assignment, representation, codification, and resistance of circum-

Atlantic identities" (Adams, "Introduction" 9). As Nancy's and Rider's possessed bodies undergo a liminal state between life and death, they resurrect circum-Atlantic pasts and transcribe them into a cultural expression beyond the scope of white understanding.

Quentin Compson narrates the events in "That Evening Sun" and focuses on his childhood experience with the Compson family's one-time servant Nancy. He recalls Nancy's fear of her husband, Jesus, who she claims is seeking revenge on her for becoming pregnant with another man's child. Despite Quentin's father's efforts to assure her that Jesus has left town, Nancy's fear of Jesus's presence intensifies: "I can feel him . . . hearing us talk, every word, hid somewhere waiting" (TES 82). At different points, Quentin remembers aspects of Nancy's strange behavior: her noise that "was like singing and it wasn't like singing"; her staring "cat's eyes" (83) and their ability to move fast "without hardly looking at all" (86); and her lack of sensation when touching a hot light bulb. Nancy's loses control of her physical body: she is unable to take in liquids, declaring, "I can't swallow it [. . .] I swallows but it won't go down me" (86). Dirk Kyuk Jr., Betty M. Kyuk, and James A. Miller argue that Nancy's actions describe the supernatural power at work within the realm of "Afro-Christianity" where "Nancy's behavior implies she has been conjured" (43). The Kyuks and Miller draw evidence from ethnographic research in the Delta and knowledge of circum-Atlantic vodou tradition to read Nancy's abnormal behavior, including her inability to consume food, as evidence of conjure and suggest that Jesus's spirit double sends Nancy the sign—"a hog-bone, with blood meat still on it" (TES 95). A similar sign also appears in *Absalom! Absalom!* and is delivered to plantation owners in Haiti as a prescient symbol of insurrection. This nontextual means of communication cannot be "read" by whites like Thomas Sutpen, who "did not know, comprehend what he must have been seeing every day" (*AA!* 203). Along with Sutpen, Quentin's father, Mr. Compson, can comprehend neither the sign in Nancy's cabin nor her declaration that it means her imminent death ("When yall walk out that door, I gone" [RN 95]). Mr. Compson can only respond, "Nonsense" (95). He repeats "nonsense" three times—denial tinged with biblical allegory—against Nancy's assertions that Jesus is present "in the ditch" and "looking through that window" (95) even though no one else can see him. However, his choice of the word "nonsense" also suggests that he cannot make sense of the situation before him, the sign and the ritual, and therefore easily dismisses Nancy's fear. By contrast, Nancy perceives herself as undead—alive within a body over which she has no control. Her liminality connects the Nancy of "That Evening Sun" to the imprisoned Nancy of *Requiem* and extends the definition of *possession* from vodou ritual to state-sanctioned ownership of her body.

In *Requiem*, Temple Stevens confesses her past transgressions to Gavin Stevens and later to the Mississippi governor in order to express a sense of culpability in Nancy's murder of her infant child, a crime that Noel Polk referred to as "the most savage and reprehensible act of violence in all of William Faulkner's fiction" (xiii). Critics, including Polk, have long debated over Faulkner's moral vision while writing *Requiem*;[3] however, I am more interested in Faulkner's method of layering narrative and legal process. Indeed, there is a moral debate at the heart of *Requiem*, but morality as a concept is subject to interpretation. In other words, Gavin Stevens must perform and continue to perform social rituals to reinforce *his* vision of morality—such as a confession. At one point during Temple's confession, she digresses into emotional observations about incarcerated blacks and retells the story of the black sawmill laborer Rider, the protagonist of "Pantaloon in Black." In the original story in *Go Down, Moses*, Rider also experiences dissociative body-spirit behavior similar to that of Nancy in "That Evening Sun." Yet, when the white deputy sheriff attempts to (re)narrate Rider's tale to his wife at the story's conclusion, he overlooks the crucial signs of supernatural forces at work on Rider's body. Temple's narrative in *Requiem*, which occurs years later, contains the same oversight. Their versions of the events provide further evidence of the failure of cross-cultural understanding. Rider transforms after he buries his wife, Mannie, in a grave surrounded by "objects insignificant to sight but actually of a profound meaning and fatal to touch, which no white man could have read" (*GDM* 132). The burial initiates a circum-Atlantic funerary ritual that extends throughout the U.S. South, the Caribbean, and locations in Africa. Soon after, Rider transcends his physical body with superhuman strength. Like Nancy, Rider is unable, despite repeated attempts, to drink liquid (in his case, alcohol), which is described as "no longer passing down his throat" (144). Notably, though, his failed efforts to hold down the liquid lead him to realize that he "just misread the sign wrong" (145). Whatever unknown "sign" Rider subsequently begins to follow leads him to further dissociation from his body, as if he is witnessing his body externally. He hears "his own voice without grief or amazement" (146) and begins repeating, "Ah'm snakebit and de pizen cant hawm me" (147). The reference to "snakebit" suggests that an external power has entered his system that should have the potential to kill him, but instead it seems to drive his actions—including the murder of a white man, Birdsong. The sheriff attempts to keep him imprisoned and thus away from violent vigilantism of white community members, yet Rider's supernaturally strong body cannot be contained and acts unconsciously, for example, breaking out of the prison while stating, "Ah aint tryin to git out" (154). The conjure-like possession of his body, along with the performance of diasporic funerary ritual, links Rider's identity to Africa and the Caribbean. In a literal reading of the title, Rider's actions are a pantaloon, or performance, of his identity where, as Jessica Adams argues, "the past travels through the bodies [, and] the body itself is a site of documentation and remembrance" (7).

His mysterious actions perform an oppressed past, and thus Rider breaks down the identity of the modern black laborer by revealing ongoing racial oppression in face of industrial labor. When the sheriff claims, "if it wasn't going to be the law, then them Birdsong boys ought to have the first lick of him" (153), he suggests the complicit relationship between the legal system and the white mob violence that eventually claims Rider's life in a lynching. In the deputy sheriff's narrative in which he misunderstands Rider's actions, he provides a racist explanation: "Because they [blacks] aint human" (149), and thereby uses the narrative to deflect blame away from the lynch mob. Temple's version draws further attention to the inability of narrative to encompass truth or natural law. Temple claims that Rider's strange actions, including his murder of a white man, were a product of exhaustion after burying his wife. Temple is more sympathetic than the deputy in "Pantaloon," yet both overlook Rider's participation in a circum-Atlantic ritual—not to mention his lynching by a white mob. Temple instead focuses on the psychology of a man in mourning. She uses narrative to position herself as sympathetic to the plight of a murder as a means to displace her own culpability in Nancy's immanent death. Yet after her telling, "[t]here are still no tears on her face; she merely takes the handkerchief and dabs, pats at her eyes with it as if it were a powderpuff" (171). Temple's attempt to remember Rider is filtered through her subjective and biased understanding of the events; her narrative is a dramatic performance rather than a realistic or objective representation of actual events. Yet beyond misreadings and misrepresentations by whites, the possessed bodies of Rider in "Pantaloon" and Nancy in "That Evening Sun" recover and reenact past diasporic histories. The failure of white characters to understand these histories—from Mr. Compson's indifference to the more violent lynching of Rider—challenges the notion of social progress through the perpetuity of racial and social injustice.

In *Requiem*, the repetition of Rider's and Nancy's stories serves to raise doubts as to whether an objective, universal justice system can be achieved. Indeed, in *Requiem* the legal system's continuing power over black lives constitutes an uncanny parallel to slavery. The jail presents a site that defies social progress through its unnatural but familiar determination over human bodies, which becomes a ritualized process. In the "The Courthouse" and "The Jail" sections of *Requiem*, which also figure as preludes to the acts of the play, Faulkner describes the creation of the jail as a mythical space that depends on performative gestures rather than inherent truth. It originates as a lock on a mail pouch described as "not even a symbol of security" but rather as a "gesture of salutation, of free men to free men, of civilisation to civilisation" (11). The lock develops into the jail yet continues to fail in its actual purpose: In a "scene resembling an outdoor stage setting," a group of prisoners easily remove a wall, "leaving the jail open to the world like a stage" (14). This theatrical imagery exposes the jail's core significance as "symbol" or "gesture" of civilization through its creation of an anticivil area where rights can be taken away from others, evident from the jail's position as "older than even the town itself" (183). The Parisian architect in charge of designing Jefferson articulates the jail's symbolism in his physical blueprint. He places the courthouse and jail at the center and claims to the nascent citizens: "In fifty years you will be trying to change it in the name of what you will call progress. But you will fail; you will never be able to get away from it" (34). The architect's prophesy extends to the legacy of slavery that contributed to the building of not only the courthouse but also the town; a blueprint of racial oppression will continue to haunt Jefferson, despite the town's economic and social progress. The history of the courthouse/jail whose "fate," the narrator of the prelude states, "is to stand in the hinterland of America" (41) marks the framework of race relations that determines the drama of Nancy's fate. Nancy's already-dead-yet-living body is symbolic of the legacy of racial oppression: suspended in spaces such as prisons, removed from the town's outward sense of progress, yet central to it.

Nancy serves as a reminder of the racist design inherent within the prison system's power to remove black civil life, which gives double meaning to Gavin Stevens's claim that, "In the eyes of the law, Nancy Mannigoe doesn't even exist" (72). Similar images of undead incarcerated blacks appeared previously in *Intruder in the Dust* (1948). In that novel, Faulkner renders incarcerated African American bodies as corpses. They lie within the Jefferson jail cell "motionless, their eyes closed but no sound of snoring, no sound of any sort, lying there immobile orderly and composed [. . .] as if they had been embalmed" (*ID* 54). The jail becomes not only a living tomb but also a site for the perpetual reaffirmation of racial oppression where black "servants" incarcerated for "drunkenness or fighting or gambling [. . .] would be extracted the next morning by their white folks." Even the "New Negro" spends his nights in jail and his days laboring for the state to work off fines (216). *Intruder* hints at how the repetitive ritual of incarceration takes black lives through the systematic removal of their social agency. This image is repeated and augmented in *Requiem*, where Faulkner presents the jail as a central character/actor with monstrous consequences for Nancy.

Moments in the text that reveal Nancy's background have the ability to garner reader/audience sympathy. Temple tells (or retells, it having previously been narrated by Quentin Compson in "That Evening Sun") the story of Nancy's public beating by the white banker, Mr. Stovall, which occurs after Nancy confronts him about his failure to pay her for her sexual services. Temple presents the audience—and the reader—with Nancy's background and the events surrounding the murder as evidence in order to raise *doubt* over whether legal arbitration should determine Nancy's life. However, it is Nancy's other background as a victim of supernatural *possession* that reveals the depth of the jail's power to control her, and especially her body. The ritual that controls Nancy's body in "That Evening Sun" defamiliarizes the legitimacy of the legal system. While Jesus's vodou may seem primitive and supernatural, his power parallels the justice system as they both possess and repress Nancy. In *Requiem*, the jail and the legal process take on a mythic religious quality in order for society to accept its power to determine lives. The history of the jail's (re)construction becomes a ritual that transforms the participants into members of a civilization: "something happened to them—the men who had spent that first long, hot, endless July day sweating and raging about the wrecked jail [. . .] in order to rebuild the new one" (27–28). The narrator stresses that the men actually did not labor so intensely: the process took only two days and employed the exploited labor of the settlement's two slaves. Yet the building of the new jail is necessary to a performance of community where "Progress" is described as a "pierceless front of middle-class morality" (194), supposedly moving away from barbaric practices of execution. Yet if we recall both Fischer-Lichte's discussions of the universal persistence of ritual sacrifice and the performative repetition of past exploitations, it becomes evident that execution will continue to exist despite supposed social progress; it is simply adapted to other forms, including those considered more humane, such as electrocution ("by electricity now [so fast, that fast, was Progress]") (216). A symbol of the past—the etching in the window of the jail, *Cecilia Farmer April 16th 1861*—haunts this sense of progress. Created by a young girl's "frail and workless hand" (197), the dated name provides the mythological presence of the real Cecilia Farmer's lack of agency as an inert body incapable of social contribution. The eternal presence of the etching suggests how the jail in its "seasonless backwater" (213) becomes a space for performance and preservation of past histories.

In the present time of *Requiem*, the jail remains a stage for the grotesque dehumanization of black bodies, as in the disembodied image of black "hands among the bars of the windows, not tapping or fidgeting or even holding as white hands would be, but lying there among the interstices, not just at rest, but even restful. [. . .] until the steel bars fitted them too without alarm or anguish" (170). The workless hand of Cecilia Farmer haunts the black lifeless hands; within the prison the workers cannot work and thus are incapable of economic contribution. Temple's narrative reduces humans to representations of their labor: "just the hands lying there among the bars and looking out, that can see the shape of the plow or hoe or axe" (170). The jail becomes a space where the long legacy of black dehumanization is performed once again, as in Nancy's weekly ritual of singing hymns with other prisoners that "folks was stopping along the street to listen to them instead of going to regular church" (228). In Faulkner's oeuvre, the image of this performance derives from *Sanctuary* (1931), where a "negro murderer" sings with a choir in prison: "they sang spirituals while white people slowed and stopped in the leafed darkness that was almost summer, to listen to those who were sure to die and him who was already dead" (*Sanctuary* 115). In both *Sanctuary* and *Requiem*, the spirituals of undead black prisoners, robbed of agency and entangled in a repetitive cycle of imprisonment, collapse the temporal distance between slavery and contemporary state containment of African American bodies. The jailor in *Requiem*, Mr. Tubbs—whose ineloquent and blunt behavior serves as a reminder of his proximity to the uncivil space—jokes that "I had a idea at one time to have the Marshal comb the nigger dives and joints not for drunks and gamblers, but basses and baritones" (229). Tubbs conflates incarceration, religious worship, and performance, adding to images that dissolve the differences between state-sanctioned ownership of life and the legal ownership of bodies dating back to the legacy of slavery. Abuse inflicted on Nancy's body comes from a variety of directions, but each represents and reveals white male power: from Mr. Stovall's sexual possession of and violence against her body to the guards in the jail that also beat her, this time for trying to commit suicide. As individual manifestations of white southern social authority, these men thwart any expression of self-determination on Nancy's behalf, be it her demand of payment from Stovall or the grim agency of taking her own life.

Nancy's traumatic experiences subvert the distinction between the legal system and disparate religious belief systems, thus categorizing due process as another ritual that depends on performative acts. For example, when Nancy responds, "Yes, Lord," to the judge who sentences her, she collapses the distinction between judicial and religious ceremony. This causes an uproar in the courtroom because it is an "unheard-of violation of procedure" (45); she speaks out of turn, and, even more, she assents to a legal decision that she should fear. The stage direction calls for the curtain to jerk down as if to "hide this disgraceful business" of Nancy's willing acceptance of her death at the hands of the state—an acceptance that parallels her eventual acceptance of her (anticipated) death at the hands of Jesus in "That Evening Sun." The relationship between Nancy's Jesus and the legal system centers on respective forms of control over her life and reveals the dual oppression of race and gender. Significantly, her identity as a prostitute cross-racially connects her to Temple, who regards her own past experience as a kept woman in a Memphis brothel as a form of imprisonment. Temple admits she hires Nancy as a housekeeper because Nancy was "the only animal in Jefferson that spoke Temple Drake's language" (136), thereby suggesting their ability to communicate with one another through their identities as reformed prostitutes "swapping trade, or anyway avocational, secrets over Coca-Colas in the kitchen" (137). While there are severe limitations to their shared experiences (Temple admits she was a prisoner who "could have climbed down the rainspout at any time" [123]), her ability to speak the "right words" (130) to Nancy that she "didn't even need a dictionary" for provide a significant exception to the cultural misunderstandings throughout the various narrations previously discussed here. Temple may miss the signs when she retells the story of Rider's plight, but she and Nancy mirror each other through their relationship to this economy of sexual commodification. As Temple states quite bluntly to Nancy, "But then, if I could say whore, so can you, can't you?" (159).

In the jail, Nancy presents sexual exploitation and religion as parallel systematic structures of oppression. She states that "I can get low for Jesus too" and claims that "Jesus is a man too" (234), hinting that her "'womanishness'" (159) will gain her access to salvation. Nancy also believes her entrance into heaven is dependent on her labor; she can be saved because as she claims, "I can work" (239). Nancy's language—what Temple calls "the only language He [God] arranged for you to learn" (235)—is actually a discourse where all of Nancy's options are determined by an oppressor looking to take advantage of her body. Here, too, Nancy suggests an uncanny homology between the law and religion as systems of power. To Nancy, Jesus (Christ) is yet another agent of male dominance defining her through her labor as a prostitute and servant for the Compsons; moreover, she has every reason to believe her position is eternal when she describes the labor she imagines she will perform in the afterlife. Nancy's choices are not really choices at all, narrowed down as they are to the diasporic ritual that possesses her body, or state-sanctioned death. She repeats the empty gesture of faith and belief, mirroring society's empty gesture of justice that fails marginal people like Nancy.

Nancy's belief is the contested issue in the last act of the play when Temple visits Nancy in the jail the night before her hanging. Temple repeatedly asks Nancy what it is she believes, to which Nancy can only reply, "I don't know. But I believes" (241). Rather than read her faith as a symbol of her endurance in the face of death, I argue for a darker reading of her belief. Nancy's insecurity regarding the Christian Jesus contrasts her absolute conviction of the other Jesus's supernatural power in "That Evening Sun," where Nancy does not doubt his unseen presence. More importantly, Nancy filters her belief in the Christian Jesus and salvation through the legacy of abuse that suggests to Nancy that she will be cleaning and performing sexual favors throughout eternity. The only enduring belief Nancy has is that she will always be subject to oppression. She might not "know" whether Jesus, religion, ritual, or law is the source of infliction, but Nancy can *believe* that any of them will exploit her body. The conclusion is ambiguous as to whether or not Temple can interpret the meaning of Nancy's cryptic last words about believing; however, the sacrifice of Nancy's life takes from Temple the only person who could understand her. Any possibility of a socially progressive cross-racial relationship between them is eradicated in the space of the jail. Nancy's crime offers Temple a release from her past association and thus she can properly reenter society, which Temple does onstage as the play concludes and the jail door locks behind her.

Nancy's undead body exposes ways in which mysterious and misunderstood rituals reenact past oppressions and challenge genuine social progress in race relations. In contrast to a "sense of Gothic space [that] remains subterranean" (Ellis, "On Southern Gothic Literature" xvi), Faulkner forces us to recognize the grotesque elements of humanity that characterize the very foundations of civilization. Through the form of a play, he distances readers by placing them in the audience of *Requiem*'s events. Morality, sympathy, and justice are not universal truths, but rather staged processes while society is a grotesque drama that must be continuously reenacted. The murder of Temple's baby, like Cecilia Farmer's etching in the jailhouse window, is a symbolic reminder of society's dependence on the antisocial space to confirm its existence. Revealing the darker desires for control over and the sacrifice of others' bodies, the jail in *Requiem* becomes a site through which ritual performance maintains those practices in the midst of a supposed "Progress" that is forever haunted by the architectural design of exploitation.

NOTES

1. See Richard Schechner, *Between Theater and Anthropology* (Philadelphia: U of Pennsylvania P, 1985), chap. 2.

2. See Roach (*Cities of the Dead* 11–12) for his discussion of Ngui Wa Thiong's concept of orature.

3. For a discussion of this critical debate, see Noel Polk, *Faulkner's "Requiem for a Nun."*

9

OF FLESH AND BONES
Incarnations of the Silenced Past in William Faulkner's and Erskine Caldwell's Early Southern Gothic Short Stories

ELSA CHARLÉTY

There is something about the South that makes it the perfect background for stories of specters, haunted mansions, and hidden secrets. An unfathomable region of the mind, it is haunted by the innumerable ghosts of its past. Slavery, Civil War, and years of segregation and racial tension have scarred the memory of the region with violence. The tormented history of the South, the obscure intertwining of its roots with racial tension and moral prejudice, feed a cosmogony where terror, as French scholar Marie Liénard puts it, is linked to the repressed knowledge of its illegitimate foundation (71). Repressed by a polished discourse of nostalgia and the myth of the "glorious Old South," the violence of the past resurfaces in southern fiction in the early 1930s in the short stories of writers such as William Faulkner and Erskine Caldwell.

Quickly labeled as "Southern Gothic" literature by critics of the time, their work depicted scenes of collective brutality, murders or lynching as well as fairly graphic representations of corpses, mutilated bodies, and physical deformities. In that sense, the Southern Gothic fiction of the early 1930s sought to emancipate itself from traditional gothic literature: instead of resorting to classical images of ghosts, apparitions, and other types of supernatural creatures, Southern Gothic fiction tackled fear in a more visceral or carnal way. It displayed with outrageous directness a carnivalesque parade of freaks, cripples, and misfits of all kind, marginals whose presence in the narrative space confronted the South with its moral contradictions and social tensions instead of comforting it with the nostalgic discourse of a long-gone glorious past. The myth of the Old South and the discourse of the Lost Cause are called into question by figures that were obliterated from the nicely polished glass of the dominant discourse: poor blacks, poor whites, physically impaired people, the mad, deviant, and indefinable. Their unruly bodies and amoral behavior stand as a tangible reminder of a past reconfigured through appalling shapes and excessive forms.

The emergent Southern Gothic fiction of Faulkner and Caldwell broke away radically from traditional gothic fiction, while still displaying some of the substantial features of the Gothic heritage. Indeed, the South in itself appears as fertile ground for the emergence of a gothic literature: great colonial houses, eerie marshes, and dark family secrets are regular fodder for stories of the uncanny, the mysterious, and the unknowable. A region "infested with psychic and social decay and coloured with the heightened hues of degeneracy," where "violence, rape and breakdown are the key motifs" (Punter 3) seems a natural background to gothic tales of horror, the bizarre, the monstrous, and the terrifying. The quasi-organic link between the South and the gothic has made the genre a typical if not distinctive feature of the region. Nonetheless, for all that southern literature owes to the gothic, both Caldwell and Faulkner also break with the codes of the genre by undermining a founding principle, identified as "the surreal imagination" by Joyce Carol Oates. According to her, the essence of the gothic is to escape the rigidity of reality by resorting extensively to the power of the imagination. It displays in a surreal mode the fantastical extravagance of the human imagination (Oates 9), transcending the mundane with phantasmagorical creations. Ghosts, ghouls, and supernatural creatures appear therefore as a means to question an otherwise sterile discourse on "reality." However, because in the South the extravagance of imagination has allowed the development of the romanticized and sterile myth of the Old South, early Southern Gothic writers work in a dynamic contrary to that defined by Oates. They challenge stock representations of the South by grounding the fictional discourse in prosaic, crude reality.

Extreme materiality is an oblique way to challenge the sanitized discourse of the Old South and reveal what has been obliterated from its romanticized image. By bringing to the surface the buried anxieties of the region, Southern

Gothic fiction thus marks a radical change in both southern literature and the gothic genre. It undermines the classic representation of gothic horror by fitting it to a southern context, outlining a new form of haunting severed from the fantastic and its creatures: a haunting that happens in the realm of words, in language itself. A celebration of death, decadence, and decay, Southern Gothic short stories expose the absent presences within their own texts, revealing the spectrality of a language haunted by the silenced voices of the past.

Graphic Violence and Abject Representations of the Body

Early Southern Gothic tales depict with unsettling realism moments of collective brutality, including murders and lynchings. The reader is not spared the violence and horror of such scenes, with vivid descriptions of decaying flesh, rotting corpses, or mutilated bodies. Stories like "Savannah River Pay Day," "Saturday Afternoon," and "Kneel to the Rising Sun," written by Caldwell in the early 1930s, illustrate in a crude way the brutality and gratuity of lynchings in small rural Georgia towns. The corpses of the victims are described with surgical precision, and a particular emphasis is put on the bloated and deformed flesh of the cadaver. In "Kneel to the Rising Sun" (1935), an old sharecropper goes missing in the night only to be found eaten alive by the share tenant's hogs: "He sat on the ground looking at the body. There had been no sign of life in the body. The face, the throat, and stomach had been completely devoured" ("Kneel to the Rising Sun" 653). Later that night, his son Lonnie witnesses the lynching of his friend Clem, a black sharecropper who helped him find the old man: "The body, sprawling and torn, landed on the ground with a thud that stopped Lonnie's heart for a moment. The crumpled body was tossed time after time, like a sackful of kittens being killed with an automatic shotgun, as charges of lead were fired into it from all sides" (663). Caldwell's unsparing prose reduces human bodies to shapeless heaps of meat, distorted and mangled in unnatural positions. The violence of the scene comes here mostly from the dehumanization of the body and the crude emphasis on it being treated like meat. In another of Caldwell's short stories, "Saturday Afternoon" (1931), a young man called Will Maxie is hunted like an animal by a lynch mob, hanged, and tortured to death. The gut-churning description of the spectacle echoes the fate of Lonnie's father and Clem: "Will Maxie was going up in smoke. When he was just about gone they gave him the lead. Tom stood back and took a good aim and fired away at Will. [. . .] They filled him so full of lead that his body sagged from his neck where the trace chain held him up" (32). Tortured to extremes, the body remains that of Will Maxie in name only and is even refused the sacred ritual of a burial when the villagers finally hang the carbonized body up in a tree for everyone to see (33).

Instead of being hidden, obliterated, or alluded to, death is thus put at the center of the narrative discourse for everyone to witness. At the same time as it repels and generates horror, the evocation of a dead body fascinates and puzzles. In "A Rose for Emily" (1930), one of Faulkner's most iconic gothic short stories, the townspeople of Jefferson stand in shock and awe when they have to face the morbid discovery of a corpse that has been rotting for the last thirty years. However horrifying the sight may be, they can't seem to take their eyes off of it, literally fascinated (*fascinere*. Latin, bewitched) by the macabre discovery: "For a long while we just stood there, looking down at the profound and fleshless grin. The body had apparently once lain in the attitude of an embrace, but now the long sleep that outlasts love had cuckolded him. What was left of him, rotted beneath what was left of the nightshirt, had become inextricable from the bed in which he lay" (130). The body belongs to the lover of a local figure, Miss Emily Grierson, who has recently passed away. It is in such an advanced stage of decomposition that it no longer even looks like a corpse. What the villagers discover are the remains of a corpse that was once the remains of a human being. The Faulknerian prose resorts to encased repetitions, further suggesting that this corpse is beyond the stage of decay: the remnant of the body is to be spotted *behind* what is left of his former clothes that have themselves rotted away ("what was left of a nightshirt"). The corpse is gradually hollowed out of its referential content: identified as a "man" at the beginning of the sentence, it falls into decay (*cadere*. Latin) and becomes a corpse ("the body"). Still keeping a faint trace of humanity—notice the use of the pronoun "him" in "what was left of him"—it finally ends up as "biting dust." The words used to define the awkward heap of flesh and bones undergo the same process of hollowing out as the corpse itself. Through language, the notion of cadaver empties itself of its referential content to remain as a linguistic trace.

An empty vessel that used to contain a human soul, the corpse stands awkwardly between life and death. It is the physical evidence that death is irrevocable, and yet it still seems to contain traces of the life it once held. The power of horror, as French philosopher Julia Kristeva explains, lies precisely in the awkward contradiction that the corpse materializes: without makeup or mask, the remains and corpses indicate what we permanently thrust aside in order to live. Nothing remains of what we were, and our entire body falls beyond the limit: *cadere,* to fall (Kristeva 3). Caldwell's and Faulkner's morbid emphasis on cadavers forces the reader to acknowledge the dirty materiality of death (rotting organs, foul smells, decomposing flesh) as well as experience the limits of the human condition. When hogs savagely devour Lonnie's father, his face, his throat, and his stomach are entirely eaten out (Caldwell, *Stories* 653). His body being beyond recognition, the old man ceases at this point to be a living being. Once dead, he is not a man anymore, nor even an identifiable subject, but something that has fallen beyond the limit of subjectivity, while remaining strangely familiar. The cadaver materializes the uncanny feeling that Kristeva identifies as *abject:* The corpse [. . .] is death infesting life. It is something rejected from which one does not part, from which one does not protect oneself as from an object. An uncanny fantasy as well as a real threat, it beckons to us and ends up engulfing us (4). The cadaver gives to self-conscious subjects the overwhelming feeling of their own downfall, a clearer sense that they are themselves one step closer to the grave. It has a reflective function for the readers, who realize as a consequence that they hold within them the ultimate other that is the corpse, while being unable to completely comprehend what this implies.

Beyond Moonlights and Magnolias: Challenging the Romantic Ideal of the Old South

The crudity and intensity of such fiction is a strong counterpoint to the romanticized image of the South. As a matter of fact, when William Faulkner and Erskine Caldwell started writing their first short stories in the 1930s, they were immediately labeled by the southern critic Gerald Johnson as "merchants of death, hell and the grave" (37) and earned the nickname of "horror-mongers in chief."[1] Ellen Glasgow, who eventually coined the term "Southern Gothic," was among the first to attack Caldwell and Faulkner for their macabre taste in writing. In a 1935 article in the *Saturday Review* entitled "Heroes and Monsters," she expresses strongly her resentment of this new type of southern literature, criticizing Southern Gothic writers for entertaining a morbid fascination for everything that is low, ugly, and morally condemnable, and exhorts them to follow her advice: that the Southern Gothic novelist should "remind himself that the colours of putrescence have no greater validity for our age than have—let's say, to be very daring—the cardinal virtues" (Bassett 358). What Glasgow considers to be a "fantasy of abominations" goes against everything she believes fiction ought to be: a means to transform and sublime reality. Because the South is "incurably romantic," all that southern writers have to do is "to deny or distort the shifting balance [they] know as reality" (358).

Glasgow perceives the romantic ideal of the South as a necessary escape from harsh reality. What she identifies as "romantic" is a linguistic frame where words have power to shape our representation of reality: they allow the imagination to cast a flattering light on what is ugly, to turn the harsh reality of life into a comforting ideal. Words offer a possibility to gloss over gruesomeness and build a reassuring discourse of compensation. This desire of escapism accounts for the success of plantation novels in the second half of the nineteenth century and later, such as Margaret Mitchell's romantic fresco of a proud and glorious antebellum South. In the wake of southern romances such as *The Planter's Northern Bride* (1857), *In Ole Virginia* (1895), or even *The Clansman* (1905), *Gone with the Wind* (1936) presents a South that stands solid and sure of its values in spite of the obstacles it must face. It offers clear landmarks and reassuring categories on which to fantasize, including the proud southern belle, the sassy but reliable nurse, and the brave gentleman. The underlying conservative discourse found in such fiction provides a fantasized and simplified answer to the hardships of the times while completely silencing dissenting and marginal voices.

Far from the representation of the ethereal southern belle and descriptions of glorious Victorian mansions of the Old South, Caldwell and Faulkner bring to light what has been hidden by the polished looking glass of myth. They put at the center of their fiction the "savage south" (Hobson, *Tell About the South* 4) and its collection of aberrations: the socially awkward, the physically impaired, the cowards, the brutes, and all other kinds of misfits that had been mostly obliterated from the fictional discourse. In the foreword he writes to Caldwell's collected stories, Stanley B. Lindberg defends such a harshness of style by demonstrating how Caldwell's "dark realistic slices of life" contain little of "the familiar romantic mix of moonlight and magnolias," focusing instead on including "unrelenting heat, sweat and lust, starving poverty, lynching sadistic white supremacist violence and exploitation of the sharecropping system" (xiv). The social and racial violence that the South inherits is a reality that writers such as Faulkner and Caldwell decide to embrace rather than avoid. Lonnie ("Kneel to the Rising Sun"), alongside other Caldwellian characters, represents those antiheroes of the Great Depression that Caldwell was among the first to fictionalize: the poor white farmer who toils on the land alongside descendants of freed slaves for the benefit of one rich white landlord. Torn between conscience of class and racial loyalty, Lonnie hates his landlord for starving out his family but can't seem to find the strength to stand up against him when the brute decides to hunt down his friend Clem, a black sharecropper who helped him find his father in the first part of the story: "Lonnie knew he could not take sides with a Negro, in the open, even if Clem had helped him. [...] He was a white man, and to save his life he could not stand to think of turning against Arch, no matter what" *(Stories* 657). Lonnie is caught in the paradox of white impoverished workers that Wilbur J. Cash, in *The Mind of the South* (1941), defined as the "proto-dorian bond": a tacit doctrine implying unconditional solidarity between rich and poor whites that grants a white dominant class, mostly coming from the antebellum planter elite, to feed the discourse of white supremacy and safeguard their privileges. By superseding solidarity of class to solidarity of race, the wealthy landed elite ensures that poor white farmers do not side with poor black farmers for fear of falling further down the social ladder.[2]

The social tension is such that it can only be released through extreme means. Resentments and jealousies inherited from the complex history of the South resurface in individual narratives through sudden outbreaks of violence. In the article he wrote about class and race in early Southern Gothic fiction, Louis Palmer highlights how Caldwell's depiction of poor rural areas of Georgia indeed challenged the mythical image of the antebellum South by putting the margins in the center of the fictional space. It is a liminal discourse that questions accepted boundaries of class and race; it emphasizes strong instincts like hunger, fear, and sex; its characters are physical brutes of strong desires, neurotics, and strong characters of broken will (Palmer

218). The obscene and *outré* aspect of early Southern Gothic tales indeed dwells extensively on amoral primary instincts; it acts like a magnifying glass for the silenced and repressed urges of mankind. The body becomes the perfect medium to express those impulses. It becomes, as Palmer points out, " a grotesque signifier of material and social condition" (137) and thus plays a key role in the assertion of a marginal discourse: impulsive brutes, neurotics, broken men, and cowards replace type characters such as the southern belle, the young gentleman, and the loving patriarch.

Spectralized Language and Other Discursive Forms of Haunting

Bodies therefore act as vessels through which the violence of history is materialized. They are catalyzers for the underlying and unspoken issues characters cannot deal with: when words fail to represent reality in an accurate way, bodies and gestures become the relay through which anguish can be expressed (*ex-pressere*. Latin, to force outside). They compensate for what French philosopher Daniel Bougnoux identifies as a crisis of representation: when language and literature feed on empty clichés, fake ideals, and used-up images, words lose their performativity. They "don't ever fit even what they are trying to say at," as Addie Bundren points out in the haunted monologue she gives from beyond the grave (Faulkner, *As I Lay Dying* 171). There is a gap between words and what they are supposed to represent, a crisis of language where the signifier is severed from the signified. As a consequence, there ensues a craving for new forms, direct actions, and challenging figures that would fill the gap in order to reconstruct meaning. Matter and bodies are the most immediate means for expressing what cannot be said, and cruelty is the default mode, which, according to Daniel Bougnoux, forces the mind to be projected on bodies by keeping the senses sharpened, and in awareness (Bougnoux 12).[3] Only action—face-to-face confrontation—can unify what has been disjointed. Unjustified constraint and meaningless pain operated on the flesh pushes bodies to extremes and contributes to the creation of a genre of excess and ostentation.

The images of the Old South are so imprinted in the southern psyche that the southern writer has to strike a big and exaggerated blow to destabilize them. As Flannery O'Connor puts it in her essay *Mystery and Manners* (1969), the South offers complex and powerful writing material; it has to be wrestled with, as Jacob did with the Angel (O'Connor 138), in an unsparing way: "When you have to assume that [your audience] does not [hold the same beliefs you do], then you have to make your vision apparent by shock, to the hard of hearing you shout—and to the almost blind you draw large and startling traits" (O'Connor 34). The more constraints that are imposed, the greater the resistance has to be. The author amplifies her gesture when facing narrow modes of expression, thus favoring intensity and condensation over length. As a consequence, excess in genre has to be matched by excess in form. The short story imposes itself as the logical form for the development of the genre: short, intense, and bold, it condenses awfulness. As brief as it is demanding, the short story requires a complete mastery of style, structure, and rhythm in order to achieve the radical effect described by Flannery O'Connor. Faulkner himself, whose fame lies mostly in his extensive Yoknapatawpha novels, recognizes the literary challenge that short stories represent: "In the novel you can be careless, but in the short story you can't. It demands absolute exactitude. You have less room to be slovenly careless. There's less room for trash. It is the hardest art form" (Gwynn and Blotner 207). The short story is neither a truncated version of a novel nor a simplified version of it: the constraint of the length forces the author to go straight to the point and not linger on unnecessary details in the narration. A couple of pages are not long enough to dwell extensively on plot development or characterization. The brevity of the story serves the unity of the narration and creates an exaggerated and excessive tone, often leading to climactic ending. "Elly," which Faulkner wrote in 1934, illustrates how the plot of a short story is built around one event to which the story leads and after which it ends abruptly. Alyana, a young girl from Jefferson, is torn between her desires and her duty. She loves and lusts for Paul, but her grandmother wants her to marry a young man from a respected Jefferson family. After a failed attempt at eloping, she has to drive back to Jefferson in the company of her grandmother and her lover, both of whom cold-shoulder her for trying, and failing, to escape. When driving up a particularly steep turn on the road, Elly turns the wheel to thrust the car over a precipice. The story ends with both the grandmother and the lover dying and Elly, injured but alive, contemplating the blood flowing from her wounds. The car crash is implied as the only way out of the moral dilemma Elly was facing. Incapable of choosing between what she wants and what she must do, she lets her body speak her mind. The accident upsets the narrative structure and fast-forwards the plot to a dramatic, graphic, and literal fall. Both realism and excess contribute to building the aesthetic so specific to Southern Gothic fiction in the early 1930s: realism forces us to see violence in a crude light, and the brevity of the short story condenses and magnifies the horror.

However, the explicit close-ups of swollen wounds and flowing body fluids only hint at what is implied by the text: the zones of shadows, the absences, the moments when language fails to represent the complex reality. Moments of ghostly absences hollow out the fabric of the narrative and suggest that the text hides as much as it reveals. Like the piece of fabric described by Gilles Deleuze in *The Fold: Leibniz and the Baroque,* the short story is "a structure endowed with an organic fabric, like a folded up texture. The creases of the text give to see either excess on the surface or mystery in the folds" (131). Behind savage violence and brutal action are moments when the text floats and language crumbles to pieces. These are the moments when remaining traces of the past come up to the surface to haunt characters. The murder of Jack Houston by Ernst Cotton, for example, is the event around which "The Hound" (1931) is built; however, the crime itself is never described as such. The third-person narrative with a clear internal focalization on Cotton only mentions the event in an oblique way: it is alluded to and evoked by other characters, but never by Cotton himself. Cotton's "omission" erases the crime from the linguistic scope of the narrative, but all in vain. In the absence of supernatural creatures, buried secrets come back to haunt the living as traces, signs, fragments of memories.

As the sheriff points out at the beginning of the story, "a fellow can't disappear without leaving no trace, can he?" (*Uncollected Stories* 156). And indeed, in spite of Cotton's efforts to hide the body, Houston leaves behind him traces that will betray Cotton's secret. The most obvious one is his dog (the hound of the title), who comes back every night to howl in front of Cotton's cabin. What was at first incidental soon becomes an obsessive motif of the story. The dog's bark turns into a lingering howl: "deep, timbrous, unmistakable and sad" (158). Insidious and invisible, the noise haunts Cotton every night, prevents him from sleeping, and finally leads him to his breaking point. Half-mad, Cotton goes back to the tree trunk to dig up the corpse. In returning to the scene of the crime, he is caught by the sheriff and sent to jail. Houston is therefore granted posthumous revenge when, in jail, Cotton finally falls into a catatonic state. Stillness and silence gradually hollow the murderer from his living substance. Locked up behind prison bars, Cotton rants about his failed plan, repeating on and on that "Hit would have been all right" (161), words finally failing him.

The trace is neither absence nor presence. As Derrida points out in "La différance," it is the representation of a presence that contains a sign of the past but that is already being hollowed out by the upcoming future (59). In other words, the dog is a physical presence that signifies the absence of his murdered owner. The animal manifests its presence through insidious but unrelenting signs (barking, scratching, sniffing). It literally comes back to *haunt* Cotton in the sense that it lingers around his house like an invisible presence that is not seen but felt. Traces guarantee the persisting presence of the past in the present under infinitesimal forms. But their accumulation finally overwhelms the present. A trace therefore has the paradoxical power of containing in its minute presence the complexity of the past.

Conclusion

The hyperpresence of bodies, organic materiality, and violence in early Southern Gothic short stories shows how traditional features of gothic fiction such as the bizarre, the horrible, and the uncanny are being reinterpreted and reworked in the early stages of the genre. In seceding from the literary heritage of "gothic fantasy," authors like Caldwell and Faulkner pave the way for a new understanding of what "gothic" means in a southern context. Instead of being projected on phantasmagorical creatures (ghosts, ghouls, vampires), the feeling of the uncanny and alienation that is inherent to the gothic is internalized within bodies and minds. Fear and horror are not displaced in time and space, but deeply inscribed in daily life and present time. Harsh confrontations with reality—with what is ugly, unpleasant, unthinkable—become a way to refuse clichés and ready-made certitudes.

In Southern Gothic fiction, all the social insecurity, racial tension, and historical wounds that cannot be expressed in words are channeled and punctuated through extreme gestures, awkward bodies, and bluntness of style. A fictional discourse that revitalizes language and modes of representation, it brings up to the surface repressed urges and silenced secrets, so that the past may never be completely dead and continues to haunt the present. The excessive materiality of early Southern Gothic short stories thus allows for the emergence of a *necro-logos,* a language of death that sketches a diffuse feeling of the uncanny, that reworks and re-presents the traces, memories, and obsessions gnawing at the flesh of the South.

NOTES

1. "T. S. Stribling, Thomas Wolfe, William Faulkner and Erskine Caldwell. These are the real equerries of Raw-Head-and-Bloody-Bones, these are the merchants of death, hell and the grave, these are the horror-mongers-in-chief. These are they who drive the conservative Confederates into apoplexy. I make no boast of my physical prowess in other respects, but I have always cherished the idea that I have a right strong stomach; yet perusal of the works of these four has shown me very definitely that there are limits beyond which I dare not to go" (Johnson, "The Horrible South" 37).

2. As W. J. Cash writes in *The Mind of the South:* "If the plantation had introduced distinctions of wealth and rank among the men of the old backcountry, and, in doing so, had perhaps offended against the ego of the common white, it had also, you will remember, introduced that other vastly ego-warming and ego-expanding distinction between the white man and the black. Robbing him and degrading him in so many ways, it yet, by singular irony, had simultaneously elevated this common white to a position comparable to that say of, the Doric knight of ancient Sparta. Not only was he not exploited directly, he was himself made by extension a member of the dominant class—was lodged solidly on the tremendous superiority which, however much the blacks in the 'big house' might sneer at him, and however much their masters might privately agree with them, he could never publicly lose" (39).

3. "A world that would only be sheer representation would be heading toward destruction: beautiful but still shapes, sanitized but sterile images make you yearn for energy, nervous connections, cruelty. We want to touch, to be touched. [. . .] Matter, bodies are the only things that are surely there when we touch them. [. . .] Therefore the representation of cruelty keeps the meaning closest to the five senses: strength remains contained in constraining forms" (Bougnoux 12–13, translated from French by E. Charléty).

10

MONSTROUS PLANTATIONS
White Zombie and the Horrors of Whiteness

AMY CLUKEY

At the same time that Hollywood studios turned to plantation romance with historical films about the antebellum South like *Jezebel* (1938), *So Red the Rose* (1935), and, of course, *Gone with the Wind* (1939), they also began producing contemporary films that featured the twentieth-century New World plantation as a site of horror. These films range from productions now regarded as classics like *White Zombie* (1932) and *I Walked with a Zombie* (1943) to a variety of less well known, usually far less tasteful, B-movies like *The Devil's Daughter* (also known as *Chloe, Love Is Calling You*) (1934), *The Monster and the Girl* (1941), *The Vampire's Ghost* (1945), *Bride of the Gorilla* (1951), *The Naked Jungle* (1954), and *The Alligator People* (1959). These films are less concerned with the plantation past of the slave-owning South than with the plantation present of the mid-twentieth-century Americas. While romance depicts a bucolic plantation destroyed by the ravages of the Civil War and the indignities of Reconstruction, horror movies depict a modern-day plantation that provides the basis for, yet poses a threat to, twentieth-century U.S. imperial capitalism.

Given the racism of romantic cinema, one might expect these films to feature a big house under siege from the typical antagonists of romance: the vengeful black masses or perhaps even the Union army and Yankee carpetbaggers. However, such films are not concerned with the threat of black insurrection; filmmakers seem assured of the permanence of white supremacy in the United States South and the West Indies. The horrific plantation is firmly racially stratified: there are few black characters beyond the odd butler or coachman. The Union army does not appear, either. In place of romantic sectional divides, in these years horror movies united the North and South around the postbellum plantation.[1] Although many characters running these plantations are recognizably "southern"—the figure of the Colonel, for instance—most are simply Americans, with a range of American accents and backgrounds. More than simply the product of lazy casting and poor acting (many of these films were hastily made), classic American cinema also shows the nation's unification behind plantation colonialism in the early to mid-twentieth century.

This essay uses Victor and Edward Halperin's *White Zombie* (1932) as a case study for a genre that I call "plantation horror." I argue that, in place of the usual foes of the historical southern plantation, the horrors of the contemporary plantation emerge from within the big house itself as modern planters uncontrollably transform into supernatural creatures. Here, white elites make choices that lead to their own monstrosity and threaten to destroy their own communities. In a perversion of planter hospitality, they welcome or at least invite "foreign" interlopers like *White Zombie*'s Murder Legendre and *Son of Dracula*'s Count Alucard into their well-appointed homes. By the 1950s, this foreign menace is replaced by the contaminations of strong, but racially impure, American whites such as *Bride of the Gorilla*'s Barney Chaves, a working-class overseer turned planter with a suspiciously Spanish surname, and *The Alligator People*'s Mannon, a drunken Cajun plantation worker. In this way, American horror registers fears of racial corruption and degeneration on the contemporary plantation. As planter elites battle it out with other white ethnic groups for control of working estates through legal wrangling and strategic marriages, they struggle to maintain the boundaries of Anglo-American whiteness against the contaminations of decadent Creole, European, and working-class strains.

The Halperin Brothers set their plantation horror story on an island that was once the most lucrative sugar colony in the world, but which by the early twentieth century was plagued by poverty and political chaos. Filmed in a Hollywood studio, *White Zombie* was produced in the final years of the U.S. occupation of Haiti that lasted from 1915 to 1934, a time when white Americans came to the island to administer both the federal government and the means of agricultural production. As was typical with Anglophone plantation colonialism, the occupation was justified by the ethos of the "white man's burden" to uphold the civilizing mission. Indeed, as Jeremy Wells has shown, the southern plantation of romantic fiction served as a model for American imperialism in the Caribbean. The dominant sentiment among Americans was that Haiti, like most of the West Indies, needed "shaping up" (Langley 219). *White Zombie* doesn't reflect any anxieties that Haitian citizens had about such an enterprise. Tellingly, black insurrection isn't a threat in the film, which seems confident of the U.S. military's ability to control the island's black citizenry. Considering the "success" that white Americans had experienced in curtailing the autonomy of ostensibly free blacks in the Jim Crow South for nearly seventy years, this confidence would not be surprising in many contexts, but it is rather odd given *White Zombie*'s setting in Haiti, a nation with a long tradition of successful black insurrection. As Mary Renda has commented, in many ways, "the film erased Haiti's blackness" (227). Although it begins with a shot of black Haitians burying their dead in the road as the title credits roll, black actors are largely absent. The film's only significant black character—if he can even be called that—is a coachman who tries to warn the newly arrived American protagonists, Neil Harker and Madeline Short, about the threat of zombies: "They are not men. They are dead bodies." Black islanders—their chanting and drumming—provide some of the film's spookiness but ultimately prove only atmospheric. In this way, *White Zombie* simultaneously evokes, contains, and disavows Haiti's violent history.[2]

The Halperins strip the island of much of its historical and cultural specificity. In place of the post-Dessalines Black Empire, *White Zombie* presents an indistinct dark rural landscape littered with palm trees and headstones, turning Haiti into a generic tropical locale. As Haitian signifiers become confused or absented, this foreign land begins to uncannily resemble the United States. Rendering Haiti more generically southern—or rather, American— *White Zombie* suggests that the United States' military and metropolitan interests are likely to be successful in occupying it, just as they were successful in "occupying" its own "domestic Africa" (to quote Jennifer Greeson), the South, after the Civil War (*Our South* 237). By the 1950s, Hollywood horror would code most of its cinematic plantations as American (that is, southern) regardless of each film's respective setting, such as the nominally South

American locale of both *Naked Jungle* and *Bride of the Gorilla*. Supposedly set abroad, these films progressively strip each location of cultural specificity and regional histories. *White Zombie* reflects the early stages of this tendency to cinematically Americanize the global plantation complex.

This begs the question: Why don't the film's protagonists, Neil and Madeline, get on well in such an Americanized terrain? Even if the film's version of Haiti mirrors the U.S. plantation, the South itself was seen as a foreign territory within the nation. As Matthew Bernstein demonstrates, in the early twentieth century, Hollywood filmmakers and executives conceptualized the South as a country within the United States to the extent that they hired "Professional Southerners" to market to this foreign audience (122). At the same time, Roosevelt declared the South the nation's number-one economy problem: for many Americans, the region clearly needed cleaning up, just like Haiti. Both Haiti and the U.S. South are characterized by historical North-South divides and civil war and remain deeply stratified by color.[3] For 1930s audiences, the Haiti of *White Zombie* could be both like home and unlike home, because the U.S. South occupied just such a liminal position within the American imaginary, "[a] space simultaneously (or alternately) center and margin, victor and defeated, empire and colony, essentialist and hybrid, northern and southern (both in the global sense)" (Smith and Cohn 9).

White Zombie and similar films show the imperial anxieties that emerge in relation to the American sense of self and identity abroad. Specifically, plantation horror questions the possibility of maintaining unequivocal U.S. control over the greater Antilles in light of ostensibly white, local competition, which it strangely plays out in a nation that (unlike most of the West Indies) does not have a significant white elite. Quite simply, it interrogates how white Americans, as agents of imperialism facilitating the neoplantation in the West Indies, can avoid becoming like the decadent, morally corrupt, racially ambiguous, vaguely European, Creole plantation elite that they seek to replace.

White Zombie maps this conflict between white Americans and foreign Others over competing versions of plantation colonialism: the historical plantation of romance embodied by Charles Beaumont, the newer plantation of industrial capitalism embodied by Murder Legendre, and a future plantation of finance capitalism embodied by Neil and Madeline. Ever a highly capitalized, highly mechanized institution, the plantation has been a central generator of transatlantic modernity since the sixteenth century. Responding to postslavery necessities, New Agriculture theories, and recent technological developments, its modes of production changed significantly in the early twentieth century, yet these changes were not evenly distributed across the global plantation complex. Far from dying out with emancipation in the New World, the always adaptable postslavery plantation shifted to Third World sites in the Pacific Rim and Africa, where natural resources had not yet been exhausted. At the same time, it also underwent significant postslavery adaptations in the United States itself. The plantation had used cutting-edge technology since the seventeenth century, but the American Civil War stunted the use of technology on southern estates and appeared to freeze them in time, so that the rural South seemed out of sync with national history. A similar dynamic occurred in the Caribbean with the abolition of slavery in the British Empire wherein British merchants, investors, and policy makers cut ties with the plantation in the West Indies after Emancipation even as they continued to profit from its agricultural products, a process depicted with gothic aplomb in Jean Rhys's *Wide Sargasso Sea* (1966). In Haiti in particular, "the counter-plantation system," a "steadfast resistance to plantation labor in all its forms" that relied on small family plots and sustenance farming, seemed out of sync with twentieth-century agricultural developments (Dubois 33). In this historical context, cinematic representations of the plantation became caught between old and new: while the early- to mid-twentieth-century plantation was largely corporate, plantation horror presents family-owned ventures in the nineteenth-century mode located in Haiti, Louisiana, and South America.

In this way, classic American horror evokes the colonial plantation past even as it charts the imperial plantation present. *White Zombie* reflects the plantation's dehumanizing potential in a famous sugar-mill scene featuring loud, groaning gear works and the shadowy bodies of silent white workers. Legendre declares, "They work faithfully. They are not worried about long hours," as the body of a zombie falls and is crumpled in the gears. The sugar mill registers the capitalist horror of utterly docile workers—of white men who toil like slaves in the modern age.[4] As Greeson shows, in the United States comparisons between the plantation and the factory go back well into the nineteenth century (*Our South* 169–92).[5] However, it was only the twentieth century that saw a real effort to optimize the industrial potential of the plantation—to Taylorize and Fordize it (quite literally in the case of Fordlandia)—through agribusiness. *White Zombie* thematizes the seeming temporal disjunction between the agrarian West Indies and industrialized America by collapsing the two.

Bela Lugosi was an obvious casting choice for Legendre after the immense success of *Dracula* (1931) the previous year. With his iconic widow's peak and half-heartedly repressed Eastern European accent, his star power is hardly contained by the weakly characterized Legendre, who even recalls Dracula with his goat-like facial hair and black tuxedo, his power over animals, and ability to hypnotize people. That Lugosi/Legendre poses a sexual danger is clear. Lugosi's allure derived not only from his role as Dracula but from his own eroticized foreignness.[6] This hodgepodge of gothic European signifiers makes Legendre out of place in the superficially Caribbean landscape of the film, but it also renders him racially ambiguous. It is unclear whether this character with the unconvincingly Frenchified surname is supposed to be a white Creole, a light-skinned black Haitian, one of the West Indies's many interstitial racial types, or something else altogether. As Gyllian Phillips observes, "it is this very ambiguity which helps to generate the fear embodied by the zombie master" (28). Such racial indeterminacy challenged the binary racial social system at home. In other words, the socioeconomic ambiguity of the mill—part plantation, part factory—is mirrored by Lugosi's racial ambiguity. Unnervingly, neither fits within American binaries.

White Zombie's plot is typical of plantation horror, which usually focuses on a new arrival on the plantation who discovers the supernatural at work there and involves a marriage plot in which the central love story is delayed or left unfulfilled due to these otherworldly forces. Madeline and Neil are optimistic and naive would-be neoplanters who find themselves starkly vulnerable to white forms of colonial otherness. Neil welcomes Madeline to "our West Indies," indicating his confidence that Haiti is firmly under American control, but the film explores their inability to control the white Creole population—or rather, the Creole population's shocking ability to control them. Madeline is a modern girl: she arrives in Port-au-Prince fashionably dressed in a sleek, yet modest suit with chic bobbed hair and flapper makeup. Yet one of the horrors posed by the film is the way that Madeline is stripped of these markers of modernity in plantation contexts. Despite her Yankee origins and wardrobe, Madeline fulfills the role of the belle whose sexual availability is offset by an innocent demeanor and staunchly guarded virginity.

With the white belle at its center, the film casts U.S. racial fears onto its Americanized Haitian setting through the familiar plantation trope of rape. Madeline's sexual vulnerability is evident, for instance, in a scene where she stands in her underwear and wedding veil as ominous drumming begins. When a maid opens the door to investigate, Madeline lays her arm defensively across her body to cover her bare midriff and protect herself against the vague exotic dangers that lurk outside. The drumming suggests that black peasant revolt is a threat to her chastity and her marriage plot, but the true threat comes from within the big house itself. Her universal desirability, as a young white metropolitan American woman, makes her a target for the morally corrupt Beaumont, who wants to marry her. Such a marriage (like postbellum romances of reunion) would unify American and Creole cultural elites. This sort of alliance might initially seem desirable for the United States, as a friendship with Beaumont initially seems desirable to Madeline, because it would allow better access to West Indian resources. Yet the film shows that West Indian elites have their own agendas and can't be trusted to advance American interests. When Madeline befriends Beaumont, she does so out of innocence of white Creole depravity and moral turpitude. In response, he hires Legendre to cast a love spell on her and, when that fails, to transform her into a zombie. Still attired in her wedding gown and veil, she is zombified immediately after being married to Neil as she gazes into a celebratory glass of wine. Thus, the marriage remains unconsummated, and she walks the line between sexual availability and chastity for the remainder of the film (as she must, since sexually active women are typically punished in American horror, as gothic narratives as diverse as *I Walked with a Zombie* and the television series *Buffy the Vampire Slayer* show).

Through Neil, the film indicates that the American hold on Haiti is tenuous. Just as Legendre mirrors Dracula, so too does Neil mirror another bureaucratic agent of empire overwhelmed by supernatural colonial forces, Jonathan Harker from Bram Stoker's novel (1897). As a banker in Port-au-Prince, Neil competes with local "whites" like Beaumont and Legendre for dominance, but he is ill-equipped to handle Creole manipulations of otherworldly forces. His white mourning suit, like Madeline's wedding dress, signals his purity, innocence, and vulnerability, and like Madeline, Neil spends most of the film prostrated, weeping, or wandering aimlessly: he collapses in the graveyard, on the beach, and in the castle. His character can be summed up by a statement he makes to the American missionary Dr. Bruner, "The whole thing has me confused. I just can't understand it." Once he's found Madeline, Neil can't comprehend that she's a zombie. "Oh my darling, what have they done to you?" he asks her empty face, before turning to Legendre with his zombie retinue to demand, "Who are you? And what are they?" Even as the films ends, and even though zombiism has been explained to him multiple times, Neil just doesn't get it.

Because the history of Haiti has been repressed both in the United States and in the film itself, Neil has no cultural context for understanding the supernatural happenings that he encounters. Accordingly, he interprets the situation in the context of American racial ideology and expects black Haitians to be a danger to white womanhood. When a local doctor explains that Madeline has been transformed into a zombie, Neil exclaims, "Surely you don't think she's alive in the hands of natives? Oh no! Better dead than that!" Certainly, images of insatiable black men preying on white women loomed large in American popular culture throughout the early twentieth century, especially in the wake of the Scottsboro Boys trial of 1931. Neil's exclamation that it would be better for Madeline to be dead than at the mercy of black peasants clearly reflects white American paranoia about the violation and contamination of the white female body, one that cloaks the far greater vulnerability of black women to white men historically under slavery and during the occupation. However, the film denies the certainties offered by this familiar narrative, and Neil's fear that black Haitians have Madeline, then, turns out to be a sign that he is unprepared for the unfamiliar dangers at hand.

While plantation horror starkly renders the sexual vulnerability of white women in plantation contexts, it substitutes romance's black rapist with the "foreign" or ethnic white rapist. In plantation horror, bourgeois American couples like Neil and Madeline are threatened by members of the white laboring class, like Mannon in *The Alligator People,* who tries to rape that film's heroine when her new planter husband morphs into an alligator-human hybrid. In place of the mythical and lynchable black rapist, *White Zombie* presents a different threat to American imperial normativity as property-owning white men drawn from West Indian plantation culture prey upon largely middle-class belles. Beaumont and Legendre effectively control the local black populace and much of the white populace as well. Now this corrupt planter elite threatens to overtake the wholesome American couple that stands in for U.S. imperial legitimacy and optimism.

Summaries of the film often describe Madeline as enslaved, but she spends most of her time wandering through a luxurious seaside castle in diaphanous gowns. In one scene, Beaumont watches the Zombie Madeline play classical music on a piano. She stares vacantly ahead, her large doll-like eyes further emphasized by dramatic cosmetics. The film tiptoes around exactly why these men might want to zombify any woman, nonetheless the sexually aloof Madeline, who remains largely untouched throughout the film. At times, it seems as though Beaumont and Legendre want to keep her merely as a willowy household ornament. In this way, her transformation into a zombie parallels her transformation from a belle into a cold, asexual plantation mistress. As if to further establish this shift, the Zombie Madeline wafts around in a catatonic state wearing a nineteenth-century-style dress with corseted bodice and full skirts. Pampered and vacuous, she loses her sexual appeal when she becomes an idle figure of decadent ennui—when she becomes, in other words, Creole.

Despite the fact that he transformed her into a nineteenth-century stereotype like himself, Beaumont realizes he wants a modern wife, not a historical aberration. Ann Kordas argues that Beaumont's rejection of the Zombie Madeline demonstrates progress in the realm of American gender relations in the 1930s: "Modern men, the [film makes] clear, do not want zombies for wives. Although a female zombie (completely controlled by her husband/master, always silent, possessing no desires of her own) would have made an ideal wife for many men during an earlier period in history, the female zombie is depicted as an imperfect wife for the modern age" (29). I think that the film's characterization of Madeline undermines this reading. Madeline loses her soul as a zombie, but as a character she's bereft of interiority from the start. In *White Zombie,* the biggest difference between a zombie doll and the perfect wife is that a zombie is unsmiling and silent, while the perfect wife is smiling and silent. When Madeline awakes from her drugged stupor in the film's final scene, her restoration is indicated with a small smile as she breathily says, "Neil, I, I dreamed. . . ." She never finishes this sentence. In the end, the film's ideal woman is little more articulate than a zombie.

Neil may stand in for Jonathan Harker and Legendre for Count Dracula, but Madeline is no rational Mina Harker or even precocious Lucy Westenra.

Instead, Madeline's zombiism reflects American weakness in the face of Creole resistance to the twentieth-century plantation—a weakness that is, naturally, gendered. In *White Zombie,* racially suspicious whites employ the racially coded black arts, and the plantation proves a dangerous place for white women and feminized Anglophone men like Neil. Legendre's ability to will Madeline to kill Neil illustrates the danger posed by women manipulated by charismatic foreign men and the lure of the plantation past. The film indicates that the imperial might of American men may be undermined by "seduced" women, who are vulnerable to exotic Otherness. The suggestion that white women are the weakness of American men, like the idea that Creoles are bad planters, absolves white American men of responsibility for imperial horrors.

White Zombie depicts the residual nineteenth-century colonial plantation epitomized by Beaumont and Legendre as horrific and the emergent twentieth-century model epitomized by Neil and Madeline as vulnerable, but nonetheless the foundation for a just and innocent U.S. imperial future. The neoplantation is bourgeois, not aristocratic; run by metropolites, not settler colonists. But what does this future plantation of finance capitalism *look* like? We're never shown. Rather, Haiti is presented as essentially rural and premodern with the exception of Legendre's sugar mill/factory. If the antebellum plantation was portrayed as a fantastic ideal in romance, then it was also portrayed as irretrievably lost: Scarlett vows to return to Tara at the end of *Gone with the Wind,* but it is still a one-horse farm financed by Rhett's money and her lumber mill. In this way, Margaret Mitchell and David O. Selznick separate the plantation from the mills that depend upon southern cotton. In *White Zombie* the two are mutually constitutive: sugarcane requires immediate processing, so the plantation and the factory are interdependent, closely situated, and almost indistinguishable. However, the postslavery plantation of finance capitalism remains elusive. *White Zombie* is haunted by the sense that not only does the plantation still exist, but that the metropole depends upon all its forms, even if the mutually constitutive socioeconomic and historical links between Beaumont's plantation, Legendre's sugar mill, and Neil's bank are invisible.

White Zombie problematizes American imperial optimism, but ultimately, if unconvincingly, upholds the plantation as a viable future. The sugar-mill-owning bocor temporarily beats the Creole plantocracy and the American bureaucrat into submission, but then Legendre's zombie army self-destructs by walking off a cliff before Beaumont pushes Legendre into the sea and inexplicably leaps to his own death. As native rivals conveniently take each other out, the threats posed by the racially suspicious Creole planter and the oddly Slavic witch doctor are neutralized, but not through the efforts of the American characters. The scene closes with Madeline's reunion with the milquetoast Neil and their implied return to bourgeois respectability and control, both over themselves and others. The loss of innocence that the Americans experience is psychologically shattering, but all too easily restored by the film's end. *White Zombie* closes on a requisite happy note, but the fitness of American imperial might is undermined. Because the film both begins and ends with Neil and Madeline being joyfully and inarticulately reunited, it leaves viewers with the sense that its heroes have learned nothing from their terrifying experiences with colonial otherness.

The cinematic plantation has largely been critically regarded as an Edenic escape for Depression-era, wartime, and postwar audiences, but classic American horror reveals that it was also a site of contemporary anxieties.[7] In these films, the plantation provides a familiar narrative arc through which to explore American imperial futures—just as it always has in the United States. The interest in the plantation as a site of horror fizzled out after the 1960s with films like *I Eat Your Skin* (1964), *The Oblong Box* (1969), *Frogs* (1972), and *Black Moon* (1975), among others. Horrific cinematic representations of plantation violence and grotesquerie reflect midcentury fears about the unstable boundaries and meanings of white identity in the context of Jim Crow segregation and American imperial expansion. Ultimately, the various monsters of horror—the evacuated zombie of *White Zombie*, the dissolute vampire of *Son of Dracula*, and the simian creature of *Bride of the Gorilla*—are white planters who cannot maintain their modernity and consequently fail to fulfill their socioeconomic roles or protect white womanhood from themselves. Shape-shifting from zombie to vampire to beast, the monsters of plantation horror register anxieties about how Americans can maintain imperial control abroad without losing self-control and their white identities. If romance idealizes the white man's burden to take up the civilizing mission, then horror suggests that the white man's own claims to civilization are tentative at best.

NOTES

1. In history, see Grace Elizabeth Hale's *Making Whiteness: The Culture of Segregation in the South, 1890–1940*; and Karen Cox's *Dreaming of Dixie: How the South Was Created in American Popular Culture*.

2. For more on the disavowal of the Haitian Revolution in Western culture, see Sibylle Fischer's *Modernity Disavowed: Haiti and the Cultures of Slavery in the Age of Revolution*.

3. See Laurent Dubois's *Haiti: The Aftershocks of History*.

4. For example, Laurent Dubois explains how the Haitian-American Sugar Company (HASCO), a corporate sugar plantation that functioned as a factory, came to the island during the U.S. occupation. In the *Magic Island*, Seabrooke called HASCO a "modern big business" and "a chunk of Hoboken" in Haiti (qtd. in Dubois 298). Haitians responded with stories of zombified workers, as Laurent Dubois comments: "It wasn't really strange at all, though: telling stories about *zonbi* workers at HASCO was probably a way for the local community to articulate the feelings evoked by the reappearance of the plantation in their midst" (298).

5. For instance, Greeson notes that in *Uncle Tom's Cabin*, "movement southward becomes progress into industrial modernity" (*Our South* 179).

6. His performance as Count Dracula had already established Lugosi's reputation as a sex symbol. Biographer Gregory William Mank observes that the ads for *Dracula* featured Lugosi posed over scantily clad women as a veritable "God of Sex": one such ad read, "Beware the Kiss of Dracula—the Caress That Burns Like a Flame of Fire!" (45).

7. Barker and McKee note that "[t]he fallen plantation, in particular the ruined house at its center, has undeniably served as a national symbol of unrepentant pride and the failure to recognize defeat and as such, it has served as a mythic repository for the shifting specters of our national wrongs, the historical legacy of U.S. slavery, and the persistent blight of poverty" (4).

11

WHEN DEAD MEN TALK
Emmett Till, Southern Pasts, and Present Demands

BRIAN NORMAN

The dead have a way of sticking around in American literature, especially in stories concerned with social justice. These are the talking dead of history. Not the stuff of zombie films and their moaning cadavers or of gothic novels and their wailing ghosts. Rather, I am concerned with dead folks who hang around the living, chatter, sing, loiter, and generally expect to be treated like anyone else. Such figures tend to be women, as I discover in *Dead Women Talking*, from Madeline Usher and Addie Bundren to Toni Morrison's Beloved, Kushner's Ethel Rosenberg, and many more who in some way speak to injustices prematurely deemed past and thereby challenge communities to recognize the dead as one of their own.

Of course, sometimes dead men also talk. This piece considers the curiously persistent literary urge to exhume Emmett Till, the fourteen-year-old notoriously lynched in Mississippi in 1955 for allegedly whistling at a white woman, followed by the acquittal of his killers by an all-white jury despite considerable evidence. Ever since Till's lynching and what Dora Apel calls his "spectacle funeral" (Apel and Smith 64), writers have retold his story more than 140 times (and counting) as a parable of racial justice, often in the register of mourning and perhaps metaphorical haunting.[1] In a few, Till himself speaks after his murder. We see this most clearly in works by Ishmael Reed, James Baldwin, and Bernice McFadden. This subtradition also includes other fictional resurrections, such as Randall Kenan's collection *Let the Dead*

Bury Their Dead, which evokes both Till and a young Joe Christmas from Faulkner's *Light in August.* These exhumations are more than hauntings. They are what Karla Holloway calls African American "mourning stories," and they respond to what cultural critic Fred Moten calls "black mo'nin'"—those needful, inchoate wails of abjection arising from injustices that continue to fester after the casualties are buried. When Till comes back from the dead, we can do more than mourn a loss: we can measure our responsibility to one of the civil rights movement's quintessential martyrs. And yet, what does it mean that we ask Till to do this work for us after his death?

Exhuming Emmett

The most controversial literary exhumation of Till is probably Ishmael Reed's antifeminist satire *Reckless Eyeballing.* The 1986 novel features a play by black male writer Ian Ball in which the corpse of Ham Hill, a lynching victim evocative of Till, is dug up so that it can stand trial for the sexual ogling of his white female accuser. The problem is that a dastardly feminist theater director demands revisions. "She wants to change your play," Reed writes, "so that the mob victim is just as guilty as the mob" (76–77). In Reed's madcap description of the resulting Broadway play, the corpse's defense attorney cross-examines the accuser by questioning her sexual past and need for male attention, arguing that she took offense when Ham Hill *wasn't* ogling her. Reed writes, "At that moment the skeleton, with a sardonic grin, began to slide to the floor; the bailiff propped it up" (95).

Reed uses Till, and the southern lynching culture for which he stands, to lend historical weight to a novel essentially about the New York City literary scene and its machinations, turf wars, and petty rivalries. The protagonist writes the play to get off the "sex-list"—a feminist blacklist—but he worries that the play ends up being his metaphorical castration. There are also frequent Holocaust references throughout the novel that serve a similar function: to lend weight by brute analogy. Reed himself is overt about the strategy of comparing African American oppression with the Holocaust, which he further aligns with the depiction of black men in Susan Brownmiller's popular feminist critique of rape and rape cultures (Zamir 254). The double-tiered analogy comes to a head when another playwright, this one Jewish, finds himself the guest of honor at a lynching party when he accepts an invitation from a southern university only to find a front for old-style white supremacists itching for a rally. The ensuing lynching of the Jewish playwright is scarcely more than a cartoon backdrop to the story of the protagonist's attempts to regain his manhood amid a New York art scene dominated by doctrinaire feminists. Reed muses in an interview, "There's a scene in that book where they dig up a corpse of this guy and read his misogynous crimes before him. Certainly it's a bizarre turn of events" (Dick 354).

Reed's satire can be shrill and prone to misfire so that the talking skeleton may seem more prop comedy than serious critique. On the one hand, John Lowe convincingly situates Reed's novel in postmodern ethnic comedy, along with trickster novels by Maxine Hong Kingston and Gerald Vizenor, and argues for the metaphorical lynching of the black playwright (esp. 105–8). Still, reviewers generally panned the novel. Michiko Kakutani complained in the *New York Times* that it is "a nasty, idiosyncratic blend of invective, satire and social criticism" (12) filled with stock characters and historical references that are all primary colors and no nuance. Reed was clearly stung by the review, calling it a "public scolding which would never be used against a white author" (Zamir 300). Black feminist Michele Wallace famously called *Reckless Eyeballing* "the most extreme enactment so far of Reed's female trouble," before chronicling how he "doesn't know his ass from his elbow when it comes to American feminism" (187). That may be why so few critics have attended to the Till exhumation. There are too many other cardboard cutouts to shoot and paranoid shadows to box.

The exhumation, it turns out, is not far from reality. About two decades after Reed's novel, the FBI reopened Till's case and exhumed his actual corpse. A proper autopsy had never been performed, and an exhumation could both confirm the identity (to rebut a defense canard) and, more important, reveal DNA evidence of other participants in the torture and murder.[2] In this way, Till's corpse held the possibility of delivering justice long after the trial and beyond the two killers, both of whom were now dead. While gruesome—if not also fascinating—the 2005 exhumation is only one late chapter in the literary unburials of midcentury America's most famous race martyr. In his study *Digging Up the Dead*, historian Michael Kammen finds that Americans often dig up famous corpses, from Thomas Paine and Abraham Lincoln to Daniel Boone and Chief Sitting Bull. Such unburials, he explains, are driven by sectional competitions to lay claim to our icons, for reasons ranging from patriotism or regional pride to more touristic desires for cultural and economic capital (esp. 8–9, 22–23). So, too, Till's literary exhumations are bids on his story, though typically for more justice-oriented concerns.

Disorienting Returns

Let's consider an earlier exhumation: James Baldwin's short-lived 1963 play *Blues for Mister Charlie,* a key influence in Reed's novel.[3] Baldwin's play opens with the violent shooting of Richard Henry and the dishonorable disposal of his body in a ditch that runs midstage between Whitetown and Blacktown, two halves of Plaguetown, U.S.A.[4] Baldwin instructs: "Lights go up slowly on Lyle, staring down at the ground. He looks around him, bends slowly and picks up Richard's body as though it were a sack. He carries him upstage drops him" (*Blues* 2). The play is "based, very distantly indeed" on the Till case, though Richard is older and more world-wise (*Blues* xiv). The play begins with the murder, and Baldwin incorporates a complicated temporal structure to provide Richard's backstory. When the actor playing Richard arises from the pit several scenes later to perform his first lines, we experience him as a dead man. We cannot forget his corpse lying in the ditch that separates Whitetown from Blacktown in Baldwin's polemical staging of American race segregation. Richard's opening-scene murder is intractable, as is Till's brutal lynching central to his place in our historical imagination. I have described the effect as an exhumation and excavation.[5] Similarly, Koritha Mitchell compellingly frames it as raising the dead. Drawing on the work of Sharon Holland, she argues that "Richard's appearances are not simple flashbacks; rather, he materializes in response to living characters" (50). For Mitchell, to "re-member" (51) is to create; the community conjures Richard.

Richard's first lines aren't even lines at all. They are song lyrics performed in Harlem well before the lynching and during his career as a musician. When the dead son finally speaks onstage, he enters contemporary time amid a southern community trying to reconstruct his death. His father, the Reverend Meridian Henry, spits out, "No witnesses!" That same stage houses yet a third time frame as Richard, now seemingly resurrected for the *audience* to witness, turns to his doting mother and declares, "You treating me like royalty, old lady—I ain't no royalty. I'm just some raggedy-assed, out-of-work, busted musician. But I sure can sing, can't I?" (*Blues* 17). Unlike most retellings, Baldwin's play conspicuously does *not* insist on Till's innocence to fashion him as a Christian martyr and thereby underscore white depravity. Rather, Richard has done some hard living in the decade since Till was lynched. He got hooked on drugs, totes a gun and lewd photographs of white women, and very much baits the woman minding the store.

All the temporal layers can be disorienting for the audience, not to mention a challenge to any director. Reviewers often criticized the play's temporal structure, along with its polemicism. One concluded, "the total pattern is erratic, with numerous flashbacks that do not seem necessary to the relatively simple narrative of the play" (Hewes 36).[6] Another early critic defended the temporal structure by comparing it to "a nightmare from which one awakes screaming." The play is not only about Till, he argued, "but it is also a distillation of all the maimed and lynched, all the brutish sadism of three centuries of Negro's American experience" (Turpin 195). After the play's brief three-month run in New York, a subsequent London production eliminated its flashback structure.[7] Such a move loses the disruptive potential: exhumation becomes mere memory once again, more akin to historical documentation or courtroom testimony.

Mitchell suggests that encounters with Richard happen in a productive "space of death" so that for living characters "his presence confirms their humanity in ways that they may not do for themselves" (Mitchell 52). So too, contemporary readers who look to the dead not for consolation or mourning but for help in imagining justice beyond the courtroom trial. Whether welcome or not, the play's elaborate temporal structure forces the audience to struggle to discern past from present. Elsewhere, I have called this a "temporal dysphoria" when the nation's Jim Crow past may not seem so passed.[8] By the end, despite the inevitable acquittal—a fact branded in historical memory—Baldwin's experiment with linear time and the resurrection of Richard's corpse suggest that the historical record need not bind us.

For a 1963 play, Baldwin exhumes Till in order to explain nascent pulls toward racial self-determination and militancy in the civil rights movement while also underscoring how separatism neatly maps onto the structures of segregation. When the play opened at the Actors Studio on April 23, 1963, the nation was on the precipice of key civil rights victories, and yet, Baldwin's play reminded, Till was only freshly buried. The recent murder of Medgar Evers, the latest of many acts of violence against civil rights activists, demonstrated with terrifying sharpness the lack of change since Till's brutal murder. In fact, some of the earliest criticism subtly implies that Baldwin exploits the cachet of civil rights martyrs. Influential black critic Darwin Turner, for instance, deemed the subject "timely and popular" because "still fresh in the minds of black people was the torture-murder of young Emmett Till," even while insisting that Baldwin's intended audience was white (191). In any case, Richard's resurrection demonstrates that 1963 may not be so different from 1955 after all.

Dead Whores and Reborn White Men

Writers exhume Till more frequently than any other slain civil rights figure. As the civil rights movement moved from national crisis to national memory in the ensuing decades, we can't stop digging him up. In Bernice McFadden's 2012 novel *Gathering of Waters,* we again encounter exhumation's twin: resurrection. Like Reed and Baldwin, McFadden reanimates familiar historical characters in Till's narrative and places them in a trajectory that spans post-Reconstruction America to Hurricane Katrina. The novel is told from the collective point of view of Money, Mississippi, the town inextricably linked with the Till lynching in our imaginations. We know nothing good can come of this story, but we proceed anyway, looking for answers to this story of never-finished justice. The novel begins in the early twentieth century with Esther, a spiteful, cheating, no-good whore. She eventually gets her due, but her devilment lives on as her spirit invades future generations, with each person she inhabits ending in a watery grave. She first invades a young preacher's daughter who seduces her father before eventually getting what's coming, a shameful death by drowning in a flood. So, too, we know that Till ends up in the Tallahatchie River. And by 2005, the water engulfs much of the Mississippi River Delta as a horrified nation watched helplessly.

In McFadden's world, Esther can cross social lines in death that are viciously policed among the living. She comes to inhabit the body not of Till, as we expect in literary retellings, but rather of J. W. Milam, one of the infamous murderers and the brother-in-law of the accuser, Carolyn Bryant. The narrating town, however, doesn't know what is to come, which creates another kind of temporal dysphoria—the historical script is set, but the novel's world is still unfolding. McFadden begins earlier: J. W. drowns as a boy, only to come back to life in the funeral home courtesy of Esther. "He had been such a sweet child," McFadden writes, "but after he died and came back again, he was different. J. W. was suddenly fond of torturing living things: cats, puppies, fledglings" (153). His evil festers and boils, awaiting an outlet: the lynching of young Till.

For the infamous encounter with Bryant, McFadden eschews magical realism and resurrection in favor of straightforward narration from the vantage of the white woman, who gazes with nostalgia at Till and his companions. She thinks of lost youth and desires to join their ice pop–licking competition:

> So after tying her hair into a knot, Carolyn skipped out into the road, cupped her hands around her mouth, and hollered, "Hey! Do that whistle for me again, would you?"
>
> And he did and the sound made Carolyn happy, it made her feel included in something free and forbidden. (170)

This scene is indebted less to Reed and Baldwin than to Gwendolyn Brooks's famous portrait of the white fairy tale underlying the lynching plot in her 1955 poem "A Bronzeville Mother Loiters in Mississippi. Meanwhile, a Mississippi Mother Burns Bacon." In McFadden's portrayal of the wistful white woman and innocent black boy, the whistle is inevitably witnessed by passersby—the lynching script necessitates it. What is less inevitable is confirming the whistle in the first place, a subject long at the center of fierce and high-stakes speculation, first in the court of law and then in the court of history.

McFadden returns to the resurrection plot when she portrays the fateful lynching through the vantage of the murderers. What is most surprising is that she emphasizes reluctance and immediate regret from signature villains of the civil rights movement—or at least from Roy, Carolyn's husband. J. W., on the other hand, is an unrepentant aggressor who threatens his brother-in-law with a gun: "He licked his fingers, smeared saliva over the nozzle, and aimed it at Roy's heart" (174). The phallic and rape imagery is not subtle. Nor is the depiction of J. W.'s depravity as he slobbers, sneers, laughs, and generally careens through the drunken torture and murder scene. But of course we cannot forget that, in McFadden's rendition, this slavering icon of white violence is really a long-dead black whore. Strangely, Exhibit A of white depravity in the civil rights imagination ends up a supernatural problem of one low-down black woman who won't stay dead.

As for justice denied in the Till case, McFadden looks for karmic just desserts in the historical record itself: the brothers subsequently encounter social ostracism and trouble getting work so that "misery became as much a part of their lives as oxygen" (192), eventually leading to Bryant's and Milam's deaths from cancer in 1980 and 1994, respectively. And as for Till, McFadden wrests a similar feeling of closure by having his spirit benevolently haunt that of his cut-short love, Tass, who shared a kiss with young Emmett on the fateful day of the ice pop–licking adventure. "When Emmett had finally opened his eyes in the here-and-now," McFadden writes, "he found that his body was no more, that the boys he'd known were now men and the girls had blossomed into women" (208). Eventually Tass returns to Money, and we are heartened that she has not forgotten the young boy. McFadden draws on sentimentalism and familiar history by calling up collective, ritualized mourning for the real Emmett Till: "But I ask you, dear reader, how could she forget him? How could she possibly forget, when year after year August 28 rolled around and *Jet Magazine* republished that horrid photo, reminding Tass and the rest of the world what had happened here during the summer of 1955?" (209). Eventually, McFadden offers Tass—and us—a feeling of closure through a sort of posthumous consummation of heterosexual romance. A mysterious young black boy appears at the now-elderly woman's door in Money—possibly a fever dream, perhaps not—only to disappear, leaving depression marks in the grass.

And yet the malevolent spirit of the dead black whore lives on. Her centuries-long rampage culminates in another iconic moment of racial injustice: Hurricane Katrina and its aftermath. This time Esther arises not in the form of a resurrected villain of history but rather the hurricane itself. Now her black body count spans lynching and Hurricane Katrina, leaving us simply to mourn their victims. McFadden's supernatural premise explains injustice through a moral lens of evil, chalks it all up to a long-dead black whore rather than white supremacism, racialized masculinity, or structural inequality. Everyone in the Till story is redeemed: the murdered boy restored posthumously to his adolescent love, the humanity of his two killers confirmed by a supernatural plot twist, and the white woman accuser remembered as a wistful romantic. Esther alone remains the grand explanation for senseless suffering and violence.

In *The South That Wasn't There*, Michael Kreyling positions memory and history as inseparable planes of a Mobius strip. He points to the southern penchant for reenactment, especially of the civil war variety, and argues for "the ways simulation never quite jettisons the real thing, and vice versa" (177). It may be that our retellings of Till vie to displace actual history. The Till story, or rather our retelling of it, shows how we fabricate history to explain the nature and origins of present injustice. McFadden's resurrection of Till and his murderers offers less historical critique than historiness, to borrow from comedian Stephen Colbert. Or, as Kreyling quips, "It may be that the past remembers us" (178).

When Dead Boys Don't Talk

Let me end with a fictional exhumation: Randall Kenan's *Let the Dead Bury Their Dead*, a delightful story sequence from 1992 set in fictional Tims Creek, North Carolina. Here, the dead chatter, gossip, consort, and generally intrude into the daily lives of the residents. A young boy converses with the dead, even plays poker with them; a hog talks; an immigrant of unknown origins falls from the sky; and an elderly woman seeks absolution from her dead gay grandson via his surviving white lover as "an interpreter for the dead" (Kenan 56). The stories would be rather familiar vignettes of life in segregated America if not for the ability of some Tims Creek residents to commune with the dead and other fantastical possibilities that come to seem as mundane and natural as Jim Crow law.

In the penultimate story, "Tell Me, Tell Me," a young black boy turns up at the bedside of elderly white widow Ida Perry. The problem this time is that he *doesn't* talk. He just stands there, immobile and staring from a bedroom corner, a roadside, the porch. Ida can barely see him but detects an "African shape: too large for his thin frame and shaped like a peanut." Moreover, "She could hardly see his eyes, but she knew he was staring at her" (247). Ida is a figure of racial paranoia. She worries over the race of the young boy and others, especially the new doctors of various backgrounds—Filipino, black— who tend to her. Ida's friend counsels that she remain mum or blame it on the oysters she ate, lest Ida find herself locked up in a home. And yet the boy returns, to Ida's amusement, which turns annoyance, and then anger.

It turns out that the "little colored intruder" (249) is the young boy murdered decades prior by Ida's husband when the boy happened upon the courting couple making love on the beach. As Ida finally remembers the incident, the scene recalls not only Till's murder but also famous scenes of interrupted sex in segregation literature. Richard Wright's "Big Boy Goes Home," for instance, includes a fatal clash of black boyhood innocence and white sexuality in an edenic swimming hole. And Toni Morrison revises that pastoral scene in her 1970 novel *The Bluest Eye* through Cholly's backstory and Pecola's first menstruation, which both feature white pairs who intrude into the bushes as adolescent black sexuality unfolds. Kenan draws on this iconic trope and brings it into the white bedroom. Ida responds with deliberate forgetting: "Then she wiped the thought from her mind, like wiping mucus from her nose, and stepped inside and about her daily life" (244). The memory, like mucus, is off-putting, inconvenient, easily discarded. As she proceeds, "she had repeatedly tossed the memory aside: just an impertinent, trespassing Negro" (248). She wanders through the story determined not to remember, not to penetrate the "luminous membrane of memory" (265). For, in the end, "some things you forget to remain innocent; some things you forget to remain free; some things you forget due to lassitude . . . She did not care to remember" (268). To remember is to accept culpability, even in inaction. To remember is to forfeit white innocence.

And yet to forget is to remain hostage to the dead who wait at one's bedside, silent and staring. To Ida's pleas to "Tell me, Tell me," the boy remains mute, dumb—leaving it to Ida to dredge up the long-buried memory of her own silent complicity in horrific violence against a young boy not unlike Till. Kenan uses the uncannily familiar murdered boy to refract contemporary sexual politics through slavery and Jim Crow. This is somewhat common in gay literature of the time. Ethan Mordden's *Everybody Loves You* (1988), Jim Grimsley's *Dream Boy* (1995), and Jonathan Strong's *The Old World* (1998), for instance, all feature ghosts of sorts in order to endow historical depth onto otherwise conventional gay coming-of-age narratives.

Kenan also draws on southern literary history for his incantation of Till. The story's title, "Tell Me, Tell Me," comes directly from William Faulkner's *Light in August*. Moreover, Kenan's silent black boy directly evokes Joe Christmas in his early days in the orphanage. In Faulkner's novel, little Joe finds himself drawn to the private room of a young dietician, especially her toothpaste. As he sneaks small bits of the strange and wondrous white substance, the dietician returns with a lover, and Little Joe must secret himself into the closet. He does not understand what he is observing and, when discovered, is certain that he will be punished. A fearful, mutual silence results with each fearing the other will tell about white female sexuality or black thievery. Little Joe comes to haunt the dietician: "Because always against her eyelids or upon her retinae was that still, grave, inescapable, parchment colored face watching her" (123). She attempts to buy Little Joe's silence with a silver dollar and the promise of more to come. And yet his silence is maddening, leading her to hound him, seize him, and demand, "Tell me, tell me, now" (127). As in Kenan's story, the boy never tells. Eventually, he must be cast out, hastily adopted to the stern Mr. McEachern.

Silence, not speech, becomes a problem. There is no easy solution to white insistence on an exculpatory black voice and the murdered boy's relegation to ghostly, mute black body. It is, of course, no surprise to find Faulkner's influence in southern literature. In conversation, Kenan confirmed that the influence was not conscious,[9] which only bolsters what Kreyling calls the "Faulkner effect" in *Inventing Southern Literature* (esp. 126–30). By resurrecting a Joe Christmas–like child and transporting him to the bedside of an old white lady who got him killed, Kenan disassembles white innocence. Even more difficult, he also dismantles seemingly empowering calls for black voice. The title's admonition to "Tell Me, Tell Me" fails to elicit a verbal response from the dead, though Ida herself is eventually moved to admission and perhaps penance of a sort.

Dead Silence

The resurrected black boy who remains resolutely, inexplicably silent breaks from the tradition of exhuming Till so that he may bring civil rights histories to bear on present injustices. What possibilities does his silence create? On the one hand, Fred Moten comes to value the unconsoled black moan in Till's story precisely because it is inconsolable by mourning.[10] Perhaps posthumous silence seeks not consolation but reflection and redress among the living. On the other hand, Ashraf Rushdy provocatively asks, "When is an American lynching?" (1). The question signals the end-of-lynching discourse that has prevailed in America since the 1940s so that each new incident of racially motivated violence is a shock, a return of an "undead past" (129). If we deem the past passed, then we have no way of understanding its legacy and its continuation. And so we are ill-equipped to understand each new horrific act, such as the 1998 dragging death of James Byrd in Texas or the fatal 2012 shooting of Trayvon Martin as the unarmed teen walked through a gated community in Florida. Rushdy helps us understand a dominant response: *Such things can't happen anymore.* Which is to say, we expect such things to happen *then.* Sociologist Avery Gordon has argued that ghost stories are the unfinished past's way of asserting its presence. In this way, literary exhumations reject historical amnesia and equip us to understand injustice in the present, and perhaps work to dismantle it. But what if the dead don't cooperate and instead remain silent as the skeletons they are?

Each exhumation of Till—be it literary or historical—fails in this way. They each look to wronged corpses to speak to our own complicity in the present. Perhaps Reed had it right: to dig up Till and demand that he talk is an absurdity and a violation. As Ida desperately pleads with the boy, "What do you want from me?" (239), we all sink into the titular repetition, "Tell Me, Tell Me." The demand itself is an intrusion. The fact that the murdered black boy *doesn't* talk may be something to celebrate. With Kenan's Cheshire-cat silence, we learn not to seek absolution by unburying our dead, especially those who died neglected, lynched, or otherwise abused. They need not rise to repair the injuries of the past. It is Ida's responsibility. It is ours.

NOTES

1. See especially Pollack and Metress, *Emmett Till in Literary Memory,* including the annotated bibliography of retellings to date. On retellings as racial justice, see especially Metress, "No Justice, No Peace." On retellings as mourning, see, for example, Mark, "Mourning Emmett." On Till's story in music, see Kohlin, "Haunting America."

2. Davey and Ruethling, "After 50 Years."

3. *Reckless Eyeballing* contains a not-so-subtle dig at Baldwin as feminist lackey: the protagonist plays one of the actresses "like a Baldwin piano" (109).

4. Elsewhere I discuss the segregated stage as an integration strategy. See my "James Baldwin's Unifying Polemic," esp. 79–83.

5. See my "James Baldwin's Unifying Polemic," esp. 86, 95. The exhumation is both literal and metaphoric.

6. For more on the reception, especially its temporal structure, see my "James Baldwin's Unifying Polemic," esp. 80, 86–92; and Mitchell, "James Baldwin, Performance Theorist," 54.

7. See Leeming, *James Baldwin,* 239.

8. See my *Neo-Segregation Narratives,* esp. 159–68

9. Kenan, personal conversation with the author.

10. For Moten, this explains why resurrection and insurrection are linked, each forever awaiting the other to commence ("Black Mo'nin'," esp. 72).

12

SECOND LIFE

Salvage Operations in Cormac McCarthy's Undead South

SUSAN EDMUNDS

Cormac McCarthy's *Child of God* (1973) opens with the image of Lester Ballard pissing like a yard animal "at the barn door" as county officials gather to auction off his family's Appalachian farm.[1] Introducing him as the inheritor of "Saxon and Celtic bloods," "a child of God much like yourself perhaps" (*CG* 4), McCarthy briefly poses his protagonist as a potential double for the reader before pushing him off home ground and into the wild. The loss of his land through a failure to pay taxes strips Ballard of the dignity conventionally accorded to the yeoman farmer and confirms his white trash status. After a brief scuffle with the law, he joins the novel's other poor white characters in a life of hunting, squatting, scavenging, and trash picking on the mountainous outskirts of postwar Knoxville. But midway through the novel, the malfunctioning exhaust system of a car parked on "the Frog Mountain turnaround" (*CG* 19) sets him on a different course. The car's exhaust fumes asphyxiate the couple inside while they're having sex, delivering two corpses to Ballard amid the other garbage strewn about the turnaround. This sudden bounty kick-starts his transformation from a trash picker to a serial killer, and Ballard spends the rest of the novel hunting down his neighbors, whose bodies he recycles along with the rest of the scraps and leavings on which he has learned to subsist.

McCarthy plays on the themes of trash and recycling central to the lives of Ballard and his other poor white Appalachian characters when he recycles long-standing literary and pseudoscientific stereotypes to create them. At the same time, he challenges the ideological premises on which these stereotypes depend when he assigns the same white trash traits to the novel's more affluent, middle-class white characters. In this essay, I want to read McCarthy's refusal to honor the conventional distinction between white trash and mainstream white Americans in *Child of God* against a wider public discourse of the 1960s and early 1970s that focused on the social and environmental costs of national prosperity in the postwar era. As old immigrant dreams of wealth decayed into unconscionable spectacles of waste, observers across the political spectrum began to question the virtue of a civilizational project that white Americans had long asserted that they, and they alone, were racially equipped to carry out.

Vance Packard inaugurated popular discussion on the topic with the publication of his 1960 book *The Waste Makers*. Building upon arguments first launched in J. K Galbraith's *The Affluent Society* (1958) and Packard's own *The Hidden Persuaders* (1957), *The Waste Makers* asserted that the "philosophy of waste" (8) governing state and market promotion of "ever-higher levels of private consumption" (8) was affecting "not just the United States economy but the drift of the United States civilization" (244). With the postwar creation of "a brand new breed of super customers" (11), people whose forebears had once made the nation proud were now "goofing off" and "wallowing in waste" (8). The young, in particular, were no longer "ambitious, dedicated, self-sufficient, individualistic idealists who hope to build a better world" (237). Focused almost exclusively on "the hi-fi set," "the outdoor barbeque," or "the game room" waiting in their futures, they showed "little apparent concern for their fellow man" (237). Aggregate consumer spending habits told a similar story: despite the persistence of poverty at home and abroad, "average American[s]" were "spending more on smoking, drinking and gambling than [. . .] on education" and "more on admission tickets to pastimes than [. . .] on foreign economic aid" (233).

Four years later, in *One-Dimensional Man* (1964), Herbert Marcuse shifted the target of critique from the degenerating American "character" (Packard 232) to the "Welfare and Warfare State" (48). According to Marcuse, the nation's technological capabilities offered an unprecedented historical opportunity to provide plenty for all—to create what the New Left would soon call the "post-scarcity society." But instead of seizing this opportunity, the welfare-warfare state was spending huge amounts of money to prop up an exploitative and profit-driven system dedicated to "the production and consumption of waste" (7). Like Packard, Marcuse defined "waste" broadly, including in that category not only the waste materials and shoddy, unsold, or quickly discarded commodities of the production process, but also the labor-time spent making those commodities and the ever-growing apparatus of market research, advertising, and public relations required to sell goods to people whose desire for them had to be manufactured alongside the goods themselves. It was in this sense that Marcuse argued that the "production of [. . .] waste" (49) had become "socially necessary" (49) to a system whose irrationality could be measured in its power "to turn waste into need, and destruction into construction" (9).[2]

Contemporary fears about overpopulation, escalating pollution levels, and dwindling natural resources, referenced in both Packard's and Marcuse's analyses, dominated headlines throughout the 1960s, reaching a fever pitch with coverage of the New York City garbage strike and Appalachian miners' black lung movement of 1968 and the Santa Barbara oil spill and burning of the Cuyahoga River the following year. By decade's end, claims about the inherent destructiveness of the American way of life were commonplace. In the international best seller *Future Shock* (1970), Alvin Toffler castigated "the throw-away society" (51) for "breeding a new race of nomads" (75) who prized "minimum involvement" (64) over all other social goods; and he predicted that "the malaise, mass neurosis, irrationality, and free-floating violence already apparent in contemporary life are merely a foretaste of what may lie ahead" (11). Murray Bookchin agreed, warning readers of his New Left manifesto *Post-Scarcity Anarchism* (1971) that "bureaucratic state capitalism" (38) was turning "man" into "a highly destructive parasite who threatens to destroy his host—the natural world—and eventually himself" (61). Offering TV audiences a gentler preview of apocalypse, the "Keep America Beautiful" ad campaign that began airing in the spring of 1970 featured the image of a Hollywood Indian moved to tears by the trash piling up on the nation's once-majestic waterways and roadsides.[3]

Though the language of "race" and "breed" plays a purely rhetorical role in these accounts, they all attribute to the "average" postwar "American" social characteristics once thought to distinguish white trash from the nation's larger, and purportedly more sound, white population. As a number of recent critical studies have established, the presence of "mean whites" or "white trash" among the nation's citizenry had long troubled attempts to link the special destiny of the United States to the innate superiority of the white race. Critic Matt Wray lists "laziness, criminality, promiscuity and licentiousness, nomadism, [and] animal-like behavior" (76) among the traits assigned to this worrisome white group, whose presence in the New World was routinely traced to "purely Anglo-Saxon" (120) bloodlines and dated to colonial times. Writing in 1861, Bayard Taylor confessed that "the white trash of the South [. . .] almost shake our faith in the progressive instinct of the Anglo-Saxon" (qtd. in Wray 59–60). Three years later, James Gilmore would assert that "the 'mean white' of the South does not *know how* to labor; he produces nothing; he is a fungous growth on the body of society, absorbing the strength and life of its other parts" (qtd. in Hartigan 67).

With the emergence of the eugenics movement in the late 1800s and early 1900s, the increasingly racialized, "cacogenic" character attributed to white trash jeopardized nativist arguments about the unique civilizational mission of "old stock" Americans, said to be grounded in native-born whites' greater racial aptitude for self-discipline, self-denial, and self-government, and thus for democracy, discovery, enterprise, and family love.[4] Such virtues are shockingly absent in the eugenic family studies of the period. Textual predecessors of *Child of God*, these studies exposed civilization-harming genetic pollutants in poor white families of both the South and the North. In his 1912 study "The Kallikak Family," Henry Herbert Goddard faults his subjects, whom he claims have "no power of control" (12) for "multiplying at twice the rate of the general population" (71) and for burdening society with "more feeble-minded children with which to clog the wheels of human progress" (78). A year later, his coworker Elizabeth Kite reaches back to Darwin in order to condemn the "Pineys" as "barnacles upon our civilization," "degenerate relative[s] of the crab" who have given up "life's stimulating struggle" for the pleasures of "kicking food into [their] mouth[s] and enjoying the functionings of reproduction" (170). In a 1930 family study entitled "The Bunglers," I. S. Caldwell bemoans the irrational consumer habits of his subjects, who starve during the week only to engage on payday in "an orgy of spending" on trifles such as "candy, snuff, bottled drinks, [and] ice cream cones" (205). Advocating sterilization as the only effective way to keep people like the Bunglers from infusing the U.S. "population" of "1964" with a "great army of delinquents" (383), Caldwell's study directly inspired the portrayal of the Lester family in his son Erskine Caldwell's famous 1932 novel *Tobacco Road*, where the methodical trashing of "a brand-new automobile" serves as a metaphor for the threat that Jeeter Lester and his kind pose to twentieth-century American progress (*Tobacco Road* 83).

McCarthy faithfully recycles all these white trash stereotypes in his depictions of Lester Ballard and his friends. Poor Appalachian whites who squat, scavenge, binge-drink, fornicate, and fight, they appear to be overblown caricatures of the literary and pseudoscientific discourses that produced them. But McCarthy also uses the same stereotypes to depict the region's growing white middle class. The corpse-laden car that Ballard finds on the Frog Mountain turnaround becomes central to his depictions in this regard. As some of the details I've cited above suggest, early-twentieth-century writers typically identified automobiles with a peerless American progress that white trash figures threatened, either by clogging their wheels, destroying their motors, or trashing their fine exteriors.[5] But in the postwar period, commentators repeatedly identified automobiles, which consumers had been taught to replace as often as once a year, as a leading index of American wastefulness.[6] Waste and wastefulness permeate the scenes McCarthy assigns to the Frog Mountain turnaround, where local couples go in their cars to get wasted.[7] When the malfunctioning exhaust system of one couple's car reroutes gasoline fumes through the passenger cabin, killing them as they make love to the blare of a radio, their cause of death abruptly reclassifies the couple as disposable waste products of their own profligate consumerism, setting up an equivalency between their spent bodies and "idling" car (*CG* 85) and "the flattened beercans and papers and rotting condoms" (*CG* 20) that litter the ground of the turnaround. In turn, Ballard's own actions on the same ground, first as a trash picker and lonely voyeur, then as a necrophiliac, and finally as a serial killer, begin to look like a curious kind of salvage operation that, like the idling automobile he finds, recycles various unwanted forms of waste and trash back through the social and economic system that produces them.[8]

Critic K. Wesley Berry usefully traces the trashed and wasted landscapes that prevail in *Child of God* to the history of northern capital investment in timber, marble, and coal extraction that stripped the Appalachian Mountains of their beauty and mountain farmers of their land, collapsing first a subsistence and then a cash economy before their own profits dried up on the eve of the Great Depression (62–63).⁹ Ballard's loss of his home, the flood that almost drowns him midway through the novel, the abandoned quarry filled with junk, and even the mountain turnaround—one road in a larger network built to carry timber out of the hills—all index the impact of this history on McCarthy's fictional world. But this history cannot account for the scattered signs of regional prosperity that also dot this landscape. First there's "the high sheriff of Sevier County" (*CG* 48) who tracks down wrongdoers in a "tailored shirt" (*CG* 48) and "pressed and tailored chinos" (*CG* 50). Then there are Ballard's male victims, who include the man who carries "eighteen dollars"[10] in his wallet and drinks "bonded," rather than bootleg, "whiskey" (*CG* 90); the "boy" who has fully "paid for" his automobile in anticipation of his marriage (*CG* 147); and three more men who die with "wristwatches" (*CG* 130) on their arms.[11] There are the good old boys who sit around a store, idly bartering to buy the same watches with cash they keep on hand (*CG* 130–32). And finally, there are the many big-ticket items—the "bloated sofa," "upturned" cars, "old stoves and water heaters," and "ruins of an old truck" (*CG* 28, 26, 39, 38)—that rust and rot next to "a burning slagheap of old rubber" (*CG* 30) in the local dump and nearby quarry.

These details speak to new sources of wealth associated with the rapid growth and transformation of nearby Knoxville and its suburbs beginning in the New Deal era, when federal funding for the TVA, the University of Tennessee, and the nuclear facility at Oak Ridge made the city a regional hub and a showcase for the kind of multipronged, government-sponsored development occurring throughout the New South. Almost entirely indebted to the welfare- warfare state for its resurgence, Knoxville became a glowing example of Sunbelt prosperity in the postwar decades, as its former exploiters to the north saw their own regional economies rust. With the creation of the 1965 Appalachian Regional Commission in the years immediately prior to *Child of God*'s publication, the Johnson administration sought belatedly to extend the same prosperity to poor mountain whites. But, as local activists charged, the region's highway systems and "perimeter metropolitan growth centers" managed to soak up most of the government money, and "the neediest areas" remained "neglected."[12]

In *Child of God*, stray hints of an affluent and mobile southern consumer class only underscore the persistent poverty and stasis of Ballard and his friends, and suggest that the predatory relationship to Appalachia, once imposed by northern capital, now persists by other means. When Ballard starts collecting bodies from the Frog Mountain turnaround, he turns this predatory relationship around, redefining his more prosperous, if temporarily wasted, fellow citizens as superfluous goods or trash produced by, but in no way necessary to, the current social order. Freeing them from one set of social relations and placing them in another, he salvages his neighbors, recovering in and from death the ideal white, middle-class existence denied him by the living before pushing beyond that ideal into a stranger communalism of his own making. In this way Ballard transforms his own social death, imposed on him by his white trash status and confirmed by his eviction, into an alternative state that makes death the condition of a new kind of sociality.

Like poor people everywhere, Ballard and his friends do not throw things out, but instead routinely salvage and recycle what they can.[13] The Lane family rigs a car roof with a light bulb to warm a brood of chicks and uses hammered food tins to cover up holes in the floor (*CG* 76, 77). The dumpkeeper names his daughters "out of an old medical dictionary gleaned from the rubbish he picked" (*CG* 26); discarded automobile parts round out the furniture in his yard and keep the "rotting sedans and niggerized convertibles" of his daughters' many suitors in motion (*CG* 110, 27). Lacking access even to a "patched up" car (*CG* 27), Ballard works on a smaller scale, using "cardboard" to pane windows and sweep the floor (*CG* 14, 66), "salvag[ing] a worn kitchen knife" and "rusty axehead" from the quarry (*CG* 39, 70), and "husbanding" forgotten ears of corn from his neighbors' fields (*CG* 40). Together with the game he shoots or steals and the unpaid tally he maintains at Mr. Fox's store, these small pickings keep Ballard alive.

But if Ballard depends on scavenging to survive, his gun provides the only means he has to make lasting attachments. Even before he begins shooting people, his skills as a marksman win him "a ponderous mohair teddybear" (*CG* 64) and two other stuffed animals at a county fair. Firelight dancing in the "plastic eyes" (*CG* 67) of these trophies of suburban comfort teaches him the time-honored middle-class habit of personifying one's possessions, and he soon blends his first female corpse into the mix as one more cherished item in a lovingly acquired collection. Having a lady in the house gives him a reason to shop and to stand about the yard, admiring the picture she makes in her new red outfit by the hearth. The pleasure Ballard takes in looking in on his own cozy domestic scene underscores both the pain of prior exclusions and the new satisfactions available to him now that he is finally able to keep up with the Joneses. At the same time, the multiple connections he sets up between spying, killing, and housekeeping rework a recurring motif in the eugenic family studies, whose white, middle-class authors repeatedly narrate acts of looking in, uninvited, upon the lives of their white trash subjects at home, only to frame the domestic scenes they encounter as breeding grounds of "human degeneracy"[14] that need to be eliminated. Ballard displays a similar aggression when he treats his victims' private cars and homes as spaces to peer into, enter, and clean out, though in taking their bodies home with him he reasserts the contagion of human belonging that eugenicists thought they could eradicate. In turn, the eerie, copy-cat relationships that Ballard forms with a class of people who would otherwise shun or even eliminate him tips McCarthy's own largely suburban readership into a new relationship with the story. Gaining through death the power to intrude upon their worlds and place them—however horrifically—in his, Ballard simultaneously affirms, parodies, and estranges the consumerist ideals on which postwar white middle-class lives were built. When an overfed fire devours his picture-perfect wife and home in a hilarious send-up of suburban consumption run wild, he patiently uses his gun to build up his collection again, inducting couples who prefer to party privately on Frog Mountain into a new world where no one gets left out.[15]

Ballard's decision to treat his more affluent neighbors as superfluous goods or trash in need of recycling resonates with Patricia Yaeger's account of a long-standing "ethos of disposability" in the white South, which defined African American lives as so replaceable that grieving for the harm and violence done to them was unnecessary.[16] But when he learns to regard Knoxville's postwar consumer class as a subset of the waste they produce, Ballard also participates in a newer, fully national discourse that was beginning to identify Americans of all types as potentially disposable. If Marx had made the fungible relationship between people and things a founding tenet of his critique of capitalism, Leftist critics of the postwar period argued that the welfare-warfare state was turning the nation's poor not just into things but into useless and unneeded things—a "surplus" in a country that already had too much. In his 1962 book *The Other America*, Michael

Harrington gives older constructions of white trash a Marcusian slant in quoting another reporter's comment that Appalachians, "a once proud and aggressively independent mountain people" now dependent on government "relief" as a "way of life," "have themselves become surplus commodities in the mountains" (42). Six years later, in 1968, the same charge surfaces in a New Left manifesto that finds that the "chronically poor and unemployed [. . .] have been treated more and more as commodities within the service sector of production" (Gilbert, Gottlieb, and Sutheim 435). These charges carried a double valence for New Left activists. Whether Appalachia's poor whites remained in the mountains or followed rural African Americans to mass unemployment and state supervision in the cities, they offered living proof that the nation not only produced but *required* the production of wasted lives along with wasted goods and resources. At the same time, after Marcuse announced the historical demise of the white working class's revolutionary agency in *One-Dimensional Man,* these same "surplus" populations began to represent a potential "vanguard" in the struggle against a new phase of capitalism.[17]

But for other commentators, the potential associated with becoming socially unnecessary was purely negative. In *The Waste Makers,* Vance Packard audibly recoils at the idea, central to the culture of planned obsolescence, that "things" (59) have a "life expectancy" (66) and are designed with built-in "Product Death-Dates" (63). He worries that "the nation faces the hazard of developing a healthy economy within the confines of a psychologically sick and psychologically impoverished society" (316). Fears left unstated in his account become explicit ten years later in *Future Shock,* where Alvin Toffler argues that in a nation whose citizens "face a rising flood of throw-away items, impermanent architecture, mobile and modular products, rented goods and commodities designed for almost instant death" (73), the promise of "minimum involvement" (64) originally proffered by the disposable commodity must now be honored by "the disposable person" (97). Significantly, Toffler's disposable person is no longer a traditionally marginalized or stigmatized figure, but just another average Joe—like "the shoe salesman" who knows to foreground his "efficiency'" with customers and not his "problems at home, or his more general hopes, dreams and frustrations" (96–97).[18]

Public discussions of human disposability dovetailed in the late 1960s and early 1970s with a growing media fascination with serial killing. As Dianne

Luce has demonstrated, McCarthy himself drew heavily on media coverage of the Ed Gein and James Blevins killings and on Alfred Hitchcock's *Psycho* in writing *Child of God* (136–53). In the years following his novel's publication, critics would begin to make routine connections between the social outlook of the serial killer and the wider values of the new "throw-away society." TV producer Kenneth Wooden testified to Congress in the early 1980s: "Children in America are treated like garbage. Raped and killed, their young bodies are disposed of in plastic bags, in trash trucks, and left in city dumps" (Jenkins 127). In a 1991 article published in the London *Sunday Times,* James Dalrymple varied the metaphor, arguing that serial killers "regard" their child victims "as free-range products on the hoof to be either bought for pleasure or taken by force, used and disposed of in shallow graves" (Jenkins 134). One year earlier, FBI agent John Douglas summed up the general sentiment: "It becomes easy when they decide to kill. It's like throwing away a piece of garbage" (125).

These comments serve to highlight a crucial difference between McCarthy's portrayal of serial killing and other portrayals that would soon follow. Like Ed Gein and Norman Bates, Ballard does not throw away his victims. Instead as Dianne Luce notes, though no one else in Sevier County seems remotely interested in their whereabouts, he preserves and cherishes them (135). In "the bowels of the mountain" where he finally makes his home, they lie "on ledges or pallets of stone," "like saints" (*CG* 135). When the flood comes, he battles madly with the rising waters, risking his own life to carry "the last rancid mold-crept corpse" (*CG* 158) to drier ground. Like a mold or like James Gilmore's fungus, Ballard uses decaying and discarded matter to start again. His actions resacralize the dead, giving them a second life in which they enjoy forms of value and community conspicuously lacking in their first. Refusing to consider his own life wasted, Ballard doesn't weep like the Crying Indian when he "walk[s] in the gray roadside grass among the beercans and trash" (*CG* 96). Nor does he head to the cities to join a New Left vanguard of the chronically poor and unemployed. He enters an underground of a different sort, inducting his neighbors into a world that has achieved post-scarcity because it has become post-need, while granting them a social neededness which the culture of abundance fails to provide. Whether this recycling process also restores to the novel's dead white consumers a moral integrity they've lost or simply redistributes a moral irony that has inhabited the historical project of U.S. whiteness all along is a question raised but never fully answered by McCarthy's text. When a sinkhole opens up in the earth shortly after Ballard dies in Knoxville's "University Hospital" (*CG* 193), the disruption is not enough to shake his former neighbors from their ease. As "the high sheriff of Sevier County" and his men enter "the sink," their "seven bodies" sleep on largely undisturbed, "arranged on stone ledges in attitudes of repose" (*CG* 196, 195).

In 1967 the *Atlantic Monthly* ran John Barth's tribute to postmodernism, "The Literature of Exhaustion." There he argues that the contemporary writer must grapple with "the difficulty, perhaps the unnecessity, of writing original works of literature" (69) in an era shaped by "the feeling" that "the novel," like "Western civilization, or the world, is going to end rather soon" (72). In its layered meditation on the art of recycling, McCarthy's novel makes a clear nod to Barth's essay and to a larger avant-garde tradition that has cycled from art to trash and back again since the beginning of the twentieth century. In fact, we might read *Child of God* as a vehicle designed to trash the postwar suburban reader—or to allow her to trash herself—on pleasures that by 1973 had become as predictable as they were unseemly. Reaching back to an earlier generation's fears of racial exhaustion and entwining them with the current generation's indictments of American wastefulness, McCarthy appeals to white suburbanites' enduring appetite for intraracial slumming, sex, murder, moral horror, and shock even as he doubles his story back on itself, catching the reader's own white trash image in the loop of his self-reflexive text. And yet it remains unclear whether he deploys this self-reflexivity in the service of a larger critique or just for kicks. Though the novel vibrates throughout with many popular political agendas of its time,[19] any moral or political message that the reader might finally take from *Child of God* seems—like so much of the text—fully disposable.

NOTES

1. McCarthy, *Child of God*, 4. Hereafter cited parenthetically as *CG*.

2. See also Gottlieb 132–33, 138. For a contemporary political analysis that has deeply influenced my reading of *Child of God*, see Povinelli, esp. chap. 3. This essay owes another general debt to my colleague Crystal Bartolovich and her work on the history of the Commons.

3 For a discussion of the decade's listed events, see Gottlieb 137–40, 177–79, 358–72; and Binkley, 163. On the more general apocalyptic tenor of the late 1960s and early 1970s, see Binkley 137–40; and Schulman 49, 93.

4. On this point, see Jacobson, chap. 1; Carter, chap. 1; and Dyer, introduction.

5. See, for instance, Caldwell's "Memorandum" and "The Automobile That Wouldn't Run."

6. See Packard 34, 78–101; Toffler 64; Bookchin 75; and Strasser 192–95.

7. The *OED* dates the first use of "wasted" in the sense of "intoxicated (from drink or drugs)" to 1968–70.

8. For other approaches to McCarthy's interest in disposable objects and landscapes of waste, see Malewitz 538–39; and Beck.

9. See also Luce 3–18.

10. Eighteen dollars in 1957, the year to which Dianne Luce dates the novel's flood (155), would be worth roughly $150 today.

11. In contrast, Ballard's female victims are consistently poorer than his male victims, overdetermining their status as bartered goods. One victim, the Lane girl, seems to measure her class distance from Ballard solely by the fact that she lives in a house and can shut him out of it. For the white trash stereotype of treating women like goods for barter (a stereotype McCarthy successfully exploits to sell his own goods), see Kite 167, 181; and Williamson 193, 206. For poor whites' tendency to project white trash status onto "other whites of similar or lower class status," see Hartigan 113, 111.

12. On Knoxville's economic revival, see MacArthur 138–44; and Luce 18–23. On the rise of the Sunbelt, see Schulman, chap. 4. For cited reactions to ARC, see Walls and Stephenson 250, 144.

13. See Strasser 115, 139. Strasser notes that reuse and recycling, long considered respectable, middle-class habits in the United States, began to be associated exclusively with poverty in the 1920s (113, 141, 170, 266). For the renewed middle-class interest in recycling in the late 1960s, see Strasser 280–85, 293; and Gottlieb 138.

14. Goddard 73. For scenes featuring a fieldworker peering into or entering a white trash home, see Goddard 72, 73, 77–78, 86–87, 89–90.

15. For related readings of this narrative segment, see Jarrett 41–42; and Madsen 23–24.

16. See Yaeger, *Dirt and Desire*, chap. 3, esp. 86. For a more recent discussion of the role that trash and "disposable bodies" play in illuminating "a culture of racial neglect" grounded in "the Southland's (and our nation's) commitment to toxic inequality," see Yaeger, "Beasts."

17. See also Gitlin and Hollander; and Gottlieb, 137.

18. For a Sartrean reading of the novel's depictions of a capitalist economy of "scarcity" in which "human life itself is constituted as a 'thing,'" see Holloway 130.

19. By the early 1970s, the verb "to trash" had itself acquired political connotations. In *Steal This Book*, Abbie Hoffman explains that the Yippie term "trashing" means "to do battle with the pigs in the street and at the same time to inflict property damage" (159).

13

LAST ROADS TAKEN
Robert Frost, Cormac McCarthy, and Dying Worlds

BRYAN GIEMZA

McCarthy's southern settings offer, as Robert Frost's poems do, abandoned homes and half-wild groves, but in McCarthy's antipastoral mode, they are places where flesh-eating quasi-zombies and berserkers roam. John Grammer once ventured that McCarthy writes in an antipastoral tradition narrowly characteristic of southern literature. To that extent, McCarthy's southern/Appalachian novels are an extension of Faulkner's imaginative universe. In Faulkner's world, moonlight and magnolias line the path to a southern heart of darkness. If anything, McCarthy sees through a still darker lens. *Suttree* offers a region where a pervert might satisfy himself in a moonlit melon patch, only to become a perennial ward of the state for his misdeeds. If that isn't antipastoral, it will do until antipastoral gets here.

Both Faulkner and McCarthy charted fictional places that might be traced to actual ones. As Allen Josephs once pointed out to me, the father and son in *The Road* arrive in a place described as "slow water in a flat country," perhaps a paean to Faulkner's contention that Yoknapatawpha means "water runs slow through flat land" (Gwynn and Blotner 74). But which flat country? A vigorous debate among McCarthyians regarding the escape route of the father and son has settled into consensus: the two follow a watershed route, since it is generally congruent with the southeastern path that rivers take as they drain from the southern Appalachians to the sea. The consensus aligns with the general description of the novel's landscapes, which go from mountain overpasses to coastal lowlands. Think of modern-day I-26 going from Asheville to Charleston and you've got the sense of it. These serpentines mark the fastest way to get to the sea, which is the origin of life and perhaps its last redoubt in an apocalyptic age. Some have tried to pin down the exact route from landmarks. It might well be sensible to pin the ruined childhood home to the McCarthys' now-burned former residence just outside Knoxville.

The most important signifier is the "See Rock City" barn (*The Road* 18), familiar to anyone who hails from the southern part of the Appalachian world that once aspired to be the State of Franklin, an area bristling with barn roofs painted to advertise the tourist spot. It serves both as a joke and a way to center the map. The joke is that the world has been reverted to something like the Stone Age. There are plenty of rock cities to see. Symbolically, the retreat of the father and son into a bomb shelter approximates a cave. McCarthy has long been interested in caves and necropolis—think Lester Ballard in *Child of God,* and the revelation of Knoxville's underworld in *Suttree*. The latter impresses upon readers that the organic evolution of cities is such that they are built upon the dead and discarded monuments of civilization. The landscape-transforming and Atlantis-generating powers of the Tennessee Valley Authority were a fixture of McCarthy's childhood via his father's employment as counsel to the Authority. McCarthy knew that these engineered wonders would pass, too. At *Suttree*'s end, as bulldozers descend on Knoxville and McAnnally flats is leveled for highway improvements, graveyards are pushed aside, and not even the dead can be assured of rest.

Suffice it to say that McCarthy's postsouthern landscapes are consummated in the postliving landscapes of *The Road*. Particularly haunting is the tendency of human settlements toward self-consumption, a principle that applies in McCarthy's fictive (or not so fictive) world and not merely to Knoxville's pretensions to civilization but to all such human endeavors. Witness the passing orders of empire in *Blood Meridian*. Rock City is to southern nostalgia what Coney Island is for New York, a symbol so fetishized that only the appetite for nostalgia has ensured its existence in any form. Around one hundred of the nine hundred barns touting Rock City are still maintained, and this metric might be said to apply very roughly to the number of southerners whose livelihood is derived from agriculture, notwithstanding the region's enduring rustic reputation.[1] The title of David B. Jenkins's coffee-table book, a collection of pastoral photographs, sums it up: *Rock City Barns: A Passing Era*. It is something of a commonplace that the appetite to sentimentalize is a form of comorbidity.

The Rock City Barn is as empty a signifier as the pastoral culture it marked, a point driven home in McCarthy's description of the now-empty stores of hayloft and farmhouse. To be undead, in the world of McCarthy's *Road,* is to be a body in search of a soul. The question McCarthy raises is, In an entropic world, how can these dry bones be made to live? Civilizations are too fragile to be relied upon to ward off the undead and prevent death-in-life. Only heroic action and moral choice can stave off incipient undeadness. Only moral discernment can permit one to know who the "right ones" are.

This essay considers how the world of the undead permits two canonical writers, McCarthy and Frost, to seek after ultimate sources of meaning when the enterprise of civilization is a vanishingly ephemeral prospect. I juxtapose two works united by an interest in a dying and subsiding world. The first, McCarthy's *The Road,* is a best-selling novel of southern horror that traces the journey of a father and son through an entropic southern landscape populated with the living dead. The second, Frost's "Directive," embarks in an apocalyptic end-time to get back to the beginnings of things. Frost would say of "Directive" and its petrified world, "The key word in the whole poem is *source*—whatever source it is" (*Robert Frost* 151). The poem culminates in a discovered Grail. *The Road* also searches for sources of human meaning in a moribund world. "Perhaps," suggests the father, "in the world's destruction it would be possible at last to see how it was made" (231). Indeed, intriguing parallels in imagery and theme connect *The Road* with "Directive." I will examine poetic influences on *The Road* and consider the importance of the epistemological notion of logos to both works. And I will maintain that the child of *The Road* represents the logos (the word made incarnate) in the novel's larger confrontation with theodicy and eschatology. In its exploration of the first and last things, the world of Frost's poem, "made simple by the loss/Of detail, burned, dissolved, and broken off," replete with a cart-pusher on an apocalyptic road, is thematically unified with the landscapes and inscapes of McCarthy's novel. Ultimately, both seek to recapture sources of meaning in moribund worlds.[2]

The Cormac McCarthy Papers in the Wittliff Collections confirm that *The Road* was originally titled "The Grail." Robert Frost's "Directive," long held to offer a grail of its own, might supply both a title and a metaphysical vision for *The Road*. The novel speaks in parables, as "Directive" was intended to do. Both works detail a deliberate journey back to the sources of things, but as is usual with McCarthy's work, allusions operate by slant. Nevertheless, there are intriguing resonances that leave open the possibility that "Directive" played on McCarthy's mind as he composed *The Road*. Like *The Road*, Frost's poem concerns "a house that is no more a house / Upon a farm that is no more a farm / And in a town that is no more a town." Such is the state of affairs for the father of *The Road*, who will revisit the ruins of a house that is no more a house, ruminate with strange specificity upon the extinction of cattle, and gaze upon the ruins of towns that once he knew. Truly, for the father of the novel, "The road there, if you'll let a guide direct you / Who only has at heart your getting lost, / May seem as if it should have been a quarry."

McCarthy's description of the road begins with a vision of the lost and undead, bearing their carts with them: "In those first years the roads were peopled with refugees shrouded up in their clothing. Wearing masks and goggles, sitting in their rags by the side of the road like ruined aviators. Their barrows heaped with shoddy. Towing wagons or carts" (28). The people are "shrouded" as if in preparation for burial. Such is the controlling image of the boy and his father, making their journey pushing a wagon, variously called a cart and a wheelbarrow. Frost's poem also concerns a road and someone "Who may be just ahead of you on foot / Or creaking with a buggy load of grain." There is pointedly no wheat to be had in the wasteland of McCarthy's road. Moreover, Frost's image of the buggy begins in geological time, from an aviator's point of view:

> And there's a story in a book about it:
> Besides the wear of iron wagon wheels
> The ledges show lines ruled southeast-northwest,
> The chisel work of an enormous Glacier
> That braced his feet against the Arctic Pole.

If Frost is the guide who recognizes the necessity of being lost in order to be found, the quarry-like world that McCarthy establishes is confounding even to the last living who must come to accept its norms. Who will guide the father? There can be little doubt that the world of *The Road* is dissolving; if a demiurge created it, it is now being uncreated. He alludes to the writings of the seventeenth-century mystic Jakob Boehme when he mentions "the salitter drying from the earth" (220)—the creative principle in retreat. For the father of *The Road* it is a world "too much for us," as Frost writes in his opening lines, where things are indeed being "made simple by the loss / Of detail, burned, dissolved, and broken off / Like graveyard marble sculpture in the weather." Or, in the analogous phrase of *The Road*, "Everything as it once had been save faded and weathered" (7). An entropic world is indeed becoming much simpler, revealing the wellsprings and hidden mechanisms of its creation. It is no accident that in its unmaking, the *logos* seems imperiled, too, as even the words for creation fall away from their vanishing referents. "Sky blue" and "ocean blue" are terms that will no longer make sense to the boy (153). And yet McCarthy seems to suggest the presence of a metaphysical something that stands apart from memory and the fragility of labels: "He thought each memory recalled must do some violence to its origins. As in a party game. Say the word and pass it on. So be sparing. What you alter in the remembering has yet a reality, known or not" (111).

Both *The Road* and "Directive" search for the ultimate sources of meaning in time of utter dissolution, and both texts are linked by Grail symbolism. The Grail appears toward the end of Frost's poem, announced by the discovery of a child's cup among abandoned trinkets:

> I have kept hidden in the instep arch
> Of an old cedar at the waterside
> A broken drinking goblet like the Grail
> Under a spell so the wrong ones can't find it,
> So can't get saved, as Saint Mark says they mustn't.

In addition to being Christ's cup, the Grail represents the mystery of incarnation. *The Road* seems to suggest that the story of the *logos* is fully within our own flesh, as the father reflects in the third passage of the text: "If he is not the word of God God never spoke"—a direct response to John 1:1 ("In the beginning was the Word, and the Word was with God, and the Word was God"), a chapter that goes on to define Jesus as the *logos* in the flesh (4).[3] For the sake of this argument, at least, we shall assume that God spoke—while acknowledging that much hangs on McCarthy's "if." If so: the *he* referred to in *The Road* is the father's son, the fulfillment of the father and the *logos*. As the "warrant" of the father, the child must be protected so the "wrong ones" cannot find him:

> Do you think they'll find us?
> No. They wont find us.
> They might find us.
> No they wont. They wont find us. (125)

To that end, the child has his own directive, or in the cliché of our time, a "moral compass" that proves to be unfailingly and instinctually correct. It will certainly be necessary as he goes in search of other light-bearers in a darkening world. Attuned as he is to the logos, he is indeed the hope of the world and the Grail-bearer. To reinforce the point, the father, stroking the boy's "pale and tangled hair," thinks, in an oddly metonymic phrase, "Golden chalice, good to house a god"—a pointed confirmation that the boy *is* the Grail (64). McCarthy's novel frames the familiar Christ story in terms of ordinary human experience: in transmitting the logos through the word made flesh lies the only hope of redemption in this world. This does not mean that McCarthy wants to literalize the second coming—though some, taking the novel in its eschatological spirit, have construed it that way. Nor is it to say that this is literally the Christ-child, but rather that the metanarrative of word-made-flesh is reenacted in the course of human events. The Christology of the novel is recognizably human and incarnate, and similar might be said of the symbolism of "Directive," ending with symbolism of crucifixion.

There are other parallels to Frost's poem, which demonstrates that he could surpass the modernists at their allusive game. Quite a few sources have been put forward for "And there's a story in a book about it," including the compelling case made by George Monteiro for *Rhymes and Legends of the Nutfields* (1919), a regional title that would have been close to Frost's tramping grounds and to his heart ("History"). It is also possible that the poet refers to the Bible or to *Le Morte d'Arthur* for the backstory, as other commentators have suggested. There's a story about it in McCarthy's book as well, emblematically in the old man encountered later in the novel: "When he looked back the old man had set out with his cane, tapping his way, dwindling slowly on the road behind them like some storybook peddler from an antique time, dark and bent and spider thin and soon to vanish forever" (147). In *The Road*, texts cannot be relied upon to transmit meaning, any more than language. Indeed, McCarthy's version of the library of Alexandria, with its "blackened books" (158), says something about the futility of scholarship. Explaining the concept of "as the crow flies" and responding to his son's question about whether crows still exist, the father of *The Road* concedes,

> No.
> Just in books.
> Yes. Just in books. (133)

As in Frost's poem, some things will be remembered only in books, and all memory seems under threat. Collapsed memory is symbolized by collapsed dwellings in both texts. "Directive" also describes the form of a vanished house:

> [Weep] Then for the house that is no more a house,
> But only a belilaced cellar hole,
> Now slowly closing like a dent in dough.

Homes, reduced to their basements, resemble graves. In *The Road*, as the man reflects on bygone Christmas celebrations in his ruined childhood home, his eye is drawn, in the Whitman way, to lilacs that bloom beyond the door. The collapsing house is surrounded by a "waste of a yard. A tangle of dead lilac" (23). At least one ruined house in McCarthy's novel resembles Frost's forgotten homestead: "They hiked out along the dirt road and along a hill where the house had once stood. It had burned long ago. The rusted shape of a furnace standing in the black water of the cellar" (76). The superfluity of the furnace in a world on fire speaks for itself.

Another instance of the grave/home in "Directive" seems to provide an inadvertent echo of *The Road*'s terrifying encounter with subterranean prisoners in the pantry cellar:

> Nor need you mind the serial ordeal
> Of being watched from forty cellar holes
> As if by eye pairs out of forty firkins.

Frost's poem calls on the legend of Ali Baba and the forty thieves; a thief and a "slutlamp" make important appearances in *The Road*, too. One might hear echoes of the *Arabian Nights* when the father finds his firkins of fuel (gasoline and oil) and goes bearing an Aladdin-style lamp into a treasure cave (the well-stocked underground shelter)—the thief and dagger come later. Significantly, the password to the treasure cave would seem to be the first words uttered by the father when he sees it: "Oh my God" (117). Writes Frost:

> As for the woods' excitement over you
> That sends light rustle rushes to their leaves,
> Charge that to upstart inexperience.
> Where were they all not twenty years ago?

Worried by the sound of a tree falling, the inexperienced boy gets reassurance from his father: "All the trees in the world are going to fall sooner or later. But not on us" (31). And the echoes continue: in Frost's poem, the woods perhaps ". . . think too much of having shaded out / A few old pecker-fretted apple trees." In *The Road* the man makes "his way down through the ruins of an old apple orchard, black and gnarly stumps, dead grass to his knees" (100). The desiccated apples he finds there will provide sustenance for father and son.

One is also reminded of the bomb shelter interlude in McCarthy's novel when Frost beckons us, through his poetic parable, to retreat: "pull in your ladder road behind you / And put a sign up CLOSED to all but me. / Then make yourself at home." Significantly, the corresponding section of McCarthy's book offers a scene where the child feels compelled spontaneously to pray. Frost suggests that children are closer to their divine source:

> First there's the children's house of make-believe,
> Some shattered dishes underneath a pine,
> The playthings in the playhouse of the children.
> Weep for what little things could make them glad.

Throughout *The Road* there are the playthings that make children glad—or, at least, that used to make children glad—but we also "Weep for what little things could make them glad." Into this group one might place the novel's recovered Coca-Cola, the glimpse of another child, quoits, the boy's flute, a few old toys. The father, visiting the wreck of his childhood home, pushes open "the closet door half expecting to find his childhood things," finding nothing but the grayness of his heart (23). In keeping with McCarthy's inverted pastoralism, there is a "playhouse" in *The Road*. It is a blind to be used for ambushing anyone unfortunate enough to wander up to the old manse:

"Coming through the canebrake into the road he'd seen a box. A thing like a child's playhouse. He realized it was where they lay watching the road" (97). Per Frost, "This was no playhouse but a house in earnest." It is interesting that when John Grady Cole is finally undone, he breathes his last in a "child's playhouse" (*Cities of the Plain* 257) where he calls for water. By contrast, the discovery of the cistern in *The Road* comes as a great blessing: "Nothing in his memory anywhere of anything so good" (103). Earlier McCarthy works reveal long-standing interest in relationships between logos, communion, and the Grail legend. Scholars have suggested that the namesake protagonist of McCarthy's novel *Suttree* in fact represents the Fisher King (O'Gorman). In *The Road*, the father will be reminded of his son-as-the-Grail just before his death: "He watched him come through the grass and kneel with the cup of water he'd fetched. There was light all about him. He took the cup and drank and lay back" (233). In the gesture there is also a suggestion of the recumbent, wounded Fisher King.

For its part, "Directive" traces the water source of a household back to its roots, all the way to the spring that feeds it, yielding an epiphanic discovery. Perhaps it is also significant that the book, like Frost's poem, ends with waters, a chalice, and a watering place. The last lines of "Directive" give: "Here are your waters and your watering place. / Drink and be whole again beyond confusion." In contrast to Frost's suggestion of healing, the closing passage of *The Road* is far more ambiguous in its description of brook trout in deep glens. It refers to the trout in the past tense ("once there were brook trout") and suggests the irreversibility of design and extinction because the "maps and mazes" on their backs are "of a thing which could not be put back"—quite the opposite of being made whole again. Similarly, the father worries about the emotional damage done to the child: peering into the boy's face, at one point, "he very much feared that something was gone that could not be put right again" (114), in line with his belief that "the things you put in your head are there forever" (10), even when words no longer sustain them.

What to make of these poetic gleanings? Given McCarthy's known fondness for a variety of poetry, they hint at larger designs. "Directive" is certainly, like *The Road*, a reflection on the last things. The fact that each of the poem's major scenes is in some fashion reenacted in *The Road* is, at the very least, a startling coincidence. It is not possible to make a watertight case that McCarthy looked to Frost as he structured his novel. Mindful that there might indeed be another chalice, another cart, and another road, it nevertheless takes nothing from the genius of McCarthy's work to meditate on its analogues. Specifically, even if one rejects the argument that McCarthy consciously or unconsciously borrowed from Frost's poem, the concerns of the two works reveal a striking symmetry, especially in the notion of the logos—that *something*, however rough hewn, scripts our ends.

What is the starting point for moral order in the world of *The Road*? Is it enough to say, "Thou shalt not eat another person"? Recall that McCarthy describes the evil man, the first person other than his son to whom he has spoken in a year, as "claggy with human flesh" (64). *The Oxford English Dictionary*, which McCarthy uses extensively in his translation notes and in his writing, notes that *claggy* most likely derives from a Norse word for clay—pointing to the common origins ("My brother at last" [64]) and common destiny of this earthly dust. The roadrat cannibals, dominated by their reptilian center, elect evil over self-destruction (or more noble forms of cooperation). They are able to gainsay the world, menacing the generative power of the logos-keeping Grail-bearers. The notion of logos-bearers accounts for an otherwise cryptic passage, with a coinage ("godspoke") peculiar to McCarthy: "On this road there are no godspoke men. They are gone and I am left and they have taken with them the world" (27). But it is merely the world that was; as long as the boy travels with the father they have not taken the logos quite yet. The godspoke are logos-commanded; the logos-effacing are like the rachitic fiend in the woods "who has made of the world a lie every word" (64). When the boy glimpses the remains of an infant roasting on a spit, the violation of deep-set taboo—the literally unspeakable—threatens the power of the word itself: "He didn't know if he'd ever speak again" (199). The destruction of creation remains within the provenance of the demiurge in the world McCarthy creates: "He stood leaning on the gritty concrete rail. Perhaps in the world's destruction it would be possible at last to see how it was made. Oceans, mountains. The ponderous counterspectacle of things ceasing to be. The sweeping waste, hydroptic and coldly secular. The silence" (231).

In *The Crossing*, the church caretaker's tale depicts a god who creates in part through destruction: "A God who seemed a slave to his own self-ordinated duties. A God with a fathomless capacity to bend all to an inscrutable purpose. Not chaos itself lay outside of that matrix. And somewhere in that tapestry was the world in its making and its unmaking was a thread that was he" (149). McCarthy's archival notes reveal his fascination with the snake that consumes its own tail (the *ouroboros* that Jung described as a variety of mandala, elaborated by John Sepich in his *Notes on Blood Meridian*), and the real possibility that the world might be self-cannibalizing/ autophagous as "a creation perfectly evolved to meet its end" (Sepich 50). In an unpublished fragment of "Whales and Men" in the Cormac McCarthy Papers, he writes, "If this looping process is the way it works then there's no need for teleology"—that is, some larger intention for the design of the universe.[4] Even if this is so, there might yet be the logos behind the script.

Last things, indeed. *The Road* is a closed loop, McCarthy's apocalyptic alpha and omega, embracing both first and last things. One might argue that the wordless calculus of the father in moving his son along the road is based on survival, more so than "mere" morality, yet his insistence that there is value in the act of living, and the transmission of the divine breath, imbues his horrific lot with meaning and dignity. In Frost's poem, movement through a desolated world unmade culminates in the Grail and, with "tatters hung on barb and thorn," a startling reminder of the mystery of a divine presence in the midst of disaster. So, too, the goodness that finds the boy at the end of *The Road*. McCarthy's book demonstrates not merely the physical design of the universe's paradoxical order-in-chaos, but something of its shadowy counterpart in the moral design of its creative force. Behind the dark glass of his parable about an unmediated encounter with last things stands a script at once familiar and yet often illegible. In the logos is the suggestion of a source that offers the only possibility of wholeness, as "Directive" suggests, an elusive grail by which one might "drink and be whole again beyond confusion."

To the extent that *The Road* can be counted a novel of the living dead, it is also a novel of the origination of life and of what McCarthy calls the "closed loop" of natural systems. It is a gothic to end Southern Gothic. It is significant, then, that it continues a trajectory established in McCarthy's opus, from the commoditized South tapped out by Faulkner's work, to another sort of South in the southwestern novels where there might still be a type of desolated frontier, to arrive finally at a place that is postsouthern and very nearly posthuman. One might compare this trajectory to that of a satellite that has moved beyond the reaches of the solar system in a search for other sources of life, into the vastness of space itself. It is fitting that McCarthy's work, which once was so preoccupied with making sense of his place in the

South, might now see those concerns across a great remove, from a place beyond the significance of human civilizations—which are entropic and might more accurately be termed necropolises—and far beyond parochial national history. From that distance he might seek to see the place and fleeting beauty of the breath of human life within the universe, that flyspeck in the amber of geological time.

NOTES

1. In the 1930s, "half of the South's labor force were farmers, and more than half of America's farmers were southerners" (Reed and Reed 53). By the time of the 2000 census, only one southern state, Louisiana, could be counted among the top ten with the highest percentage of "people working agriculture, forestry, fishing and hunting, and mining," with little more than 4 percent of the populace so engaged.

2. Readers might find it useful to review the text of Frost's "Directive" in order to absorb the textual parallels that follow.

3. Christ is also described as "the word of God" "in the New Testament (John 1.1–3; Heb. 4.12–13; II Pet. 3.5; I John 1.1–3; 5.7) and [. . .] in the Old Testament (Ps. 138.2)" (Tyburski 125).

4. Manuscript in San Marcos, box 97, Cormac McCarthy Papers, Southwestern Writers Collection, The Wittliff Collections, Alkek Library, Texas State University.

14

UNDEAD GENRES/LIVING LOCALES
Gothic Legacies in *The True Meaning of Pictures* and *Winter's Bone*

LEIGH ANNE DUCK

Hardly the bloodiest film set in the southern mountains, John Boorman's *Deliverance* (1972) is nonetheless the most notorious (Harkins 206). Described by Carol Clover as "the influential granddaddy" of the rural horror "tradition" (126), it lacks the goriness of *The Texas Chain Saw Massacre* (1974) and *The Hills Have Eyes* (1977). Still, it proffers what Linda Ruth Williams calls "an antediluvian nightmare of pursuit" in which "monstrous hillbillies" perform "unnatural" acts on urban travelers (17). Previous films, such as 1964's *Two Thousand Maniacs!* and *Moonshine Mountain*—both by exploitation filmmaker Herschel Gordon Lewis, dubbed the "godfather of gore"—had also portrayed deranged rural settings "at the end of their own death throes," in David Bell's terms (Von Doviak 76–79; Bell 106). But *Deliverance* boasted high production values, literary cachet, and a well-known cast: a Warner Bros. release based on the first novel (1970) by the famous poet James Dickey, it starred a recent Oscar-nominee in Jon Voight (for *Midnight Cowboy*, 1969) and the already popular Burt Reynolds, whose celebrity would subsequently skyrocket. The film was nominated for several major awards, not least for its visual effects, which combined on-location shooting with film printed to provide an "ominous" tone to an otherwise verdant springtime landscape; Boorman also hired a local resident to scout out decaying buildings and persons with visible deformities (Gentry 25–26; Williamson 163–66). Edited to emphasize the peril of the travelers—the obscure expressions of mountain dwellers, the vastness and danger of the landscape, and the terror in protagonists' closely framed faces—*Deliverance* provided mainstream cinema an indelible image of a degenerate mountain society, the sinister opposite of the wholesome, comic realms featured on the era's televisions (Harkins 205–6).

This essay considers why tropes from *Deliverance* appear in the work of filmmakers with contrasting aesthetic commitments. In the famous and admittedly imprecise dichotomy of André Bazin, these directors "put their faith in reality": rather than seeking to "impose [an] interpretation on the spectator," their films encourage "reality [to lay] itself bare" and "reveal its structural depth" (24, 26, 27). Documentarian Jennifer Baichwal states this goal explicitly: exploring the controversial photographs of Shelby Lee Adams, whose images of poor Appalachians are accused of promulgating stereotypes, *The True Meaning of Pictures* (2002) "spends time with a number of subjects" in the hope that expanded context will overcome viewers' potential impulses to "objectify or caricature" Adams's human subjects. Debra Granik describes the art and costume directors of *Winter's Bone* (2010) as "visual anthropologists" and professes her affinity for "observational films," as demonstrated by her neorealist use of an unobtrusive directorial approach, natural lighting, diegetic sound, a largely unaltered mise-en-scène, and local residents as cast (Macaulay; Shiel 2). Each film features moments, however, where image, sound, and editing diverge from mimesis to become uncanny, even portentous.

As explained in this essay's first section, I use the term "gothic" *not* to delineate a mountain-bound version of the oft-cited regional genre but rather to explore how representational practices interact across periods and media. Baichwal cannot escape reference to "Southern Gothic," as Adams's photographs are often described that way; in her documentary, critics, photographic subjects, and Adams himself debate whether the poverty, theatricality, and physical infirmity in his oeuvre exploit living subjects through undead aesthetics. Rather than simply displaying that quandary by lingering over images of uncanny intimacies, monstrous poses, failing bodies, or shadowed mirrors, Baichwal uses gothic techniques to implicate the viewer and her film in a similar dilemma, dislodging the uncanny from Appalachian spaces and attaching it instead to artistic production and circulation. While *Winter's Bone* diverges from Daniel Woodrell's novel (2006) to articulate the space of the Ozarks more thoroughly within the contemporary nation, it also borrows from that strain of the gothic which has, historically, been used to criticize exploitative social relations.

The Lives of Undead Genres

In its contemporary profusion, the gothic is impossible to locate: Catherine Spooner argues that "its imagery and narrative strategies are everywhere" (2). But accounts of a national or regional gothic could never rest securely: identifiable chiefly through human extremity (social, psychological, and/or physical) and a gloomy tone, the gothic relates closely to other categories and always threatens to mutate (Fiedler 28–29; Simpson). This raveling process is endemic to any genre: each entry resembles its forebears while introducing new elements and generic relations (Cohen 204, 207). While this unruliness is rarely used to justify examining genres across diverse modes of circulation, Wai Chee Dimock argues that empiricism demands such inquiry: observing how the ancient epic *Ramayana* has transformed from poem to prose, novel, "work song," "street theater, song-and-dance cycles, [and] shadow-puppet shows," she urges scholars to recognize genre as a "runaway reproductive process: offbeat, off-center, and wildly exogenous" (1383–84, 1379).

Such an approach well suits films of the southern mountains. The tropes used to represent residents of the latter exhibit a formidable consistency across literature, travel writing, cartoons, advertising, television, film, and other media: whether virtuously unspoiled, stalwart, and traditional or dangerously dysfunctional, lazy, and backward, purported "hillbillies" have been portrayed as inhabiting an amorphous space, in which differences between Appalachia and the Ozarks are typically effaced but isolation from the changing nation appears stark and definitive (Harkins 4; Martin viii). Conversely, Rick Altman argues that film genres are far more variable than has generally been supposed, developing through implicit dialogue among filmmakers, critics, and audiences; once genres are recognized, Hollywood films mix their "building blocks" and internal relationships (such as between soundtrack and mise-en-scène) in order to attract diverse fan groups (30–142). No longer believed to emerge directly from genres in other media (Altman 30–31), film genres nonetheless interact with continuing developments in music, visual, and print culture.

Deliverance demonstrates this interactive potency. Adapted from a novel, the film features the kind of instrumental music that national audiences have associated with Appalachia since at least the 1920s (Becker 34–38); it also draws on multimedia stereotypes of the "savage mountaineer"—complete, in the character Bobby's terms, with "genetic deficiencies" (Harkins 33–39, 58–61, 110–12, 133–36, 142–50). From the perspective of early reviewers, however, *Deliverance* mixed these elements with those of adventure films, the Western, melodrama, and realism; Michel Ciment particularly praised Boorman's relentless exploration of American film genres (Ebert; Canby; Ciment 65). Criticism has since been shaped by the context of the film's release: between *Straw Dogs* (1971) and *The Texas Chain Saw Massacre* (1974), *Deliverance* encapsulated "urbanoia," Carol Clover's term for horrifically violent (usually horror) films that depict rural dwellers as primitives eager to destroy urban travelers' "civilized" status (and often the travelers themselves) (124–37). Combining this plot with well-established tropes in representations of Appalachia, *Deliverance* tied the area securely to rural horror, an affiliation which, as Emily Satterwhite has shown, the region retains. (The Ozarks, whose representational history shares much with that of Appalachia, have hosted fewer such films.) To this day, questions of genre shape viewers' thoughts on *Deliverance,* as can be seen in Rabun County, Georgia, where it was filmed. In 2012, when organizers of the inaugural Chattooga River Festival celebrated the film's fortieth anniversary, residents protested: one felt that the novel emerged from Dickey's "wrestling with darkness in its own soul" but complained, "he never stepped up to make clear the distinction from reality and his own artistic representation"; the resulting film, in another's words, "really did a number on my people" (Thomas 210–11).

This danger that stylized representations might supplant audiences' awareness of geographic actualities has been central to the Southern Gothic since its first articulation. Ellen Glasgow's "Heroes and Monsters," published in *Saturday Review of Literature* in 1935, flaunts political and aesthetic conservatism, aligning social critique with callowness and rejecting trespass across generic boundaries (Glasgow 3–4; Palmer 120). But her concerns about generic indeterminacy remain trenchant: conceding that "the Gothic as Gothic" serves an aesthetic function, she argues that Southern Gothicists, in their prevalence and vigor, beg the question of whether "Southern life—or is it only Southern fiction—[has] become one vast, disordered sensibility?"

(4, 3). Situating a genre in a region may inevitably blur boundaries between sociology and aesthetics, but where later critics, such as Lewis Simpson and Tennessee Williams, attributed Southern Gothic to the region's intellectual or artistic cultures, Glasgow feared her contemporaries might believe southern writers were exposed only to "moral and physical degeneration" (4). After all, numerous forms of discourse—in different ways and for many reasons—described such a South in the 1930s.

Such alignments between fictional and other genres can occlude the gothic's imaginative inventions, leading audiences to perceive mimetic representation of a region in ruins. This possibility heightened Appalachians' concerns in 1972, as they had recently been featured in numerous televised documentaries. Both *The True Meaning of Pictures* and *Strangers and Kin: A History of the Appalachian Image* (1984) excerpt Walter Cronkite's *Depressed Area, USA* (1964) as well as *Deliverance* in order to contextualize anti-Appalachian stereotypes; in Baichwal's film, Adams—who grew up in Appalachia—argues that War on Poverty documentaries imbued him with shame.[1] Today, difficulties distinguishing between gothic aesthetics and the uneven economic development that inspires them may confound understanding of mountain spaces even more than overt stereotype. David Pratt argues that "most Americans are aware and wary of" the latter (99), and those of mountain slasher films have been gleefully mocked by the parody *Tucker and Dale vs. Evil* (2010). But as some reviews of *Winter's Bone* demonstrated, audiences can become so accustomed to seeing "hermetically-sealed" mountain cultures that alternate approaches fail to register (Nochimson 53; Wilding; see also French; and Macauley 29).

This concern about how previously circulated images shape viewers' interpretations is central to Baichwal's documentary and appears prominently in Granik's commentary concerning *Winter's Bone*. Granik's presentation of landscape diverges somewhat from Woodrell's novel, which emphasizes family ancestry: there, merely looking at a stone fencerow enables the protagonist, Ree Dolly, to "conjure" and relate to her forerunners' "pioneer lives," and her problems are similarly linked with "bloodline customs" (loc. 364, 794). Woodrell's less condensed and often focalized narrative enables him to combine this fascination with the past with more contemporary referents: Ree tends to make such observations when high, for example, and also modulates her mood through such ambient audiorecordings as "*Alpine*

Dusk" (140). Granik, in contrast, feared that her compressed visual tale might struggle to overcome its antecedents: "you put three children on a porch in clothing that is well used and you've got [Depression-era photographer] Walker Evans!" (Macaulay 31). From the outset, she presents a region in which contemporary commodities and cultural traditions coexist—or where, as she noted in her initial research for the film, "wild game was being consumed for dinner" by a family whose "grandmother [. . .] works as a greeter at Wal-Mart" (29). Accordingly, the opening shot reveals children playing on trampolines and skateboards while the soundtrack features an a capella solo of what sounds—in theme and performance—like a traditional lullaby.[2]

Neither Granik nor Baichwal seeks to stop the gothic from haunting documentary and realism; rather, they pursue more fulfilling entanglements. Clover argues that in early rural gothic films, "the city approaches the country guilty," and gothic representations—horror plots and hauntings—suit the ensuing "blood feud" (128). Certainly, such critique is foregrounded in *Deliverance*. When the mountain sheriff (played by Dickey) says that he would "like to see this town die peaceful," he refers not to degenerate residents but to an imminent flood: the river, as established early in the narrative, is being dammed to provide energy for Atlanta. As the character Ed leaves the area, he sees coffins being unearthed for reburial elsewhere; relations between city and country have disturbed even the dead, who, the closing scene suggests, may forever disrupt Ed's rest also. As more recent scholars celebrate how early rural slasher films highlighted exploitative economic, ecological, and even international relations, they question whether contemporary entries hew to this purpose; what seems certain is that recent horror films offer their pleasures chiefly to a generic community, which now has—in festivals, Internet activities, remakes, sequels, and parodies—unprecedented means to cohere (Soles; Bell; Blake 128–47; Middleton; Craig and Fradley 85–86).[3] By pursuing what Dimock calls the exogenous connections of rural gothic, however, we can find alternate mutations where undead elements appear in films overtly concerned with mountain lives.

Uncanny Relations

Baichwal's opening uncannily combines an impassioned, chanting voice and an empty black screen; while the voice's source remains mysterious, the words distinguish between people who will and will not get to heaven. If, as Michel Chion argues, such "acousmatic sound [. . .] constitut[es] a dramatic technique in itself"—which, in fiction films, often introduces "evil, awe-inspiring, or otherwise powerful characters"—Baichwal's usage suggests even greater potential for alarm (72). Viewers affiliated with charismatic faiths—particularly as practiced in Appalachian accents—might brace themselves for stereotypical depiction; others, meanwhile, might expect a theme of apocalyptic cultural hostility.

Ultimately, this introduction prepares viewers to explore representation and stereotype by alluding to a film that flaunted the latter. As the voice continues, the screen fades into images of thick forest, presented first from above and then from amid using a tracking shot to produce a sense of undecipherable depth: trees in the foreground relentlessly prevent the eye from determining what might be hidden behind. This disjunction between scenery and soundtrack echoes *Deliverance*'s opening,[4] and the formal echo becomes thematic as the film shifts to Adams's photographs. Shot with a large-format camera using often extreme angles and stark illumination, some of these human figures resemble shiny dolls while others lurk in shadow. Like the local residents sought out for *Deliverance,* many of Adams's subjects feature distinct physiognomies due to congenital defect, age, or performative flair. Meanwhile, on the film's soundtrack, the preacher's voice yields to birdsong, which heightens the gothic tone; matching much of *Deliverance*'s soundtrack, these chirps underscore the uncanny coexistence of the natural and the *"unearthly"* (Welling 27).

The last in this series of shots, however, foregrounds the stakes of such representation by revealing an exhibit of Adams's photographs at Chicago's Catherine Edelman Gallery. The sequence's editing suggests that these diverse realms, whether geographic or representational, connect across a chasm. With each shift of locale—from mountain greenery to photographic space to art gallery—the image zooms into a dark detail as the screen fades to black and then fades in from yet another obscure space: a bit of bark, a photographic shadow, an urban alley. The fact that scene and soundtrack finally coincide in the gallery—the sounds of patrons as they mill about and chat—announces the film's focus on how these images circulate, from their origins in Adams's shooting sessions through their reception.

Throughout, interpretations vary according to experience. The sister of two of Adams's developmentally disabled subjects, for example, argues that "the true meaning of pictures" emerges from the photographer's effort to understand life in an economically depressed region. Some art critics, however, confess to wondering whether the persons photographed might have incestuous parentage, would prove dangerous in a dark alley, or could even comprehend their own photographs. Dwight Billings, a senior scholar in Appalachian studies, worries that "the stories" told in Adams's photographs "are left to the reader to imagine," a challenge approached through the influence of "100 years of stereotypes."

Such disagreements concerning the images' "meaning" are exacerbated by generic instability. Adams refuses categorization, claiming to produce "authentic" images of hardship while repudiating any "limits" to documentary: "a portrait of a culture" can also be "a self-portrait"—"conscious and subconscious together, for me." This overlap between the mimetic and the uncannily imaginative—Adams, though not specifically psychoanalytic in his self-assessment, emphasizes the influence of memories, associations, and affects—complies with aesthetic theory: Tzvetan Todorov argues that "uncanny" literature does not defy "the laws of reason" but only feels as if it must, because it introduces a sinister strangeness to readers' understanding of the world (46). Adams, too, seeks to disorient: sensitive to anti-Appalachian stereotypes and identifying with the region, he suggests that greater understanding must result from urban residents' questioning their worldview. But the photographs' disturbing peculiarity could be thwarted if viewers understand them as typical of their region.[5]

Baichwal's documentary works to avert that problem. As Laura Mulvey argues of the relationship between still and moving images, situating Adams's photographs amid film of Adams's subjects conveys that the latter more effectively capture actuality, which is "animate, moving, alive" (52). This distinction is intensified by the qualities of Adams's images—black-and-white and shaped by pointedly artificial light. The photographs' status as documentary record is effaced as we observe their subjects in richly vocal action, noting that even the moving images are incomplete. When we see the descendants of a family also represented in Adams's archival film, for example, we note who has died over the passing of years; as another family gathers to be interviewed, this animated domestic occasion reveals the camera's inability to frame the event. Amid these unavoidably limited records, viewers can better appreciate photography's distinct power, which is to capture what Roland Barthes calls "a closed field of forces" at an isolated moment: an array of social and imaginative relationships—between the posing subject and that subject's interiority, the posing subject and surrounding persons (in and outside of the photographic scene, especially the photographer), and all of these and eventual viewers (13–15, 20). Observing how Adams's images come into being, the film—in contrast to Adams's book titles *Appalachian Legacy* (1998) and *Appalachian Lives* (2003)—resists the idea that they represent a social category.

Freed from such responsibility, their uncanniness—which, in Sigmund Freud's formulation, emerges from a familiar but repressed fear—can aptly be located in what they evoke for viewers ("The Uncanny" [2003] 147–48). In one scene, for example, siblings Homer and Selina—whose developmental distinctness is such that family members call them "the kids" even as they approach middle age—are posing for a photograph that requires them to approach each other closely, mouths open as if for erotic embrace. Despite their previously displayed affection for Adams, they seem, at that moment, inhibited, as if uncertain what they should do, what Adams wants, or whether those mandates align. Accordingly, any discomfort viewers feel as the photographs evoke issues of sexuality, propriety, or surveillance aligns us with Selina and Homer; we receive the vision they uneasily participated in creating. Rather than simply consuming images of distant bodies, we recognize our mutual participation in a pictorial economy that vexes and stimulates thought. Without condoning or condemning Adams's art, the film highlights how his gothicism assembles rural and metropolitan persons and places in relation—connections too often imagined thoughtlessly and practiced exploitatively.

Weight on the Living

Where Baichwal's documentary questions whether aesthetic practices exploit social hierarchies, *Winter's Bone* explores the more classically gothic concern of economic exploitation. Jacques Derrida observes this linkage even in Karl Marx's oeuvre, which is marked by a "rich spectrology"; these philosophers, however, differ concerning how to treat gothic hauntings. For Derrida, writing after the triumphantly proclaimed capitalist "end of history," Marx functions as a ghost (*revenant*) in himself, a critique and vision that must return (105, 14, 10). This investment in mourning trauma, which creates "ghost[s] [. . .] which give one the most to think about—and to do," aligns well with recent literary studies—perhaps especially concerning the U.S. South—and has long shaped scholarship on the U.S. gothic novel (Derrida, *Specters* 98; Gwin; Fiedler). But Marx preferred "exorcism [. . .] in the name of living presence": rather than submitting to past social and economic structures which seek to haunt the living—contemplating the ghost with such compassion as to identify with it—those who seek social change must "have the ghost's hide [. . .] possess it without letting oneself be possessed by it" (Derrida, *Specters* 106, 170, 132). This latter approach better matches that of *Winter's Bone*'s teenaged heroine, whose problem is not only, in Marx's words, that "the tradition of all dead generations weighs like a nightmare on the brains of the living" but also that her father, Jessup, has offered her home as collateral for his bail bond (595). The property sustaining the lives of her two young siblings, her near-catatonic mother, and herself has been usurped, in effect, by a ghost, as Jessup has disappeared—murdered for "snitching," as she soon deduces. In order to evacuate his legally constituted debt to the system that tried to contain and discipline him, Ree must situate Jessup definitively beyond its grasp: that is, in the realm of the dead. Largely forswearing the mourning process, she seeks and ultimately dismembers his corpse.

Much as Ree defies the mandate—repeatedly encountered in her quest—to accept Jessup's newly ineffable and unlocatable status, the film repeatedly evokes gothic tropes only to repudiate them. Slasher elements detailed by Clover—the individualized (stalking) point of view of the camera, the abjectly terrified and somewhat androgynous heroine, the monstrous family, and the "Terrible Place" (30–47)—abound in *Winter's Bone,* but never with quite the effects expected in the genre. As Ree trudges across the gray, hilly wooded landscape so familiar in cinematic horror, the camera—despite the ominous music in these scenes—never assumes the position of an attacker. Far less sexual and feminine than her novelistic counterpart, who has had diverse sexual experiences and seems to own only dresses,[6] this Ree is swathed in denim and sweatshirts with no apparent time to think of sex. (The same may not be true of her male kin, who routinely—and alarmingly—squeeze her face and gaze into it as if trying to determine what to do with her.) But where the "Final Girl" responds to threats with fear and violence, Ree—who is, after all, part of the dangerous family—negotiates almost unflappably. At one gothic apex, Ree seeks the syndicate's patriarch, Thump, at a cattle auction, where camera movement, editing, motion, and soundtrack align her with the whirling animals awaiting slaughter. Immediately afterward, when she appears in his yard, she is attacked, beaten past consciousness, and awakens in a barn; the first shots are of chains and meat hooks. Ree, however, merely argues that Jessup has paid—she suspects with his life—for his infractions and that her family should not be left to suffer. Eventually, the matriarchs who tortured her agree—showing some kindness even as one of them removes Jessup's hands with a chain saw.

These generic reversals situate Ree in a world of financial exigency but allow her to imagine a future. Holding Jessup's arm above the water where his corpse lies (evoking the end of *Deliverance*), she convulses in grief and horror but ultimately accepts the view—voiced by Thump's wife, Merab—that dead bodies, like living ones, cannot be extricated from economic relations. (Assuring Ree that Jessup would support her actions, Merab also details the law's exacting standards of proof: "You'll need both hands or sure as shit they'll say he cut one off to keep from going to prison. They know that trick.") Packing the limbs in a plastic bag and claiming they were left on her porch, she delivers them to the sheriff and later smiles triumphantly when her deed is cleared. The film unequivocally establishes her as a compassionate character, but familial feeling—especially for her younger siblings—requires that she defeat the plotline, noted by scholars of the gothic, in which living characters fail to expunge the dead's claim on their property (Watkiss 2; McClanahan). Where Jessup's brother, Teardrop, expects to end "toes up" because he cannot resist vengeance, Ree jettisons even mementos when she expects her family to become homeless. Her success in reclaiming the deed links the film to the coming-of-age tradition, as she manages to claim a distinct identity nonetheless affiliated with her extended family: "a Dolly, bred and buttered." But it does not negate the burdens of the present: as she lovingly says to her siblings in the film's final line, "I'd be lost without the weight of you two on my back."

In 2010, such precariousness was hardly unique to the Ozarks. In his State of the Union address—delivered the week *Winter's Bone* won the Grand Jury Prize at Sundance—President Obama compared the nation's continuing economic "test" to those confronted during World War II, the civil rights movement, and the Great Depression. He did note that "small towns and rural communities have been hit especially hard," and seven months earlier, Nick Reding's widely reviewed book *Methland: The Death and Life of an American Small Town* made the same point in terms relevant to Granik's film. Reports concerning methamphetamine, like those surrounding many drugs, tend to overstate use in ways that demonize people demarcated by race, class, and/or locale as threats to normative citizens; because meth is deemed a "white-trash drug," stereotypes used to promote greater social control often stem from the savage-hillbilly tradition (Linnemann 39–46).[7] But Reding, to his credit, situated meth amid economic changes that required longer, harder labor amid dwindling pay, globalization, and corporate abuse; such views resonated with an audience still reeling from the financial crisis of 2007–8. Related concerns were abundantly represented at Sundance in domestic and global documentary and fiction films; journalism concerning the festival focused on financial threats facing independent cinema itself (Lippard; Barnes; McClintock and Swart). To revisit Clover's account of geographic relations, by this era "the city approaches the country" less guilty, on the whole, than in a state of somewhat shared—if imperfectly recognized—vulnerability.

Granik's film, focused closely on Ree's story line, offers little sociological reflection beyond what can be gleaned from mise-en-scène, which is not insubstantial: in the few scenes shot at the local school, for example, we see teenagers learning infant care and practicing military drills. But the one segment directly concerned with economic relations is, fittingly, the film's most gothic; overtly referencing cinematic history, it is shot in monochrome and matted to a smaller aspect ratio. Here, the soundtrack is relentlessly grating, combining minor chords with a chain saw's sporadic raging; unlike the relatively long deep-focus shots elsewhere in the film, camera movement and editing for this brief passage are rapid and erratic, featuring close-ups of twitchy forest animals and vertiginous shots of trees that seem to spiral above the lens. At this diegetic moment, Ree has taken a painkiller after her beating, and her dreams are haunted by Teardrop's warning that, when she loses her property, the next owners will "go out and cut them 100 year old woods down to nubs." Believing her situation hopeless, she nonetheless refuses to sell this timber and thereby destroy the landscape that, throughout the film, has provided what little nutritional and emotional sustenance she receives. Her nightmare, however, exceeds this narrative exposition to provide what Adam Lowenstein, referring to horror film, calls an "allegorical moment," "a shocking collision of film, spectator, and history where registers of bodily space and historical time are disrupted, confronted, and intertwined" (2).

Here, Granik manages both to differentiate her film from the representational history that marginalizes mountain residents and to rescue the ecological and economic critiques embedded in those films. While this nightmare's cinematic codes cite the rural-slasher tradition, the referent is more mundane: rather than human evisceration, we witness only the trembling and fleeing of squirrels, the flapping of roadside crows, and the billowing of smoke. But this banality paradoxically intensifies the scene's dual encapsulation: in an era when the future of the human species—let alone our social geographies—is in doubt, those palpitating squirrels emblematize the history of resource extraction in rural areas, which leaves residents with a devastated ecology and no economic opportunities. More broadly, the camera's movements suggest the contemporary confusion that leaves individuals and communities worldwide whirling, uncertain how to secure a livelihood.

This is not to say that the film forges a sense of imagined commonality across space: its method is subtle and probably requires time to process. As Steve Neale argues, generic systems "provide spectators with a means of recognition and understanding [. . .] becoming a form of cultural knowledge," and this disruptive, vigorously multigenre film left reviewers admiringly debating how to classify the work (158–59; Denby; O'Hehir; Scott; Turan). In an era where consumption often takes place long after production—and in contexts that allow for interrupted playback—viewers' verdicts may be delayed. (*Deliverance*, as it happens, was released long before the technologies that facilitated its notoriety.) Meanwhile, though aesthetic innovation may stimulate geographic insight, broader social change may be required also—and may come. Awaking from her nightmare, Ree continues to pursue options for her family, but her fate ultimately depends on the emergence of some decency in her erstwhile persecutors. One would prefer a more reliable resource.

NOTES

I thank Emily Satterwhite for drawing my attention to the representational legacy of rural horror through her terrific conference paper years ago, Barbara Ching for urging me to analyze Shelby Lee Adams's work, the University of Mississippi graduate students in my class on southern documentaries for their willingness to explore *The True Meaning of Pictures*, and the editors of this volume—and the audience at the MLA panel they organized in 2013—for encouraging me to pursue this project.

1. *Strangers and Kin* was produced by Appalshop, a regional film workshop located in Whitesburg, Kentucky, and dedicated to countering damaging images of the region. In documentary, as in horror, Appalachia has received greater attention than the Ozarks—both during the War on Poverty (Blevins 221) and in government efforts to promote Tennessee Valley Authority initiatives. Elsewhere, Adams explains that he collaborated with filmmakers, only later discovering that his neighbors found the results offensive (Adams 11–16).

2. Sheet music to "Missouri Waltz," later chosen as Missouri's state song with racial epithets removed, was first published in 1914; it may have been adapted from an existing song (Studwell and Schueneman vii, 48).

3. For the workings and significance of generic communities, see Altman (156–94).

4. There, acousmatic voices speak *about* Appalachia, while a tracking shot reveals thick forest yielding to dam construction. This section of Baichwal's soundtrack may have been taken from Adams's archive, which is incorporated into the documentary: Hort Collins, one of Adams's photographic subjects, maintains a small church.

5. I have made a similar argument concerning Erskine Caldwell's use of the grotesque, which is often linked with Southern Gothic, and Adams cites Caldwell's aesthetics as an inspiration (Duck 87–96; Adams 18).

6. Woodrell's Ree is not stereotypical either, but flashbacks allow him to explore her particularities—including a mostly lesbian erotic life—more fully. Both characters hunt, gut their prey, and nurture their siblings, though the novelistic version is sometimes impatient.

7. For this reason, analyses that link criminality in *Winter's Bone* strictly to local history and culture—such as Moon and Talley's discussion of the Ozarks as a "shatter zone" at the periphery of governed, capitalist society—seem too readily to accept popular narratives concerning drug syndicates and usage without considering how local markets in methamphetamines link to broader distribution networks and consumption patterns. Attending also to the representational history of crime—as in Harrison's description of the Dolly family as "rural Corleones"—better enables critics to appreciate the film's naturalistic style while also recognizing its relations to fictional genres.

15

BURYING THE (UN)DEAD AND HEALING THE LIVING
Choctaw Women's Power in LeAnne Howe's Novels

KIRSTIN L. SQUINT

In the poem "Evidence of Red," from LeAnne Howe's collection of the same name, the importance of the female in the matrilineal, matrilocal Choctaw society is evidenced in this line describing the moment of emergence: "In minutes we tunneled through / corn woman's navel into tinges / of moist red men and women" (5). Here, Choctaw peoples are depicted as coming into existence through a birth by Corn Woman, Ohoyo Osh Chisba. Historian Michelene Pesantubbee details the interdependent relationship of the feminine, the earth, and the corn plant for the Choctaw: "Corn itself not only provided sustenance for the people of this world, but through its roots and stalks tied the three parts of the world together—Above, Below, and This World. Because the corn plant crossed the boundaries of the three worlds it was considered powerful. It was beloved. It was beloved woman. And because women had primary responsibility for the corn, they were the mediators between the fertility and power of the corn and the Choctaw people" (119–20).

The disconnection of Choctaws from the sacred ideal of corn began with the collapse of the Green Corn Ceremony, an annual period of diplomacy, as a result of a severe population reduction in the eighteenth century. English and French colonialism had led to disease, slave raids, civil war, and intertribal wars, which made it difficult to hold a ceremony that required the contribution of an entire community and its neighbors. The collapse of the

Green Corn Ceremony for the Choctaws meant a lost opportunity to purify the community and to carry out the annual reinforcement of the importance of women to society (Pesantubbee 132–33).

Pesantubbee's central thesis in her historical study of Choctaw women is that the role of "beloved women" declined because of contact with European patriarchal cultures;[1] however, she also contends that the importance of women to Choctaw society can be traced historically through other cultural practices such as funeral rites. LeAnne Howe has taken issue with Pesantubbee's claim, arguing that "today, there isn't an organization [. . .] or community group at home that isn't run, or managed by women. You want something done, go to the women. I see that as a continuance of something very old" ("Choctawan Aesthetics" 220). Howe's novels, *Shell Shaker* and *Miko Kings: An Indian Baseball Story*, highlight centers of female power mobilized against patriarchal European colonizers and their cultural legacies, illustrating the author's conviction that Choctaw women have maintained their traditional position of cultural strength.

Both *Shell Shaker* and *Miko Kings* are novels replete with women working individually and in groups to heal people and communities from the pain and division resulting from European and U.S. settler colonialism. *Shell Shaker*'s Auda Billy sees herself as a continuation of women leaders in her family, and it was her backing of Redford McAlester, along with the other women in the community, including the Choctaw women's society, the Intek Aliha, that got him elected chief (21). The power of the Intek Aliha is also referenced in the section of the novel set in the eighteenth century, when Anoleta is plotting to kill Red Shoes (181). In *Miko Kings,* Howe describes how the Four Mothers Society, "an organization that boasts twenty-four thousand Choctaws, Creeks, Chickasaws, and Cherokees as members" (116), works to fight the allotment of Indian lands by organizing at stickball games and "burning the Indian agent's outhouses, sand houses, and train depots all over Indian Territory" (107). Rooted in the Cherokee Keetoowah Society, the Four Mothers Society emerged when members of the Choctaw, Creek, Chickasaw, and Cherokee tribes organized to fight plans for allotment and find ways to return to traditionalism (Fogelson 169). Though the Four Mothers Society was not strictly a women's society, its name reflects the reverence of women's political and cultural strength by Southeastern Indian nations.

While Howe's novels depict a number of powerful individual Choctaw women, two of the most notable are Ezol Day of *Miko Kings* and Shakbatina of *Shell Shaker*. Both women are ancestors and spirits who find ways to effect change in the contemporary era, ameliorating the painful histories of individuals and communities torn apart by colonialism, racism, or greed. Even though they are not referred to as such, Ezol and Shakbatina are kinds of *alikchi*, or healers, intervening in the lives of their descendents, guiding them to paths of reconciliation with their pasts. The *alikchi* figure is discussed most in *Miko Kings,* and it is Ezol Day who explains the complexity of Choctaw healing practices to her descendent, Lena. Lena remembers going to see a Choctaw *alikchi* for a healing ceremony when she was ten years old, and she describes what happened when tornado clouds appeared: "Grandmother and I had to hold on to a big cottonwood tree to keep from blowing away. I was terrified, but the *Alikchi* kept on pitching his ax into the ground until the earth opened up a large crater. Then, as the winds died down, he walked counter-clockwise around and around the crater. After awhile the clouds disappeared and the sky was blue again" (42). When Ezol, an autodidactic (meta)physicist, explains that mathematical codes at the heart of rituals make it possible to control the cosmos, Lena is skeptical. Ezol argues that the Western distinction between scientific and sacred knowledge does not apply to Choctaw beliefs and uses another example to drive her point home: "Indians in North and South America built cosmic observatories in the form of mounds and pyramids, very complicated structures that require geometry. A stomp dance and a baseball game mimic natural phenomena, such as tornado winds, that are counter-clockwise. Why can't you believe that the *Alikchi* knew how to interact with the chaos?" (43).

Ezol, herself, has found a way to "interact with the chaos," by virtue of her physical presence in a room with her cousin's granddaughter nearly a hundred years after her death. Her interest in the topic of exploring the dimensions of time and space manifested as a young woman when she wrote a paper called "Moving Bodies in Choctaw Space," the premise of which was that Choctaws and Euro-Americans experienced time and space differently, given their differing linguistic expressions of time, particularly through verbs and verb tenses (38). She exemplifies her theory through the word *Okchamali*, meaning "both blue and green" (38). Her extended argument is that the word also signifies "life," given that it might also suggest "the blue sky and green swamplands" of the emergence place of the Choctaw peoples, attributing a temporal quality to the term (38). She tells Lena: "After I understood that there might be other spacetime terms embedded in our language, I looked for them in plants that contain sacred geometric expressions. I studied the patterns in our stomp dances and baseball games. Words make equations the same way that numbers connect us to other dimensions and to *okchamali*" (39). Lena begins to understand when she remembers her own departure from Jordan, where she lived as a freelance journalist. After her Palestinian lover, Sayyed, is killed in a terrorist bomb, she hears a voice accompanying the call to prayer, repeating the phrase, *"The time has come to return home"* (41). Lena believes that her own repetition of the phrase four times, followed by her return home, gives credence to Ezol's theory about a relationship between speech acts, time, and space.

Using her understanding of linguistic power, Ezol transcends time, space, and even death to visit her descendent in order for the story of the Miko Kings all-Indian baseball team to be told. The two women write the story together, Ezol giving Lena clues about the events of the past and life in early-twentieth-century Indian Territory, while Lena researches Ezol's diary and other artifacts she finds in a satchel in the wall of her grandmother's house, which she is renovating. In fact, the renovation of the house is a central symbol of the "renovation" of the Miko Kings' story, which comes about as a result of Ezol and Lena's joint efforts. The story they write together is itself a healing ceremony, one that is a balm for Ezol's pain, Lena's isolation, and at least some of the suffering caused by the allotment of Indian lands.[2]

Ezol's desire to heal herself and Lena likely comes from the painful events of her own childhood and her own experience with an *alikchi* as a child. Her father was killed by "invading *Nahollas* [white people] [. . .] for twenty five cents" (147), and she also lost both her mother and sister to illness, ultimately living in an orphanage. Before she was sent away, however, her Aunt Fancy took her to an *alikchi* who healed her from attacks by an eye tree, which she illustrates in her journal (135). The healer "winnowed the branches and sucked out places of its bark from within that plagued [her]" (137). Both her friend Justina Maurepas and Lena think the eye tree may be akin to cataracts, which Justina has experienced; however, Lena explores the idea more closely: "Normally cataracts would have blurred her vision not enhanced it, as the drawing suggests. The eyes almost look like seven angry fish. When I look up 'cataract' in the dictionary I find it means floodgate (of heaven)" (185). This passage suggests that the eye tree has given Ezol the ability to see and possibly even exist in multiple times and spaces, a seemingly supernatural ability.

Ezol was an isolated child, and she sees Lena living a similar existence, which is part of the reason she travels through time to help her descendent write the story of the Miko Kings, explaining at the novel's end: "I may not be your blood grandmother—but I should have been. And I have always been with you in spirit. That is the true story I came to tell" (221). Ezol had planned to marry Lena's grandfather, Blip Bleen. Instead, Blip was seduced by Cora, Ezol's cousin, whose ulterior motive was to entice Blip to throw the final game of the Twin Territories' series against Ft. Sill's Seventh Cavalry on behalf of her gambler boyfriend, Beau Hash. Not only did Cora betray Ezol, but she also appears to have had a hand in her death. Per a 1907 newspaper clipping, the authorities suspect that Cora was involved in starting the fire that burned the Miko Kings' office, and where, unbeknownst to her, Ezol was trying to save the book of shares from gamblers who would take over the baseball team (205–6). Ezol's spirit reaches out to her descendent to ameliorate what she sees as a cycle of trauma. Lena had run from her life in Oklahoma because her mother died, her father was often physically absent, and her grandmother spent a lifetime punishing herself for the betrayal and possible homicide of her cousin. Lena doesn't return until the voice urged her back during a call to prayer in Jordan. Chanette Romero argues that the beliefs of people of color, as depicted in the works of LeAnne Howe and others, "in an ever-present link among themselves, ancestors, spirit beings, deities, and the animate earth, provide a meaningful connection to the past and future necessary for survival" (58). The link between Ezol and Lena creates a temporal and discursive space for them to recover and rewrite the story of the Miko Kings, thus healing themselves and their tribe.

Like Ezol Day, Shakbatina is the spirit *alikchi* of *Shell Shaker* who sacrifices herself for her daughter in the eighteenth century and who saves her twentieth-century female descendent, Auda Billy. Funeral ceremonies bookend the narrative, highlighting the importance of death rituals for the Choctaw and affirming the words of Horatio Bardwell Cushman, who, in 1899, claimed that "no people on earth paid more respect to the dead, than the Choctaws did and still do; or preserved with more affectionate veneration the graves of their ancestors" (191). Pesantubbee asserts that Choctaw women were often responsible for traditional funeral rites because of their relationship to corn and its annual cycle of life and death: "The roots of corn reached into the Below World, the world of fertility (or life) and death. [. . .] Women were associated with that power because Ohoyo Osh Chisba, a woman, became corn, and women of This World were responsible for the cultivation of corn as well as other plants" (152). Menstruation, an embodiment of fertility and death, underscored this relationship. Pesantubbee describes the role of women in Choctaw funeral rites such as eighteenth-century bone-picking rituals, nineteenth-century pole-pulling ceremonies, and periods of intense wailing that would help the spirits unite with ancestors in the afterworld (154, 165).

The first funeral ceremony represented in the novel is the bone picking of Shakbatina, who has transcended time in order to come to the aid of her female descendents and to heal her tribe as a whole. Shakbatina has sacrificed her own life for that of her daughter, Anoleta, the eighteenth-century doppelganger of the twentieth-century character Auda. Shakbatina embraces her coming death, declaring: "On this day I will follow our Choctaw ancestors to our Mother Mound at Nanih Waiya. When released from the bone picking, I will grow and sprout up like green corn. From the mound I will watch over our people. Do not cry for me, I am a fast grower" (8). Shakbatina's speech links her to the power of Ohoyo Osh Chisba. The bone-picking ceremony that follows Shakbatina's death is one of the most striking moments in a novel replete with the violence of war, murder, and rape. Monika Siebert describes the multifaceted language of the scene, concluding: "Howe offers plenty of opportunities to assimilate what is taking place, even to deeply appreciate the terrifying—and sublime—beauty of the ritual. At the same time, however, she thwarts such assimilation, giving unrelenting play to the gruesomeness, potential horror even, of the traditional Choctaw practices she describes. She forces her readers to visualize crushed skulls, half-decayed bodies coming apart in other people's hands, and necrophilic sex" (110). For Siebert, the bone-picking ceremony is designed to upset attempts at cross-cultural understanding, a goal of multiculturalism, instead, creating a kind of "epistemological gap" (112) that resists full comprehension of Choctaw rituals by a mainstream audience. This is an interesting point, given the types of balancing acts many American Indian writers perform when envisioning an audience for their creative works;[3] however, I would argue that Howe's objective in her explicitly detailed representation is less about obfuscating ritualistic practice for non-Native readers and more about centering the text within a Choctaw worldview. In particular, the necrophilic elements of the ceremony underscore a relationship between fertility and death that begins with Ohoyo Osh Chisba, whose legacy is performed in the bodies of women.

True to Shakbatina's pledge prior to the bone-picking ceremony to remain with her people, her spirit arrives on the 1991 autumnal equinox to help Auda, who has been raped by her former lover and the current Choctaw tribal leader, Redford McAlester. Shakbatina extends herself to her descendant, uniting past and present, in a shell-shaking ceremony: "Auda watches the spirit woman with turtle shells strapped to her ankles. She's big-breasted and wears a deerskin dress, bloodied at the neck and hem. Smoke rises from the turtle shells and forms a constellation on the ceiling. Auda knows the dance. Every spring she shakes shells with the other Indian women in Southeastern Oklahoma" (18). The ceremony has already linked the women symbolically through its continued practice, but Shakbatina's dancing creates a physical link between the two.

Shakbatina's shell-shaking ceremony also connects her own history and that of her descendent back to a much earlier female ancestor. The first conflict between Choctaws and Europeans referenced in the novel is the 1540 battle that pitted the forces of Hernando de Soto against those of Tuscalusa (Howe, "Author's Note" 226). Howe's fictional representation of the meeting is a creation story in which a woman becomes the first shell shaker, both mythic and powerful, through her ceremonial act of love. Shell shakers are traditionally women in Eastern Woodland tribes who "stomp dance" at various ceremonies, providing rhythmic accompaniment to the singing and dancing with their turtle-shell leg rattles (Howard and Kurath 1). The first shell shaker of whom Howe writes is the wife of Tuscalusa and who Shakbatina calls Grandmother of Birds. Because Tuscalusa has heard that De Soto is a dangerous enemy, an *Osano* (bloodsucker), he prepares for a battle with the Spanish in order to lure the invaders away from his people.[4] According to Shakbatina, Grandmother of Birds danced "for four days and nights [. . .] extolling the heroics of the man she loved" (2). Grandmother's ankles bleed from the continuous dancing, and this sacrifice moves Miko Luak, the fire's spirit, to take her prayers to the Autumnal Equinox, Itilauichi, who in turn, gives her a song to "make things even" (2). This ceremony is passed down matrilinealy through the novel and operates as a tool for "evening out" personal, social, and cultural injustices. In the case of Tuscalusa's battle with De Soto, the Choctaw men were defeated and their bodies mutilated. Grandmother does not mourn her husband; rather, she sings the song given to her by Itilauichi, and she and her sisters take flight in the form of birds to found the seven original Choctaw towns.

The second funeral ceremony represented in *Shell Shaker* is held in the late twentieth century for Redford McAlester, the incarnation of the eighteenth-century character Red Shoes, and is presided over by Delores Love. Red Shoes had claimed to be the figure known as Imataha Chitto, translated as "the greatest giver" (22), the Choctaw leader who would unite the tribe. Despite his claims, Red Shoes' actions prove that he is not this figure; in fact, his relationship with the English colonizers actually divides the tribe. His contemporary iteration sells out his people by dealing with the Mafia. Given the power of women in Choctaw society, Shakbatina does not believe the Imataha Chitto would be a man (185). Though many tribal traditions have changed as a result of European and U.S. settler colonialism, the twentieth-century character Isaac Billy notes that his sister Susan, Auda's mother, still follows the matrilineal tradition by caring for the personal possessions of their powerful shell-shaker ancestor (60). Howe's presentation of strong female figures reclaiming their roles as leaders in Choctaw society subverts a historically patriarchal European and Euro-American culture, and the murder of McAlester following his act of sexual violence against Auda suggests that the women will not succumb to a colonizing male superstructure.

Delores Love is, in fact, the Imataha Chitto, uniter of her tribe, and another of the novel's *alikchi* figures. She has experienced her people's varied stages of history: tribalism, dispersal, colonization, and decolonization. In the eighteenth century, she is Mantema,[5] the Imataha Chitto who is bayoneted to death in the battle against Red Shoes and the *Inkilish Okla* (English people). During her childhood in the twentieth century, she first runs away from a government boarding school and then again away from her tribe in Oklahoma with her sister. Delores and Dovie become actresses in California who bill themselves as "The Love Maidens of The Five Civilized Tribes" (117). Even though Delores despises her Indianness (155), she is willing to exploit it, buying into the role of a Hollywood stereotype for material gain. That changes when her mother dies, and she returns to the tribe and learns the funeral traditions from Nowatima—Susan and Isaac Billy's grandmother—a descendent of Shakbatina. The matrilineal sharing of this knowledge speaks to the connection between women and death rites through their original association with corn.

After Delores learns the pole-pulling ceremony[6] and traditional songs from Nowatima, she conducts her mother's funeral and begins to sing for others, creating a resurgence of interest in Choctaw traditions. Delores has come full circle from her tribal self, through an internally colonized self, to a decolonized self, inspiring other Choctaws to embrace their cultural beliefs. Delores believes that "her role as modern *foni miko*, bone picker, is the only useful thing she's ever done" (146). This adherence to and faith in her cultural traditions leads to her vision of what must be done with the body of Redford McAlester in order for tribal healing to commence. Delores takes McAlester's body to the sacred ground near the mound of Choctaw emergence, Nanih Waiya, also known as Oholiptopa Ishki, or Beloved Mother (Pesantubbee 23; Swanton 30). She is accompanied on her journey by Isaac, her lover in both the eighteenth and twentieth centuries, and teenagers from the Oklahoma Choctaw Nation; they are met by relatives from the Mississippi Band of Choctaws. Echoing the actions of Grandmother of Birds, seven shell-shaking women from Oklahoma, Mississippi, Louisiana, Texas, and Alabama aid Delores in the ceremony, one that also includes burying Red Shoes/Red McAlester with numerous material possessions so that his spirit will remain in the sacred mud of the Nanih Waiya. According to Pesantubbee, it was not uncommon for Choctaws to be buried with possessions and even spouses and friends who would accompany them to the afterlife (153). In the case of McAlester, Delores Love and Isaac Billy will be his companions, sacrificing themselves to guard over his spirit.

The journey eastward, upon which Delores, Isaac, and many other Choctaws embark is one that represents a community united with the goal to make itself whole, rather than one divided by death, disease, and enemy arms. It is significant that Delores learned the traditional funeral songs from Nowatima, who was also keeper of the oral history of her people's displacement from their homelands. At the same time that Delores gains the knowledge to bury the dead, she learns of the terrors of the Trail of Tears, in which her ancestors suffered from disease, malnutrition, hopelessness, and death (Howe, *Shell Shaker* 148). In "Weeping for the Lost Matriarchy," Kay Givens McGowan argues that Removal failed, citing the fact that Southeastern Native peoples maintain communities throughout the region (62). Though this is true in the sense that the Southeast was not entirely ethnically cleansed of its Indigenous peoples, it is also true that Removal succeeded, as evidenced by the many Indian nations in Oklahoma, what was to be "Indian Territory." *Shell Shaker* both demonstrates the failure of Indian Removal and performs what Eric Gary Anderson has termed "a strategic counter-removal" by representing the journey back east to the mother mound in the original Choctaw homelands.

In her study of contemporary Native American literature of the South, Melanie Benson Taylor takes issue with such an optimistic reading of the return of Howe's characters to the Nanih Waiya, making the cogent point that Delores and Isaac are "killed by the casino overlords who follow them in pursuit of the dirty money they have taken from Redford's stash" (64). Yet, Taylor's focus on the novel's failure to "slay the demons of materialism" (62) misses the mark when considering the novel's spiritual dimension. At least two major characters in the novel are actually spirits, and nearly all the major characters are linked across the centuries by spiritual aspects of themselves that transcend whatever material body they may inhabit. According to Pesantubbee: "Prior to the 1800s the Choctaw [. . .] believed that a person had two spirits, one that went to the afterworld and one that remained on earth restlessly wandering about its former habitation [. . .] if the spirit did not have everything it needed to travel and live in the afterworld, it would remain behind as it sought those desired items" (161–62). Clearly, Shakbatina's descendents, the Billy family, and Redford McAlester were spirits with unfinished business, and that business could not be finished until the novel's eighteenth-century wrongs were righted in the twentieth century. Isaac and Delores are aware that their deaths are self-sacrifices in order to "help [Red McAlester] stay put" (212) in his burial mound, saving the tribe from his greedy spirit.

As *Shell Shaker* suggests, unification of the Choctaws in the eighteenth century would have been the most dangerous scenario for the English colonizers; Shakbatina's survivance[7] has made this unification possible in the twentieth century. The implication is that a contemporary unification of the Choctaws is a step toward decolonization, continuing resistance against the descendants of English colonists. At the novel's end, Shakbatina acknowledges: "My story is an enormous undertaking. Hundreds of years in the making until past and present collide into a single moment" (222). Like Ezol Day, Shakbatina has found a way to transcend time and space in order to heal her descendents individually and communally. *Shell Shaker* is a novel comprising numerous ceremonies, all of which work toward the larger ceremonial event of the novel itself.[8] Shakbatina's (and the novel's) final words are "*Hekano*, I am finished talking" (222); thus, language signals the ceremony's end. Similarly, *Miko Kings* conflates language and ceremony in its last line, "the sacred [. . .] manifest in the flesh of the page" (221).

LeAnne Howe's powerful Choctaw ancestor spirits provide an interesting response to dominant cultural depictions of Indian ghosts in American literature. Renée Bergland has argued that in the early nineteenth century, "Indian ghosts shaped the nation and the national literature, constructing America as a haunted community rather than a simply imagined one" (102). Similarly, Annette Trefzer makes the point that in modernist southern fiction, "Native American presence is eclipsed and yet rendered in the signifier of the mound grave as a historical spirit that leaves its imprint on the land and its people" (3). In these contexts, it is significant that LeAnne Howe's ghosts are not haunting Euro-Americans; instead, they are helping to heal Choctaw communities haunted by a history of genocide and the continuing implications of U.S. settler colonialism. Achille Mbembe's conception of necropolitics or "contemporary forms of subjugation of life to the power of death [. . .] [that] profoundly reconfigure the relations among resistance, sacrifice, and terror" (39) is relevant when considering American Indian literatures. For Mbembe, singular examples of necropower are the plantation and the colony in which inhabitants are a kind of "*living dead*" (40), citing the current occupation of Palestine as "the most accomplished form of necropower" (27). Howe's depiction of a Choctaw journalist losing her Palestinian boyfriend to a terrorist bomb and then immediately choosing to return home to Oklahoma in *Miko Kings* is an urgent linking of diverse global sites of necropower. Chickasaw critic Jodi Byrd extends Mbembe's argument to Native Americans, claiming that "Indians [are] the original necropolitical affect of the living dead brought back to haunt cosmopolitan colonialism," and that it is only through the decolonizing works of LeAnne Howe and other Indigenous American writers and thinkers that "settler, arrivant, and native [can] apprehend and grieve together the violences of U.S. empire" (229). For Howe, one way to work through that grief is to represent sites of female power in the face of these violences, such as the women healers in her novels. As the author observed in a recent interview: "I'm trying to write myself healthy [...] by losing the wounds of these two hundred years, three hundred years [...] that I carry" ("The Native South").

NOTES

1. Pesantubbee explains that the honor of "beloved" would apply to "any person who had distinguished herself in any number of ways, [but] the most common descriptions of women are those who had participated in councils or became peace leaders" (2).

2. The General Allotment Act of 1887 is regarded by historians as one of a number of laws enacted throughout U.S. history with the goal of disenfranchising Native Americans of land, in this case, resulting "in a decrease of Indian-owned land from 138 million acres in 1887 to 52 million acres in 1934" (Ulrich 4).

3. See Jace Weaver's *That the People Might Live: Native American Literatures and Native American Community* and James Ruppert's *Mediation in Contemporary Native American Fiction* for more nuanced discussions of American Indian writing and audience.

4. Patricia Galloway elaborates in *Choctaw Genesis* on the historical evidence of the truly dangerous nature of Hernando de Soto's expedition through the Gulf Coast region: "The Spaniards' only consistent actions, by their own testimony, were demands for obedience to their king, questions about gold and other stones, abuse of hospitality through seizing and chaining bearers and raping women, and capture and imprisonment of chiefs or people they perceived as chiefs" (108).

5. A word meaning an official female messenger or someone "to go and carry or deliver something sacred or particular" (Pesantubbee 170; Swanton 121).

6. Sometime in the eighteenth century, pole pulling, which involved placing poles around a grave and then later removing them, replaced bone picking. More Christian-like ceremonies became dominant near the end of the nineteenth century (Pesantubbee 154).

7. One of Anishinaabe writer Gerald Vizenor's numerous neologisms, "survivance" suggesting both survival and resistance, through "an active sense of presence, the continuance of Native stories" (vii).

8. Leslie Marmon Silko's *Ceremony* is the seminal novel in American Indian literature read as ceremonial text.

16

THE INDIGENOUS UNCANNY
Spectral Genealogies in LeAnne Howe's Fiction

ANNETTE TREFZER

The South's cultural and historical identity has often been depicted in gothic terms, as a "benighted landscape, heavy with history and haunted by the ghosts of slavery" (Goddu 76). This perception of the South as the nation's abject, its uncanny oppositional image, a place of "gothic excesses and social transgressions" (76) has produced a literary tradition haunted by ghosts specific to this geopolitical location.[1] Scholars of southern literature, including Houston Baker and Patricia Yaeger, have long established that the South is a space made uncanny by a history of physical and political violence, racial and sexual trauma, and bodies left unburied. More recently, scholars of the indigenous South have begun to summon the region's "most deeply repressed ghosts" (Taylor 15) in an attempt at what Eric Anderson has termed "strategic counter-removal" ("South to a Red Place" 8).[2] While southern native texts are coming to life as part of a formerly ghosted regional canon and contributions by native women writers have been noted, I wish to examine more specifically the gendered nature of these women's texts. If southern women's literature represents a world whose thin veneer of everyday life cannot hide the "fantastic, unexpected and perpetually uncanny" as Yaeger so convincingly argues (*Dirt and Desire* 13), then the same is true for Indigenous women writers who also make their fictional homes in the South. Yaeger's study draws particular attention to the "occluded knowledge" in stories by southern women writers: "for white women, the gender and race practices that their characters know by heart and yet rarely acknowledge, for black women, a longing for lost epistemologies—the names, customs, revenants, and remnants for Africa" (*Dirt and Desire* 13), and for Indigenous women, we might add, the history of colonial violence and displacement. Native American women writers, like Choctaw writer LeAnne Howe, also have stories to tell about haunted homes and bodies.[3]

In Howe's fiction, the figure of the ghost hails from the spectral landscape of the native South to settle old scores and unsettle contemporary readers. Her novels *Shell Shaker* (2001) and *Miko Kings* (2007) sound gothic resonances and engage with the region's traumatic wounds as spirits ill at rest point at Indigenous dispossession and disrupt official historical narratives. Zooming in on the physical and psychological unsettlement from the Choctaw homelands, Howe's depiction of the colonial South in *Shell Shaker* confirms its abjection. However, zooming out from the origin lands of the Choctaws in Mississippi to their postremoval location in Oklahoma and other places in the world, she represents the South not as an embarrassing aberration but as part of a continuum of American colonialist and imperialist violence marked by the continued abuse of political power. On the one hand, Howe's novels draw on the Southern Gothic to address the trauma to the collective body of the community and to women's bodies more specifically. On the other hand, the narratives attempt to reformulate the workings of the Southern Gothic not only by invalidating the region's apparent exceptionalism, but by revising and adapting the literary strategies of the gothic genre.[4]

There are several types of haunting in Howe's fiction that directly connect with our expectations of the gothic: both *Shell Shaker* and *Miko Kings* feature family homes in which spirits go about. There are settings like the funeral scaffold where Koi Chitto is sinking his six-inch-long fingernails into the corpse of his dead wife to strip her flesh from her bones. Or the dank basement at Hampton School where Hope Little Leader watches a spider eat her lover: "First she peels back his head from his body, then cherishes his hands as food" (67), a horrifying vision that foreshadows the violent loss of his own hands. There are characters, like Hope's young mother, who "wastes away" and whose death scene is dramatically charged with classic gothic elements: the cabin became luminous, the wind howled violently, the house shook and rattled, her body had become almost transparent and her mouth hung open (64). But although both novels capitalize on the gruesomeness of gothic details, the narratives only partially embrace them and even mock them: think, for instance, of the humorously conspicuous name Lucius Mummy, the first baseman of the Miko Kings, or of the shape-shifting native spirits and their antics. We learn that cranky porcupine spirits are "the nervous types, prone to fits" (99) and see government agents morph into sniffing and barking Doberman pinschers in the blink of an eye (60). Clearly, Howe's fiction, though saturated with traditional gothic elements that produce anxiety, fear, and even terror, also includes ghostly voices, spirit appearances, and haunted places that do not attempt to produce this effect.

If we take as a classic Southern Gothic text, Poe's "The Fall of the House of Usher" (1839), with is decaying mansion and nerve-wracked protagonist, with its brooding family secrets and inward sense of the past as burden, we realize that there is a very different dimension to the uncanny in Howe's fiction: ghosts appear as shadowy traces of an absence—the absence of Lena's mother, for instance—and they appear not to destroy but to restore the southern native family. Spirits mend ruptured genealogies, restore powerful female ancestors, and provide a vital link to Indigenous histories. Thus, the appearance of the ghost in Howe's fiction leads us beyond the Southern Gothic and away from the American tradition's ubiquitous Indian burial grounds. When ghosts arise, they do so in direct opposition to the technique of literal and literary Indian removal.[5] The spirits in *Shell Shaker* and *Miko Kings* do not eulogize a bygone time and people; they do not support a "colonialist politics of mourning" over their absence or death.[6] On the contrary, these spirits produce a "healthy" haunting that reinstates memory and ancestry crucial to Indigenous survival in the present and moves beyond the gothic to embrace what I call the "Indigenous uncanny."

The uncanny is that which haunts, that which is frightening, eerie, spooky, and unsettling, what Sigmund Freud calls "unheimlich." As such it seems to stand in opposition to its antonym "heimlich," which refers to the homelike, familiar, and intimate. But because "heimlich" also means "secretive" and "sly," the seeming antonyms are in fact synonyms, as Freud points out in his famous 1919 essay "The Uncanny." An encounter with the uncanny thus relates to the rediscovery of something that is at once familiar and unsettling. "The sense of unsettledness in the word *unheimlich* is important," according to Bergland, "because it evokes the colonialist paradigm that opposes civilization to the dark and mysterious world of the irrational and savage" (11). But whereas Indians might seem to be "unheimlich" to settler cultures, the term, when used in the context of Native American fiction, gains new significance. When Howe claims access to the uncanny, it is not only to revise familiar colonialist hierarchies, but to redefine the condition of being un-settled in order to find a new home in it. In other words, in Howe's novels, the Indigenous uncanny is the unsettling process by which the un-homed find a new entrance to the original home, the womb, the "homeland." The guide figures to this home are spectral women who harness an uncanny power and potency as bearers of native culture.[7]

The opening chapter of *Shell Shaker* is written in the disembodied voice of Shakbatina, who traces Choctaw history back to precolonial times and up to the day of her execution in 1738. Shakbatina's blood sacrifice, for a crime the corrupt leader Red Shoes committed, saves the peace among the neighboring Choctaws and Chickasaw, and the life of her daughter, Anoleta. But her spirit cannot rest and resurfaces in 1991 in Durant, Oklahoma, where she haunts Auda Billy, who also battles a greedy chief who has turned on the Choctaws. Possessed by the spirit of Shakbatina, Auda kills Red McAlester (a reincarnation of Red Shoes), and her mother, Susan Billy, shoulders the crime. This irruption of the past into the present creates the effect of the uncanny whose structural function in *Shell Shaker* is the involuntary return to the same situation: a chief's betrayal of his people causing female sacrifice and revenge.[8] McAlester is seized by the hubris of Red Shoes when he shouts "I am the *Imataha Chitto*, the greatest leader" (24). Such acts of unconscious repetition compulsion occur throughout the novel as characters are possessed by the dead. The ghost of Shakbatina, the female ancestor, haunts all the women of the Billy family and forges powerful matrilineal connections that shape the contemporary political life of the Choctaw nation. The sisterhood, "intek aliah," reasserts itself specifically against patriarchal and chauvinistic abuses. As Auda Billy knows, "if you want to get elected in Choctaw Country, you must have the women on your side" (21). It was the women who helped elect Red McAlester and supported him until he turned his "dirty tricks." After McAlester's murder, all the Billy women—Susan Billy and her daughters Auda (Choctaw historian and assistant tribal chief), Tema (successful actress), and Adair (the stock broker and "Wall Street Shaman") with their aunts Delores and Dovie—are converging at the family home in Durant, Oklahoma. Here they are joined by the spirits of their ancestors.

Shakbatina's spirit slips into the kitchen while the women of the Billy family are preparing the funeral feast, much of which is explicitly coded as "southern." There are plenty of references to fried chicken and to the "droplets of a greasy elixir only Southerners appreciate" (151). In this Oklahoma home space smelling of southern foods, a spirit from the South enters the conversation between two generations of women who are doing the cooking: "Suddenly there is a gust of wind, a hint that someone has entered the room. A clock strikes four. A voice calls from afar. Footsteps barely audible touch the floor. There is a spirit. A loving compassion circles the room" (146). It is from this ancestral spirit—presumably Shakbatina herself—that Delores is receiving the gift of the home soil and the message that they must bury Red McAlester in the mound at Nanih Waiya, the Choctaw origin mound in Mississippi. In her trance reinforced by the rhythmic kneading of the dough, Delores hears many voices and understands the spirit message in several languages. Her mind becomes a conduit through which history flows all the way back into "prehistoric" times. She experiences "Memories dressed in thick bear skins with ice in their hair. Thoughts with gorgets made of mastodon toes around their necks. Voices with long black braids and flint hoes give rise to ancient arguments on how best to move the Earth" (159). This ancient race memory—N. Scott Momaday calls it "blood memory"—takes her back to the Mississippian mound-building era and the homelands of the modern Choctaws.[9] Delores's vision blurs mythological time, when "grandparents of tribes part clouds with their blow guns and assist the digging crews," with modern times, when a warrior helps with the mound construction by driving a "giant yellow Caterpillar with four wheels the size of houses" (159). Modern technology blends with ancient blow guns: the present fuses with the past. When Delores awakes from her trance and takes her hands out of the dough for the chicken dumplings, she has "black sticky fingers" and realizes the dough has turned into Mississippi mud.

Clearly, Choctaw women have their hands in the sticky dough of history and their fingers in the black fertile soil of the South. In the Billy kitchen, cooking and baking jobs have a myriad of political consequences: women still shape and mold native history, and they are able to decode the spectral messages hailing from the South. Howe's contemporary Choctaw women are literate in the signs they receive and empowered by the spectral ancestral history. Nobody seems to panic at the miracle of the multiplying dough in their midst. The specter is welcome. The dough passing through Delores's fingers is different from the "dough" passing through Red's greedy hands. The dough miracle provokes surreal manifestations of a different kind of "dirt"—that dirt beckons from the mother mound, Nanih Waiya. Instead of producing the effect of the uncanny with its sense of dread, unease, or horror, the specter in Howe's fiction is canny (in the sense of shrewd and knowing) in its ability to reveal a layer of occluded knowledge. An encounter with the uncanny thus relates to the rediscovery of something that is very ancient and familiar.

In *Shell Shaker*, the specter brings the Choctaws home to the womb-like space of their emergence, to Nanih Wayia.[10] In Delores's vision, she sees the mound builders: "with a thousand hands they help the warrior open Mother Earth's beautiful body. Slowly and lovingly Mother Earth turns herself inside out and a gigantic platform mound emerges out of the ground. When this sacred ovulation rises to meet the Sun, a private blush sweeps over Mother Earth and becomes grass. A gift" (159). Choctaws were said to have originated from this *mother mound*, a sacred location closely linked with origin stories and ceremonies such as the Green Corn Dance.[11] Delores explains that the "whole Nanih Waiya area represents the cradle of Choctawan civilization. A long time ago, people came from all directions to settle there. It takes a sacred space like that to heal a troubled spirit" (161).

For a firm grasp of female Choctaw identity, this Mississippi homeland cannot be forgotten and must be reimagined in literature and regained in political and cultural life. Howe gestures at the reunification of the Mississippi and Oklahoma Choctaws as they are reclaiming political and geographical space. Howe's characters claim Nanih Waiya, the ancestral land in the South, as a site of political activism and historical reconciliation. These mound-building sites testify to Indigenous presence, history, and ingenuity as well as to the survival and transformation of southern native people. The mounds are crucial reminders that being Native American is not an ethnicity in the panoply of other contemporary ethnicities, but evidence of southern Indigeneity. By returning her narrative to Nanih Waiya, Howe has three goals: first, she uses the mounds as physical artifacts testifying to an original cultural and historical context that grounded Choctaws in the Southeast two thousand years ago; second, she intervenes in contemporary cultural and political discussions about ownership, access, and preservation of Indigenous sacred space. Nanih Waiya was a Mississippi state park until the Mississippi Legislature Senate Bill 2803 officially returned control to the Choctaws in 2006, and they bought it back.[12] And third, she sketches a gendered landscape that links women to a sacred cosmological geography that reaches well beyond the ghosts of Ibsen's stage. To the Choctaw, "the earth work is still gendered as 'Great Mother'" (Nabokov 47); it is, in other words, the place of origin and return, the womb and the tomb.

Like *Shell Shaker*, *Miko Kings* begins with violent death from which a haunting emanates. The narrative present takes place in a haunted home space: Lena's grandmother's home in Ada, Oklahoma, which is being renovated. The tearing down of plaster walls, the whack of the sledgehammer, and the thick plaster dust in the air—in short, the physical violence of the destruction—transport Lena back to Amman, Jordan, where she worked as a journalist for a number of years. Traumatized by a terrorist bombing of the Days Inn (protesting the U.S. invasion of Iraq in 2003) and her sudden horrifying recognition that her friend had died and was buried under the rubble, Lena is haunted by voices sounding from the minaret urging her not to prayer but to return home to the United States. Lena learns what the female characters in *Shell Shaker* know, that her "native connections" run so deep they cannot be purged. The "restoration" of her home is the mending, renewal, and symbolic reinstatement of her Indigenous identity and history.

This restoration necessitates an encounter with the uncanny as a way to rediscover communal and personal history. As in *Shell Shaker*, the haunting in *Miko Kings* is not terrifying; on the contrary, Ezol Day's spirit is welcome and invited to help with the writing of the story. Haunting, Jeffrey Weinstock writes, "indicates that beneath the surface of received history, there lurks another story, an untold story that calls into question the veracity of the authorized version of events" (5). In *Miko Kings,* that story is that America's national pastime—baseball—is in fact a Native American game. This lost story, the "occluded knowledge," comes to the surface with the help of Ezol Day, a female spirit who visits Lena nightly as she pieces together the story of the Miko Kings and what became of them, and in the process learns about her own identity and family history. The fate of the Miko Kings, who played their last game in the summer of 1907, is tragically entwined with the historical moment of Oklahoma statehood. The change from Indian (and Oklahoma) Territories to statehood, conferred on November 16, 1907, meant the removal of all U.S. governmental restrictions on originally allotted Indian lands. As a result, more than 12 million acres of Indian land became immediately subject to taxation and sale (Debo 180). This resulted in a frenzy of buying land from Native Americans who held allotments and in irreversible changes to Choctaw life. Ezol remembers when large numbers of whites applied to the U.S. Dawes Commission for a place on the rolls of the Choctaw and Chickasaw Nations in order to receive sections of tribal allotment lands (29). "Allotment brought financial loss to all classes of Indians," Debo writes (128), and statehood increased the pressure to sell or lose their lands, so that many native people ended up destitute.

Howe fictionalizes this historical time period when, with the influx of settlers and land speculators, Ada became a boomtown rampant with characteristic corruption, gambling, drinking, and prostitution. In this climate of social change, Ezol's uncle, Henri Day, organizes an all-Indian baseball team and invests in a ballpark as a business opportunity. The team, consisting of players from the "Five Civilized Tribes," represents political and social resistance to the colonizing and militarizing forces of the United States as well as Henri's vain hope to save his landholdings and native sovereignty. When the Miko Kings play the championship game against the U.S. Seventh Cavalry, the stakes are high. Unfortunately, the all-Indian team gets ensnared in the capitalist machinations of the economic boom, and gambling on the team's futures leads to its demise when Hope Little Leader, its star pitcher, purposely loses the championship game in a desperate attempt to make money and save his relationship with his beloved Justina Maurepas. This mistake results in tragedy: a battle between the players of the Miko Kings and the gangsters who "played them" leaves all of them dead except for Hope, whose hands were chopped off by his teammates and who will never again play baseball. Haunted by his betrayal, Hope experiences the phantom pain of his mutilation in his "sea horses" arms and his deep regret for his weakness and the loss of his love. However, aptly named Hope, he is living out his life until he ends up in the tribal nursing home in Ada in 1969 where he relives all the glorious moments of baseball history and shares his stories with his nurses. In his mind, time moves back and forth as he slips in and out of consciousness, and past and present blur.

In both *Miko Kings* and *Shell Shaker*, the elders live in a retirement center that becomes the modern location for tribal memory and the ancestral knowledge. In *Shell Shaker*, Hoppy and Nick are disappointed when they pull up in front of a nursing home to visit Divine Sarah. "I thought we were going out in the deep woods to visit the spirits" says Nick (67). The elders may be physically weak and live in modern homes, but they have power. Sarah is linked with the seven ancestral grandmothers through her crazy bird menagerie; those birds, we may recall, were the ones that dropped excrement on the heads of the Hispanos in protest of early exploitation and colonization, further proof of women's uncanny power. Retirement homes are quite literally portals into the past, places whose temporal borders are unstable and haunted by tricksters and shape-shifters.

This is not to say that there are no terrifying gothic spaces in Howe's novels: they are conspicuously present, for instance, in the boarding schools that played such prominent roles in the cultural dispossession, the so-called "civilization," of Indians. Both novels feature traumatic boarding school experiences that force Howe's characters to abandon native knowledge, traditions, and languages while attempting to teach them their own cultural inferiority. In *Miko Kings*, Hampton Normal School for Blacks and Indians is a carceral environment that traps Hope as a young boy in 1896. Punished for his repeated attempts to run away, he is thrown in his dark solitary cell, "yakni kula," where "ghosts meander unperturbed" (61). At the Hampton "Reservation," he is traumatically separated from his sisters in a violent assimilation effort. The sneering principal of the school is a stock gothic character whose "words floating out of the fecal dust inside the cell" make it clear that "confinement is sometimes necessary even among *family*" (63). In *Shell Shaker*, Dovie and Delores also run away from the Indian boarding school but not before being so traumatized that Delores did not "want to be Indian anymore" (155). Lacking medical care or attention to proper hygiene, the girls barely survive. Delores tried to comfort a dying Ponca girl who shared her bed and whose bed-wetting was blamed on Delores. The child was sick, and Delores was trying to keep her arms around the girl to keep her warm at night, but she failed to save her. When Delores woke up, "the bed was stone cold and the girl's face was yellowish gray, swollen and contorted" (155). Even many years later, Delores cannot share her experiences of the terrifying night when she was sleeping with a corpse of a girl in her arms. The dead body of the Ponca girl is an example of the political work of the gothic, which displays, in this case, the social injustice and tyranny of an education system that kills its students.

The chilling horror of death, so important to gothic fiction, is also central in Howe's novels that render death from inside the characters' consciousness at the moment when they surrender to its violence. In *Shell Shaker*, Shakbatina is clubbed to death, and the narrative perspective is hers: "I suck in my breath. I feel an icy hot explosion in my head. Deafening. Blood gurgles from my mouth. My hands spring to my head involuntarily, blood is seeping out of my head and flecks of bone are strewn through my hair" (16). Noting the anachronistic execution method, Monika Siebert argues that Howe engages with cultural binaries of savagery and civilization, a tradition from which the writer has "inherited a specific representational difficulty, one shaped by a long history of Europeans playing Indian" (95). Indeed, Howe activates a representational framework of gothic horror that includes fear of "savages" peculiar to the American imagination. But in depicting violent death from the "inside," she signifies more broadly on pervasive fears about the loss of the stability of the self, so characteristic of the gothic. Here the self is narrating its absolute physical and mental disintegration. Howe uses this technique again in *Miko Kings* when Ezol narrates her own death in a fire: "So with my arms across my face, my eyes shut tight, I see the glowing red. The trunk of the eye tree is on fire, its limbs detach from my body and I am truly burning up" (209). The body, whose image provides individuals with a sense-integrated being, is literally torn apart in violent death. Crossing the line between being and not being, Shakbatina and Ezol have already stepped outside of their bodies to narrate their own demise in the ghostly voices that will live for centuries. Both novels insist that the loss of the body is not a limitation to Indigenous existence, nor is the loss of native land because the remembered stories remain part of the living tradition of the Choctaws. Spirits who preserve the stories open up new ways of being and knowing in this uncanny liminal space from which new opportunities emerge for those haunted by them. Because these native ghosts do not eulogize a lost past, but connect it to the present, southern Indigeneity is (the) undead.

And this is why in Howe's novels, time rewinds and history is getting a second chance. As Siebert has argued for *Shell Shaker*, there are two solutions to the murder plot; the first one is based on a "rational explanation of the mystery" of Red McAlester's death that exonerates Auda for the murder; the second one is based on "Choctaw cosmology" that implicates Auda, aided by Shakbatina, in the murder. The novel, Siebert claims, "aligns itself with Shakbatina because she gets the last word" (105). Using the gothic framework, we might say that the novel privileges the Indigenous uncanny by revealing the unsettling events and irrational processes through which characters and readers accept the closure offered by a ghost. Like *Shell Shaker*, *Miko Kings* offers two endings: the first ends in loss and death because of Hope Little Leader's tragic choice to "sell out." The second, a repetition of the game played on October 5, 1907, at the Fort Sill Military Reservation, ends in victory for the Miko Kings as "Hope winds up, looking straight into the Sun as if in prayer to *Hashtali,* the Choctaw's source of power" (218) and throws the winning ball—and the Indians win over the cowboys!

In situating the temporal and spatial dimensions of the gothic, Eric Savoy argues that common to the genre is "a narrative site that tends to be an epistemological frontier" (6). In the double take on history, its rewinding and replaying, Howe's narratives directly engage with the question of epistemology and the production of native knowledge. Howe explains that her characters "link the stories they've heard about their ancestors with the stories they are living" ("Blind" 331), and she argues that Native American writers tell a story that "includes a collaboration with the past, present, and future" ("Blind"). When the spectral Ezol collaborates with Lena in *Miko Kings,* Howe demonstrates that temporal modes and changing sociopolitical landscapes are integral to each other, not in a sequential or chronologically linear way but in a dynamic and flexible relation. "Different times nest within each other and draw meaning from each other," writes anthropologist Barbara Bender (S104), an insight that applies exactly to the political hauntings in Howe's novels. The specter herself articulates a theory about time that is central to the events in the novel: she argues that "universal time in space could not exist because there are no universal verb tenses," ergo "time must flow at different rates for English speakers and for tribal peoples" (38). This theory of linguistic and epistemological difference is reinforced not only by the shifting narrative temporalities of the novel, but also by the idea that baseball is a Native American game. "How plausible is it that white people, who live by the clock and sword, would invent a game without time, one that must be played counter-clockwise?" Ezol asks provocatively (42). The idea that baseball, the national pastime, is very literally past time—beyond time—is integral to the haunted plot and the political message of its specter. In her last appearance, Ezol says, "[R]eality is manifest from what we see and how we speak of it" (219), and Lena concurs, "[S]uch is the sacred made manifest in the flesh of the page" (221).

It is this manifestation of the imagination in the act of writing the story—making manifest on the page—or of telling a story that is central to the survival of Choctaw culture. Howe's specters bring the past into the present to render the uncanny "canny" and in doing this they link the mummy (death) to the mommy (mother),[13] not like Freud, who feminizes and eroticizes death, but more like N. Scott Momaday, whose invocations of the venerable woman Ko-Sahn provide a link to the individual and racial experience of the Kiowas. Howe's own invocations of Choctaw ghosts, in the shape of Shakbatina or Ezol, attempt to invert the contemporary cultural conditions in native homelands not only to reveal the original possessors of the place, but to reinvest them with authoritative power.

NOTES

1. On the South's oppositional relation to the nation, see Greeson, *Our South;* and Duck.

2. Renée Bergland argues that "the ghosting of Indians is a technique of removal" (4).

3. I allude to the title of the landmark essay collection "Haunted Bodies" edited by Jones and Donaldson, which examines African American and white women's writing in the South.

4. Boyd and Thrush argue that native hauntings perform a wide range of political and cultural work.

5. Bergland argues that to write of Indians as ghosts is to remove them from the land and replace them with figments of the American imagination (4).

6. See Burnham, who has made this argument for Sherman Alexie's *Indian Killer*, which she characterizes as part of an "Indigenous gothic" that serves an "anti-liberal politics" and "an anti-colonial ethics" (6).

7. Brogan's *Cultural Haunting* also focuses on the return of specifically female ancestor spirits and their help in restoring connections between generations. See especially her chapter on Louise Erdrich's *Tracks*.

8. Freud discusses the uncanny feeling that an involuntary return to the same place can cause.

9. For a discussion of Momaday's use of the phrase "blood memory," see Chadwick Allen's *Blood Narrative*.

10. The mound and cave are in present-day Winston County, Mississippi, about fifteen miles northeast of Philadelphia, Mississippi.

11. On Nanih Waiya creation stories, see Mould; Galloway; Swanton; and Pesantubbee.

12. See "Choctaw Regain Mother Mound" by Andrea Williams, www.wtok.com/home/headlines/34488274.html. Text of the Senate Bill 2803: http://billstatus.ls.state.ms.us/documents/2006/html/SB/2800-2899/SB2803IN.htm.

13. I borrow this phrase from Nicholas Royle's *The Uncanny*.

17

CROSSIN' THE LOG
Death, Regionality, and Race in Jeremy Love's *Bayou*

RAIN PRUD'HOMME C. GOMÉZ

"They think we're all going to drown down here. But we ain't going nowhere." The heroine of *Beasts of the Southern Wild*, the fearless, philosophical, powerful, yet bruised Hushpuppy, whose journey intersects both physical and metaphysical spaces of memory and concepts of time in the geographical space of southern Louisiana, makes this claim. In the face of erasure and expected removal, she asserts a testament to stubborn survival. This line encapsulates not only the attitude of the peoples who call southern Gulf lands home, but the peoples and lands themselves; it is a tenacious reminder that land, people, and memory will not—despite natural or man-made disasters, floods, attempts of burial, erasure, and removal—be written over: "We ain't going nowhere."

Anumpa nan anoli sa'bvnna.[1] I want to tell a story. I want to tell a story because like all good southerners, I was formed by storytellers, tall tales, familial narratives, funny fables, and soulful speakings, haunting in their Spanish moss imagery. I come into this essay as a summation of stories—syllables woven together from Indians, Creoles, and the Gulf lands of my father's people—forming my brackish bayou basket of memories: a Southeastern Indigenous descended story. These stories rise up from our land into our people. As a person formed by Gulf spaces, I like to think I recognize a good story. A good story carries the intersections of pasts, presents, futures, and cultures in its narratives. Behn Zeitlin's *Beasts of the Southern Wild*

(2012), adapted from Lucy Alibar's screenplay with the input of locals from Terrebonne Parrish, Louisiana, is such a narrative. The film also created a heroine, Hushpuppy, whose journey was evocative of yet another recent addition to the southern textual repertoire of race, memory, and land in the Louisiana/Mississippi Delta: Lee Wagstaff of Jeremy Love's serial comic *Bayou* (2007–10).

Love pens a comic (story and illustrations with colors by Patrick Morgan) whose horrors are confronted on the page in present reading spaces, illustrating that the past is never past and that the experiences of Indians, Africans (enslaved, free, and segregated), and disenfranchised people of color are forever emblazed on the land, not to be forgotten. In 1933, Lee leaves her family in "fictional" Charon, Mississippi, to save her father from the lynch rope, and with a swamp-colored man-mammoth, hoodoo, blues-singing guide named Bayou, passes into "Dixie," a parallel space where events know no chronological history. Love's "fictional" Charon, like Faulkner's Yoknapatawpha County, is made up of real places, landscapes, and events. Additionally, the parallel space of Dixie stands in for *the South* without the convention of compartmentalizing historic horrors: a communal memory representation of the mythic Deep South. Therefore the text becomes its own landscape tied to race and memory within very real southern geographic Mississippi and Louisiana homeplaces.

In this essay I read *Bayou* from an Indigenous perspective and ask us as critics to consider the incessancy of trauma.[2] Trauma not as a historic haunting but an ever-present reality linked to place, race, and regionality, in the case of *Bayou*, the Deep South of Louisiana and Mississippi, where Indigenous and African American horrors collide on paracolonial occupied lands.[3] Locating *Bayou* within intersections of present and past, using a lens of Indigenous concepts of *place/space* rather than Western concepts of time, I follow the example of Kimberly (Roppolo) Weiser (of Cherokee, Choctaw, Creek descent), who affirms in the first chapter of her manuscript "Back to the Blanket: Reading, Writing, and Resistance for American Indian Literary Critics," that we as Indigenous scholars need to privilege Native epistemologies as theoretical discursive practices for reading texts produced in the Americas, on Native ground. Reading *Bayou* from an Indigenous epistemology highlights that the horrors occurring within the text based on "historical" racial tensions are decidedly beyond gothic haunting tropes, reflecting ever-present strains still within literature and land as contemporary fissures and frictions of ongoing assertions and reclamations.

Southern lands are inscribed with literary allusions and rich historical tapestries, from Faulkner's tales set in the "fictional" Yoknapatawpha county to Kate Chopin's efforts to capture Creole dialect in Natchitoches Parish.[4] However, these narratives, for all their complexity and even their horrors, are part of a dominant colonial discourse where the colonial project claims "the territory [. . .] as the colonizer's own [. . .]" (Spurr 28), assuming authorship of the land for itself, writing over the presence and events of Indian peoples first and other peoples of color second. Colonial authorship of land creates a narrative of *the South* that maintains a white/black binary structure solidifying ideas of white land claim. Therefore, Indigenous land is subsumed and erased in favor of paracolonial narratives and the bifurcation seen in an overwhelming majority of southern literature that erases Native occupation. Despite this, Indian Removal is both a "towering historical fact and an oddly invisible one within the field of Southern literature" (Anderson, "Presence" 285). The shadow of Indian Removal haunts perceptions of Indigenous presence in both American literature and our southern homelands. Renée L. Bergland's work examines Indian hauntings (as characters, apparitions, spirits) that haunt American literature, noting that, from Nathaniel Hawthorne to Stephen King, "spectral Indians appear everywhere in our national literature" (159). Similarly, Annette Trefzer links the archeological project of the early twentieth century to this haunting literary phenomenon, locating spectral and peripheral Indigenous presences as signifiers: "The exercise of archeology plays a major role in awakening this ghost and in recovering in literature the traces of an Indian presence" (3). While current scholarship in American literature and Native American studies has sought to draw attention to the haunting absent/presence of Indigenous peoples in southern literature, I would suggest it is time we address this absent/presence not as a haunting but as still *present* contestations, contentions, and traumas against both Native American and other peoples of tribal descent in the Americas.[5] If we think of events that take place not as historical, but as acts on land, then time is not a linear factor linking happenings; those events become land-based, linked to the peoples who occupy its space.

Native stories "pull all the elements together of a storyteller's tribe, meaning their people, the land, and multiple characteristics and all their manifestations and revelations and connect these in past, present and future milieus" (Howe, "The Story" 42). In essence, LeAnne Howe (Oklahoma Choctaw) is connecting the nature of Native story and meaning-making inheritance with geography, the lands we inhabit, and distilling them into a simple terminology, or philosophy: "tribalography." Event, land, tribe, memory are interconnected; and memory of an event is inherently, intrinsically connected to the land on which it occurs and the bodies of the peoples to whom it occurs. In her interview with Kirstin Squint, Howe describes Native concepts of time as being land-based: "[L]and is past tense and present tense at the same time. The land actually is a wonderful space in physics that is all things at once—past, present, and future" (qtd. in Squint 219). Rather than land as chronologically time-based, something that can be subsumed, erased, and written over, place-centered events as understood through tribalography allow for a more holistic picturing of events, rather than a fractured echo of historical happenings. Tribalography connects land, people, storyteller, listener, past, present, future, and their continual interactions. Western concepts of time cause events to be historicized and therefore compartmentalized, seen as removed, and when they rise up in contemporary literature, they become echoes or hauntings, not actualized, relevant, meaningful events connected to geographic places. Chickasaw scholar Jodi Byrd asserts that "within American Indian epistemologies *where* something takes place is more important than when, and the land itself [. . .] remembers" (118). Like Howe, with her concept of tribalography, Byrd stresses that for Indigenous people, place holds memory and that events are encountered, reencountered, or re-counted through our interactions with land memory.

Thadious M. Davis observes that "Southscapes" are "a social, political, cultural, and economic construct" acknowledging "the connection between society and environment as a way of thinking about how raced human beings are impacted by the shape of the land" (2). This definition of regionality is particularly relevant to Louisiana and Mississippi as Indigenous spaces first and bifurcated spaces second. It is additionally useful in conceptualizing the trauma of race and death as actualized horror narratives in the Deep South setting of Love's *Bayou*. Lee's travels through landscapes of Mississippi and Louisiana during Jim Crow and Love's dense play on regionality and race remain in the forefront of the narrative, rather than removed, testifying to the reality that history is present, not past, or as Faulkner wrote: "The past is never dead. It's not even past" (73). From the opening panels that include a field of cotton (Love 1:1), to the Confederate flag welcome sign that reads, "Welcome to Charon, Mississippi," the crow perched on the "colored entrance" sign, and a panel of faceless white men and swinging feet of a lynched black victim in the swamp (which we will later learn is the youth Billy Glass) (1:2–4),[6] the setting is rife with a juxtaposition of the calm pastoral (cotton fields) and the depths of racial violence (lynching). As Brannon Costello and Qiana Whitted address in their collection *Comics and the U.S. South*, graphic novels and comics by and about southern spaces and subjects shift the focus from oral/written only to include the visual. Emphasizing the visual alongside the oral South highlights how "intensely *visual*" southern culture is historically, from colorisms of racial construction, to signage of inclusion and exclusion (x). This is evident in the opening panels of *Bayou*, where signage highlights segregation as clearly as the panels of violence show the split between the pastoral agrarian and the liminality of the swamp.

Early in the story, Lee wades into the depths of dark mutable bayou water to fetch the body of Billy Glass. Glass's adolescent body has been lynched, maimed (in particular his eye gouged out and neck strangulated), and weighted down, thrown into the murky, mysterious, swamp waters (Love 1:13–14; 2:201–9). If the lynching of Billy Glass sounds familiar, it is no accident, as the circumstances are decidedly modeled after the Emmett Till case. Like Till, Glass has been found "guilty" of harassing a white woman, in this case whistling at the local storekeeper's wife (1:25). Newpapers report this incident, we later learn, as "assaulting Mrs. Georgia McAllister," a seeming justification for his lynching and the subsequent disposal of his body, which Lee Wagstaff retrieves from the Yazoo River (2:201–2). Till's body was found in the Tallahatchie River, a tributary of the Yazoo. Therefore, the site of Till's massacre overlaps the imagined space of Love's Charon, Mississippi, a "fictionalized" space marked by real Mississippi geography bearing Indian names.[7] Glass's mirroring of Till strategically keeps alive the event of racial horror within Mississippi Delta landscape. Moreover, revisualizing the violence of Till's death through Glass within the graphics of the page offers evidence "of racism's sadism and the symbol of a nation's shame" in much the same way as Till's open casket at his public funeral does for national memory (King 58). The setting of Glass's murder predates Till's actual murder, and the publication of *Bayou* is decidedly later. Past (the textual setting), future

(Till's murder), present (the reader) intersect in the landscape of text, much like the events intersect the landscape of the Mississippi Delta. This intersecting of place-specific horror events is not only indicative of Indigenous epistemologies of place memory but is also enhanced by the nature of the textual structure in comics. As Costello and Whitted note: "[T]he comics page, after all, is frequently a collection of images that are at once separate and interdependent [. . .] and can thus represent an infinitely wide range of places and times both serially and simultaneously and can suggest an enormously complex tangle of connections and relationships" (xi). The structure of comics is naturally nonlinear and dialogic, allowing its framework to fit into an Indigenous place-centered epistemological discursive structure.

The seeming bifurcation of race is played out in the bifurcation of the land, from calm sharecropping scenes featuring Calvin Wagstaff (Love 1:62–63) to pastoral fields (1:1; 1:59) and swamp panels with bodies in the bayou, and to scenes of flooding swampland juke joints in both volumes (1:12–14; 2:201–10; 1:39; 2:138–39;). Lee says, "The Bayou is a bad place" (Love 1:6), as she retrieves Billy Glass's body. Death, liminality, and horror are often associated with swampland, as Anthony Wilson notes: "In the South [. . .] the swamp remained more than anything else a physical reminder of the barrier between the actual and the ideal, an obstacle to the creation of an idealized agrarian society" (xiii). The swamp in Love's *Bayou* is a transient, liminal space. While evocative of actual problematic geographic spaces that have stood as gothic horror tropes in stark defiance to southern gentility, it has also represented actual escapism and livelihood to raced bodies outside the South's hegemonic classifications. To capture this mutability, the bayou is depicted in murky green-gray tones, surrounded by sticky mud banks that cling like hands (Love 1:113), harboring cypress limbs, large catfish (1:10), and deep depths, (1:10–11), and including a golliwog, which attempts to literally drag Lee into the pits of the bayou.

In *Bayou*, land/space factors are at the center of the story. This allows for the reencountering of violence enacted against bodies of color. While walking from the field to the bayou, Lee and Lily pause amid tall grasses, butterflies, and ladybugs (Love 1:32). Lee hears a chorus of voices in the wind and asks Lily if she hears "[f]olks singing, like it's coming from the trees." Lily responds, "I don't hear nothin'" (1:32). Lee, the black raced body, hears voices, while Lily, the white body, cannot hear the singing. The voices that have been singing out to Lee become visible in the next panels as she runs from the bayou away from Cotton Eye Joe, who has swallowed the young Lily whole and disappeared into the waters (1:118–26). Lee runs through a field of trees from which she had heard singing voices echo "go down, go down, down to the bayou" the previous day (1:102–05), Into this same grove of trees Lee, her face registering shock, stops just short of smacking into a pair of dangling feet (1:130). The next panel pulls back to show a broad view of Lee standing before six lynched bodies, swinging from the trees, including two teenagers, a girl and a boy (1:31). Qiana Whitted discusses this scene through use of Toni Morrison's concept of "rememory," or the present being haunted or inscribed by traces of the past (188). For Whitted, history breaks through the present, intruding on the living with the dead: "What Lee has stumbled upon is not a single moment, but a temporal dislocation of borrowed memories" (208). While I agree with Whitted that this is not a single moment, I would contend that the notion of the past being remembered, or traces intruding, haunting, or surfacing again, regulates the notion of trauma to the realm of historical. I would argue that the events, the lynchings, are always present, always visible and part of the land. Lee is connected to the land. She is able to navigate the bayou, swampland often seen as menacing and "navigable by those that society rejects" (Wilson 14). Lee Wagstaff is such a character, racially outside the norm, endowed with the ability to see Billy Glass's spirit in the depths of the bayou (Love 1:15–16; 2:213) and likewise the continual spirits of lynched bodies in the trees. She is inscribed by the land as a raced body and thereby continuously connected to the events and narratives that take place on the land. In this scene, key components converge: place, person, memory. There is no past—just event, land, race, and trauma.

The presence of rich allusions such as those to Emmett Till, golliwogs, juke joints, and other literary, event, and cultural traditions are the result of Love's carefully crafted southern tapestry.[8] Land keeps events current: pain, joy, even horror are not relegated to the annals of forgetting or written over by new experience. Space triggers a multitude of communal memories tied geographically to raced bodies. Keith Cartwright addresses how concepts of land, bodies, and memory are tangled in national memory: "[W]e must recognize that we are dealing with at least two different but historically blended forces. We are looking at a landscape infused with the cultural presence of Africans and their descendants .[. . .] [H]owever, we are looking at a landscape shaped by racial ideologies that have worked to deny African humanity" (*Reading Africa* 4). Cartwright's claim is equally true of Indigenous peoples. Land is foremost Native and has retained its inscription despite attempts of paracolonial erasure. Likewise, arrivals of other raced bodies, particularly African/African American bodies in the South, have woven deep shared cultural presences alongside Indigenous bodies onto Native homelands. The colonial project Cartwright describes works to deny both Indian and African humanity and their narratives—shared, divergent, and contested—as well as ongoing, active Indian and African narrative presences. Destabilizing linear time concepts upsets the notion that what are typically seen as "the worst" atrocities against bodies of color are past; instead, it relocates them in the present, as they are within the sensibilities, action, and governing systems that dictate Southscapes. That is to say, "[s]pace is inextricable from social processes and the phenomena that occur in the specified South as place" (Davis 4). So, while Love highlights southern binary separatism, rather than erase Indigenous occupation from Southscapes, he allows Indigenous presence to leak into the text from the land itself through the ways that Lee and other characters encounter and oppose concepts of horror, death, and dying, uniting geographic spaces to memory and resistance.

Indian land, memory, and presence are never absent but rather are couched within southern land spaces and aligned with African American experiences against settler-colonialism. Many critics such as Qiana Whitted have called *Bayou* suggestive of *Alice in Wonderland* or a mix of "*Alice in Wonderland*, American folklore, and early twentieth century racial politics" (Knowlton). However, I find *Bayou* far more suggestive of Choctawan and African American roots than of Anglo-European tales of Alice. Beginning with Lee's entrée to Dixie through the bayou where she once waded to fetch the body of Billy Glass, she again heads through murky water to the log where Billy's body was lodged (Love 1:13; 1:235). To cross into the other reality Lee must forge through water and then the slick hole in the submerged log, surfacing on the other side, where she is pulled from the swamp by Bayou, her lumbering guide to Dixie (1:247). This is no rabbit hole Lee has fallen down. This American southern tale takes place on Indigenous soil. Swimming through the opening in the log, a golliwog spirit attempts to drag Lee down and stop her crossing from one realm to the next. The golliwog is an allusion to the literary minstrel character created by Florence Kate Upton and further popularized by Enid Blyton's negative racial constructions.[9] The golliwog's grotesque blackface parody of racial minstrelsy latches onto Lee as she crosses from the bayou in Charon to the parallel realm of Dixie (1:240–42).

Unlike Alice chasing the white rabbit through its hole, Lee's journey is evocative of Choctaw or Choctawan spiritual crossing over, or Crossing the Log. To cross into the spirit world or afterlife, "it was necessary to cross a wide river filled with rapids by crossing on a perfectly round slippery log. [. . .] [When] spirits tried to cross the river, they were met by two guardian spirits. [. . .] [G]uardian spirits pushed bad peoples spirits into the river. [. . .] Good people's spirits crossed the river, where they were met by relatives and friends" (Innes 248). Other variations of this narrative tell of spirits that impede all travelers, or throw rocks at travelers, where only worthy travelers make it to the other side.[10] Like the Choctaw crossing over, water acts as both a conduit and test of spiritual and physical strength. Lee must brave the rigors of water and survive the golliwog, a representation of all that has been stereotypically reprehensible and inscribed on black bodies, manifested in solid form. The log is both a physical impediment and passageway to the next world; as a tree, its roots connect it to earth, its limbs, to sky. This tree being in water or over water becomes symbolic of all three Mvskogean worlds: Upper, Lower, and Middle.[11] That Lee moves through the water rather than over the water, and through the log rather than on the log, shows, I would argue, more a mutability of the nature of story than differences. What is significant is the presence of *both* the *water* and *log* elements in her *crossing* from one plane of reality to the next. Not only does Lee cross in a manner similar to Choctawan tradition, but she carries with her a symbol of Choctaw culture. This helps ground the narrative both in Choctawan land base through place-names, literal geographies of Choctaw Mississippi homelands, and through evoking a crossing-over narrative that mirrors the traditional rite of passage within Choctawan religious complexes.

Lee carries the axe of her Uncle Bedford's great-grandfather Enoch.[12] Bedford describes Enoch as the child of a Choctaw warrior and a runaway African slave woman who took shelter in an "old Spanish fort" in Florida during the First Seminole War (Love 1:188–90). The panels of Bedford's recollection are in black, white, and sepia, varying from high-contrast inks, such as his great-great-grandmother and child hiding in foliage (1:188), to detailed portraiture of Enoch's parents on sepia-toned paper in pencils, charcoal, and white chalk (1:189–90). Uncle Bedford paints a familial narrative of a Choctaw warrior and his runaway slave wife who have joined with other Mvskogean peoples, along with runaway slaves, free slaves, and maroons in Florida.[13] This is before "Old Hickory" (Jackson) comes to "blast" them out with cannon fire (1:90–91). Enoch is saved, along with a few women and children, by a Choctaw warrior, but his parents die in the fort (1:193). Love depicts the Choctaw warrior who rescues Enoch as wearing a Southeastern turban with feathers, bandolier, belted trade shirt, and with hair highlighting his sharp cheekbones; though Love's image is sepia-toned, it bears a resemblance to the 2001 portrait of Pushmatah painted by Katherine Roche for the Mississippi Choctaw and donated to the Mississippi Hall of Fame.[14] According to Lee's uncle: "The warrior gave him [Enoch] this blessed axe. Told him it was for chopping wood and killing men" (1:194). So the axe travels through the family, not only keeping Enoch safe as he builds his home with the Choctaw people. Passed to Bedford's grandfather, who had it with him in South Carolina when he helped "storm Fort Wagner" (1:96).[15] Bedford tells his niece: "This axe was baptized in the blood of the Negro and the mighty Choctaw," and rather than pass it to his son, he gives it to Lee with his final advice: "keep it with you and the spirits will watch over you" (1:197–98). While Love's depiction of African-Indian solidarity and spirituality is certainly not without its flaws, both historically and in its moments of overromanticism, what is of note is the deftness of the mutability of cultural narrativity within the evolution of *Bayou* from its inclusion of Choctawan specificity to acknowledging Southeastern Indigenous reciprocity historically from war to land trauma.[16]

Reading Native literatures means locating them within their histories, traumas, and geographic spaces. The South and notions of the South are exceedingly complex and cannot be delimited by singular definitions or engagements with ideals of history, land, or people—it is groundless yet grounded (Anderson, "South" 29). As evidenced in this essay and the work *Bayou*, the South is complex and built on and around multitudes of events on Original land, occupied by Indigenous peoples, wherein settler-colonialism has enacted its own events, and the bodies and peoples have *reacted*. The tales, stories, and emotions of peoples involved raced bodies, colonizer, colonized, free, slaved, and disenfranchised: all have a multitude of relationships, interactions, and narratives that build networks of stories around, about, and with these events. Some are deeply personal, some removed, yet all are part of the region, and all are complex. The South is not isolated; it is a global, transracial, transnational space (Regis 1). Moreover, the spaces occupied share histories of trauma and survival, and those bear fruits of creativity, hostility, and survivals. Melanie Benson Taylor (Herring Pond Wampanoag) notes: "[T]he crossing and alteration of multiple communities by and in one another's stories is a reality that needs to be reckoned with. [. . .] [T]he transformative force of this pluralism is something that few studies of southern literature have managed to do" (174). The reality of the ways in which "cultural, and racial practices, bloodlines, and experiences have long bled fluidly into one another" (174) is apparent in the delicately interwoven narrative fabric of *Bayou*, which merges African American experience with Indigenous narrative presence and practice, creating a third space that mirrors the homespace of southern soil, Dixie, but yet is one where the horrors of a bifurcated South and Indigenous "assumed" absence can be confronted. Frictions and fissures linked to racial trauma are embedded in the text and storied in the narratives of the land. They are ongoing reclamations, confrontations, and assertions because they are not historic, but ever-present, as their persistence in Love's text attests. Love allows a space for trauma to be present, not historic, because land functions as the unifying force, the communal memory for Black, Red, and Red-Black bodies; a truly Original American Southern narrative. After all, "American is a tribal creation story" (Howe, "The Story" 42).

NOTES

1. Choctaw.

2. This essay is drawn from my dissertation, "Gumbo Banaha Stories: Locating Louisiana Indians and Creoles in the Indigenous Diaspora of the American South" (University of Oklahoma, 2014), which looks much more closely at the allusions of the text. For more discussion, see "Red/Black Culture and Pain: 'Certified' Creoles and Red/Black Bodies" in that work.

3. I capitalize Indigenous, Indigeneity, Indian, and all language associated with Native American/First Peoples/Indigenous peoples in my work. Throughout not only the history of the Americas but of American literature, Indigenous peoples have been scripted as "less than," and while it has become common practice to capitalize various designations of other ethnicities and races, Indigenous (the designation that includes all First Peoples of the Americas) is often left in lowercase. In capitalizing these terms, I assert proper-noun status.

4. I use quotation marks around "fictional" to call into question just how fictionalized Faulkner's literary landscape is. I echo the work of such critics as Phillip Carroll Morgan (Chickasaw/Choctaw), Charles S Aiken, Melanie Benson Taylor (Herring Pond Wampanoag), and Geary Hobson (Arkansas Cherokee/Quapaw).

5. I, too, have drawn in various ways upon the absent/presence of Indian hauntings within southern literature. Ultimately, I use the argument in my dissertation to move away from the notion of hauntings and toward an idea of presences as understood through place-centered time, as discussed in this essay. For my work drawing on absent/present (via Baudrillard and Vizenor), see my dissertation, "Gumbo Banaha Stories."

6. Notes on my citations of serial comics: the first number represents the volume, and the number after the colon represents the panel. Hence (1:10) indicates volume 1. panel 10. *Bayou* was first presented by Zuda comics, a division of DC online in 2007, allowing for only volumes and panels. It was the first of the online series to move to print in 2009, with volume 1. Volume 2 followed suit, moving from online format to print in 2010. The third volume has yet to be released.

7. The Yazoo River being named for the Yazoo people, a nation related to the Tunica; and the name Tallahatchie River is taken from its original Choctaw name, tali, meaning rock, and hacha or hachi, meaning river.

8. Love's text is full of event allusions as well as cultural/literary allusions. Space constraints prevent me from listing them or explicating them thoroughly in this essay. The text is densely packed with references from the 1922 flood and Katrina, and with musical references such as "Go Down, Moses" and Stag Lee.

9. Upton's first children's book, *The Adventures of Two Dutch Dolls and a Golliwogg* was published in 1885 and served to start the series. Blyton's *Here Comes Noddy Again* (1951) showcases the golliwog as a car-stealing villain. Additionally, the depictions in *Three Golliwogs* (1944), *The Proud Golliwog* (1951), and *The Golliwog Grumbled* (1953) include racial slurs and stereotyping constructs. For critical work, see MacGregor "The Golliwog"; and Klein, *Reading into Racism*.

10. Variations of this religious narration also appear in Cushman's *History of the Choctaw, Chickasaw and Natchez Indians;* Swanton's *Source Material for the Social and Ceremonial Life of the Choctaw Indians;* and Kidwell's (Oklahoma Choctaw), *The Choctaws in Oklahoma: From Tribe to Nation, 1855–1970*.

11. By Mvskogean, I mean to be inclusive of those tribal groups whose languages and or cultural complexes are tied by unified features such as, but not limited to, Choctaw, Mvskoke Creek, Seminole, Chickasaw, Houma, Koasati, Natchez. In referencing the Upper, Middle, and Lower worlds of Mvskogean peoples, I refer to the greater cosmological worldview.

12. The story line seems to imply that Uncle Bedford married into the Wagstaff family and that Aunt Lucy is Calvin, Lee's father's sister. This reading seems affirmed when Uncle Bedford likens Lee's stubborn temperament to that of his wife, Lucy (Love 1:184).

13. Given the First Seminole War, we can assume Seminoles, Creeks from the Red Stick uprising, and remnant Choctaw supporters are part of the Indian refugees and resistance.

14. See Katherine Roche, *Portrait of Pushmataha*. 2001, oil on canvas, Mississippi Department of Archives and History, http://mshistorynow.mdah.state.ms.us/articles/14/pushmataha-choctaw-warrior-diplomat-and-chief.

15. Love's allusion to the Second Battle for Fort Wagner is accompanied by a sepia charcoal of Bedford's grandfather in Union uniform with his buckle monogrammed "US," a rifle in one hand, and the axe in the other, dripping blood. Love does not differentiate or give background on how his grandfather, a man raised with the Mississippi Choctaw, came to be in South Carolina, or how he would be part of the Fifty-Fourth Massachusetts or the First South Carolina Volunteers, which were mostly Gullah.

16. Space constraints prevent me from explicating the complications involved in Love's oversimplifications of such topics as the Seminole War, the history of Southeast Indian slaveholding, and the attachment of spiritual significance to Indian figures and objects (e.g., the "blessed axe"). For more on these topics, see Taylor, "Red Black and Southern: Alliances and Erasures in the Biracial South," in her *Reconstructing the Native South;* and Byrd, "Been to the Nation, Lord, But Couldn't Stay There" in her *Transit of Empire*.

18

"LIFE REFUSING TO END"
The Transformative Gothic in Shani Mootoo's *Cereus Blooms at Night*

JAMEELA F. DALLIS

In spring of 2012, I attended a friend's annual garden party in the pastoral town of Graham, North Carolina. After touring a fraction of his ten-acre property and admiring the native and exotic trees he raises, the afternoon sun began to fade and rain was imminent. I prepared to leave, and, to my surprise, my host offered me a night-blooming cereus. (He felt he had neglected the plant, and, bemoaning its impending death, he wanted to find it a proper home.) After some prodding, I accepted, admitting that I did not know if I would be able to care for it successfully either. Without blooms, the cereus is not the loveliest to behold. It is large and unwieldy. Its serpentine feelers shoot out from the plant's base and branches in search of a support, a wall, something to hold onto, something for grounding, or something to which it can bond. That summer, something began to happen: tubular buds formed, and my anticipation for the cereus's blooming increased. I had an idea of how the flower would look based on the cover of Mootoo's novel, but I was not truly prepared. When the plant bloomed midsummer—two ghostly white blooms on one night and another fist-sized bloom a week later—the event was magical. Conveying a sense of ecstasy, the blooms' scent perfumed my entire home. Those spectral blossoms were truly exquisite, almost profane in their beauty.[1]

Witnessing the effusion of this plant, I now understand why Shani Mootoo chose the cereus as the centerpiece of *Cereus Blooms at Night*, her daring, disturbing, and decidedly gothic 1996 debut novel set in Paradise, Lantana-camara, a locale modeled on Trinidad, where Mootoo grew up. The night-blooming cereus is native to Sri Lanka and now can be found in Central and South America (some sources claim it is native to these "New World" locations) (Purak). The cereus's sublimity is in its form and production. It is unassuming, wild, and weed-like with its propensity for climbing and escaping the boundaries of its container; yet, it is extraordinary. Its duality mirrors the novel's form as Mootoo's text is one in which we must acknowledge and embrace the potential within the unexpected that transforms into something terribly beautiful, something nearly sublime.

Mootoo consciously engages recognizable gothic aesthetics, discourse on the Caribbean at the height of European imperialism in the "New World"—discourse that is still recognizable today—and the problem of women and other traditionally marginalized groups existing within both contexts. Mootoo's employment of the cereus and the figuration of its promised blooming encapsulates a larger message and suggests a new way to think about the long-standing relationship and tension between beauty, terror, horror, and sublimity within the gothic and the Caribbean. Perhaps what makes this novel so different from other gothic novels, or other literature about the Caribbean, is the way in which Mootoo uses the gothic mode, its violence, its decay, its tangled overgrown gardens populated with exotic flora and fauna, to provide the psychological and material space of transformation. She revises and rehabilitates these feared and maligned gothic aesthetics and provides a haven, a sort of paradise, for the novel's protagonist, Mala Ramchandin, its gothic heroine. Mala lives an embodied experience within a decay-filled, gothic garden, and within that space, she is not bereft of the transcendental. Indeed, she embraces the ecstatic experience. This space of the terrific sublime becomes a necessary avenue to dealing with and transforming the pain of her traumatic past—specifically her abandonment by her mother and her aunt (her mother's lover), which leads to more traumas: incest, physical and psychological abuse, and additional abandonments by her sister, Asha, and lover, Ambrose.

The Caribbean has long been associated with picturesque beauty and represented as a virgin paradise ripe with potential. Late-eighteenth-century landscapes convey idyllic locales with laborers surrounded by plantation buildings in the foreground and an endless expanse beyond suggesting even more lands to be conquered and tilled.[2] Of course, the dark edge of such aesthetic discourse is the reality of the massive clearing of vegetation to make way for plantations, the removal of Indigenous peoples from their lands, and the importation of slave labor to work fields of cane, tobacco, and other cultivated commodities. Hence, with the figuration of paradise, there is the taint of ruthless imperialism, ravaged landscapes, the horrors of slavery, the threat of slave revolt (as the Haitian Revolution exposed the fragile fabric of the system on which an enormous amount of capital was based), and the hazard of flora and fauna in vast not-yet-colonized territories. An interesting account of the tension between paradise and its bitter underpinnings is found in Leonara Sansay's semi-autobiographical gothic novel *Secret History; or, The Horrors of St. Domingo* (1808) set in post-Revolution St. Domingo (present-day Haiti) and the surrounding islands. Sansay reflects: "St. Domingo was formerly a garden. Every inhabitant lived on his estate like a sovereign ruling his slaves with despotic sway, enjoying all that luxury could invent, or fortune procure" (70). It is apparent that such excess breeds terrible horrors and scenes just as perverse and sinister as those of gothic fiction. Sansay writes of a Creole wife who orders a slave to cut off the head of her black maidservant because she "thought she saw some symptoms of *tendresse* in the eyes of her husband" toward the woman; the wife then proceeds to serve the severed head to her husband at dinner (70). Later, Sansay travels to the Basilica de Nuestra Señora del Cobre in Cuba and comments, "The site of the temple is picturesque, and the scenery, that surrounds it, beautiful beyond description, standing near the summit of a mountain at the foot of which lies the village" (142).

Yet, a few pages later, Sansay notes the contrast between Cuba's landscape and St. Domingo's ground that "was in the highest state of cultivation" (144). And, in observing such difference, she gestures toward what Jill Casid, in *Sowing Empire: Landscape and Colonization* (2005), calls colonial relandscaping, which involved the transplantation of plants, people, machines, "tools of violence," and building materials from Asia, Africa, Europe, and other parts of the Americas. It also involved European methods of clearing, "boundary division, and signs of authority" that created a "gardenlike spectacle of variety and harmony, a union of the decorative and the useful that turns the sugar plantation into a site of aesthetic consumption by the device of converting the planter's or colonist's gaze into that of a traveler, a stranger distanced from the violence of colonization" (87). Even though such colonial relandscaping reshaped and permanently altered the Caribbean landscape, in contrast to the increasing industrialization of Britain and western Europe, the Caribbean remained a seductive new Eden, full of lush beauty and opportunities for capital for the prospective planter. But, again, Eden has two aspects.

In the earliest British gothic novels, such as Horace Walpole's *The Castle of Otranto* (1764) and Matthew Lewis's *The Monk* (1796), false nobles, Italians, and other European foreigners are villains who disrupt social order and often succeed in bringing about terror, murder, and betrayal. However, by the 1790s, the expanding British Empire introduced a new host of potentially threatening characters into the literary landscape: the racial, social, and natural *others* of the colonies (Hogle 5). In *The Monk*, the main character, Ambrosio, is bitten by the deadly "Cientipedoro"—a "serpent," as it were, "[c]oncealed among the Roses" (71)—in a garden with his malevolent seductress, Matilda (who has been masquerading as Rosario, a young initiate of the monastery Ambrosio oversees). After this bite, and Matilda's subsequent saving of his life, Ambrosio falls from grace and, in the end, rapes and murders Antonia, who is none other than his sister. What's interesting about this trajectory is that Lewis adds the footnote: "The Cientipedoro is supposed to be a Native of Cuba, and to have been brought into Spain from that Island in the Vessel of Columbus" (*The Monk* 72). Thus, as Lizabeth Paravisini-Gebert explains: "With the inclusion of the colonial, a new sort of darkness—of race, landscape, erotic desire and despair—enters the Gothic genre" (229). At the zenith of European imperial expansion, powers such as the British Empire became increasingly dependent on the economic successes of its colonies principally through African slave labor and then later, in the wake of Britain's Slavery Abolition Act in 1834, indentured servitude with the first arrival of East Indian laborers in 1845 (Leonce 1).[3] Elizabeth Abbott terms indentured servitude a "peculiar new institution," and notes that in Trinidad, for example, conditions were so horrid that it was common for laborers to endure twenty-two-hour workdays and unremarkable to find workers' corpses in the cane fields and surrounding forest (316).[4]

In Mootoo's novel, Mala is the granddaughter of Indian indentured servants who gave up their son, Chandin Ramchandin, to be raised by the Thoroughlys, white Christian missionaries, in the hope that he would live a successful life outside of cane field labor. Chandin falls in love with his adoptive sister, Lavinia, and his desire for her is rebuked and forbidden by his adoptive parents. Lavinia leaves for the mainland and plans to marry her white adoptive first cousin. Feeling confused and betrayed, Chandin marries Sarah, a West Indian woman, and they have children: Mala and Asha. An unmarried Lavinia returns to the island and rekindles her friendship with Sarah. The women fall in love and plan to run away together with the children, but an unfortunate series of events prevents their success. Namely, Mala runs back to the house for a bag she had prepared full of seeds, shells, and a night-blooming cereus cutting originally given to her by Lavinia (62). Chandin, devastated, succumbs to alcoholism and begins to rape his daughters nightly. Asha escapes, Mala endures, and when Mala becomes a young woman, she falls in love with Ambrose, a West Indian childhood friend. The consummation of their love leads to some of the most traumatic events in Mala's life: the most physically violent rape she ever experiences by her father, Ambrose's discovery of the truth and his subsequent abandonment of her, and Mala's killing of her father. Mala drags her father's still-dying body into her mother's former sewing room and shuts him up there. After these events, Mala never passes another night in the house and sleeps on the verandah or in her garden instead.

Through the novel's representation of incest in explicit, excessive detail, Mala's characterization, and Mala's excessive garden landscape, Mootoo creates a distinctly gothic mood. And, because a substantial amount of *Cereus Blooms at Night* invokes the gothic, the narrative choice to employ excess is apropos. Fred Botting puts forth simply, "Gothic signifies a writing of excess" and gothic writing "remains fascinated by objects and practices that are constructed as negative, irrational, immoral, and fantastic" (1–2). He explains further: "Gothic excesses transgressed the proper limits of aesthetic as well as social order in the overflow of emotions that undermined boundaries of life and fiction, fantasy and reality," and from the "often incestuous tendencies of Gothic villains there emerges the awful spectre of complete social disintegration in which virtue cedes to vice, reason to desire, law to tyranny" (4–5). We see Chandin's dream of an ideal life, his design, crushed, and we witness the collapse of virtue into vice, which brings to mind characters like Lewis's Ambrosio and Faulkner's Thomas Sutpen. Furthermore, in the tradition of ghastly, violated women of earlier gothic and U.S. Southern

Gothic novels, Mala becomes witchlike: a woman deemed both inscrutable and dangerous. After Ambrose abandons her, Mala ages overnight and keeps "her hair as wild as a worn-down, coconut-fibre broom" and screams "sounds that [have] no meaning" (235).

By the novel's present "[e]veryone in the village seemed to have finally forgotten about Mala. The generation of children who harassed her by calling names and pelting her with mango seeds had grown up. Their children preferred to chase each other within the confines of their own yards" (113). But when children do pass by her yard, they walk on the "other side of the street, glancing through her fence—not to see her but to make sure she did not see them" because the children's parents claim Mala "possess[es] the ability to leap her fence, track an offending child into its hiding place and tear out its mind" (113). Children swear they see her on occasion, and "their sightings became the substance of frenetic dreamings at night" (114). Here we see how Mootoo operates within and outside of established paradigms. Unlike the early gothic, which placed ancient castles and drafty manor houses in secluded mountainsides or forgotten forests, and more like her literary predecessors of the U.S. South, Mootoo invokes the gothic in an otherwise average community of people, thus bringing to mind the anxieties about the secrets and dangers within one's own community that may bleed through perceived boundaries.[5] The community's disrespect, fear, and strategic forgetting of Mala and her untamed garden demonstrate further the fear of contamination by Mala, who comes to represent the material proof of her father's sexual violence and becomes akin to a gothic monster. For Paradise, Mala embodies the threat of the impure, the inexplicable, and the unspeakable. She is imprisoned, virtually buried alive—undead—and relegated to the community's psychological space of things they would rather forget.

Mala eventually refrains from speaking (until her nurse Tyler at Paradise Alms House works to coax her life's story from her silence). In her nonverbal phase, Mala becomes deeply embodied and acutely aware of her environment: "Every muscle of her body swelled, tingled, cringed or went numb in response to her surroundings—every fibre was sensitized in a way that words were unable to match or enhance. Mala responded to those receptors, flowing with them effortlessly, like water making its way along a path" (127). In her gothic, countercolonial garden space, Mala thrives against all odds. (Casid describes "countercolonial" gardens as spaces that contest the "terrain of imperial landscaping" [191].) Mala's garden marks a significant departure from the space of first enslaved and then indentured labor in Lantanacamara's cane fields that yield cathected phantoms—unquiet ghosts born from unjust social institutions, both transhistorical and transnational—that continue to haunt the present: animated remains that sociologist Avery Gordon names "ghostly matters." Instead of becoming a place that leads to her downfall, like the garden that held the Cientipedoro that corrupted Ambrosio, Mala's Caribbean garden becomes the space in which she circumvents the fate of a violated, abused gothic heroine—the type of heroine such as Lewis's Antonia, who, after being kidnapped, imprisoned in catacombs, and then raped and mortally wounded, "resigned herself to the Grave without one sigh of regret," because, alas, she had been "deprived of honour and branded with shame" and saw death as "a blessing" since she could have never been her beloved's wife (392). (Mala also escapes the fate of women like Faulkner's Clytie, or Welty's Clytie or Mrs. Larkin.) Mala defies generic conventions by encountering ecstasy and using the space of the terrible sublime to work through the weight of the past. We witness the commingling of awe-full beauty and exquisite pain, a space that reflects the two poles—one of beauty and the other of terror—that are characteristic of literature about, and representation of, the Caribbean.

One such scene in the novel that reveals the necessity of an excessive, near sublime experience is when Mala ingests "flaming red [bird-pepper] sauce" (132). In a manner so common in gothic writing, Mootoo purposefully sets the scene and describes in detail the architecture and environs. She creates a gothic atmosphere that exemplifies the degradation and decay of her mudra house, but instead of casting Mala as fearful of such gothic trappings, Mootoo brings attention to the promise of beauty held within the cereus plant:

> [Mala] enjoyed the smell of rotting, water-bogged wood. It had been at least a decade since the eaves trough came away from the roof over the back stairs. [. . .] [T]he top steps were coated in a dangerous green and black slime. [. . .] Before her was the wall of climbing cereus, foliage scaly with age and striped with the mucous trails of buff-periwinkles. The succulents, half a dozen plants in all, had raged over the side of the house, further concealing the boarded-up window of the [sewing] room downstairs. Scattered over the network of spiny, three-sided stems and fleshy leaves were countless buds, each larger than her fist. The sight of the buds made her giddy. She so looked forward to the night

of their opening that she decided not to sit idly and wait but to enjoy every moment until then. (130)

Next we see Mala completing a preparation of bird peppers she will allow to ferment for weeks before use in her ritual; the peppers are so hot that handling them causes the "lining of her nostrils [to become] raw" (131). Mala employs the ritual during the rainy season when the memory of the day her mother and aunt left her and Asha behind arrests her: "The time of day would come upon her and deafen her. [. . .] Insects spawning in pools of water, their drones shouting, *Sarah!* [. . .] Time would collapse. Every inhaled breath was a panicked tremble sustained and each exhale a heavy sob" (131–32). Mala then ingests the bird pepper sauce and through the physical pain she is transported out of her scene of originary trauma. She speaks for the first time "in ages" and cries out for her mother not to leave her. The ritual is deliberate:

> Mala looked down at the cerise blossoms of the pomerac trees and braced herself [. . .] scooped out a heavy clump of raw pepper and shoved the finger into her mouth. [. . .] She didn't swallow, keeping the fire on her tongue [. . .] so blistered that parts of the top layer had already disintegrated and other areas had curled back like rose petals dipped in acid. [. . .] She gasped for air. [. . .] A thousand bells clanged. Then all sound stopped. [. . .] [B]lossoms of the pomerac swayed in the breeze. [. . .] Her flesh had come undone. But every tingling blister and eruption in her mouth and lips was a welcome sign that she had survived. She was alive. (133–34)

The pomerac tree and its lovely blossoms are not incidental, and, like the cereus, its presence in the Americas is due to the mechanisms of imperialization as the pomerac is native to Malaysia (Morton, "Malay Apple"). The pomerac—object of beauty—contrasts starkly with the terrible spectacle of Mala's physical anguish yet elucidates Mootoo's unification of the two poles of Caribbean aesthetic representation—the region's beauty and its horror—into one sublime figuration. Indeed, Mala's intrusive rememory[6] of trauma, her experience that cannot be fully assimilated, her moment of (to quote from Julia Kristeva) "violent, dark revol[t] of being, directed against a threat that seems to emanate from an exorbitant outside or inside," the tenebrous fabric of a memory that Mala has "ejected beyond the scope of the possible, the tolerable, the thinkable"—is "edged with the sublime"

(Kristeva 1, 11).⁷ Of course, the sublime, the simultaneous play of terror and pleasure, is yet another way Mootoo employs the gothic in addition to the work she performs with representations of the Caribbean. Botting explains that terror and horror are the emotions most associated with the gothic, and that "[t]error, in its sublime manifestations, is associated with subjective elevation, with the pleasures of imaginatively transcending or overcoming fear and thereby renewing and heightening a sense of self and social value: threatened with dissolution, the self, like the social limits which define it, reconstitutes its identity against the otherness and loss presented in the moment of terror" (9). Mala's experience resonates with Kristeva's sublime:

> The "sublime" object dissolves in the raptures of a bottomless memory. It is such a memory, which from stopping point to stopping point, remembrance to remembrance, love to love, transfers that object to the refulgent point of the dazzlement in which I stray in order to be. [. . .] I then forget the point of departure and find myself removed to a secondary universe, set off from the one where "I" am—delight and loss. [. . .] [T]he sublime is a *something added* that expands us, overstrains us, and causes us to be here, as dejects, and *there*, as others and sparkling. (Kristeva 11–12)

Mala's gruesome ritual imbues her with awe and inspiration, as it takes her to the edge of being and back again; she is released from her abject state as an abandoned daughter, sister, and niece; an abandoned lover; and a victim of repeated incest and violent rape. Within that sublime moment there is "*something added* that expands" Mala.

Mala is a gothic heroine, yet she is able to step outside that confining space through the ecstatic sublime. Furthermore, Mala's bird pepper ritual happens in the space of excess—in the physical space of her overgrown garden, and in the psychological space of the sublime—but it does not bring harm to any other person as so much of the excess within more conventional gothic narratives. Thus, Mootoo challenges and rehabilitates our expectations for the typical gothic heroine who has suffered such profound physical and sexual abuse. To outsiders, Mala's garden is far from the conception of a Caribbean Paradise, and to readers familiar with the gothic aesthetic, her garden is easily understood to be a place of danger, a space of rape and death. Yet, Mala's garden is a space of both splendor and peril, as her garden is the place where cereus flowers bloom and the place where she experiences ecstasy that brings her to the brink of physical collapse, release. For Mala, her wild, gothic garden is a space of transformation. The disintegration that usually signals a dangerous or hopeless environment for the gothic heroine becomes a source of renewal for Mala. For example, "every few days, a smell of decay permeate[s] [Mala's] house" (115). This scent is no doubt that of her father's decomposing body, among other things. In order to avoid being overwhelmed by the stench, Mala brews "an odour of her own design" (115). The scent is created by boiling empty snail shells, which envelops the house with the "aroma of a long-simmering ocean into which worm-rich, root-matted earthiness was constantly being poured and stirred," and, as a result, the "aroma obliterated, reclaimed and gave the impression of reversing decay. [. . .] A pin prick of fresh blood to sharpen the snails' scent [. . .] [makes] it almost tangible" (115). The ritual rejuvenates the air for days at a time and "[weaves] itself though Mala's hair and penetrate[s] her pores" (115). The ritual also reveals a positive reimagining of what we may call the "undead." In Mala's experience of the world, things and people are not fully obliterated by physical death. Decay, in this sense, brings solace and transforms perspectives.

Mala also repurposes detritus in the sewing room where she has hidden her father's body. Measuring a "full hand deep," Mala carries a bucket filled with "every visible corpse off her property, the heap included ants, beetles and cockroaches, different kinds of spiders" (128). Unlike her efforts to neutralize the scent of her decaying father, "[s]he [pays] no attention to the odour rising out of the bucket. The scent of decay was not offensive to her. It was the aroma of life refusing to end. It was the aroma of transformation" (128). In a most revealing passage, we learn that for Mala, "[s]uch odour was proof that nothing truly ended, and she reveled in it as much as she did the fragrance of cereus blossoms along the back wall of the house" (128). Mala's perception that the odor is the one of "transformation" echoes the novel's emphasis on the cathected, undead nature of what is thought to be over or dead, but simultaneously underscores the space in which such animated remains can be countervailed. Mala takes the carcasses from the bucket and pins them to the wall of the sewing room, crushing fallen insects beneath her feet. These fallen corpses become "fodder for a vibrating carpet of moths, centipedes, millipedes, cockroaches and unnamed insects that found refuge in Mala's surroundings"; it is the sublime representation of "[d]eath feeding life" (130). Mala's conception of "death feeding life"—or "life refusing to end"—is even more salient when her father's corpse is discovered. She encounters her past and its frightful, undead reality. The corpse transforms into an undead entity beckoning Mala with "grey" then "red" stretched skin and a "purplish tongue" flickering from "parted black gums" (183). Even though the discovery of the body leads to exile from her garden, her home, Mala is effectively reborn with the help of Tyler, who tends to her ghostly matters, those ghostly matters being the persistent state of hauntedness that her rituals have helped her abate—that "animated state" in which Gordon says "repressed or unresolved social [and physical] violence [. . .] mak[es] itself known" (xvi).

Nevertheless, in the novel's final pages, Mala has reached the pinnacle of her recovery sitting in a new garden, reentering the world of human relationships and interaction, waiting with four other characters for the rare, exotic cereus plant, born from clippings salvaged from her former garden, to bloom. In a way, Mala is like the cereus, a plant that must rest for a season, and sometimes for many years, before it will bloom again. During its rest, the plant needs warmth, water, and manure in order to flourish again. (The appearance of my own plant during its resting season oscillates in some interstitial space between a vivacious weed and a strained, unkempt houseplant on the precipice of death.) After reading numerous accounts of others who have witnessed the cereus's effluence, a common theme emerges: when the cereus blooms at night, one witnesses a magical happening. From at least Victorian times until the present, people have held viewing parties waiting for the plant's tubular buds to erupt into amazing, perfume-heavy flowers.[8] As the characters await the transplanted cereus's first blooming, they have faith that the plant will transform from something gangly and unremarkable into something exquisite and extraordinary. They believe in its promise, its potential. That promise frames and births so many layers of Mootoo's novel. And within its depths is the proof that from cathected remains of trauma, from the depths of gothic decay, something else may emerge—something transformed, *something added*, something sparkling.

NOTES

Special thanks on my first publication to the editors of this volume, Eric Gary Anderson, Taylor Hagood, and Daniel Cross Turner; my dissertation directors, Minrose Gwin and Shayne

Legassie; colleagues and friends including Kelly Bezio and Christin Mulligan; the Literatures of the Americas Working Group (UNC–Chapel Hill); and María DeGuzmán and Ruth Salvaggio.

    1. Esteemed gardener Irene Virag describes the night-blooming cereus cactus, *Epiphyllum oxypetalum*, as "strange but romantic" (G15). There are many species of night- blooming cereus, but this particular species has green, gangly leaves, as Mr. Hector, the Paradise Alms House gardener, describes (Mootoo 5).

    2. See Casid's study of late-eighteenth-century landscapes and their meticulous compositions (e.g., 57–74) in *Sowing Empire: Landscape and Colonization*.

    3. East Indian indentured servitude ended in 1917 (Leonce 1).

    4. See Abbott 313–48 for more information about the conditions and practices of indentured servitude in the Caribbean and specifically in Trinidad.

    5. U.S. South fiction such as Faulkner's "A Rose for Emily," Welty's "Clytie," and "A Curtain of Green," and Lee's *To Kill a Mockingbird*, for example, draw much of their power from the tension between community and the aberrant.

    6. The phrase "rememory" refers to the phenomenon Sethe experiences in Toni Morrison's *Beloved* (e.g., 7, 43). In brief, rememory is the memory and the physical site of memory imprinted by the psychic energy of people, events, or things. I note that rememory is akin to "emotional memory—what the nerves and the skin remember as well as how it appeared" that Morrison describes in her essay "The Site of Memory" (77).

    7. This passage from Kristeva's *Powers of Horror: An Essay on Abjection* and the one that follows fall in line conceptually with Mala's transcendental, transformative ritual space.

    8. See, for example, Sudhadra Devan's "Cereus Magic" in *New Straits Times*, www.nst.com.my/life-times/health/cereus-magic-1.132911, which includes Asian folklore about the plant; Virag's "Cereus Reigns as Queen for a Night" in *Newsday*, www.irenevirag.com/media/cereus.pdf; or a whole collection of night-blooming cereus stories and photos at Ken Druse's gardening site *Real Dirt*, http://kendruse.typepad.com/ken_drusereal_dirt/2006/09/opening_night.html.

19

"MORE DEAD THAN LIVING"
Randall Kenan's Monstrous Community

WADE NEWHOUSE

In a recent article calling for the development of a "philosophy of the monstrous," Dominique Lestel describes a contemporary condition in which humanity has created so many monsters (biological, cybernetic, medical) that monstrosity has ceased to be a recognizably distinct category of ontological or epistemological difference. In philosophy at least, claims Lestel, "what is most likely the major problem of our time" has therefore become "the normalization of the monstrous and the jubilation that results from it" (265). For Lestel, ours is increasingly a culture that seeks out and delights in its confrontation with the uncanny—so much so that Lestel can claim that "we have come to share our life with monsters without even knowing it" (265). The uncanny is in this analysis no longer a threatening Other disguising desire but an open acknowledgment of that desire; the presence of the monstrous becomes a means of publicly accessing, rather than deferring, direct confrontation with traumas.

Randall Kenan's fiction thrives on the attitude toward monstrosity that Lestel maps out. His 1989 novel *A Visitation of Spirits* and 1992 short story collection *Let the Dead Bury Their Dead* seem to require ghosts, demons, zombies, and other unnamable haunts for his most basic analysis of small-town southern life. In Kenan's little town of Tims Creek, North Carolina, race, gender, sexual orientation, and religious affiliation provide markers of individual identity and community standing, but these markers are tested and (sometimes) affirmed almost always through characters' experiences with a supernatural that fits so seamlessly into "normal" life that Kenan's fundamental narrative structures cannot function without it. If, to cite a common view of such tales, the genre of the American gothic is about "a narrative site that tends to be an epistemological frontier in which the spatial division between the known and the unknown, the self and the Other, assumes temporal dimensions" (Savoy 6), then Kenan's particular deployment of gothic conventions misses a central feature of the genre by downplaying the distinction between the known and unknown: Kenan's monsters are always already part of the available fabric out of which his communities and characters define themselves, evoking a sort of spooky magical realism in which the everyday is more haunting than the abject.

The central theme of Kenan's work in *A Visitation of Spirits* and *Let the Dead Bury Their Dead* is the relationship between individuals and their community—specifically, the various degrees to which the community of Tims Creek allows individuality to function. *A Visitation of Spirits* tells the story of teenager Horace Cross, whose homosexuality prevents him from participating in the community traditions his own family has established over the generations, while *Let the Dead Bury Their Dead* showcases an array of tormented figures who struggle to articulate their subjectivity amid the restrictive boundaries created by the town's stifling racial and sexual standards, what Maisha Wester calls its "communal definition of survival" (1036). All of these stories use figures of the monstrous to emphasize the extreme passions and prejudices that lie at the edges of community norms—as such, almost all of them investigate Scott Romine's question about whether a community must coerce in order to cohere (*Narrative* 2). The titular story in *Let the Dead Bury Their Dead*, however, presents Kenan's most comprehensive analysis of not only the formation of community itself but the apparent need of a southern black community to hold onto its monsters rather than exorcise them. As in Lestrel's analysis of monstrous humanity, Kenan's community of Tims Creek cannot exist without its monsters, cannot tell its own story without recourse to an imagery of undeath that grounds its sense of contemporary reality. Kenan's monstrosity, however, works in surprising ways, effectively distancing the material concerns of the present from the traumas of black history. Rather than affirming a productive connection to the past and using its lessons to build a future in which individual agency can express itself, Kenan's polyphonic, ghoul-ridden oral history emphasizes a rupture between the black South's understandings of its past and its sense of itself going forward.

In gothic fiction, writes Judith Halberstam, "multiple interpretations are embedded in the text and part of the experience of horror comes from a realization that meaning itself runs riot. Gothic novels produce a symbol for this interpretive mayhem in the body of the monster" (2). For Halberstam, the figure of a monster in a gothic text represents a fear that comes from confronting too much meaning—presumably contradictory, irreconcilable meanings clashing in a limited textual space. Therefore, the appearance of demons (in *A Visitation of Spirits*) and ghosts and zombies (in *Let the Dead Bury Their Dead*) indicates Kenan's recognition that narrating the contemporary southern black experience is not one of simply testifying and signifying on tradition but of recording and managing ontological chaos. What Halberstam refers to as "the body of the monster" is less the physical manifestation of the undead that populate Kenan's work than the more fundamental problem of representing a community that is uncomfortably bound to the darkest parts of its heritage even while it claims a new cultural identity in the present day.

Kenan lays the groundwork for his vision of monstrous community in *A Visitation of Spirits*, in which the unhappy Horace Cross summons a demon to free him from the horrors of being a homosexual black teenager in Tims Creek.[1]

In a night of Dickensian travel through history and space, the demon forces Horace to confront painful scenes from his own unhappy life and that of his pious, hypocritical family, reinforcing Horace's belief that the moral structure of the town is too insular and judgmental to allow him any space to be himself. The novel ends with Horace's suicide and the even bleaker suggestion that the community's life and norms will continue on, never registering his sacrifice:

> *Most importantly,* the day did not halt in its tracks: clocks did not stop. The school buses rolled. The cows mooed. The mothers scolded their children. Plows broke up soil. Trucks were unloaded and loaded up. Dishes were washed. Dogs barked. Old men fished. Beauticians gossiped. Food was eaten. And that night the sun set with the full intention of rising on the morrow. (254, emphasis added)[2]

I note this moment near the novel's end to suggest the true subject in his stories is not only the individual characters, but the potential (however often unfulfilled) that those characters might influence the destinies of those around them. Kenan uses ghosts and monsters to signify an uncanny instability in such influences.

In *A Visitation of Spirits,* Kenan's monsters equivocate, but they are not exactly deceptive: like Scrooge's ghosts, the demons who force Horace to face his community and his church do speak truths—about Horace as well as about what it means to belong in Tims Creek. When they lead Horace into a vision of his congregation as it was in days gone by, Horace is at first unable to accept the fact of the dead returned to life before him.[3] "But how can these people be here?" he asks. "I mean . . . are they ghosts?" The demon's response is as instructive for us as it is dismissive of Horace: "Ghosts? Yeah, you might call them ghosts. Ghosts of the past. The presence of the present. The very stuff of which the future is made. This is the effluvium of souls that surround men daily" (73).

This concept of ghostly power summarizes much of Kenan's project. First, it announces that in Kenan's supernatural world, past, present, and future are assumed to mingle with and supplant one another. This blurring of distinct temporal labels ensures that the prejudices and repressive gendered norms of one era become fixed and reincarnated (so to speak) in each new generation. As Éva Tettenborn notes, Horace's destiny is already defined for him, since the history of the Cross family is one of "repeat[ing] life experiences of their fathers" (252). For Horace's demon, all times are one. More significantly for my reading of "Let the Dead Bury Their Dead," this passage suggests that it is the *presence* of the ghosts that allows time to be seen in this way—which is to say that hauntings are necessary in Kenan's fiction to get beyond a simplistic view of history as linear and "progress" as teleological. Put another way, Kenan's monsters testify not simply to crimes in the past but injustices still to come; there can be no surmounting of trauma, no healing power of time, because the present and future, as we have seen, are *together* the "effluvium" of life, ultimately indistinct from one another and each subject to constant revision by the other.

"Let the Dead Bury Their Dead" is a more direct exploration of this idea's implication for an entire community. This final tale of Kenan's collection pulls the key themes from Horace's night of black magic—Christian hypocrisy, the allure of an Afrocentric alternative, tradition's need to suppress homosexuality, and the relationship between individual expression and community narrative—and applies them to a potential history of Tims Creek. A multilayered nest of tales and tellings presented as a newly published work collected before his death by the Reverend James Malachai Greene, the central action of "Let the Dead Bury Their Dead" takes the form of a debate between Greene's aging great-aunt and -uncle in which they attempt to explain how a "maroon" settlement for escaped slaves eventually became the town in which all of Kenan's stories have unfolded. At the heart of the stories spun by these competing tellers is the struggle for supremacy between two mysterious religious leaders: the African chieftain Pharaoh, raising an army of runaway slaves in the swamp, and Preacher, who seeks to bring the local citizens back to the Gospel. The historical struggle between these two ideologies is paralleled by a textual struggle between competing accounts of this competition: in addition to the oral history argued by Zeke and Ruth, the reader must contend with a range of outside commentaries, such as scholarly footnotes to trace the historical inaccuracies of the tall tales and journal entries that allow lesser historical personalities to speak for themselves against the grain of the contemporary reconstruction.

Though the story ends with a zombie apocalypse writ small that wipes out one iteration of the town to prepare the ground for a new one, both Kenan's subject and style struggle, monster-like, against conventions that seek to bind them to established systems of meaning. Kenan's story is thus as much an exercise in rhetorical monstrosity as it is a story about how monsters function in the black southern imaginary. The past, he seems to say, might very well simply unroll into the eventual present, but describing that historical process—and assigning meaning to the darkest parts—is fraught with peril. Choices must be made, and people in the present (like Horace Cross) can get hurt.

The tone of "Let the Dead Bury Their Dead" is playful, although the content is not, and this disparity between material history and the language of remembering suggests for Kenan a real tension underlying black southerners' options for building on their shared past. The story that James Greene's great-aunt and -uncle tell begins with a mystery: the tale telling is prompted by a question Greene has apparently asked about the history of a strange mound on the outskirts of town. "That mound," says Uncle Zeke, "was the center of town, a long long time ago" (283)—thus the ultimate point of the story is to explain how something central became something peripheral, how (and why) the community in which these characters speak moved away from its own origins.

The mysterious mound—and the fact that it disappears from Zeke's account until the very end of the story—grounds Kenan's tale in a particular theory of storytelling's role in sustaining community. On the face of it, "Let the Dead Bury Their Dead" seems to be an example, albeit an overly baroque one, of the black "porch talk" tradition in which tale telling and exaggerations connect generations and give agency to the storytellers and their audience. In such a reading, the process of relaying Tims Creek's legendary history would give Zeke and Ruth some personal stake in shaping and passing on their interpretations of their heritage, and the younger James Greene might feel some kinship to a lost era even amid the more frantic postmodern reality of his day-to-day life.[4]

On the contrary, the mound whose mysterious origin prompts the story indicates neither empowerment through storytelling nor a reverence for community but, in fact, distance, a widening gap between the remembered past and the material present. Tims Creek, we eventually learn, is emphatically *not* located where its history began; the horrors (both likely and unlikely) of the story Zeke and Ruth will tell have pushed the contemporary community away from the site (sight) of its earliest shared history. Moreover, as we will see, Kenan presents no evidence that either telling or hearing such oral history has any effect on the lives of black southerners in the present. At best, Kenan dramatizes an impulse to tell, to listen, and to understand horror that carries few lessons and little tangible impact.

The story Zeke tells involves a legendary slave named Pharaoh who leads a violent uprising against the Cross plantation and then escapes into the swamps, gathering his followers and growing numbers of runaways around him. As long as it represents an escape from slavery, Pharaoh's new community signifies the opportunity for a society built on pre-Christian mystic power. In addition to the obvious symbolism of his name, Pharaoh "was some kind of chief or witch doctor or medicine man or wizard or something" in Africa (294) and also brings "something powerful from the Waccamaw medicine man" to Tims Creek (297). Once in his swamp refuge, Pharaoh preaches a precolonial ideology of independence: "Told em to remember that they come from a great land and a great people and such-like. Wont preaching he done, more like learning, learning em to love themselves and the world round em. Said a time gone come when they'd all reclaim their glory. And the town kept a-growing" (305). After emancipation, this community of outlaws becomes a real town: "Folk commenced to build," says Zeke. "They got a post office. Cleared land. Drained parts of the swamp, started farming, cotton, corn, and indigo. Raised livestock. But Pharaoh was still the head of the community, you know, still looked up to" (305).

At first, Pharaoh embodies the iconic Rebellious Slave archetype, representing not the existential evil of the slave system itself but an exaggerated fantasy of black power and vengeance that rises to confront it. Surely a "monster" in the slaveholding system (the mistress of the Cross plantation describes a nightmare in which Pharaoh violates her not sexually but by forcing her to do manual labor), Pharaoh also represents the conflicting multiplicity of meanings that Halberstam described. Since the Civil War removes the necessity of waging a complete war against slavery, the overly powerful, impossible-to-read magician Pharaoh becomes not the leader of a conquering army but rather the locus of a peaceful community, safely hidden and removed from white interference. Predictably the scholarly footnotes provided by the story's fictional editor manage to remove Pharaoh from legends of mystical power and pin him instead to mundane materialism: bills of sale, government documents, shipping logs.

Thus history and circumstance conspire to tamp down the monstrosity that could have emerged from Pharaoh's story. It returns in an unlikely place, however, when the community's new savior, the mysterious light-skinned Preacher, arrives after Pharaoh's death. Unlike the vengeful Pharaoh in his earlier days, the Preacher appears to represent moral order and a return to (white) Christian certainty. He urges the members of the community to reject Pharaoh's teachings and embarks upon a crusade of evangelizing, building churches, baptizing, teaching Sunday school: "And that Preacherman he say he'd been sent by the Lord thy God, said he heard tell of a bunch of Negroes living way out in the backwoods like animals wallowing in they heathen ways and he'd been sent, Praise Jesus, to deliver they souls, to make thee worthy vessels for the Lord thy God" (315). The Preacher, however, turns out to be monstrous in his own ways, eventually scandalizing the emerging town of Tearshirt with extravagant sexualities, a strangely rapacious appetite, and rumors of magical powers. "It was like the town had a new Pharaoh," admits Zeke (316).

The implicit competition between these magicians' influence comes to a head when the Preacher orders the men of Tearshirt to dig up Pharaoh's grave to retrieve a reputed treasure. In apparent retaliation, the town's dead rise from their graves and wreak havoc upon the living. "Oh, it was a mess," says Zeke (328). After an orgy of undead violence, a rain of fire from the sky destroys the town, leaving only the mysterious mound whose presence inspired the storytelling at the outset. Two survivors (in Zeke's version of the story) then establish the current town of Tims Creek, "but this time for both the black and the white" (333). Ruth's version of the story denies the zombie apocalypse and insists that the town's founder acquired the land through a business transaction. The mysterious mound, she insists, is either an old Indian burial mound or a feature of natural geology: "But it sure as the devil wont the Lord destroying devils and dead folk and suchlike. And you know it yourself, you old fool" (334).

The fundamental disagreement between Zeke and Ruth represents a debate about the proper role of the gothic in narrating Kenan's vision of black southern history, but that debate also implicates other textual strategies that slyly encode normative attitudes toward such slippery issues as "truth." Scott Romine, for instance, finds that the story's use of footnotes—some fictional but many referencing "actual historical sources"—undermines the power of the narrative to imagine a useful alternative to established historical tropes; for Romine, "the regime of the footnote, for which there is only one kind of real," creates "a narrative apparatus that locks folk history into the prison house of empiricism" (*The Real South* 151). Like Zeke, Romine is suspicious of a narrative insistence upon material reality, especially when we have access to the powerful image of the restless dead as a tool for understanding—and not merely depicting or representing—social evils. "How can one make use of the dead?" he muses earlier in his chapter on novelist Lewis Nordan (150).

How, indeed? In their most literal appearance, the dead in Kenan's story kill almost every living member of the town, effectively destroying rather than improving the community that had created itself out of the horrors of slavery. Whatever a maroon community such as Tearshirt represents for the evolving history of the postbellum black South, Kenan's worldview will not allow it to pursue a straight line from then to now—the zombie apocalypse breaks the community's history in half and leaves an un-narrated gap between the black Tearshirt that was and the heterogeneous Tims Creek that is.

Contrasting Kenan's community ethos with that of the traditionally conservative black church, Uzzie Cannon argues that Kenan's use of the oral storytelling trope is "subversive" and ultimately allows Kenan to suggest "that the African American community gains cohesion not through conformity but through difference" (107). The problem with this analysis is that it shows Kenan simply replacing one kind of community (traditional, judgmental, binary) with another (experimental, accepting, open-ended). Cannon seems entirely comfortable using the label "real community" to describe both the illusory sense of place and circumstance bound up in traditional folk histories and the newer, more postmodern set of associations that "maintains cohesion through a negotiation of ideas, thoughts, and reality" (111). Of course, Cannon is correct to argue that Kenan's goal is to expand the black experience of itself—to preach for acceptance of difference and tolerance of identities and potential cultural situations outside the limits imposed by older models of thinking. To simply suggest that Tims Creek is more "real" once it has done so, however, is to fall back into the old canard of using the binary of real/unreal in an attempt to claim diversity as a legitimate, rather than aberrant, social condition. Hoefer, by contrast, recognizes the key role of the monstrous in erasing a sense of linear progress in the road from Tearshirt to Tims Creek, pointing to apocalyptic imagery as a "signal of deferral, of trauma, and of productive instability" that allows competing narratives of community to share cultural authority, rather than simply overtake one another (127). The final effect of Kenan's monstrous narrative form is to "[create] a space for meaningful discussion of the possibility of difference within community" (129), where the past serves "not in order to maintain a stable identity but rather in order to create a usable history that will guide those exchanges and that will be accessible to all who wish to claim it" (129).[5]

To fully appreciate how far Kenan goes in redrawing community as an unstable, yet accessible dynamic requires that we more fully conceptualize the presence of the living dead in the story's final apocalyptic scene and that scene's relationship to the present-day in which Kenan's tale is narrated. Brian Norman claims that Kenan's larger goal is to "imagine new models of community made possible when the living commune with the returned dead" (53)—though in "Let the Dead Bury Their Dead" specifically, that "communion" is brief and violent and destructive; it does not seem to be the stuff of community building.[6] Yet the orgy of violence serves a purpose in Kenan's architecture of story by acknowledging and owning the fact of shared monstrosity in the black southern past.

Zeke suggests that "the Horror" was "let aloose" by the Preacher to purge Tearshirt of its sin for following the pagan (Africanist) teachings of Pharoah (319). The army of the dead that rises to slaughter the town's inhabitants, however, is not comprised of outsiders or special deceased commandos chosen for this mission: they are, according to Zeke, "[e]very last one of them what died and been buried in Tearshirt or Snatchit going back to the first who died when Pharoah first brung em out of bondage. Some of em dead twenty, fifteen years" (327). The risen dead, in other words, represent the entire history of the town as a self-sustaining community, everything that has been gained and lost in the transition from slavery. "And wont nowhere safe," says Zeke, "cause there was more dead than there was living" (238).

If we read the murdering dead not literally but as a discursive strategy—as a need within the town's narrative of itself to confront a monstrosity that is internal rather than external—then this is a crucial moment in Tims Creek's communal memory. I suggest that a town such as Tims Creek needs the monstrous version of the story, for its identity as a racially heterogeneous community in the present requires a horrific origin in which the dead (that is, the horror of memory, the trauma of return) actually outnumber the living (those who might endure and survive). Or perhaps such a community needs the *rejection* of such an origin to justify its status as a legitimate mixed-race modern town that no longer needs to believe such tales.[7] Zeke claims, after all, that the current town of Tims Creek was founded by a survivor of the apocalypse "not wanting to remember the town before" (333), intentionally separating the new community from the myth of its beginnings. The Preacher's bloodthirsty zombies present a uniquely stark vision of unrelenting black-on-black violence and signify an ontological horror already implicit in the community itself. The dead rising from their graves to kill off the town's residents therefore testify to the uncanny nature of the entire enterprise. Maroon community, self-governance, rule by Pharoah or by Preacher: all must be accepted as monstrous.

To the degree that, in Romine's original articulation, cohesive communities depend on coercion, the black community's history of oppression—by slavery itself, certainly, but afterward by competing predatory liberation narratives—has ultimately allowed a folk culture in which tale telling, jockeying for rhetorical position, parodies the violence of its own past. Lestel's admonition that "we have come to share our lives with monsters without even noticing" (265) points to an important distinction: in Kenan's tale, many monsters are noticed—but most are eventually dismissed. In his final account of the battle between good and evil that established the community of Tims Creek, Zeke mentions that the mysterious mound (all that remains of the original maroon community) "goes all the way down to hell" (332). But as I noted at the beginning of this chapter, that mound is *not* the site of the present-day community, which is defined in both versions of the story by its *distance* from that mound. Thus, in its eagerness to begin its oral tradition in the realistic horror of slavery but to then shift to more imaginary horrors, Kenan's contemporary black tale-telling experience is founded on an access to hell but has apparently decided to move on.

NOTES

1. Kenan's novel is not entirely clear about whether the demon actually exists or is a figment of Horace's imagination. As Wester notes, however, "real or imagined—the text suggests its actuality doesn't matter because the nightmare points to the real, lived horror" (1035).

2. "In other words," notes Anthony Hoefer in his discussion of this paragraph, "the Apocalypse does not come" (121).

3. Trudier Harris notes a distinction between fearing God and fearing "the *people* who profess belief in God" as a tool for indicting religious hypocrisy (*Scary* 127). For more on Kenan's tale as a commentary on the black church, see Tuire Valkeakari, *Religious Idiom and the African American Novel, 1952–1998*.

4. As Jean-François Lyotard explains: "Thus the narratives allow the society in which they are told, on the one hand, to define its criteria of competence and, on the other, to evaluate according to those criteria what is performed or can be performed within it" (20). Harris notes that the "porch talk" tradition emphasizes a process by which the voice of a speaker "enters into the minds of the readers, finds fertile ground in a commonality of philosophies, characters, activities, and approaches to the world" (*Power* 58)—a commonality that Zeke doesn't seem to care much about.

5. Hoefer defines "the unmistakably apocalyptic nature of Zeke's story" as the fact that "the dead rise to mete out justice to their kin"—essentially, in my opinion, aligning his label of "apocalyptic" to the presence of the monstrous I have been tracking here (127).

"MORE DEAD THAN LIVING"

6. Norman's analysis focuses upon young Clarence's apparent ability to talk to the dead in the story that opens Kenan's collection, but I am borrowing his sense of "communion" with the dead to see how far it will go when applied to wanton destruction.

7. Wester nicely notes that transgressive bodies are made monstrous by the gothic in order to emphasize "the shudder, and not the desire" (1038), suggesting that there might be an element of the fetishistic in the images of violent black bodies risen from their graves.

20

GOING TO GROUND
The Undead in Contemporary Southern Popular Culture Media and Writing

TAYLOR HAGOOD

The essays in this volume show the many ways that subtle metaphorical and cultural incarnations of undeadness have lurked in southern literature from its beginnings. This essay turns to the explicit employment of literal undead southern figures in what may or may not be considered southern places in current popular writing and media. While undead figures from and in the South have appeared before in popular culture, the current incarnation of southern undeadness, which is part of a larger popular culture explosion of the undead, offers a significant site for observing ongoing redefinitions of what the South is and what its people are or could be like. I will be focusing on three generically diverse textual clusters: (1) Charlaine Harris's Sookie Stackhouse novels and their adaptation in the HBO series *True Blood*; (2) Robert Kirkman's comic book series *The Walking Dead* and its adaptation as an AMC television series of the same name; and (3) Eric Powell's comic book series *The Goon*. In both form and content these text-media groups distill southern space and performance, and the undead characters function to articulate a foundational active discourse and presence of what can be conceived of as southern "ground."

I would situate this discussion within the larger one of postsouthernness, which continually characterizes theorizations of contemporary southern literature and culture. For some years now, distinctly poststructural conceptualizations of a post-South have been developed in contradistinction to more conventional notions of southern space and identity. The latter tend toward autochthony, the idea of southern grounds producing certain kinds of individuals and situations; examples include the writings of the Agrarians (especially the Twelve Southerners' *I'll Take My Stand*) and Richard Weaver.[1] Postsouthernness exposes the mystification inherent in such theories, posing instead more fluid, Derridian, cultural materialist conceptualizations. Three important conceptualizations of postsouthernness are useful in orienting discussion of the undead. One is Michael Kreyling's parody thesis in *Inventing Southern Literature* that the South (whatever it ever was) at some point ceased to exist as an actual thing so that writers must now work within the forms of its former existence in self-conscious parody—a markedly undead-inflected concept. In *The Postsouthern Sense of Place*, Martyn Bone teases out Kreyling's implied rupture, itself first promoted by the Agrarians, of postsouthernness to show how southern white ideas about small-time agriculture have been and are mere mythologies in the face of a space dominated in reality by finance capitalism and real estate. Most recently and effectively Scott Romine in *The Real South* has taken a different tack from Bone and Kreyling, seeing southern literature and culture's postmodern surfaces as purely a simulacrum of myths that are capitalist-driven repeated fetishizations. Of course, popular media readily embrace the capitalistic goals Bone and Romine discuss, and the undead carry their own layering of signification in the history of those media, from the urbane Dracula to George Romero's stumbling mob. Still, however much the texts I want to examine are the creations of people digging hungrily into the flesh of a cash-cow, they also reveal ongoing conceptions of southern place, space, and performance. The southern undead go far in showing how inextricable popular media and conceptions of (post)southernness are.

In fact, the undead in the current popular culture productions I am considering display postsouthern visions that are no less aware of poststructuralism and economic and cultural factors but nevertheless see "ground" as efficacious. There flows through and around these productions a kind of endemic energy that can inundate both "natural" and "virtual" planes of grounding. This energy might best be contextualized in the framework of Bruno Latour's "action network theory" and in Jane Bennett's discussion of what she calls "vibrant matter." The latter is especially useful in examining the undead, for it offers some of the most radical possibilities for nonhuman actants and redefinitions of being alive. Especially intriguing to me are the ways that an aura of southernness is created within popular fiction, the panels of comics, and television screens that negotiate already-compromised planes of simulacrum (in Baudrillard's sense) in order to evoke and negotiate as it were (which is to say imagined or not-so-imagined) planes that might be labeled "authentic." The elements interacting are not just the images, bodies, and words within these media but the media themselves and the actants who produce them as well as the places in which they are produced. For Latour, every "thing" is fair game—for example, in an office space computers, walls, desks, dust, and silverfish all interact with humans to create an environment. As Bennett notes, things can act in ways that defy conventional anthro-centered ideas of what action is. Approaching the creation of fiction, comics, and television with such a variously complex interactive model in mind, we might think about how southernness and undeadness operate on what might normally be seen as metalevels of production in which questions about the identity and attitudes of agents, publishers, directors, and actors come into play. These matters are especially true of current popular culture productions, which proliferate in multiple forms of social media and metacommentary; for example, each episode of *The Walking Dead* is followed immediately on AMC by *The Talking Dead,* in which the foregoing episode is discussed with the series' screenplay writers, actors, and nonaffiliated fans.

Southernness—whether thought of spatially or as a spatially defined, variously performed identity—pervades the "grounds" of these layers, from literal southern soil to the simulacra of film sets to metadiscussions of writers, producers, and actors. Present in these layers is, among other things, an at times explicit and at other times implicit element of authenticity, and it is in this element that undeadness functions in important ways pertaining to history and identity. Even when at its most obviously postmodern, southernness nevertheless requires an implied authenticity, even if it is one of authenticated pure simulation—the simulation itself requires recognizable forms, a matter that Kreyling discusses in terms of memory and specifically the "southern memory market" in *The South That Wasn't There.* The undead represent many things in the texts here examined, but they particularly articulate different things that the South and southernness may be considered to be. In a postmodern moment, these various layers of ground compete with each other for authenticity even as they manifest anxiety about the impossibility and strategic pragmatism of the very concept of authenticity itself. My effort is to deal with texts that progressively alienate a recognizable version of southernness using the undead as enabling figures. Freed from the functioning of humans (lacking the operation of vital organs and even brainwaves), the undead can exemplify authenticity even as they by nature always already exemplify the inauthentic. What I mean by the latter is that within their fictional contexts they are disconnected from human functioning and history however much they may affect those things, while on a metalevel their being mythical places them on a different authenticity scale. It is also worth noting that they can represent things "living" in different ways from animated life and so register those traditionally less visible actants and modes of acting that Latour and Bennett present.

The first textual cluster I want to examine is that consisting of the Sookie Stackhouse novels by Charlaine Harris and HBO's series *True Blood*.[2] A Mississippian, Harris sets her novels in the small fictional north Louisiana town of Bon Temps, allowing herself to focus on a traditional rural southern space in explicit contrast with the New Orleans vamp scene of Anne Rice's imagination. The premise of the series, beginning with *Dead until Dark*, is that because scientists have developed and marketed synthetic blood, vampires are no longer forced to kill and drink human blood and so can "come out of the coffin" and coexist with humans.[3] The narrator of the novels is a young waitress named Sookie Stackhouse, whose gift (or, as she puts it, "disability") of hearing other people's thoughts constantly tortures her until one night a vampire appears in Merlotte's restaurant-bar where she works. This vampire is William Compton, a former slave owner and Confederate soldier with a name that evokes Faulkner's aristocratic Compson family. Vampire Bill, as he is sometimes called, represents a figure largely and multivalently eroticized, the desire of multiple generations of white southern nostalgists, for like the Confederacy and the so-called Old South he fought for, he ceased to live in the 1860s only to go on living as not-alive ever since. The reader may well hear in the background of Bill's existence the popular culture cry of "The South Shall Rise Again!" and Bill's speaking to the Descendents of the Glorious Dead provides unassailably authentic information and validation for the largely neo-Confederate white community of Bon Temps. In the larger context of the novel's portrayal of southernness, Bill's presence in a recognizable and conventional southern rural space seems to confirm the concept of a South with an unbroken history of which the living whites are strikingly conscious and knowledgeable.

At the same time, though, many things in Harris's southern space are not what they seem, a fact that the television series *True Blood* makes even more explicit. The series announces its determination to play with stereotypes from its opening scene, when two college students stop at a convenient store for a bottle of the *True Blood* brand of synthetic blood, and the conventionally vampy-looking cashier pretends to be a real vampire while a redneck in overalls and a cap rummages in the coolers. By the scene's end, the traditional campy black-clad vampire proves a fake while the equally campy redneck reveals himself to be a real vampire. The maneuver in this case involves a layering of stereotypes that blends southernness and vampirism, but where Bill stands in for the not-so-surprising undead aristocrat, the redneck vampire outrages the expectations of both vampness *and* southernness. On one hand, this layering asserts an alternative kind of "authenticity" of vampire essence which the show does also by presenting "real" vampires as being able to appear in mirrors, immune to garlic, and capable of being photographed. At the same time, the redneck character's vamp status causes him to signify as more than what he seems: while being a vampire might accentuate the image of a poor white man as violent, the fact is that he not only does not kill the people in the store, he is actually "mainstreaming" as a distinctly nonmainstream human who buys and drinks the not-very-tasty *True Blood*.

By the end of season one, *True Blood* establishes a doubledness of authenticity that holds two different concepts of southern authenticity together and in tension with one another. In some ways the novel that the season loosely follows, *Dead until Dark,* does this too, but the series makes it sharper. For example, in the television series, Sookie's friend Tara is black, and she ironically jokes that she was named for the O'Hara plantation of Margaret Mitchell's *Gone with the Wind,* which the audience knows never existed. Later she and her mother visit a mysterious black woman exorcist named Ms. Jeanette only for Tara later to find she is no voodoo medicine woman living in the woods but a clerk in a small-town drugstore pretending to be an exorcist for extra cash to support her family. The result is a doubledness in which an authentic presentation of a southern African American woman in the twenty-first century underlies and anchors the more mythical and historically antecedent postsouthern "authentic" performance. In a similar vein, the murderer Rene is shown to be a fake Cajun who learned his accent from a cassette tape course for actors: his falseness adds to the general horror of authenticity (an uneasiness of the stability of autochthony) that ultimately drives the early seasons of the series. These examples make it clear for viewers how thoroughly elements of southernness can be and are performative. Nevertheless, underlying these cases is the autochthonously authenticated Bill and the "Old South" he represents. In other words, however much one layer of authenticity unsettles southern authenticity, the series remains, as it were, authentically "southern."

Rene's learning from actors' lessons deftly points to another layer of authenticity-performance in the series that lies in its production. Where Harris's being a native of Mississippi and working within traditional fictional forms carries a certain authorial autochthonous authentification, the television series is collaborative and performative in the many ways any television series or film is. As Tara McPherson has argued, "the real action [of *True Blood*] may actually be taking place offscreen, as capital reconstitutes itself in an era of networked globalization" (336). McPherson goes on to show that *True Blood*'s true place is "Premium Cable" as she traces the issues of film-industry labor that the series encodes. What is intriguing is the way a shaping force that can be called "southernness" moves through filmic space, fictive space (the space of the story), the space where filming happens, and the spaces with which different figures are connected or through which components of the film and its products pass . The series producer, Alan Ball, is from Atlanta, and none of the core cast members are from Louisiana. A few are not even from the United States: for example, Anna Paquin (Sookie) is from Canada, Stephen Moyer (Bill) from England, Ryan Kwantan (Sookie's brother Jason) from Australia. Viewers are treated to the presence of Memphis native William Sanderson as the Bon Temps sheriff, and there are other actors from the South, but *True Blood* is finally a performance of people playing within the postsouthern plane of surfaces. The possibility of sheer performance only of southern identity finds illustration within the series in season three in the form of Mississippi vampire king Russell Edgerton, who, unlike the southern-if-not-Cajun Rene, originated in another place altogether even as he enacts white southern aristocratic southern speech and manners. At the same time, though, even as the vampires' coming-out references everything from race to third-wave feminism to LGBTQ rights, these figures are also stand-ins for modes and performances of southernness that will not die.

However performative southernness or Louisiana-ness appear, there remains an anchoring of southern ground. While most indoor scenes are Hollywood sets, the exteriors were filmed in Louisiana, and there is in season one especially a strong implication of the power of ground itself. Two cases stand out: in episode six ("Cold Ground"), Bill burrows into the ground to survive a daytime attack of humans, and in episode eleven ("To Love Is to Bury"), Bill must be buried with Jessica, whom he has been ordered to turn, for the human-to-vampire transformation to take place. Pam discusses the necessity of this Christ-echoing burial imagery as Bill digs the grave, an ironic fact in light of the right-wing Christian "Fellowship of the Sun" response to the vampires in the series. For all its social progressiveness (especially the HBO series, which especially emphasizes gay characters, not least of which is the flamboyant Lafayette, brilliantly portrayed by Nelsan Ellis), ultimately the Sookie Stackhouse novels/*True Blood* series is somewhat backward-looking in its use of undeadness, which tends to stand in for all kinds of things of varying and even clashing sociopolitical motivations that refuse to expire, whether neo-Confederate platforms, conservative Christian ones, civil rights of a distinctly 1960s African American variety, or gay culture and the fight for its promotion. In the logic of the series' images and characters, including the montage that opens each episode to the sound of Jace Everit's "Bad Things," there stands a persistent, interactive series of things, sounds, icons, people, animals, vegetation, and, on a metalevel, film and audience memories that work together in a large affirmation of never-deadness of a conventional, recognizable southernness. They are the products and producers of a shaping southern ground, grounding, groundedness.

The Walking Dead, a comics series created and written by Kentuckian Robert Kirkman beginning in 2003, largely eschews established southern signifiers even while situating its distinctly September 11, 2001, brand of apocalyptic imagery and themes within a southern United States setting. Kirkman sends the message early on in the series: although the protagonist Rick Grimes is a small-town sheriff from Kentucky, he is no Andy Taylor, and when he wakes up from a coma and discovers that the town has been overtaken by zombies, he finds himself rescued by an African American man and his son with apparently no interracial tension. Then, as if writing with the current interests of southern literary scholars in mind, Kirkman has Rick go to none other than Atlanta to start trying to find a way to rid the countryside of the undead and restore a state of normality. Atlanta, the self-proclaimed international city, has occupied much attention as an urban space that disrupts monolithic notions of southern space, with Bone citing it as an under-the-radar epitome of the kind of finance capitalist–driven space that has been the southern reality instead of the Agrarian-based southern dream, and Scott Romine asking, "Is Atlanta part of the real South, the New South, the No South, or (as Tony Horowitz maintains) the anti-South?" (*The Real South* 10). What is interesting about Kirkman's work is that he feels no need to reference Atlanta's "southern" aspects at all. In *The Walking Dead*, Atlanta signifies in terms of its consciously asserted generic urbanness, as though Kirkman is using the city's cosmopolitanism against itself. Kirkman seems to want to employ Atlanta as a place that specifies itself *as* generic, a kind of postmodern blank space upon which anything can be projected. Kirkman simultaneously makes it an Old West town by having Rick wear a cowboy hat as he rides a horse into the city *and* a devastated 9/11 New York City where Rick encounters the Yankees baseball cap–wearing Asian American Glenn. Although a character in a later volume ventures that this zombie crisis results from government testing on the people of the region, suggesting a southern specificity, the reality is that there is no obvious reason this story *has* to happen in Atlanta beyond the fact that Atlanta provides the kind of general urbanness and urbanity that Kirkman seems to be after.

Interestingly, the zombies in *The Walking Dead* represent the very "Real South" Romine describes—a mass-produced mob wandering mindlessly through a series of capitalist-repeated signs and products. Kirkman's avoidance of explicit southern signs or the attempt to evoke an authentic southernness among almost all of the living characters is a deliberate showing of those signs to be rootless and inauthentic (at least in the naïve sense of authenticity). Gregory A. Waller has argued that in the encounter of the living and the undead, it is the similarity and relation of the undead to the living as having been once the living that is so revealing, and in *The Walking Dead* it is the zombies who represent the present-day southern world caught up in the sterile, generic landscape that Atlanta represents. These flip-flop-,

T-shirt-, and shorts-wearing zombies are the mindless, popular culture–drugged, mass-produced mob—the unmarked southern middle class, as Jon Smith has put it in "Southern Culture on the Skids." This is the very industrialized South the Agrarians feared, and it seems reasonable to discern a latent pro-Agrarian or at least pro–small town ethic in *The Walking Dead* that sees not the so-called Old South as the undead (as Harris does in William Compton) but rather the Real South, post-South, Atlanta South as the undead that has lost the value of "helping folks out." While Rick Grimes is no corny Sheriff Taylor, viewed a different way, Mayberry values struggle to overcome the heartless mass.

The AMC television series produced by Frank Darabont, however, infuses the story with far more explicit signifiers of southernness. Evidently suspicious of whether viewers will buy the idea that Rick gets all the way from Kentucky to Atlanta, Darabont has Rick come from a town in Georgia. The southern accents are thick, even though, again, few of the cast members are from the South (Andrew Lincoln, who portrays Rick, is British). As early as episode two of season one, the interracial group of survivors in Atlanta are at each other's throats, with the poor white Merle beating up the African American Tito until Rick steps in to save him. What is intriguing about this adaptation is that Darabont comes of Hungarian parents who settled in Chicago and then Los Angeles. So far as I know, Darabont has no connection to the South or Atlanta (although he seems to be friends with Eric Powell, who features a cartoon version of him in an issue of *The Goon*), yet although Darabont explicitly evokes Atlanta's Center for Disease Control as a nonregionalized touchstone for Atlanta's relevance to a zombie epidemic, he is more eager to juice up the southernness of the series than the Kentucky resident Kirkman, who seems to want to negotiate the poetics of the specific and the generic. Atlanta becomes a significant point of intersection, too, between the Sookie Stackhouse/*True Blood* textual cluster and *The Walking Dead* cluster because, as mentioned earlier, Alan Ball is from Atlanta. It is as if at the same time that the city signifies generic urbanity it also licenses the kind of play and repetition of signs that Romine discusses in his conception of the "Real South." Ground here is crucial and endowed with shaping power, whether one sees the city as possessing a quasi-mystical ability to form and shape or one understands Atlanta's engines of performance of *habitus* (in the Bourdieu sense) as inculcating its inhabitants with and/or somehow allowing for certain strategies of signification that accomplish this strange blend of the specific and the generic, the southern and the nonsouthern. Either way, one might wonder if Scarlett O'Hara's land is still imagined as all-powerful in southern popular culture?[4]

It is this nebulous performance-place nexus that makes the third textuality especially compelling; *The Goon* is a comic series created, written, illustrated, and initially even published by Tennessean Eric Powell. The overall premise and setting of the comic can hardly be called "southern" according to any conventional signs. It concerns a muscle-bound personage known only by the sobriquet of "Goon," who is the crime lord of a noir urban space usually referred to only as "this burg." Accompanied by a fiendish little fellow named Franky, the Goon spends the bulk of the early issues of the comic fighting the Zombie Priest and his legions of undead, who mostly occupy the area of Lonely Street. The Goon's world is an unabashedly, playfully postmodern conglomeration of mid-twentieth-century elements, ranging from Cold War aesthetics to 1930s-style nightclub scenes. This space may seem to make Powell what Fred Hobson, pondering postmodernism and the South, calls a "No South Writer." Yet the inclusion of "Lonely Street" from Elvis Presley's "Heartbreak Hotel" signals the kind of vague bubbling up of southern signs in Powell's work.[5] However nonsouthern this burg is, Powell takes care never to let the reader forget that it is imagined by someone who lives in a southern space.

Take, for example, the story in the second trade volume of the series, entitled *My Murderous Childhood (and Other Grievous Yarns)*. This story narrates Goon's meeting up with Franky when they are children, but it begins with a section of photographs of a boy in a rural setting that may be supposed to be Tennessee who is running away from home. The kid finds a comic book, reads the story of Goon and Franky, and declares: "That picture book done opened my eyes. Back Home I got a loving family, a community of loyal, hardworking friends and neighbors, and a lush, peaceful countryside for buildin' a home with a family of my own one day. Screw that crap! Good thing I got set straight before I went cryin' home with my tail between my legs. Yes, sir! After I get a tattoo across my face, I gotsta find me some of them easy women." Powell takes care in presenting a circumscribed world outside the comic panels themselves: his presentation of himself and his home setting are part of his creative project. Even the introductions by various hands included in practically every trade volume mention Powell's being a Tennessean. For example, William Stout, the production designer for *Return of the Living Dead*, writes: "I gotta admit it—I've got a thing for zombies. And hillbillies. That makes Eric Powell's comic, *The Goon*, just my cup of inbred anthrax." Frank Cho writes in his introduction to trade volume two, "What else is scary is that [Powell's] from Tennessee. [. . .] This just goes to show you that geniuses come in all sizes and shapes—and places."

The logic here is that somehow the very *grounds* of Tennessee shape Powell and his creation, infusing it with a high level of abstracted southernness. Literal southern ground and a forceful, inescapable ethos find themselves wedded in a deep layer of authenticity that functions to anchor the otherwise blatantly fictitious setting and population of the comic. The result may well even be so abstract that applying the term "southern" to a collection of guiding attitudes, sensibilities, and spaces seems too constrictive (one could of course just as well tag this abstract force "Appalachian"). Without falling prey to the constrictiveness of that label, it seems, however, appropriate to perceive a kind of strategic intersecting in which abstractions of southernness, which may well resemble abstractions of Americanness, function in unique if fluid ways. In a comic so invested in postmodern repetition, there is no reason to see this underlying ground of authenticity as rigidly or naively conceived. Rather, it is as if Powell replicates within the panels as well as in the space outside those panels and that of the comic's production the kind of self-other abstract projectioning that Scott McCloud argues is central to cartoon images in comics. McCloud asserts that the more abstract the drawing of a face, the more the reader identifies with, blends into, projects upon, and strategically interfaces in relation to it: "The comics creator asks us to join in a silent dance of the seen and the unseen. The visible and the invisible. This dance is unique to comics. No other artform gives so much to its audience while asking so much from them as well" (92). Genre and form, then, allow for the kind of southern space of performance abstractions that permeate *The Goon*, even when it seems farthest from the South.

In *The Goon*, this quasi-Lacanian exchange intersects with southern grounds and authenticity in the form of zombies. Where Kirkman's zombies bear the specific marks of the living, Powell's zombies look like monsters unmarked beyond their monstrosity. More importantly, Powell's zombies actually come from the ground: instead of being living folks bitten by zombies who die and then immediately come back to undeadness, these zombies are dead and buried people resurrected by the Zombie Priest. In the same way that the ground yields these marauding creatures, it also brings forth concepts of southernness. But where the older autochthony models of southernness see the land as a static presence and force producing recognizable southern spaces and performances, Powell's ground is itself characterized by fluidity and postmodern play. Southernness is not either-or in *The Goon*: the burg can have recognizable southern elements along with many others. Powell, partly through the freedoms of visual texture that the comic form allows, thus offers arguably the most liberated as well as abstracted vision of what the South and southernness can be even as he realizes a radical incarnation of postsouthernness.

Powell's comic makes explicit what can be extrapolated from the undead generally in these texts—including the Sookie Stackhouse/*True Blood* cluster, with its vampires that sometimes go to ground. Specifically, when thinking about how the undead figure in the context of southern place and performance, the ground of the South and the poetics of autochthony it has long promoted, along with its implications of authenticity and southern identity, remain undying persistent monsters. These monsters have many heads, from marketing to creative self-fashioning, and we can find in these texts of popular culture that negotiate both the specific and generic, the southern and nonsouthern, the persistently undead and indestructible grounds of southern authentification. It could well be argued that the things these undead monsters expose should be destroyed with a bullet to the head, a hatchet in the brain, or a stake through the heart. At the same time, though, southern ground conceived as an actant also provides the kinds of liberating energies that can imagine new Souths, themselves predicated on undead foundations but with much promise for the living. It is a striking thing that the United States' consumer appetite for the southern undead in media remains strong, suggesting that the nation's region (as Leigh Anne Duck has described it) continues to be a gauge for reading national desires. These textual clusters are continuing as strong elements in popular culture, showing little sign of abating. Ultimately, the undead South of popular media production can well be read as a mirror-gazing undead United States, horrified by its own abjection, in the Kristevan sense, and thrilled by not just the persistence but the refashioning of its cherished other. Most fascinating, and unsettling, is the seeming joy that attends the undeadness of the South in media and the raising of it and the southernness encoded in it to an abstraction that can be turned into an infinite number of things. In this potentially endless proliferation lies the possibility that "the South," in some form or another, chilling or thrilling as the thought is, may live forever.

NOTES

1. For a useful discussion of theoretical autochthonous and postsouthern arguments, see Scott Romine's "Where Is Southern Literature? The Practice of Place in a Postsouthern Age."

2. An earlier text that anticipates the textual clusters I explore is Alan Moore's story sequence "Southern Change" and "Strange Fruit" in the comic *Swamp Thing* (1995), in which a soap opera crew prepares to film a series of episodes at an abandoned plantation. Although the stars of the show resist the stereotypes they are to portray—a slave owner, his wife, and a slave—a mysterious power from the past located in the plantation ground overtakes their bodies and has them reenacting the real-life events that occurred in the past on this actual plantation in which a cruel slave owner catches his wife in an intimate moment with a slave and skins the slave and kills other slaves who protest. In this reenactment, African Americans of multiple generations rise out of the ground and walk as sentient talking zombies to demand their freedom from the slave owner, who refuses to give them that freedom all over again. The British Moore evokes Faulkner by having Swamp Thing respond to the situation by rushing into the big house with his mossy body afire to burn it to the ground and end the cycle of African American subjugation and slavery. Qiana J. Whitted well detects the connection of undeadness and ground in Moore's story sequence, writing that the comic asks "if there is any land below the Mason-Dixon Line not touched by 'old and cherished horrors'" (203).

3. One of the challenges of writing about serial publications still in production is that they lack the kind of closure that simplifies scholarly treatment. I am choosing to focus on the initial novels, television series seasons, and comic trade volumes as most impactful for the context of this essay.

4. My repeated mention of *Gone with the Wind* gestures to its being another complicated text-film (and other popular culture productions) cluster that focuses on ground and forms of resurrection that interface in striking ways with undeadness.

5. Elvis also appears as an undead figure in the Sookie Stackhouse novels (although not in the television series), in which he was turned into a vampire just before he died and now appears as a cognitively disabled vamp named Bubba. As Bill observes, "Now you know at least some of the sighting stories are true" (C. Harris 238).

MAKING DARKNESS VISIBLE
An Afterword and an Appreciation

SUSAN V. DONALDSON

In a 1973 interview with Alice Walker, Eudora Welty reacted with quick anger when Walker asked the Mississippi writer if she had ever been called a gothic writer. "They better not call me that!" Welty declared and then admitted a bit wearily: "Yes, I have been, though. Inevitably, because I'm a Southerner. I've never had anybody call me that to my face. I've read that I'm Gothic, or I get asked by students to explain why I am" (Walker 152). By the 1970s, before the explosion of feminist theory, critical theory, and our own millennial fascination with zombies, vampires, and other denizens of the undead, the label Southern Gothic literature was something of a hoary chestnut, a relic of literary wars dating back to the early 1930s, when William Faulkner was regarded by eminent critics like Henry Nash Smith as the founder of a literary trend defined by its penchant for decay, decadence, and grotesquerie.[1] By the early 1940s, when Welty herself began publishing—and fending off the label—Southern Gothicism was generally considered a term of opprobrium and dismissal, shorthand for monolithic categorizations for the region's backwardness, violence, and injustice.

Indeed, Southern Gothic appeared to be something like a rusty metamaster narrative attempting to make sense of a regional literature obsessed with monologic histories of an ever-retreating past and with accompanying legacies of death, loss, and mourning. That particular perspective shaped the decision Anne Goodwyn Jones and I reached in the mid-1990s when we were working on our interdisciplinary essay collection on gender, race, region, and texts and decided on the title *Haunted Bodies*. The title was inspired, though, not by Edgar Allan Poe or by images of traditional southern ruins, but by the new scholarship on sexuality and gender emerging in the early 1990s and by a writer for the *New Left Review*, Maurice Godelier, who had declared in the 1980s, "Our conclusion must be that it is not sexuality which haunts society, but society which haunts the body's sexuality" (17). Godelier's pronouncement struck us as the perfect metaphor for a collection of essays demonstrating the oppressive weight of inherited and rigidly defined narratives upon social constructions of gender, race, and class in the nineteenth- and twentieth-century South. We had in mind in particular the southern rape complex that W. J. Cash denounced as the defining story of the postbellum white South—white anxieties about black autonomy articulated in paranoid scenarios of black rapists forever preying upon white women interchangeable with the white South itself. Despite the collection's focus on gender as an analytic category—terminology borrowed from historian Joan W. Scott[2]—the essays did surreptitiously borrow from the vocabulary of Southern Gothicism as a master narrative defining, among other things, the mysterious coupling of race and gender in the region, their mutual haunting as compelling as the haunting of southern bodies by inherited, time-worn narratives. Were we ultimately resorting to literary and regional clichés that tended to consolidate rather than disrupt textual conventions of individual and regional identity? Were we reenacting and reinscribing exclusions and strategies of repression that Dominick LaCapra warned the academy three decades ago almost inevitably results from the transferential engagement all too often accompanying scholarly analysis?[3] Were all the clichés of Southern Gothicism—haunted houses, secret histories, incarceration, uncanny revelations—reemerging in our own critical discourse like revenants from nearly forgotten critical arguments from the past?

One of the contributors to our collection, Patricia Yaeger, who sadly passed away in the summer of 2014, suspected as much, or at least seemed to hint as much in her essay, "Beyond the Hummingbird: Southern Women Writers and the Gargantua," which pointed the way to her brilliant monograph *Dirt and Desire: Reconstructing Southern Women's Literature* (2000) and her equally brilliant postscript in a 2005 issue of *South Central Review*—"Ghosts and Shattered Bodies, or What Does It Mean to Still Be Haunted by

Southern Literature?" In "Beyond the Hummingbird," Patsy (I really can't do justice to her achievements and their personal meaning for me by referring to her impersonally as Yaeger) revives an old cliché often coupled with Southern Gothicism—the Southern Grotesque—that critics and reviewers in the mid-twentieth century often wielded to make sense of freakish, frightening, and distorted characters and representations in fiction by William Faulkner and Carson McCullers in particular. Relying on emerging scholarship on the body and in particular Peter Stallybrass and Allon White's *The Politics and Poetics of Transgression,* her essay evokes grotesque and gargantuan bodies as emblems of female rebellion against the confining ideologies and boundaries of race, gender, and class. These were issues that she would explore with wit and élan in *Dirt and Desire,* which nearly single-handedly broke southern literary studies out of its own incarcerating critical vocabulary and concerns by addressing the rhetoric of monstrosity, violence, and grotesquerie configuring the fiction of black and white southern women writers at a time when traditional definitions of race, gender, and class were slowly dissolving under the pressures of social, economic, and political change.[4]

Nowhere more so, though, was Patricia Yaeger's path-breaking reconceptualization of Southern Gothicism more on display—and more influential—than in her 2005 *South Central Review* essay, where she asks, almost as an afterthought in the title, ". . . What Does It Mean to Still Be Haunted by Southern Literature?" Building on Jacques Derrida's concept of hauntology in his 1993 volume *Spectres of Marx,* Patsy exposes the specters haunting black and white writers alike who must contend with the residue of racism in everyday life and with the difficulties of navigating what she calls "the racial repressed." These are writers, she contends, who are defined by "a refusal of the ordinary techniques of the gothic" and resort instead to everyday "acts of haunting"—to half-repressed white memories of complicity in oppression and to willed resurrections of loss and oppression shaping black memories. What these ghosts reveal, Patsy asserts, are "'ways of knowing' the different terrors that cross white and black cultures" ("Ghosts" 99, 101, 92). Accordingly, the writers with whom Patsy is concerned—Ellen Douglas, Flannery O'Connor, Alice Walker, Zora Neale Hurston, Eudora Welty, and Sarah E. Wright, among others—address hauntings in what Avery Gordon calls "the *world of common reality*" (54). Rather than resorting to gothic dramas and gothic voyeurism, they settle for the odds and ends of the everyday, and in doing so they try "to make a few of these ghosts visible"—Patsy's words about Ellen Douglas writing in the 1960s ("Ghosts" 87). From Patsy's perspective, southern women writers have both aimed lower—resorting to the everyday and the ordinary rather than the epic—and multiplied the ways those efforts can be charted. Hence in *Dirt and Desire* Patsy offers an ever-widening rubric to capture a plurality of stories inspired by ever-multiplying clusters of images—white bodies, secret black mothers, bodies as refuse, bodies of knowledge brought up short, "crossover objects" exchanged in interracial contact zones, the trauma of daily labor, and blackness confined to lists and objects (12).

Patsy's rubric, I suspect, has inspired a good many of the marvelously inventive essays making up this collection on undead Souths. Like Patsy, these essays resist and dismantle inherited master narratives about the region and its gothic legacy and pose in good postmodern fashion the possibility of multiple micronarratives splintering off from the region's boundary-bound master narrative of loss, death, and mourning. By venturing into the Caribbean, Native American studies, critical race theory, and redefinitions of horror, haunting, and affect in the aftermath of trauma, they carry on Patsy's legacy of disrupting and dynamiting the rails of the Dixie Express looming down on us still. Like Patsy, the writers of these essays—and all of us in southern cultural studies as it metamorphoses under the pressure of the transnational turn in American literary studies—still have to contend with a long tradition of imposing boundaries, limits, and rigid classifications dating back to antebellum efforts to define southern literature as the first line of slavery's defense. And like Patsy again, the writers here seek to explore and reconfigure the regional imaginary, "to make darkness visible," in the words of the volume's three capable editors, "not as an escape into an alternate reality or fantasy world, but as an unruly means of political and social confrontation." In doing so, of course, they engage in dialogue with those pioneers who have already cross-pollinated the Southern Gothic with ventures into vodou and conjure, into those "discredited" areas of knowledge that writers and scholars like Toni Morrison, Natasha Trethewey, Joan Dayan, Teresa Goddu, and LeAnn Howe—to name just a few—are already busy reclaiming and restoring for collective remembrance and re-memory, as Morrison herself would declare. But in the end, having lost Patsy as a cherished friend and colleague this past summer, I think of these essays—

daring, iconoclastic, and sophisticated—as testimony to her power and grace as a scholar and to her courage in braving the territory of the undead marking so much of the southern imaginary. These essays take up the task of confronting the undead square on—and in a spirit that Patsy herself would appreciate and applaud.

NOTES

1. See, in general, Inge, ed.
2. See, in general, J. W. Scott 28–50.
3. See LaCapra 71–94.
4. See Yaeger's "Beyond the Hummingbird: Southern Women Writers and the Southern Gargantua"; *Dirt and Desire: Reconstructing Southern Women's Writing, 1930–1990;* and "Ghosts and Shattered Bodies, or What Does It Mean to Still Be Haunted by Southern Literature?"

WORKS CITED

Abbott, Elizabeth. *Sugar: A Bittersweet History.* Toronto: Penguin, 2008.

Ackermann, Hans W., and Jeanine Gauthier. "The Ways and Nature of the Zombi." *Journal of American Folklore* 104.414 (1991): 466–94.

Adams, Jessica. "Introduction: Cirum-Caribbean Performance, Language, History." *Just Below South: Intercultural Performance in the Caribbean and the U.S. South.* Ed. Adams, Michael P. Bibler, and Cecile Accilien. Charlottesville: U of Virginia P, 2007. 1–24.

Adams, Shelby Lee. *Appalachian Legacy.* Jackson: UP of Mississippi, 1998.

Alegría, Ricardo E. "An Introduction to Taíno Culture and History." *Taíno: Pre-Columbian Art and Culture from the Caribbean.* Ed. Fatima Bercht, Estrellita Brodsky, John Alan Farmer, and Dicey Taylor. New York: El Museo del Barrio/Monacelli, 1997. 18–33.

Allen, Chadwick. *Blood Narrative: Indigenous Identity in American Indian and Maori Literary and Activist Texts.* Durham: Duke UP, 2002.

Allewaert, Monique. *Ariel's Ecology: Plantations, Personhood, and Colonialism in the American Tropics.* Minneapolis: U of Minnesota P, 2013.

Altman, Rick. *Film/Genre.* London: Palgrave Macmillan/BFI, 1999.

Anderson, Eric Gary. "On Native Ground: Indigenous Presences and Countercolonial Strategies in Southern Narratives of Captivity, Removal, and Repossession." *Southern Spaces: An Interdisciplinary Journal about Regions, Places, and Cultures of the American South and Their Global Connections.* 9 Aug. 2007.

———. "The Presence of Early Native Studies: A Response to Stephanie Fitzgerald and Hilary E. Wyss." *American Literary History* 22.2 (2010): 280–88.

———. "South to a Red Place: Contemporary American Indian Writing and the Problem of Native/Southern Studies." *Mississippi Quarterly* 60.1 (Winter/Spring 2007): 5–32.

WORKS CITED

Apel, Dora, and Shawn Michelle Smith. *Lynching Photographs*. Berkeley: U of California P, 2007.

Baichwal, Jennifer. "Synopsis." *The True Meaning of Pictures*. Mercury Films Inc. Web. 30 June 2013.

Bailey, Cornelia. *God, Dr. Buzzard, and the Bolito Man: A Saltwater Geechee Talks about Life on Sapelo Island*. With Christena Bledsoe. New York: Doubleday, 2000.

Baker, Houston. *Turning South Again: Re-Thinking Modernism /Re-reading Booker T.* Durham, N.C.: Duke UP, 2001.

Baker, Houston A., Jr., and Dana D. Nelson. Preface. *Violence, the Body and "The South."* Spec. issue of *American Literature* 73.2 (2001): 231–44.

Baldick, Chris. Introduction. *The Oxford Book of Gothic Tales*. Ed. Baldick. Oxford: Oxford UP, 1992.

Baldwin, James. *Blues for Mister Charlie*. New York: Dial, 1964.

Barad, Karen. *Meeting the University Halfway: Quantum Physics and the Entanglement of Matter and Meaning*. Durham, N.C.: Duke UP, 2007.

Baringer, Sandra K. "Brer Rabbit and His Cherokee Cousin: Moving Beyond the Appropriation Paradigm." Ed. Jonathan Brennan. *When Brer Rabbit Meets Coyote: African-Native American Literature*. Urbana: U of Illinois P, 2003. 114–38.

Barker, Deborah, and Kathryn McKee. "The Southern Imaginary." Introduction. *American Cinema and the Southern Imaginary*. Athens: U of Georgia P, 2011.

Barnes, Brooks. "Putting the Indie Back in Sundance." *New York Times* 21 January 2010.

Barrett, Faith. *To Fight Aloud Is Very Brave: American Poetry and the Civil War*. Amherst: U of Massachusetts P, 2012.

Barth, John. *The Friday Book: Essays and Other Nonfiction*. New York: Putnam, 1984.

Barthes, Roland. *Camera Lucida: Reflections on Photography*. Trans. Richard Howard. 1981. New York: Hill and Wang, 2010.

Bassett, John E., ed. *Defining Southern Literature: Perspectives and Assessments, 1831–1952*. Madison, N.J. : Fairleigh Dickinson UP, 1997.

Baudrillard, Jean. *Simulation and Simulacra*. Trans. Sheila Faria Glaser. Ann Arbor: U of Michigan P, 1995.

Bazin, André. "The Evolution of the Language of Cinema." 1950, 1952, 1955. *What Is Cinema?* Trans. Hugh Gray. Vol. 1. 1967. Berkeley: U of California P, 2005.

Beasts of the Southern Wild. Screenplay by Lucy Alibar. Dir. Behn Zeitlin. Perf. Quvenzhané Wallis and Dwight Henry. Icon, 2012. BluRay.

Beatty, Jack. *Age of Betrayal: The Triumph of Money in America, 1865–1900*. New York: Knopf, 2008.

Beck, John. *Dirty Wars: Landscape, Power and Waste in Western Literature*. Postwestern Horizons. Lincoln: U of Nebraska P, 2009.

Becker, Jane S. *Selling Tradition: Appalachia and the Construction of an American Folk, 1930–1940*. Chapel Hill: U of North Carolina P, 1998.

Beecher, Jonathan. "Echoes of Toussaint Louverture and the Haitian Revolution in Melville's 'Benito Cereno.'" *Leviathan* 9.2 (2009): 43–58.

Bell, Alden. *The Reapers Are the Angels*. New York: Holt, 2010.

Bell, David. "Anti-Idyll: Rural Horror." *Contested Countryside Cultures: Otherness, Marginalisation and Rurality*. Ed. Paul Cloke and Jo Little. London: Routledge, 1997. 94–108.

Bender, Barbara. "Time and Landscape." *Repertoires of Timekeeping in Anthropology*. Supplement to *Current Anthropology* 43 (2002): S103–12.

Benfey, Christopher. *Degas in New Orleans*. Berkeley: U of California P, 1997.

Benjamin, Jessica. *The Bonds of Love: Psychoanalysis, Feminism, and the Problem of Domination*. New York: Random House, 1988.

Bennett, Jane. *Vibrant Matter: A Political Ecology of Things*. Durham: Duke UP, 2010.

Bergland, Renée L. "Diseased States, Public Minds: Native American Ghosts in Early National Literature." *The Gothic Other: Racial and Social Constructions in the Literary Imagination*. Ed. Ruth Bienstock Anolik and Douglas L. Howard. Jefferson. N.C.: McFarland, 2004.

———. *The National Uncanny: Indian Ghosts and American Subjects*. Hanover, N.H.: Dartmouth/UP of New England, 2000.

Bernstein, Matthew. "A 'Professional Southerner' in the Hollywood Studio System: Lamar Trotti at Work, 1925–1952." *American Cinema and the Southern Imaginary*. Ed. Deborah Barker and Kathryn McKee. Athens: U of Georgia P, 2011.

Berry, K. Wesley. "The Lay of the Land in Cormac McCarthy's Appalachia." *Cormac McCarthy: New Directions*. Ed. James D. Lilley. Albuquerque: U of New Mexico P, 2002. 47–69.

Berry, Stephen, ed. *Weirding the War: Stories from the Civil War's Ragged Edges*. Athens: U of Georgia P, 2011.

Binkley, Sam. *Getting Loose: Lifestyle Consumption in the 1970s*. Durham, N.C.: Duke UP, 2007.

Bishop, Kyle William. *American Zombie Gothic*. Jefferson, N.C.: McFarland, 2010.

Blair, William A. *Cities of the Dead: Contesting the Memory of the Civil War in the South, 1865–1914*. Chapel Hill: U of North Carolina P, 2004.

Blake, Linnie. *The Wounds of Nations: Horror Cinema, Historical Trauma and National Identity*. Manchester: Manchester UP, 2008.

Blanco, María del Pilar. *Ghost-Watching American Modernity: Haunting, Landscape, and the Hemispheric Imagination*. New York: Fordham UP, 2012.

Blevins, Brooks. *Hill Folks: A History of Arkansas Ozarkers and Their Image*. Chapel Hill: U of North Carolina P, 2002.

WORKS CITED

Bolton, Joe. *The Last Nostalgia: Poems 1982–1990*. Fayetteville: U of Arkansas P, 1999.

Bone, Martyn. *The Postsouthern Sense of Place in Contemporary Fiction*. Baton Rouge: Louisiana State UP, 2005.

Bookchin, Murray. *Post-Scarcity Anarchism*. 1971. Palo Alto, Calif.: Ramparts, 1977.

Botting, Fred. *Gothic*. New York: Routledge, 1996.

Bougnoux, Daniel. *La crise de la représentation*. Paris: Découverte, 2006.

Bourdieu, Pierre. *Outline of a Theory of Practice*. Trans. Richard Nice. Cambridge: Cambridge UP, 1977.

Brodhead, Richard H. Introduction. *The Conjure Woman and Other Conjure Tales*. By Charles W. Chesnutt. Ed. Richard H. Brodhead. Durham: Duke UP, 1993. 1–26.

Brogan, Kathleen. *Cultural Haunting: Ghosts and Ethnicity in Recent American Literature*. Charlottesville: U of Virginia P, 1998.

Brooks, Peter. *The Melodramatic Imagination: Balzac, Henry James, Melodrama, and the Mode of Excess*. New Haven: Yale UP, 1976.

Buck-Morss, Susan. *Hegel, Haiti, and Universal History*. Pittsburgh: U of Pittsburgh P, 2009.

Burnham, Michelle. "Sherman Alexie's Indian Killer as Indigenous Gothic." *Phantom Past, Indigenous Presence: Native Ghosts in North American Culture and History*. Ed. Colleen E. Boyd and Coll Thrush. Lincoln: U of Nebraska P, 2011. 3–25.

Byrd, Jodi. *The Transit of Empire: Indigenous Critiques of Colonialism*. Minneapolis: U of Minnesota P, 2011.

Cabeza de Vaca, Alvar Nuñez. *Chronicle of the Narvaez Expedition*. Trans. David Frye. Ed. Ilan Stavans. Norton Critical Edition. New York: Norton, 2013.

Cable, George Washington. "Café des Exiles." *Old Creole Days*. Gretna, La.: Pelican, 2009. 85–117.

———. *The Grandissimes*. New York: Penguin, 1988.

———. "Jean-Ah Poquelin." *Old Creole Days*. Gretna, La.: Pelican, 2009. 179–209.

———. "The 'Haunted House' in Royal Street." *Strange True Stories of Louisiana*. Freeport, N.Y.: Books for Libraries Press, 1970.

Cabrera, Lydia. *Afro-Cuban Tales*. Trans. Alberto Hernandez-Chiroldes and Lauren Yoder. Lincoln: U of Nebraska P, 2004.

Caldwell, Erskine. "Kneel to the Rising Sun." 1953. *The Stories of Erskine Caldwell*. Athens: U of Georgia P, 1996. 641–64.

———. *The Stories of Erskine Caldwell*. Athens: U of Georgia P, 1996.

———. *Tobacco Road*. 1932. Athens: U of Georgia P, 1995.

Caldwell, I. S. "The Bunglers: A Narrative-Study in Five Parts." *Eugenics: A Journal of Racial Betterment* 3.6 (June 1930): 203–10; 3.7 (1930): 247–51; 3.8 (1930): 293–99; 3.9 (1930): 332–36; and 3.10 (1930): 377–83.

Canby, Vincent. Rev. of *Deliverance*. *New York Times* 31 July 1972. Web. 12 July 2013.

Cannon, Uzzie T. "Disturbing the African American Community: Defamiliarization in Randall Kenan's *Let the Dead Bury Their Dead*." *Southern Literary Journal* 42.1 (2009): 102–21.

Cantor, Steven, dir. *What Remains: The Life and Work of Sally Mann*. Zeitgeist Films, 2008. DVD.

Carter, Julian B. *The Heart of Whiteness: Normal Sexuality and Race in America, 1880–1940*. Durham, N.C.: Duke UP, 2007.

Cartwright, Keith. *Reading Africa into American Literature: Epics, Fables, and Gothic Tales*. Lexington: UP of Kentucky, 2002.

———. *Sacral Grooves, Limbo Gateways: Travels in Deep Southern Time, Circum-Caribbean Space, Afro-creole Authority*. Athens: U of Georgia P, 2013.

Casey, Edward S. "How to Get from Space to Place in a Fairly Short Stretch of Time: Phenomenological Prolegomena." *Senses of Place*. Ed. Steven Feld and Keith H. Basso. Santa Fe: School of American Research P, 1996.

Cash, W. J. *The Mind of the South*. 1941. New York: Vintage, 1991.

Casid, Jill H. *Sowing Empire: Landscape and Colonization*. Minneapolis: U of Minnesota P, 2005.

Césaire, Aimé. *The Collected Poetry*. Trans. Clayton Eshleman and Annette Smith. Berkeley: U of California P, 1983.

Chesnutt, Charles W. "Po' Sandy." 1888. *The Conjure Stories*. Ed. Robert B. Stepto and Jennifer Rae Greeson. Norton Critical Edition. New York: Norton, 2012. 14–22.

———. "Post-Bellum—Pre-Harlem." 1931. *The Conjure Stories*. 221–27.

Chinitz, David. *T. S. Eliot and the Cultural Divide*. Chicago: U of Chicago P, 2003.

Chion, Michel. *Audio-Vision: Sound on Screen*. Trans. Claudia Gorbman. New York: Columbia UP, 1994.

Cho, Frank. Introduction. *The Goon: My Murderous Childhood (and Other Grievous Yarns)*. By Eric Powell. Milwaukie, Ore.: Dark Horse, 2004. n.p.

Ciment, Michel. "Voyage au bout de la nuit." *Positif: Revue Mensuelle de Cinéma* (Oct. 1972): 64–67.

Cleman, John. *George Washington Cable Revisited*. New York: Twayne, 1996.

Clover, Carol. *Men, Women, and Chain Saws*. Princeton: Princeton UP, 1992.

Cohen, Ralph. "Genre and History." *New Literary History* 17.2 (1986): 203–18.

"Cold Ground." *True Blood: The Complete First Season*. Screenplay by Raelle Tucker. Dir. Nick Gomez. HBO, 2009.

Colebrook, Claire. "Queer Vitalism." *New Formations* 68 (Spring 2010): 77–92.

Coleman, Christopher K. *Dixie Spirits: True Tales of the Strange and Supernatural in the South*. Nashville: Cumberland House, 2008.

Colten, Craig E. *An Unnatural Metropolis*. Baton Rouge: Louisiana State UP, 2005.
Comaroff, John, and Jean Comaroff. "Alien-Nation: Zombies, Immigrants, and Millennial Capitalism." *South Atlantic Quarterly* 101.4 (2002): 779–805.
Conquergood, Dwight. *Cultural Studies: Performance Ethnography and Praxis*. Ann Arbor: U of Michigan P, 2013.
Cooppan, Vilashini. *Worlds Within: Narratives and Global Connections in Postcolonial Writing*. Stanford: Stanford UP, 2009.
Costello, Brannon, and Qiana J. Whitted. Introduction. *Comics and the U.S. South*. Ed. Costello and Whitted. Jackson: UP of Mississippi, 2012. vii–xvi.
Craig, Pamela, and Martin Fradley. "Youth, Affective Politics, and the Contemporary American Horror Film." *American Horror Film: The Genre at the Turn of the Millennium*. Ed. Steffen Hantke. Jackson: UP of Mississippi. 77–102.
Cushman, Horatio Bardwell. *History of the Choctaw, Chickasaw, and Natchez Indians*. Ed. Angie Debo. New York: Russell and Russell, 1972.
Das, Satyajit. "Dead Hand of Economics." *Naked Capitalism*. 20 Apr. 2011, www.nakedcapitalism.com/2011/04/satyajit-das-dead-hand-of-economics.html.
Davey, Monica, and Gretchen Ruethling. "After 50 Years, Emmett Till's Body Is Exhumed." *New York Times* 2 June 2005.
Davis, Thadious M. *Southscapes: Geographies of Race, Region, and Literature*. Chapel Hill: U of North Carolina P, 2011.
Dayan, Joan. *Haiti, History and the Gods*. Berkeley: U of California P, 1998.
Debo, Angie. *And Still the Waters Run: The Betrayal of the Five Civilized Tribes*. Norman: U of Oklahoma P, 1984.
Deleuze, Gilles. *The Fold: Leibniz and the Baroque*. 1988. Rev. ed. London: Continuum, 2006.
Deleuze, Gilles, and Félix Guattari. *Anti-Oedipus: Capitalism and Schizophrenia*. Minneapolis: U of Minnesota P, 1983.
Deliverance. Dir. John Boorman. Perf. Ned Beatty, Burt Reynolds, Jon Voight. Warner Bros., 1972. Warner Home Video, 2007. DVD.
Denby, David. "Thrills and Chills." Rev. of *Knight and Day* and *Winter's Bone*. *New Yorker* 5 July 2010.
Derrida, Jacques. "La difference." *Marges de la philosophie*. 1967. Paris: Éditions de Minuit, 1972.
———. *Specters of Marx: The State of the Debt, the Work of Mourning, and the New International*. Trans. Peggy Kamuf. Routledge: New York, 1994.
Devan, Sudhadra. "Cereus Magic." *New Straits Times*. 1 Sept. 2012. 7 Aug. 2013, www2.nst.com.my/nation/extras/cereus-magic-1.132911.
Dick, Bruce. "Ishmael Reed: An Interview." *Conversations with Ishmael Reed*. Ed. Bruce Dick and Amritjit Singh. Jackson: UP of Mississippi, 1995. 344–56.

Dimock, Wai Chee. "Introduction: Genres as Fields of Knowledge." *Remapping Genre.* Spec. issue of *PMLA* 122.5 (2007): 1377–88.

Diop, Birago. "Spirits." *The Negritude Poets.* Ed. Ellen Conroy Kennedy. New York: Thunder's Mouth, 1989. 152–54.

Druse, Ken. "Opening Night and Reader's Responses." *Real Dirt.* June 2009. 7 Aug. 2013, http://kendruse.typepad.com/ken_drusereal_dirt/night-blooming-cereus/.

Dubois, Laurent. *Haiti: The Aftershocks of History.* New York: Metropolitan, 2012.

Duck, Leigh Anne. *The Nation's Region: Southern Modernism, Segregation, and U.S. Nationalism.* Athens: U of Georgia P, 2006.

Durrant, Samuel. "Hosting History: Wilson Harris's Sacramental Narratives." *Jouvert* 5.1 (2000).

Dyer, Richard. *White.* London: Routledge, 1997.

Ebert, Roger. Rev. of *Deliverance. Chicago Sun-Times* 9 Oct. 1972.

Edwards, Justin D. *Gothic Passages: Racial Ambiguity and the American Gothic.* Iowa City: U of Iowa P, 2003.

Eliot, T. S. "Tradition and the Individual Talent." *The Sacred Wood: Essays on Poetry and Criticism.* 1920. By Eliot. Gloucester, U.K.: Dodo, 2009. 30–39.

———. *The Waste Land: A Facsimile and Transcript of the Original Drafts.* Ed. Valerie Eliot. New York: Harcourt Brace Jovanovich, 1971.

Ellis, Jay. *No Place for Home: Spatial Constraint and Character Flight in the Novels of Cormac McCarthy.* Studies in Major Literary Authors. New York: Routledge, 2006.

———. "On Southern Gothic Literature." *Southern Gothic Literature.* Ed. Jay Ellis. Ipswich, Mass.: Salem, 2013. xvi–xxxiv.

Ellison, Ralph. *Invisible Man.* New York: Vintage, 1995.

Faulkner, William. *Absalom, Absalom!* New York: Vintage, 1991.

———. "American Drama: Eugene O'Neill." *Mississippian* 3 Feb. 1922.

———. "American Drama: Inhibitions." Pt. 1. *Mississippian* 17 Mar. 1922.

———. "American Drama: Inhibitions." Pt. 2. *Mississippian* 24 Mar. 1922.

———. *As I Lay Dying: The Corrected Text.* New York: Vintage, 1990.

———. *Collected Stories of William Faulkner.* New York: Vintage, 2010.

———. *Go Down, Moses.* New York: Vintage, 1991.

———. "Idyll in the Desert. *Uncollected Stories of William Faulkner.* Ed. Joseph Blotner. New York: Random House, 1979.

———. *If I Forget Thee, Jerusalem [The Wild Palms].* New York: Vintage, 1990.

———. *Intruder in the Dust.* 1948. New York: Random House, 2011.

———. *Requiem for a Nun.* 1951. New York: Random House, 1975.

———. "A Rose for Emily." 1930. *Collected Stories of William Faulkner.* New York: Vintage International, 1995. 119–30

———. *Sanctuary.* New York: Cape and Smith, 1931.

---. "That Evening Sun" (1931). *Selected Short Stories.* New York: Random House, 2012. 76–98.

---. *The Uncollected Stories of William Faulkner.* New York: Vintage, 1997.

Faust, Drew Gilpin. *This Republic of Suffering: Death and the American Civil War.* New York: Random House, 2008.

Fiedler, Leslie A. *Love and Death in the American Novel.* 1966. 2nd ed. Champaign, Ill.: Dalkey Archive, 2003.

Fischer, Sibylle. *Modernity Disavowed: Haiti and the Cultures of Slavery in the Age of Revolution.* Durham, N.C.: Duke UP, 2004.

Fischer-Lichte, Erika. *Theater, Sacrifice, Ritual: Exploring Forms of Political Theater.* Abingdon, U.K.: Routledge, 2005.

Fisher, Benjamin F. "'To Shadow Forth Its Presence': Simms's Gothic Narrative Poems." *Southern Quarterly* 41.2 (2003): 60–72.

Fogelson, Raymond. *Handbook of North American Indians: Southeast.* Vol. 14. Washington, D.C.: Smithsonian Institution, 2004.

Foote, Horton. *Genius of an American Playwright.* Waco, Tex.: Baylor UP, 2004.

Foster, Gaines M. *Ghosts of the Confederacy: Defeat, the Lost Cause, and the Emergence of the New South 1865–1913.* New York: Oxford UP, 1987.

Frassanito, William A. *Antietam: The Photographic Legacy of America's Bloodiest Day.* New York: Scribner, 1978.

French, Philip. Rev. of *Winter's Bone. Observer* 18 Sept. 2010.

Freud, Sigmund. "The Uncanny" (1919). *The Uncanny.* Trans. David McLintock. London: Penguin, 2003. 121–62.

---. "The Uncanny." *Studies in Parapsychology.* Ed. Philip Rieff. New York: Collier, 1963. 19–62.

Frost, Robert. "Directive." In *The Poetry of Robert Frost: The Collected Poems.* Ed. Edward C. Lathem. New York: Holt, 1969. 377–79.

Fruscione, Joseph. "'What Is Called Savagery': Race, Visual Perception, and Bodily Contact in *Moby-Dick*." *Leviathan* 10.1 (2008): 3–24.

Fukuyama, Francis. *The End of History and the Last Man.* New York: Avon, 1992.

Galloway, Patricia. *Choctaw Genesis: 1500–1700.* Lincoln: U of Nebraska P, 1995.

Gardner, Alexander. *Gardner's Photographic Sketch-Book of the Civil War.* 1866. New York: Dover, 1959.

Gentry, Ric. "Vilmos Zsigmond: An Interview." *Post Script: Essays in Film and the Humanities* 24.1 (2004): 3–40.

Gilbert, Dave, Bob Gottlieb, and Susan Sutheim. "Consumption: Domestic Capitalism." *The New Left: A Documentary History.* Ed. Massimo Teodori, 425–37. Indianapolis: Bobbs-Merrill, 1969.

Gitlin, Todd, and Nanci Hollander. *Uptown: Poor Whites in Chicago.* New York: Harper and Row, 1970.

Glasgow, Ellen. "Heroes and Monsters." *Saturday Review of Literature* 12.1 (4 May 1935): 3–4. Rpt. in *Defining Southern Literature: Perspectives and Assessments; 1832–1952.* Ed. John E. Bassett. Fairleigh Dickinson UP, 1997. 295–306.

Gleason, William A. *Sites Unseen: Architecture, Race, and American Literature.* New York: New York UP, 2011.

Glissant, Édouard. *Faulkner, Mississippi.* Trans. Barbara Lewis and Thomas C. Spear. New York: Farrar, Straus and Giroux, 1999.

Goddard, Henry Herbert. *The Kallikak Family: A Study in the Heredity of Feeble-Mindedness.* 1912. New York: Macmillan, 1914.

Goddu, Teresa A. *Gothic America: Narrative, History, and Nation.* New York: Columbia UP, 1997.

Godelier, Maurice. "The Origins of Male Domination." *New Left Review* 127 (1981): 3–17.

Goméz, Rain C. "Gumbo Banaha Stories: Locating Louisiana Indians and Creoles in the Indigenous Diaspora of the American South." Diss. University of Oklahoma, 2014.

Gordon, Avery F. *Ghostly Matters: Haunting and the Sociological Imagination.* Minneapolis: U of Minnesota P, 1997.

Gottlieb, Robert. *Forcing the Spring: The Transformation of the American Environmental Movement.* Rev. and updated ed. Washington, D.C.: Island, 2005.

Grainge, Paul. *Monochrome Memories: Nostalgia and Style in Retro America.* Westport, Ct.: Praeger, 2002.

Grammer, John M. "A Thing against Which Time Will Not Prevail: Pastoral and History in Cormac McCarthy's South." *Perspectives on Cormac McCarthy.* Ed. Edwin T. Arnold and Dianne C. Luce. Jackson: UP of Mississippi, 1999. 29–44.

Granberry, Julian. *A Grammar and Dictionary of the Timucua Language.* Tuscaloosa: U of Alabama P, 1993.

Greeson, Jennifer. "Expropriating *The Great South* and Exporting 'Local Color': Global Hemispheric Imaginaries of the First Reconstruction." *Hemispheric American Studies.* Ed. Caroline Levander and Robert Levine. New Brunswick, N.J.: Rutgers UP, 2008. 116–39.

———. *Our South: Geographic Fantasy and the Rise of National Literature.* Cambridge: Harvard UP, 2010.

Gwin, Minrose. "Introduction: Reading History, Memory, and Forgetting." *Southern Literary Journal* 40.2 (2008): 1–10.

Gwynn, Frederick L., and Joseph L. Blotner, eds. *Faulkner in the University.* Charlottesville: U of Virginia P, 1995.

Halberstam, Judith. *Skin Shows: Gothic Horror and the Technology of Monsters*. Durham: Duke UP, 1995.
Harkins, Anthony. *Hillbilly: A Cultural History of an American Icon*. New York: Oxford UP, 2004.
Harman, Chris. *Zombie Capitalism: Global Crisis and the Relevance of Marx*. Chicago: Haymarket, 2010.
Harman, Graham. *Towards Speculative Realism: Essays and Lectures*. Ropley, U.K.: Zero, 2010.
Harrington, Michael. *The Other America: Poverty in the United States*. New York: Macmillan, 1962.
Harris, Charlaine. *Dead until Dark*. New York: Ace, 2001.
Harris, Trudier. *The Power of the Porch: The Storyteller's Craft in Zora Neale Hurston, Gloria Naylor, and Randall Kenan*. Athens: U of Georgia P, 1996.
———. *The Scary Mason-Dixon Line: African-American Writers and the South*. Baton Rouge: Louisiana State UP, 2009.
Harris, Wilson. *The Infinite Rehearsal*. Boston: Faber and Faber, 1987.
———. *Jonestown*. Boston: Faber and Faber, 1996.
———. *Palace of the Peacock*. 1960. Boston: Faber and Faber, 1998.
———. "Tradition and the West Indian Novel." *Selected Essays of Wilson Harris: The Unfinished Genesis of the Imagination*. Ed. Andrew Bundy. New York: Routledge, 1999.
Harrison, Andrew. "Ozark Mountain High." Rev. of *Winter's Bone*. *Word* (Oct. 2010): 94. 27 Jan. 2010.
Hartigan, John, Jr. *Odd Tribes: Toward a Cultural Analysis of White People*. Durham: Duke UP, 2005.
Hegel, G. W. F. *The Phenomenology of Mind*. Trans. J. B. Ballie. New York: Harper, 1967.
Heimert, Alan. "*Moby-Dick* and American Political Symbolism." *American Quarterly* 15.4 (Winter 1963): 498–534.
Henninger, Katherine. *Ordering the Façade: Photography and Contemporary Women's Writing*. Chapel Hill: U of North Carolina P, 2007.
Hewes, Henry. "A Change of Tune." *Saturday Review* 2 May 1964: 36.
Hobson, Fred C. *The Southern Writer in the Postmodern World*. Athens: U of Georgia P, 1991.
———. *Tell About the South: The Southern Rage to Explain*. Southern Literary Studies. Baton Rouge: Louisiana State UP, 1983.
Hoefer, Anthony Dyer. *Apocalypse South: Judgment, Cataclysm, and Resistance in the Regional Imaginary*. Columbus: Ohio UP, 2012.
Hoffman, Abbie. *Steal This Book*. New York: Pirate Editions/Grove, 1971.
Hogle, Jerrod. "Introduction: The Gothic in Western Culture." *The Cambridge Companion to Gothic Fiction*. Ed. Hogle. New York: Cambridge UP. 2002.

Holland, Sharon Patricia. *Raising the Dead: Readings of Death and (Black) Subjectivity.* Durham: Duke UP, 2000.

Holloway, David. *The Late Modernism of Cormac McCarthy.* Contributions to the Study of World Literature No. 115. Westport, Ct.: Greenwood, 2002.

Holloway, Karla FC. *Passed On: African American Mourning Stories.* Durham, N.C.: Duke UP, 2003.

hooks, bell. "Representing Whiteness in the Black Imagination." *Cultural Studies.* Ed. Lawrence Grossberg et al. London: Routledge, 1992. 338–42.

Horowitz, Gregg M. *Sustaining Loss: Art and Mournful Life.* Stanford: Stanford UP, 2001.

Howard, James H., and Gertrude P. Kurath. "Ponca Dances, Ceremonies, and Music." *Ethnomusicology* 3.1 (January 1959): 1–14.

Howe, LeAnne. "Author's Note." *Shell Shaker.* San Francisco: Aunt Lute, 2001.

———. "Blind Bread and the Business of Theory Making, by Embarrassed Grief." *Reasoning Together: The Native Critics Collective.* Ed. Craig Womack, Daniel Heath Justice, and Christopher B. Teuton. Norman: U of Oklahoma P, 2008. 325–39.

———. "Choctawan Aesthetics, Spirituality, and Gender Relations: An Interview with LeAnne Howe." By Kirstin L. Squint. *MELUS: Multi-Ethnic Literature of the U.S.* 35.3 (Fall 2010): 211–24.

———. "Evidence of Red." *Evidence of Red: Poems and Stories.* Ed. Janet McAdams. Earthworks Series. Cambridge, U.K.: Salt, 2005.

———. *Miko Kings: An Indian Baseball Story.* San Francisco: Aunt Lute, 2007.

———. "The Native South, Performance, and Globalized Trans-Indigeneity: A Conversation with LeAnne Howe." Interview with Kirstin L. Squint. 23 Mar. 2013.

———. *Shell Shaker.* San Francisco: Aunt Lute, 2001.

———. "The Story of America: A Tribalography." *Clearing a Path: Theorizing the Past in Native American Studies.* Ed. Nancy Shoemaker. New York: Routledge, 2002. 29–50.

Hurston, Zora Neale. *Tell My Horse.* New York: Harper Collins, 1990.

Hutchison, Coleman. *Apples and Ashes: Literature, Nationalism, and the Confederate States of America.* Athens: U of Georgia P, 2012.

———. "Surplus Patriotism: William Gilmore Simms's *War Poetry of the South* and the Afterlife of Confederate Literary Nationalism." Introduction. *War Poetry of the South.* Ed. William Gilmore Simms. Columbia: U of South Carolina P, 2013.

Hutchisson, James M. "The South." *Edgar Allan Poe in Context.* Ed. Kevin J. Hayes. New York: Cambridge UP, 2013. 13–21.

Inge, M. Thomas, ed. *William Faulkner: The Contemporary Reviews.* New York: Cambridge UP.

Ingle, Sarah. "The Terrain of Chesnutt's Conjure Tales." *The Conjure Stories.* By Charles Chestnutt. Ed. Robert B. Stepto and Jennifer Rae Greeson. Norton Critical Edition. New York: Norton, 2012. 147–64.

Inglis, David. "Putting the Undead to Work: Wade Davis, Haitian Vodou, and the Social Uses of the Zombie." *Race, Oppression and the Zombie: Essays on Cross-Cultural Appropriations of the Caribbean Tradition.* Ed. Christopher Moreman and Cory James Rushton. Jefferson, N.C.: McFarland, 2011. 42–59.

Innes, Pamela. "The Life Cycle from Birth to Death." *Choctaw Language and Culture: Chahta Anumpa.* By Maricia Haag and Henry Willis. Vol. 1. Norman: U of Oklahoma P, 2001. 245–49.

Jacobson, Matthew Frye. *Whiteness of a Different Color: European Immigrants and the Alchemy of Race.* Cambridge: Harvard UP, 1998.

James, C. L. R. *The Black Jacobins.* New York: Vintage, 1989.

———. *Mariners, Renegades, and Castaways: The Story of Herman Melville and the World We Live In.* New York: n.p., 1953.

Janney, Caroline E. *Burying the Dead but Not the Past: Ladies' Memorial Associations and the Lost Cause.* Chapel Hill: U of North Carolina P, 2008.

Jarrett, Robert L. *Cormac McCarthy.* Twayne's United States Author Series, no. 679. New York: Twayne, 1997.

"Jeff Davis Reaping the Harvest." *Harper's Weekly* 26 Oct. 1861: 688.

Jenkins, Philip. *Using Murder: The Social Construction of Serial Homicide.* Social Problems and Social Issues. New York: de Gruyter, 1994.

Johnson, Charles. "A Phenomenology of the Black Body." *Michigan Quarterly Review* 32 (Fall 1993): 590–614.

Johnson, Gerald. "The Horrible South" (1935). *Defining Southern Literature: Perspectives and Assessments; 1831–1952.* Ed. John E. Bassett. Fairleigh Dickinson UP, 1997.

Jones, Anne Goodwyn, and Susan V. Donaldson, eds. *Haunted Bodies: Gender and Southern Texts.* Charlottesville: U of Virginia P, 1997.

Kakutani, Michiko. "Gallery of the Repellent." Rev. of *Reckless Eyeballing. New York Times* 5 Apr. 1986: 12.

Kammen, Michael. *Digging Up the Dead: A History of Notable American Reburials.* Chicago: U of Chicago P, 2010.

Kanigher, Bob (story), and Sam Glanzman (art). "The Haunted Tank: The Saints Go Riding On." *DC Comics' G.I. Combat* 23:180 (July 1975): 12.

Karcher, Carolyn. *Shadow over the Promised Land: Slavery, Race and Violence in Melville's America.* Baton Rouge: Louisiana State UP, 1980.

Keeney, Bradford. *The Flying Drum: The Mojo Doctor's Guide to Creating Magic in Your Life.* New York: Atria, 2011.

Kenan, Randall. *Let the Dead Bury Their Dead.* San Diego: Harcourt Brace, 1992.

———. Personal conversation with the Wade Newhouse. 12 Nov. 2012.

———. *A Visitation of Spirits.* 1989. New York: Vintage Contemporaries, 2000.

Kidwell, Clara Sue. *The Choctaws in Oklahoma: From Tribe to Nation, 1855–1970.* Norman: U of Oklahoma P, 2007.
King, Debra Walker. *African Americans and the Culture of Pain.* Charlottesville: U of Virginia P, 2008.
Kirkman, Robert, and Tony Moore. *The Walking Dead:* Vol. 1: *Days Gone Bye.* Berkeley: Image Comics, 2008.
Kite, Elizabeth S. "The 'Pineys.'" 1913. *White Trash: The Eugenic Family Studies: 1877–1919.* Ed. Nicole Hahn Rafter. Boston: Northeastern UP, 1988. 164–84.
Klein, Gillian. *Reading into Racism: Bias in Children's Literature and Learning Materials.* London: Routledge and Kegan Paul, 1985.
Knowlton, Katie. "Alice in Wonderland for the American South." *The Stony Brook Press.* Sbpress, 20 Sept. 2009, http://sbpress.com/2009/09/alice-in-wonderland-for-the-american-south/. 10 June 2012.
Kolin, Philip C. "Haunting America: Emmett Till in Music and Song." *Southern Cultures* 15.3 (2009): 115–38.
Kordas, Ann. "New South, New Immigrants, New Women, New Zombies: The Historical Development of the Zombie in American Popular Culture." *Race, Oppression and the Zombie: Essays on Cross-Cultural Appropriations of the Caribbean Tradition.* Ed. Christopher M. Moreman and Cory James Rushton. Jefferson, N.C.: McFarland, 2011.
Kreyling, Michael. "Fee, Fie, Faux Faulkner: Parody and Postmodernism in Southern Literature." *Southern Review* 29.1 (1993): 1–15.
———. *Inventing Southern Literature.* Jackson: UP of Mississippi, 1998.
———. *The South That Wasn't There: Postsouthern Memory and History.* Baton Rouge: Louisiana State UP, 2010.
Kristeva, Julia. *Powers of Horror: An Essay on Abjection.* 1980. New York: Columbia UP, 1982.
Kuebrich, David. "Melville's Doctrine of Assumptions: The Hidden Ideology of Capitalist Production in 'Bartleby.'" *New England Quarterly* 69.3 (1996): 381–405.
Kuyk, Dirk, Jr., Betty M. Kyuk, and James Miller. "Black Culture in William Faulkner's 'That Evening Sun.'" *Journal of American Studies* 20.1 (1986): 33–50.
LaCapra, Dominick. *History & Criticism.* Ithaca, N.Y.: Cornell UP, 1985.
Langley, Lester. *The Banana Wars: United States Intervention in the Caribbean, 1898–1934.* Lanham, Md.: Rowman and Littlefield, 2001.
Larner, John P. "North American Hero? Christopher Columbus 1702–2002." *Proceedings of the American Philosophical Society* 137.1 (1993): 46–63.
Latour, Bruno. "On Actor-Network Theory: A Few Clarifications" *Soziale Welt* 47 (1996): 369–81.

———. *Resembling the Social: An Introduction to Actor-Network Theory.* Oxford: Oxford UP, 2005.

Lauro, Sarah Juliet, and Karen Embry. "A Zombie Manifesto: The Nonhuman Condition in the Era of Advanced Capitalism." *boundary 2* 35.1 (2008): 85–108.

Lee, Anthony W., and Elizabeth Young. *On Alexander Gardner's "Photographic Sketch Book of the Civil War."* Berkeley: U of California P, 2008.

Leeming, David. *James Baldwin: A Biography.* New York: Penguin, 1995.

Leonce, Helena. "Shared Memory: East Indian Immigration." 15th International Congress on Archives, August 23–29: Networking —Shared Memory (1). Ed. Erwin Gibbes, Helena Leonce, Victoria Borg O'Flaherty, and Nolda Romer-Kenepa. CARBICA.org. 2004: 1–4. 7 Nov. 2014, http://tinyurl.com/o4x2snl.

Leslie, Joshua, and Sterling Stuckey. "The Death of Benito Cereno: A Reading of Herman Melville on Slavery." *Journal of Negro History* 67 (1982): 287–301.

Lestel, Dominique. "Why Are We So Fond of Monsters?" *Comparative Critical Studies* 9.3 (2012): 259–69.

Levander, Caroline, and Robert Levine, eds. *Hemispheric American Studies.* New Brunswick, N.J.: Rutgers UP, 2008.

Lewis, Herschell Gordon, dir. *Two Thousand Maniacs!* Jacqueline Kay, Inc., 1964.

Lewis, Matthew. *The Monk.* Oxford: Oxford UP, 1998.

Lewis, Pierce. *New Orleans: The Making of an Urban Landscape.* Santa Fe: Center for American Places, 2003.

Liénard-Yeterian, Marie. "On the Gothic." *Nouvelles du sud: Hearing Voices, Reading Stories.* Ed. Liénard-Yeterian and Gérald Préher. Palaiseau: École polytechnique, 2007. 69–72.

Lindberg, Stanley B. Foreword. *The Stories of Erskine Caldwell.* 2nd ed. Athens: U of Georgia P, 1996. ix–xvii.

Linnemann, Travis. "Governing through Meth: Local Politics, Drug Control and the Drift toward Securitization." *Crime Media Culture* 9 (2012): 39–61.

Lippard, Chris. "Sundance Film Festival: Missing Fathers and Women Without Men." *Cinema Journal* 50.1 (2010): 126–30.

Love, Jeremy. *Bayou.* Vol. 1. New York: DC Comics, 2009.

———. *Bayou.* Vol. 2. New York: DC Comics, 2010.

Lowe, John. "Monkey Kings and Mojo: Postmodern Ethnic Humor in Kingston, Reed, and Vizenor." *MELUS* 21.4 (1996): 103–26.

Lowenstein, Adam. *Shocking Representation: Historical Trauma, National Cinema, and the Modern Horror Film.* New York: Columbia UP, 2005.

Lowery, Malinda Maynor. "Ghost Stories." Lumbee History: UNC's "Native American Tribal Studies" course. 8 May 2010.

———. *Lumbee Indians in the Jim Crow South: Race, Identity, & the Making of a Nation.* Chapel Hill: U of North Carolina P, 2010.

Luce, Dianne C. *Reading the World: Cormac McCarthy's Tennessee Period.* Columbia: U of South Carolina P, 2009.

Lyotard, Jean-François. *The Postmodern Condition: A Report on Knowledge.* Trans. Geoff Bennington and Brian Massumi. 1979. Minneapolis: U of Minnesota P, 1984.

Lytle, Andrew Nelson. *A Wake for the Living.* Nashville: J. S. Sanders, 1992.

MacArthur, William J., Jr. *Knoxville: Crossroads of the New South.* American Portrait Series. Tulsa: Continental Heritage P, 1982.

Macaulay, Scott. "A Daughter's Tale." Interview by Debra Granik. *Filmmaker: The Magazine of Independent Film* 18.3 (2010): 29–32, 75–76.

MacGregor, Robert M. "The Golliwog: Innocent Doll to Symbol of Racism." *Advertising and Popular Culture: Studies in Variety and Versatility.* Ed. Sammy R. Danna. Bowling Green: Bowling Green State U Popular P, 1992. 124–32.

Mackenthun, Gesa. *Fictions of the Black Atlantic in American Foundational Literature.* New York: Routledge, 2004.

Madsen, Michael. "The Uncanny Necrophile in Cormac McCarthy's *Child of God*; or, How I Learned to Understand Lester Ballard and Start Worrying." *Cormac McCarthy Journal* 9, 1 (2011): 17–27.

Malchow, H. L. *Gothic Images of Race in Nineteenth-Century Britain.* Stanford: Stanford, UP. 1996.

Malewitz, Raymond. "Regeneration through Misuse: Rugged Consumerism in Contemporary American Culture." *PMLA* 127.3 (2012): 526–41.

Mann, Sally. *What Remains.* New York: Bulfinch, 2003.

———. "Why the Civil War Still Matters to American Art." Smithsonian American Art Museum, Washington, D.C. 13 Mar. 2013. Lecture. www.youtube.com/watch?v=IN-WFjz8xL8.

Marcuse, Herbert. *One-Dimensional Man: Studies in the Ideology of Advanced Industrial Society.* Boston: Beacon, 1964.

Mark, Rebecca. "Mourning Emmett: 'One Long Expansive Moment.'" *Southern Literary Journal* 40.2 (2008): 121–37.

Martin, C. Brenden. *Tourism in the Mountain South: A Double-Edged Sword.* Knoxville: U of Tennessee P, 2007.

Marx, Karl. "The Eighteenth Brumaire of Louis Bonaparte." 1852. *The Marx-Engels Reader.* 2nd ed. Ed. Robert C. Tucker. New York: Norton, 1978. 594–617.

Matthiessen, F. O. *American Renaissance: Art and Expression in the Age of Emerson and Whitman.* New York: Oxford UP, 1941.

Mbembe, J.A. "Necropolitics." *Public Culture* 15.1 (2003): 11–40.

McAlister, Elizabeth. "Slaves, Cannibals, and Infected Hyper-Whites: The Race and Religion of Zombies." *Anthropological Quarterly* 85.2 (2012): 457–86.

McCarthy, Cormac. *All the Pretty Horses*. New York: Vintage International, 1992.

———. *Blood Meridian*. New York: Vintage International, 1992.

———. *Child of God*. New York: Vintage International, 1993.

———. *Cities of the Plain*. New York: Vintage International, 1999.

———. *The Crossing*. New York: Vintage International, 1995.

———. *The Road*. New York: Knopf, 2006.

———. *Suttree*. New York: Random House, 1979.

McClanahan, Annie. "Dead Pledges: Debt, Horror, and the Credit Crisis." *Post45: Peer Reviewed* 7 May 2012, http://post45.research.yale.edu/2012/05/dead-pledges-debt-horror-and-the-credit-crisis/.

McClintock, Pamela, and Sharon Swart. "Sundance's Roots Are Showing." *Variety* 417.11 (1–7 Feb. 2010): 6–7.

McCloud, Scott. *Understanding Comics: The Invisible Art*. New York: Harper Collins, 1993.

McCurry, Stephanie. *Confederate Reckoning: Power and Politics in the Civil War South*. Cambridge: Harvard UP, 2010.

McFadden, Bernice. *Gathering of Waters*. New York: Akashic, 2012.

McGowan, Kay Givens. "Weeping for the Lost Matriarchy." *Daughters of Mother Earth: The Wisdom of Native American Women*. Ed. Barbara Alice Mann. Native America: Yesterday and Today Series. Westport: Praeger, 2006. 59–68.

McPherson, Tara. "Revamping the South: Thoughts on Labor, Relationality, and Southern Representation." *American Cinema and the Southern Imaginary*. Ed. Deborah E. Barker and Kathryn McKee. Athens: U of Georgia P, 2011. 336–51.

Melville, Herman. "Bartleby, the Scrivener: A Story of Wall-Street." *Moby-Dick, Billy Budd, and Other Writings*. Ed. G. Thomas Tanselle et al. New York: Library of America College Editions, 2000. 639–78.

———. "The Bell-Tower." *Piazza Tales and Other Prose Pieces*. Ed. Harrison Hayford et al. Evanston: Northwestern UP and Newberry Library, 1987. 174–87.

———. *Billy Budd, Sailor*. Ed. Harrison Hayford and Merton M. Sealts. Chicago: Chicago UP, 1962.

———. *The Confidence-Man, His Masquerade*. New York, Norton, 1971.

———. *Moby-Dick*. New York: Penguin, 2003.

———. *Moby-Dick, Billy Budd, and Other Writings*. Ed. G. Thomas Tanselle et al. New York: Library of America College Editions, 2000.

———. "The Paradise of Bachelors and the Tartarus of Maids." *Piazza Tales and Other Prose Pieces*. Ed. Harrison Hayford et al. Evanston: Northwestern UP and Newberry Library, 1987. 316–35.

---. "Redburn," "White-Jacket," "Moby-Dick." Ed. G. Thomas Tanselle. New York: Library of America, 1983. 1–340.

---. "Typee," "Omoo," "Mardi." New York: Library of America, 1982.

Metress, Christopher. "'No Justice, No Peace': The Figure of Emmett Till in African American Literature." *MELUS* 28.1 (2003): 87–103.

Middleton, Jason. "The Subject of Torture: Regarding the Pain of Americans in *Hostel*." *Cinema Journal* 49.4 (2010): 1–24. Project Muse. 23 Dec. 2012, http://muse.jhu.edu/journals/cj/summary/v049/49.4.middleton.html.

Mitchell, Koritha. "James Baldwin, Performance Theorist, Sings the *Blues for Mister Charlie*." *American Quarterly* 64.1 (2012): 33–60.

Mitchell, Margaret. *Gone with the Wind*. 1936. New York: Warner, 1993.

Momaday, N. Scott. "The Man Made of Words." *Nothing but the Truth*. Ed. John L. Purdy and James Ruppert. Upper Saddle River, N.J.: Prentice Hall, 2001. 82–93.

Monteiro, George. "History, Legend, and Regional Verse in Frost's 'Directive.'" *New England Quarterly* 75.2 (June 2002): 286–94.

---. *Robert Frost and the New England Renaissance*. Lexington: UP of Kentucky, 1988.

Moon, Michael, and Collin Talley. "Life in a Shatter Zone: Debra Granik's Film *Winter's Bone*." *Southern Spaces* 6 Dec. 2010, http://southernspaces.org/2010/life-shatter-zone-debra-graniks-film-winters-bone.

Moore, Alan. "Southern Change." 1985. *Swamp Thing:* Vol. 3: *The Curse*. New York: Vertigo, 2000. 143–66.

---. "Strange Fruit." 1985. *Swamp Thing:* Vol. 3: *The Curse*. New York: Vertigo, 2000. 167–89.

Mootoo, Shani. *Cereus Blooms at Night*. New York: Grove, 1996.

Moreman, Christopher, and Cory James Rushton. Introduction. *Race, Oppression and the Zombie: Essays on Cross-Cultural Appropriations of the Caribbean Tradition*. Ed. Moreman and Rushton. Jefferson, N.C.: McFarland, 2011. 1–14.

Morrison, Toni. *Beloved*. New York: Vintage, 2004.

---. *Playing in the Dark: Whiteness and the Literary Imagination*. New York: Vintage, 1992.

---. "The Site of Memory." *What Moves at the Margin*. Ed. Carolyn C. Denard. Jackson: UP of Mississippi, 2008. 65–80.

Morton, Julia F. 1987. "Malay Apple." *NewCROP: The New Crop Resource Online Program*. Purdue University Center for New Crops and Plant Products. n.d. 7 Aug. 2013, www.hort.purdue.edu/newcrop/morton/malay_apple.html.

Morton, Timothy. *Hyperobjects: Philosophy and Ecology after the End of the World*. Minneapolis: U of Minnesota P, 2013.

Moten, Fred. "'Black Mo'nin'.'" *Loss: The Politics of Mourning*. Ed. David Eng and David Kazanjian. Berkeley: U of California P, 2003. 59–76.

Mould, Tom, ed. *Choctaw Tales*. Jackson: UP of Mississippi, 2004.
Mulvey, Laura. *Death 24x a Second: Stillness and the Moving Image*. London: Reaktion, 2006. Kindle ebook.
Murphy, Kieran M. "White Zombie." *Contemporary French and Francophone Studies* 15.1 (2011): 47–55.
Nabokov, Peter. *Where the Lightning Strikes: The Lives of American Indian Sacred Places*. New York: Viking, 2006.
Neale, Steve. "Questions of Genre." 1990. *Film and Theory: An Anthology*. Ed. Robert Stam and Toby Miller. Malden, Mass.: Blackwell, 2000. 157–78.
Night of the Living Dead. Dir. George A. Romero. Image Ten, 1968.
Nochimson, Martha P. Rev. of *Winter's Bone*. *Cineaste* 36.1 (2010): 52–54.
Nolan, Alan T. "The Anatomy of the Myth." *The Myth of the Lost Cause and Civil War History*. Ed. Gary W. Gallagher and Alan T. Nolan. Bloomington: Indiana UP, 2000. 11–34.
Norman, Brian. *Dead Women Talking: Figures of Injustice in American Literature*. Baltimore: Johns Hopkins UP, 2013.
———. "James Baldwin's Unifying Polemic: Racial Segregation, Moral Integration, and the Polarizing Figure of Emmett Till." *Emmett Till in Literary Memory and Imagination*. Ed. Harriett Pollack and Christopher Metress. Baton Rouge: Louisiana State UP, 2008. 75–97.
———. *Neo-Segregation Narratives: Jim Crow in Post-Civil Rights American Literature*. Athens: U of Georgia P, 2010.
Oates, Joyce Carol, ed. *American Gothic Tales*. New York: Plume, 1996.
Obama, Barack. "Remarks by the President in State of the Union Address." Office of the Press Secretary. The White House. 27 Jan. 2010.
O'Connor, Flannery. *Mystery and Manners: Occasional Prose*. Ed. Sally Fitzgerald and Robert Fitzgerald. New York: Farrar, Straus and Giroux, 1969.
O'Gorman, Farrell. "Joyce and Contesting Priesthoods in *Suttree* and *Blood Meridian*." *Cormac McCarthy Journal* 4 (2005): 100–117.
O'Hehir, Andrew. "*Winter's Bone*: American Film of the Year?" *Salon.com* 12 June 2010.
Oloff, Kerstin. "'Greening' The Zombie: Caribbean Gothic, World-Ecology, and Socio-Ecological Degradation." *Green Letters: Studies in Ecocriticism* 16.1 (2012): 31–45.
Packard, Vance. *The Waste Makers*. New York: McKay, 1960.
Palmer, Louis. "Bourgeois Blues: Class, Whiteness, and Southern Gothic in Early Faulkner and Caldwell." *Faulkner Journal* 22.1–2 (2006/7): 120–39.
Paravisini-Gebert, Lizabeth. "Colonial and Postcolonial Gothic: the Caribbean." *The Cambridge Companion to Gothic Fiction*. Ed. Jerrold E. Hogle. New York: Cambridge UP, 2002.
Patterson, Orlando. *Slavery and Social Death: A Comparative Study*. Cambridge: Harvard UP, 1985.

Peeples, Scott. *The Afterlife of Edgar Allan Poe.* Rochester: Camden House, 2004.

Pesantubbee, Michelene. *Choctaw Women in a Chaotic World: The Clash of Cultures in the Colonial Southeast.* Albuquerque: U of New Mexico P, 2005.

Phillips, Gyllian. "White Zombie and the Creole: William Seabrooke's The Magic Island and American Imperialism in Haiti." *Generation Zombie: Essays on the Living Dead in Modern Culture.* Ed. Stephanie Boluk and Wylie Lenz. Jefferson, N.C.: McFarland, 2011.

Pochmann, Henry A. *German Culture in America: Philosophical and Literary Influences 1600–1900.* Madison: U of Wisconsin P, 1961.

Poe, Edgar Allan. *The Complete Tales and Poems of Edgar Allan Poe.* New York: Modern Library, 1965.

———. "The Fall of the House of Usher." *Collected Works of Edgar Allan Poe. Vol. 2: Tales and Sketches, 1831–1842.* Ed. Thomas Ollive Mabbott. Cambridge: Harvard UP, 1978. 392–416.

Polk, Noel. *Faulkner's "Requiem for a Nun": A Critical Study.* Bloomington: Indiana UP, 1981.

Pollack, Harriet, and Christopher Metress, eds. *Emmett Till in Literary Memory and Imagination.* Baton Rouge: Louisiana State UP, 2008.

Povinelli, Elizabeth A. *Economies of Abandonment: Social Belonging and Endurance in Late Liberalism.* Durham: Duke UP, 2011.

Powell, Eric. *The Goon:* Vol. 1: *Nothin' but Misery.* Milwaukie, Ore.: Dark Horse, 2003.

———. *The Goon:* Vol. 2: *My Murderous Childhood (and Other Grievous Yarns).* Milwaukie, Ore.: Dark Horse, 2004.

Pratt, David. "*Squidbillies* and White Trash Stereotypes in the Corporate Postmodern South." *Appalachian Journal* 40.1–2 (2012/2013): 94–110.

Punter, David. *The Literature of Terror: A History of Gothic Fictions from 1765 to the Present Day.* New York: Longman, 1996.

Purak, Ichha. "Epiphyllum oxypetalum (Brahmakamal): Orchid Cactus—An Interesting Plant." *Indian Botanists Blog-o-Journal: Interdisciplinary Plant Sciences Blog Cum Journal* 24 Apr. 2013. 7 Aug. 2013, www.indianbotanists.com/2013/04/epiphyllum-oxypetallum-brahmakamal.html.

Rash, Ron. *Burning Bright.* New York: Ecco, 2010.

Reding, Nick. *Methland: The Death and Life of an American Small Town.* New York: Bloomsbury, 2009. Kindle ebook.

Reed, Ishmael. *Reckless Eyeballing.* New York: St. Martin's, 1986.

Reed, John S, and Dale V. Reed. *1001 Things Everyone Should Know about the South.* New York: Doubleday, 1996.

Regis, Helen A. *Caribbean and Southern: Transnational Perspectives on the U.S. South.* Athens: U of Georgia P, 2006.

Renda, Mary. *Taking Haiti: Military Occupation and the Cultures of U.S. Imperialism 1915–1940*. Chapel Hill: U of North Carolina P, 2000.

Rhodes, Gary Don. *White Zombie: Anatomy of a Horror Film*. Jefferson, N.C.: McFarland, 2001.

Rice, Anne. *Interview with the Vampire*. 1976. New York: Ballantine, 1997.

Rice, Stephen. *Minding the Machine: Languages of Class in Early Industrial America*. Berkeley: U of California P, 2004.

Ridgely, J. V. *William Gilmore Simms*. New York: Twayne, 1962.

Roach, Joseph. *Cities of the Dead: Circum-Atlantic Performance*. New York: Columbia UP, 1996.

Roche, Katherine. *Portrait of Pushmataha*. 2001. Oil on canvas. Mississippi Department of Archives and History, http://mshistorynow.mdah.state.ms.us/articles/14/pushmataha-choctaw-warrior-diplomat-and-chief.

Rogin, Michael. *Subversive Genealogy: The Politics and Art of Herman Melville*. New York: Knopf, 1983.

Romero, Channette. *Activism in the American Novel: Religion and Resistance in Fiction by Women of Color*. Charlottesville: U of Virginia P, 2012.

Romine, Scott. *The Narrative Forms of Southern Community*. Baton Rouge: Louisiana State UP, 1999.

———. *The Real South: Southern Narrative in the Age of Cultural Reproduction*. Baton Rouge: Louisiana State UP, 2008.

———. "Where Is Southern Literature? The Practice of Place in a Postsouthern Age." *South to a New Place: Region, Literature, Culture*. Ed. Suzanne W. Jones and Sharon Monteith. Baton Rouge: Louisiana State UP, 2002. 23–43.

Roopnarine, Lomarsh. "East Indian Indentured Emigration to the Caribbean: Beyond the Push and Pull Model." *Caribbean Studies* 31.2. (2003): 97–134.

Rosenheim, Jeff L. *Photography and the American Civil War*. New York: Metropolitan Museum of Art; New Haven: Yale UP, 2013.

Royle, Nicholas. *The Uncanny*. New York: Routledge, 2003.

Rubin, Louis D., Jr. "The Historical Image of Modern Southern Writing." *Journal of Southern History* 22.2 (1956): 147–66.

Ruppert, James. *Mediation in Contemporary Native American Fiction*. Norman: U of Oklahoma P, 1995.

Rushdy, Ashraf. *The End of American Lynching*. New Brunswick, N.J.: Rutgers UP, 2012.

Ruttenburg, Nancy. *Democratic Personality*. Stanford: Stanford UP, 1998.

Sansay, Leonora. *Secret History; or, The Horrors of St. Domingo*. Ed. Michael J. Drexler. Buffalo, N.Y.: Broadview, 2007.

Satterwhite, Emily. "Horror in Appalachia, or, What Happens When Suburban Whites Take a *Wrong Turn*." Presentation at American Studies Association Annual Conference. Baltimore. 20 Oct. 2011.

Saunders, George. *CivilWarLand in Bad Decline*. New York: Riverhead, 1997.

Savoy, Eric. "The Face of the Tenant: A Theory of the American Gothic." *American Gothic: New Interventions in a National Narrative*. Ed. Robert K. Martin and Savoy. Iowa City: U of Iowa P, 1998. 3–19.

Schulman, Bruce J. *The Seventies: The Great Shift in American Culture, Society and Politics*. 2001. Cambridge, Mass.: Da Capo, 2002.

Scott, A. O. "Where Life Is Cold, and Kin Are Cruel." Rev. of *Winter's Bone*. *New York Times* 10 June 2010.

Scott, Joan W. *Gender and the Politics of History*. New York: Columbia UP, 1988.

Seabrook, William. *The Magic Island*. New York: Harcourt, Brace, 1929.

Sepich, John. *Notes on Blood Meridian: Revised and Expanded Edition* Austin: U of Texas P, 2008.

Sheinkin, Steve. *Lincoln's Grave Robbers*. New York: Scholastic, 2013.

Sheller, Mimi. *Consuming the Caribbean: From Arawaks to Zombies*. London: Routledge, 2003.

Shelley, Mary. *Frankenstein*. London: Vintage, 2007.

Shiel, Mark. *Italian Neorealism: Rebuilding the Cinematic City*. London: Wallflower, 2006.

Siebert, Monika Barbara. "Repugnant Aboriginality: LeAnne Howe's *Shell Shaker* and Indigenous Representation in the Age of Multiculturalism." *American Literature*. 83.1 (March 2011): 93–119.

Simms, William Gilmore, ed. *War Poetry of the South*. New York: Richardson, 1866.

Simpson, Lewis P. Introduction. *3 by 3: Masterworks of the Southern Gothic*. By Doris Betts, Mark Steadman, and Shirley Ann Grau. Atlanta: Peachtree, 1985. vii–xiv.

Smith, Jon. *Finding Purple America: The South and the Future of American Cultural Studies*. Athens: U of Georgia P, 2013.

———. "Southern Culture on the Skids: Punk, Retro, Narcissism, and the Burden of Southern History." *South to a New Place: Region, Literature, Culture*. Ed. Suzanne W. Jones and Sharon Monteith. Baton Rouge: Louisiana State UP, 2002. 76–95.

Smith, Jon, and Deborah Cohn. "Introduction: Uncanny Hybridities" *Look Away! The U.S. South in New World Studies*. Durham, N.C.: Duke UP, 2004.

Smith, Paul Chaat. *Everything You Know about Indians Is Wrong*. Minneapolis: U of Minnesota P, 2009.

Soles, Carter. "Sympathy for the Devil: The Cannibalistic Hillbilly in 1970s Rural Slasher Films." *Ecocinema Theory and Practice*. Ed. Stephen Rust, Salma Monani, and Sean Cubitt. New York: Routledge, 2013. 233–50.

Spark, Clare L. *Hunting Captain Ahab: Psychological Warfare and the Melville Revival.* Kent, Ohio: Kent State UP, 2006.

Spooner, Catherine. "Introduction: Gothic in Contemporary Popular Culture." *Gothic Studies* 9.1 (2007): 1–4.

Spurr, David. *The Rhetoric of Empire: Colonial Discourse in Journalism, Travel Writing, and Imperial Administration.* Durham: Duke UP, 1993.

Squint, Kirstin. "Choctawan Aesthetics, Spirituality, and Gender Relations: An Interview with LeAnne Howe." *Crime, Punishment, and Redemption.* Spec. issue of *MELUS* 35.3 (Fall 2010): 211–24.

Stein, Melissa. "'Nature Is the Author of Such Restrictions': Science, Ethnological Medicine, and Jim Crow." *The Folly of Jim Crow: Rethinking the Segregated South.* Ed. Stephanie Cole and Natalie J. Ring. College Station: Texas A&M UP, 2012. 124–49.

Stout, William. "Down at the End of Lonely Street." *The Goon: Nothin' but Misery.* By Eric Powell. Milwaukie, Ore: Dark Horse, 2003.

Strangers and Kin: A History of the Hillbilly Image. Dir. Herb E. Smith. Appalshop, 1984. DVD.

Strasser, Susan. *Waste and Want: A Social History of Trash.* New York: Holt, 1999.

Stuckey, Sterling. *African Culture and Melville's Art: The Creative Process in "Benito Cereno" and "Moby Dick."* New York: Oxford UP, 2009.

Studwell, William E., and Bruce R. Schueneman. *State Songs of the United States: An Annotated Anthology.* Binghamton, U.K.: Haworth, 1997.

Sundquist, Eric J. *To Wake the Nations: Race in the Making of American Literature.* Cambridge: Harvard UP, 1993.

Swanton, John R. *Source Material for the Social and Ceremonial Life of the Choctaw Indians.* Smithsonian Institution Bureau of American Ethnology Bulletin 103. Washington, D.C.: GPO, 1931.

Sweet, Timothy. *Traces of War: Poetry, Photography, and the Crisis of the Union.* Baltimore: Johns Hopkins UP, 1990.

Tate, Alan. "Ode to the Confederate Dead." *The Fugitive Poets: Modern Southern Poetry in Perspective.* Edited by William Pratt. Nashville: J. S. Sanders, 1991. 67–69.

Taylor, L. B., Jr. *Civil War Ghosts of Virginia.* Lynchburg, Va.: Progress Printing, 1995. 71–82.

Taylor, Melanie Benson. *Reconstructing the Native South: American Indian Literature and the Lost Cause.* Athens: U of Georgia P, 2012.

Tettenborn, Éva. "'But What if I Can't Change?': Desire, Denial, and Melancholia in Randall Kenan's *A Visitation of Spirits.*" *Southern Literary Journal* 40.2 (2008): 249–66.

Thomas, Brandee A. "A River, a Past, and a People." *Gainesville [Ga.] Times* 7 Jan. 2012. Rpt. as "Famous Last Words: 'It Was Just a Movie.'" 208–11. "Signs of the Times" (compilation). *Appalachian Journal* 39.3–4 (2012): 208–23.

"To Love Is to Bury." *True Blood: The Complete First Season*. Written and dir. Nancy Oliver. HBO, 2009.

Todorov, Tzvetan. *The Fantastic: A Structural Approach to a Literary Genre*. Trans. Richard Howard. Cleveland: P of Case Western Reserve U, 1973.

Toffler, Alvin. *Future Shock*. 1970. New York: Bantam, 1981.

Trefzer, Annette. *Disturbing Indians: The Archaeology of Southern Fiction*. Tuscaloosa: U Alabama P, 2007.

Trethewey, Natasha. *Native Guard*. Boston: Houghton Mifflin, 2006.

Troost, Linda. "The Undead Eighteenth Century: 2010 EC-ASECS Presidential Address." *Eighteenth-Century Intelligencer* (Mar. 2011): 1–11.

True Blood: The Complete First Season. Prod. Alan Ball. DVD. HBO, 2009.

True Blood: The Complete Third Season. Prod. Alan Ball. DVD. HBO, 2011.

The True Meaning of Pictures: Shelby Lee Adams' Appalachia. Dir. Jennifer Baichwal. Perf. Shelby Lee Adams. Mercury Films, 2002. Docurama/New Video Group, 2003. DVD.

Turan, Kenneth. Rev. of *Winter's Bone*. *Los Angeles Times* 11 June 2010.

Turner, Darwin. "The Dilemma of the Black Artist." *James Baldwin: A Critical Evaluation*. Ed. Therman B. O'Daniel. Washington, D.C.: Howard UP, 1977. 189–94.

Turpin, Waters E. "A Note on *Blues for Mister Charlie*." *James Baldwin: A Critical Evaluation*. Ed. Therman B. O'Daniel. Washington, D.C.: Howard UP, 1977. 195–96.

Tutuola, Amos. "*The Palm-Wine Drinkard*" and "*My Life in the Bush of Ghosts*." New York: Grove, 1984.

Twelve Southerners. *I'll Take My Stand: The South and the Agrarian Tradition*. Baton Rouge: Louisiana State UP, 1977.

Tyburski, Susan J. "'The Lingering Scent of Divinity' in *The Sunset Limited* and *The Road*." *Cormac McCarthy Journal* 6 (2008): 121–28.

Ulrich, Roberta. *American Indian Nations from Termination to Restoration, 1953–2006*. Lincoln: U of Nebraska P, 2010.

United States. Census Bureau. "Vicksburg (city), Mississippi." Washington, D.C.: U.S. Census Bureau. 6 June 2013.

Van Brussel, Hendrik. "Robots: The Sorcerer's Apprentice Broom?" *European Review* 20.3 (2012): 256–64.

Vidler, Anthony. *The Architectural Uncanny: Essays in the Modern Unhomely*. Cambridge: MIT P, 1992.

Virag, Irene. "Cereus Reigns as Queen for a Night." *Newsday* 28 May 2000: G15.

Vizenor, Gerald. *Manifest Manners: Narratives on Postindian Survivance*. Lincoln: U of Nebraska P, 1994.

Von Doviak, Scott. *Hick Flicks: The Rise and Fall of Redneck Cinema*. Jefferson, N.C.: McFarland, 2005. Kindle ebook.

Wald, Alan. "The Subaltern Speaks." *Monthly Review* 43.11 (1992): 17–29.

Wald, Priscilla. *Contagious: Cultures, Carriers, and the Outbreak Narrative*. Durham: Duke UP, 2008.

Walker, Alice. "Eudora Welty: An Interview /Summer 1973." *Conversations with Eudora Welty*. Ed. Peggy Whitman Prenshaw. New York: Washington Square/Pocket Books, 1984.

Walker, David. *David Walker's Appeal to the Coloured Citizens of the World*. University Park: Pennsylvania State UP, 2000.

The Walking Dead: The Complete First Season. Prod. Frank Darabont and Gale Ann Hurd. AMC, 2011. DVD.

Wallace, Michelle. "Female Troubles: Ishmael Reed's Tunnel Vision." *The Critical Response to Ishmael Reed*. Edited by Bruce Allen Dick. Westport, Ct.: Greenwood, 1999. 183–91.

Waller, Gregory A. *The Living and the Undead: From Stoker's "Dracula" to Romero's Dawn of the Dead*. Urbana: U of Illinois P, 1986.

Walls, David S., and John B. Stephenson, eds. *Appalachia in the Sixties: Decade of Reawakening*. Lexington: UP of Kentucky, 1972.

Watkiss, Joanne. *Gothic Contemporaries: The Haunted Text*. Cardiff: U of Wales P, 2012.

Watson, Jay. *Reading for the Body: The Recalcitrant Materiality of Southern Fiction, 1893–1985*. Athens: U of Georgia P, 2012.

Weaver, Jace. *That the People Might Live: Native American Literatures and Native American Community*. New York: Oxford UP, 1997.

Weaver, Richard M. *The Southern Essays of Richard M. Weaver*. Ed. George M. Curtis III and James J. Thompson Jr. Indianapolis: Liberty P, 1987.

———. *The Southern Tradition at Bay: A History of Postbellum Thought*. Ed. George Core and M. E. Bradford. New Rochelle: Arlington House, 1968.

Weinstock, Jeffrey A, ed. *Spectral America: Phantoms and the National Imagination*. Madison: U of Wisconsin P, 2004.

Weiser, Kimberly (Roppolo). "Back to the Blanket: Reading, Writing, and Resistance for American Indian Literary Critics." Manuscript. Native Writers' Circle of the Americas First Book Award for Prose. Forthcoming.

Welling, Bart H. "'Squeal Like a Pig': Manhood, Wilderness, and Imperialist Nostalgia in John Boorman's *Deliverance*." *Green Letters: Studies in Ecocriticism* 6.a (2005): 24–38.

Wells, Jeremy. *Romance of the White Man's Burden: Race, Empire, and the Plantation in American Literature, 1880–1936*. Nashville: Vanderbilt UP, 2011.

Wester, Maisha. "Haunting and Haunted Queerness: Randall Kenan's Re-inscription of Difference in *A Visitation of Spirits*." *Callaloo* 30.4 (2007): 1035–53.

What Remains: The Life and Work of Sally Mann. Dir. Steven Cantor. Zeitgeist Films, 2008. DVD.

White Zombie. Dir. Victor Halperin. United Artists, 1932. Film.

Whitted, Qiana J. "Of Slaves and Other Swamp Things: Black Southern History as Comic Book Horror." *Comics and the U.S. South*. Ed. Brannon Costello and Whitted. Jackson: UP of Mississippi, 2012. 187–213.

Wilding, Philip. Rev. of *Winter's Bone*. *Empire* Oct. 2010: 54. International Index to Performing Arts Full Text. 28 Dec. 2012, www.empireonline.com/reviews/reviewcomplete.asp?FID=136935.

Wilentz, Amy. "A Zombie Is a Slave Forever." *New York Times* 30 Oct. 2012.

Williams, Linda Ruth. "Blood Brothers." *Sight and Sound* 4.9 (1994): 16–19.

Williams, Tennessee. Afterword. 1950. *Reflections in a Golden Eye*. By Carson McCullers. 1941. New York: Mariner, 2000. 129–36.

Williamson, J. W. *Hillbillyland: What the Movies Did to the Mountains and What the Mountains Did to the Movies*. Chapel Hill: U of North Carolina P, 1995.

Wilson, Anthony. *Shadow and Shelter: The Swamp in Southern Culture*. Jackson: UP of Mississippi, 2006.

Winter's Bone. Dir. Debra Granik. Perf. Jennifer Lawrence, John Hawkes. Roadside Attractions, 2010. DVD.

Woodrell, Daniel. *Winter's Bone*. New York: Little, Brown, 2006. Kindle ebook.

Wray, Matt. *Not Quite White: White Trash and the Boundaries of Whiteness*. Durham: Duke UP, 2006.

Yaeger, Patricia. "*Beasts of the Southern Wild* and Dirty Ecology." *Southern Spaces* (13 Feb. 2013), http://southernspaces.org/2013/beasts-southern-wild-and-dirty-ecology2013.

———. "Beyond the Hummingbird: Southern Women Writers and the Southern Gargantua. *Haunted Bodies: Gender and Southern Texts*. Ed. Anne Goodwyn Jones and Susan V. Donaldson. Charlottesville: U of Virginia P, 1997.

———. *Dirt and Desire: Reconstructing Southern Women's Writing, 1930–1990*. Chicago: U of Chicago P, 2000.

———. "Ghosts and Shattered Bodies, or What Does It Mean to Still Be Haunted by Southern Literature?" *South Central Review* 22.1 (2005): 87–108.

Young, Elizabeth. *Black Frankenstein: The Making of an American Metaphor*. New York: New York UP, 2008.

Zamir, Shamoon. "An Interview with Ishmael Reed." *Conversations with Ishmael Reed*. Ed. Bruce Dick and Amritjit Singh. Jackson: UP of Mississippi, 1995. 271–302.

Zieger, Susan. "The Case of William Seabrook: *Documents*, Haiti, and the Working Dead." *modernism/modernity* 19.4 (September 2012).

Žižek, Slavoj. *The Fragile Absolute*. London: Verso, 2000. 92–98.

CONTRIBUTORS

ERIC GARY ANDERSON is associate professor of English at George Mason University, where he teaches Native and Southern Studies and directs the interdisciplinary minor in Native American and Indigenous Studies. In addition to his book, *American Indian Literature and the Southwest: Contexts and Dispositions* (1999), he has published many essays in edited volumes and scholarly journals. His most recent work includes contributions to *Critical Terms for Southern Studies*, the Cambridge *Robert Frost in Context*, and *The Oxford Handbook to the Literature of the US South*.

KEITH CARTWRIGHT teaches in the English Department at the University of North Florida. His books include *Reading Africa into American Literature* (2002) and *Sacral Grooves, Limbo Gateways: Travels in Deep Southern Time, Circum-Caribbean Space, Afro-creole Authority* (2013). He has published articles on southern and Caribbean culture and literature in journals such as *Callaloo, Yinna,* and *American Literature*, among others, and has written essays published or forthcoming in many scholarly collections.

ELSA CHARLÉTY is a Ph.D. candidate in American literature at the Sorbonne University in Paris and a Ph.D. student in the Department of Comparative Literature at Brown. Her work focuses on the representation of bodies and voices in nineteenth- and twentieth-century American literature, the literary history of gothic and horror narratives, collective trauma, memory, and loss, as well as traces of the Civil War in southern history.

CONTRIBUTORS

AMY CLUKEY is assistant professor of transnational literature in the Department of English at the University of Louisville. Her work on global modernisms has appeared or is forthcoming in the *New Hibernia Review, Modern Fiction Studies,* and *American Literature,* among other venues. Her article "Plantation Modernity: Gone with the Wind and Irish-Southern Culture" was awarded the Louis D. Rubin, Jr. Prize for the best article on southern literature published in 2013 by the Society for the Study of Southern Literature.

JAMEELA F. DALLIS is a Distinguished Teaching Fellow and Ph.D. candidate in the Department of English and Comparative Literature at the University of North Carolina at Chapel Hill. She is also a William Neal Reynolds Fellow in the Royster Society of Fellows and consulting managing editor of the *Southern Literary Journal*. Her dissertation examines the prevalence of anachronistic gothic themes and aesthetics in representations of gender, sexuality, and space in a selection of American, British, and Caribbean texts from 1959 to 2003.

SUSAN V. DONALDSON is National Endowment for the Humanities Professor at the College of William and Mary, where she has taught American literature and American studies since 1985. She is the author of *Competing Voices: The American Novel, 1865–1914* (1998), which won a *Choice* Outstanding Academic Book award, and of over fifty essays on southern literature and culture. She has coedited, with Anne Goodwyn-Jones, *Haunted Bodies: Gender and Southern Texts* (1997) and has guest-edited or coedited special issues of the *Faulkner Journal* and *Mississippi Quarterly*.

LEIGH ANNE DUCK is associate professor of English at the University of Mississippi, where she edits the journal the *Global South*. Her research concerns literary and visual representations of the U.S. South, often using comparative and transnational methodologies to analyze representations of economic and racial exploitation. She is the author of *The Nation's Region: Southern Modernism, Segregation, and U.S. Nationalism* (2006) and has published essays in the *Journal of American Folklore* and *American Literary History,* among other venues.

SUSAN EDMUNDS is professor of English at Syracuse University specializing in the fields of U.S. modernism and twentieth-century U.S. fiction. She is the author of *Out of Line: History, Psychoanalysis, and Montage in H. D.'s Long Poems* (1994) and *Grotesque Relations: Modernist Domestic Fiction and the U.S. Welfare State* (2008). She teaches graduate and undergraduate courses on U.S. modernism, the Harlem Renaissance, and the European avant-garde as well as on modern American fiction, postwar U.S. fiction, and twentieth-century U.S. immigrant fiction.

ELIZABETH RODRIGUEZ FIELDER is a Ph.D. candidate in the English Department at the University of Mississippi. Her research interests include performance and ethnic nationalist theater groups, including how the Black Arts Movement helped further globalize the U.S. South.

ELIZABETH BRADFORD FRYE is a Ph.D. candidate at the University of Texas at Austin, where she is completing a dissertation on the twentieth-century persona poem. She is also a published poet. Her most recent poetic project is a collection of ekphrastic poems on Sally Mann's photographs of the U.S. South.

BRYAN GIEMZA lives, writes, and teaches in Chapel Hill, where he is director of the University of North Carolina's Southern Historical Collection. He is the author of the literary history *Irish Catholic Writers and the Invention of the American South* (2013) and editor of *Rethinking the Irish in the American South: Beyond Rounders and Reelers* (2013). He also is an editor of *Southern Writers* (2006) and the coauthor of *Poet of the Lost Cause: A Life of Father Ryan* (2008). His new edition of E. P. O'Donnell's *The Great Big Doorstep* is forthcoming in 2015.

RAIN PRUD'HOMME C. GOMÉZ is assistant professor in humanities/English at St. Gregory's University in Oklahoma. She is the former Sutton Doctoral Fellow in Literary and Cultural Studies from the University of Oklahoma and winner of the First Book Award in poetry for *Smoked Mullet Cornbread Crawdad Memory* (2012) from Native Writers' Circle of the Americas. She is a Louisiana méstiza of Choctaw-Biloxi, Louisiana Creole, and Mvskoke descent. Her creative and critical work has appeared in *American Indian Culture and Research Journal, Southern Literary Journal,* and *SING: Indigenous Poetry of the Americas,* among other publications.

CONTRIBUTORS

TAYLOR HAGOOD is associate professor of American literature at Florida Atlantic University. His publications include *Faulkner's Imperialism: Space, Place, and the Materiality of Myth* (2008); *Secrecy, Magic, and the One-Act Plays of Harlem Renaissance Women Writers* (2010); and *Faulkner, Writer of Disability* (2014). He also edited *Critical Insights: The Sound and the Fury* (2014). His essays have appeared in *African American Review, European Journal of American Studies*, and other journals.

SARAH HIRSCH recently completed an appointment as Research Fellow for the Interdisciplinary Humanities Center at UC Santa Barbara, where she is currently a full-time lecturer for the writing program. Her field is nineteenth-century and early-twentieth-century American literature, yet her work follows an interdisciplinary model as her projects engage with maritime, transnational, and cultural studies.

COLEMAN HUTCHISON is associate professor of English at the University of Texas at Austin, where he teaches courses in nineteenth-century U.S. literature and culture, bibliography and textual studies, and poetry and poetics. He is the author of *Apples and Ashes: Literature, Nationalism, and the Confederate States of America* (2012), which offers the first literary history of the Civil War South, and the coauthor of *Writing about American Literature* (2014).

SASCHA MORRELL is lecturer in English at the University of New England, Australia. Her research and publications examine dialectics of labor dependency and racial identity in a range of nineteenth- and early-twentieth-century fictions, and she has a particular interest in symbolic appropriations of Haitian history and culture in the United States.

WADE NEWHOUSE is associate professor of English at William Peace University in Raleigh, North Carolina, where he has taught a wide range of courses on southern literature, children's literature, law and literature, and American hauntings, among other topics. He has published studies of such diverse writers as Faulkner, Evelyn Scott, Ambrose Bierce, and Neil Gaiman. He is also assistant director of Raleigh's Village Idiots, a long-standing improvisational comedy troupe that performs and teaches in the Raleigh area.

CONTRIBUTORS

BRIAN NORMAN is associate professor of English and founding director of African and African American studies at Loyola University Maryland. He works on questions of identity, belonging, justice, and the role of literature and writers in helping us ask such questions. He is the author of *Dead Women Talking: Figures of Injustice in American Literature* (2013), *Neo-Segregation Narratives: Jim Crow in Post–Civil Rights American Literature* (2010), and *The American Protest Essay and National Belonging* (2007).

KIRSTIN L. SQUINT is assistant professor of English at High Point University, where she specializes in U.S. multiethnic literatures. She has written on American Indian, African American, and Caribbean-American texts, her work appearing in journals including *MELUS, Mississippi Quarterly,* and *Studies in American Humor,* among others.

MELANIE BENSON TAYLOR is associate professor of Native American Studies at Dartmouth College. In addition to numerous articles on southern literature, film, economics, and Native American writing both in and out of the South, she is author of *Disturbing Calculations: The Economics of Identity in Postcolonial Southern Literature, 1912–2002* (2008) and *Reconstructing the Native South: American Indian Literature and the Lost Cause* (2012). In 2012, she received the John M. Manley Huntington Award for Newly Tenured Faculty at Dartmouth.

ANNETTE TREFZER is associate professor of English at the University of Mississippi, where she teaches American literature. She is the author of *Disturbing Indians: The Archaeology of Southern Fiction* (2007) and the coeditor, with Ann J. Abadie, of several volumes of critical essays on William Faulkner. She is also the coeditor, with Kathryn McKee, of "Global Contexts, Local Literatures: The New Southern Studies," a special issue of *American Literature* (2006).

DANIEL CROSS TURNER is associate professor of English at Coastal Carolina University. His scholarly publications focus on regional definition vis-à-vis national and global contexts, cultural memory, object-oriented ontology, and interactions between emergent media. He is the author of *Southern Crossings: Poetry, Memory, and the Transcultural South* (2012). His numerous essays appear in *Mosaic, Genre,* and *Mississippi Quarterly,* among other venues, as well as in edited collections.

INDEX

Abbott, Elizabeth, 227
Achebe, Chinua, 15
Adams, Jessica, 105
Adams, Shelby Lee, 174, 177, 179–80, 181
Adler, George, 67
African American studies, 4
African Americans, 6, 31, 37, 44, 65, 98, 113, 221, 252, 254–55; culture, 35n5, 218, 244; historical burdens, 28; oppression, 137, 212, 218; writing/writers, 25, 137. *See also* Afro-Christianity; Afro-creole narratives; black bodies; black insurrection; civil rights movement; colonialism: African Americans; color line; Faulkner, William: African Americans; race relations
Afro-Christianity, 103
Afro-creole narratives, 14
agrarianism, 53
Agrarians, 249, 256
Aiken, Charles S., 222n4
Alibar, Lucy, 212
Allewaert, Monique, 6
Alligator People, The (1959), 124, 125, 131
Altman, Rick, 175
amputations, 56
Anderson, Eric Gary, 196, 199
Anglo-Protestant gaze, 11
Angola Prison, 12
anti-pastoralism, 161

Apel, Dora, 136
apocalypticism, 170
Appalachia, 3, 149–50, 151, 153–55, 157, 161, 162, 174–75, 177, 179, 185, 258
Appalachian Regional Commission (1965), 154
Arabian Nights, 167, 168
Arawak-Taíno, 21
Atlanta, GA, 254, 256
Avilés, Pedro Menéndez de, 22

Baichwal, Jennifer, 174, 177, 178–79, 180, 186n4
Bailey, Cornelia, 14
Baker, Houston, 11, 199
Baldwin, James, 136, 139–40, 140–41, 142, 147n3
Ball, Alan, 253, 256
Baraka, Amiri, 14
Barker, Deborah, 135n7
Barth, John, 159
Barthes, Roland, 181
Baudrillard, Jean, 59, 250
Bayou, 3, 212, 214–20, 222n7, 13; Indigenous space/time concepts, 212, 214, 218, 220; racial politics, 218, 221
Bazin, André, 174, 177
Beasts of the Southern Wild, 211–12
Bell, David, 173
Bender, Barbara, 209
Benfey, Christopher, 80

INDEX

Bennett, Jane, 6, 8n3, 249, 250, 251
Bergland, Renée, 32, 197, 201, 210n2, 210n5, 213
Bernstein, Matthew, 127
Berry, Wesley, 154
Billings, Dwight, 180
Birth of a Nation, The, 52, 89
black bodies, 218, 247n7; containment, 109, 126; corpses, 107, 139; imprisoned, 100, 106, 107, 108
black insurrection, 124, 126
Black Moon (1975), 134
blackface, 219
Blair, William, 63n6
Blanco, María del Pilar, 26, 34
Blevins, James, 158
Blyton, Enid, 219, 222n10
bodily disposability, 139, 156, 157, 215
Boehme, Jakob, 164
Bolton, Joe, 12
Bone, Martyn, 59, 249
Bookchin, Murray: *Post-Scarcity Anarchism*, 151
Boone, Daniel, 138
Boorman, John, 173, 176. See also *Deliverance* (1972 film)
Botting, Fred, 228, 232
Bougnoux, Daniel, 119, 123n3
Brady, Mathew, 41
Brer Rabbit, 12
Bride of the Gorilla (1951), 124, 125, 127
Brodber, Erna, 14
Brodhead, Richard, 30
Brooks, Gwendolyn, 142
Brooks, Peter, 86
Brownmiller, Susan, 137
Buck-Morss, Susan, 75n6
Buffy the Vampire Slayer, 130
burial rituals, 115
Byrd, James, 147
Byrd, Jodi, 197, 214

Cable, George Washington: gothicism, 77, 81; *The Grandissimes*, 76, 77, 78, 82–83, 84–85, 86, 87n5, 87n6; New Orleans, 77–78, 79, 80, 81, 83–86; *Old Creole Days*, 77, 79, 81, 86; *Strange True Stories of Louisiana*, 77, 81, 83, 86
Cabrera, Lydia, 14, 15, 22
Caldwell, Erskine: gothicism, 113, 153, 186n5; "Kneel to the Rising Sun," 114, 118; "Saturday Afternoon," 114, 115; "Savannah River Pay Day," 114
Caldwell, I. S., 152
Camus, Albert, 102
cannibalism, 19, 20, 59, 91, 170, 171
capitalism, 15, 71, 91, 93, 95, 97, 127, 152, 157
Cartwright, Keith, 15, 217–18
Cash, W. J., 118, 123n2, 261
Casid, Jill, 226
Centers for Disease Control (CDC), 256
Césaire, Aimé, 18
Chamoiseau, Patrick, 14
Chariandy, David, 14
Cherokee Keetoowah Society, 188
Chesnutt, Charles W., 2, 35n5; conjure tales, 23, 24, 25, 31, 33–34; "The Goophered Grapevine," 32; gothicism, 27; Indigenous people's absence, 32–33, 34; "Po' Sandy," 27, 29–30, 31; Poe connections, 23–24, 25, 31–32, 33, 34; racial consciousness, 23, 25
Chinitz, David, 16
Chion, Michael, 179
Chloe, Love Is Calling You. See *The Devil's Daughter* (1934)
Cho, Frank, 258
Choctaws, 2, 94–95, 189, 194, 200, 202–4, 210, 210n10, 212, 214, 220, 222n8, 228n12, 228n14, 223n16; ancestor spirits, 197, 208–9, 210, 218, 219; corn sanctity, 187–88, 192, 195, 204; European relationships, 193, 194, 196–97; funeral rituals, 191–93, 195; removal, 196, 200, 204, 206; spatiality, 189; women, 187–89, 192, 193, 194, 203, 204
Chopin, Kate, 213
Ciment, Michel, 176
civil rights movement, 20, 59, 137, 140 141, 142

300

INDEX

Civil War, 36, 50, 112, 124; Antietam, 41, 44; battlefield photographs, 41, 42, 43, 44, 45–46, 50n3; Cold Harbor, 46; commemorations, 38; Fifty-Fourth Massachusetts Voluntary Infantry, 48, 223n16; Second Battle of Fort Wagner, 48, 219, 223n16; Siege of Charleston Harbor, 48, 58
Clover, Carol, 173, 176, 178, 184
Colbert, Stephen, 144
Colonel figure, 125
colonialism, 20, 21, 76, 77, 113, 128, 130, 152, 213, 226–27; African Americans, 6, 89, 98, 218; Indigenous peoples, 32, 97, 98, 200, 218; zombies, 129, 133, 134
color line, 23, 25, 31
Colten, Craig, 78
comic books, 2, 248, 257
Confederacy, 2, 52, 55, 58; nostalgia, 61, 251; spectral remediations, 52, 55; undeadness, 53, 54, 62–63
Confederate battle flag, 52, 215
Confederate remediations, 52, 53
consumerism, 150, 154, 155
contagion, 7, 9n4, 16, 92, 156. *See also* disease; infection
contamination, 7, 17, 91, 125, 131, 229
corpses, 1, 137, 138–39, 140, 182, 183; Civil War, 41, 56, 60–61, 63n4, 63n7; Faulkner's fiction, 89, 90, 93, 107, 112, 114, 115–16, 121; Howe's fiction, 200, 207; McCarthy's fiction, 149, 153, 155, 158; Melville's fiction, 64, 67, 69, 73, 75n12; Mootoo's fiction, 227, 233–34; rotting, 114, 115, 116
Costello, Brannon, 215, 216
creole contact knowledge, 13. *See also* Creoles
Creoles, 87n3, 132, 133, 134, 211, 213, 226. *See also* creole contact knowledge
critical race theory, 264
Cronkite, Walter, 177
cross-cultural space, 11
Cuba, 226
culture of death, 50

culture of denial, 89
Cushman, Horatio Bardwell, 191

daguerreotypes, 3
Dalrymple, James, 158
Dante, 16, 17
Darabont, Frank, 256
Daughters of the Confederacy, 39
Davis, Jefferson, 53, 60
Davis, Thadious M., 40, 214
Dawes Allotment Act, 33, 206
Dayan, Joan, 264
decadence, 114, 125, 127, 132, 261
decay, 43, 113, 114, 115, 158, 234, 261; bodies, 1, 44, 46, 53, 61, 114, 115, 192, 233; landscapes, 39, 41, 76, 79–80, 83, 100, 173, 201, 225, 230, 233
Deleuze, Gilles, 54, 89, 121
Deliverance (1972 film), 173–74, 176, 177, 178, 179, 183, 185
departure/return stories, 27, 28, 34
Derrida, Jacques, 181, 182, 249, 263
Devil's Daughter, The (1934), 124
Dickey, James, 173, 176, 178. See also *Deliverance* (1972 film)
Dimock, Wai Chee, 175, 178
Diop, Birago, 12, 13
discourse, 88, 117, 150, 153, 156, 248; colonialism, 213, 225, 226; gothicism, 101, 122, 177, 262; nostalgia, 112, 113, 115; racial, 9n4, 65, 110, 113, 117–19, 146
disease, 7, 9n4, 21, 79, 89, 93, 96–97, 187, 195. *See also* contagion; infection
dismemberment, 1, 6, 23, 24, 34n2, 46, 56, 112, 182, 194
Dixon, Thomas F., 117
Douglas, Ellen, 263, 264
Douglas, John, 158
Dracula (1931), 129, 135n6
Duck, Leigh Anne, 63n5, 186n5, 259
Dumas, Henry, 16
Durrant, Samuel, 18

Edwards, Justin D., 101
Eliot, T. S.: "Tradition and the Individual Talent," 15, 16; *The Waste Land*, 3, 15, 16, 17, 18, 28–29
Ellis, Jay, 100
Ellis, Nelsan, 254
Embry, Karen, 72
Endore, Guy, 74
escapism, 4, 117, 216
eugenics, 152, 156
Evans, Walker, 178
Everit, Jace, 254
Evers, Medgar, 140
excess, 120, 121, 122
exploitation films, 173

false/premature burial, 27, 29
Faulkner, William, 1, 2, 13, 88, 95, 98, 99n3, 99n7, 107, 112, 116, 123n1, 161, 171, 212, 213, 214, 222n4, 260n2; *Absalom, Absalom!*, 75n9, 90–92, 98, 103, 228, 230, 251; African Americans, 98, 107, 108, 118; *As I Lay Dying*, 119; corpses, 115, 116; "Elly," 120, 121; *Go Down, Moses*, 99n8, 104, 105, 106; gothicism, 101, 102, 111, 113, 115, 121, 122, 261, 263; "The Hound," 121, 122; *Light in August*, 137, 145–46; Native Americans, 94, 95, 96, 97, 98, 99n8; nostalgia, 94, 97, 117, 161; *Requiem for a Nun*, 100–104, 106, 107, 108, 109, 111; "A Rose for Emily," 115, 235n5; *Sanctuary*, 108, 109; "That Evening Sun," 100, 101, 102, 103, 104, 106, 107, 109, 110; *The Uncollected Stroies*, 95; undead, 89, 90–92, 98, 99n2; *The Wild Palms*, 92–94, 96, 99n7
Faust, Drew Gilpin, 50
fertility, 187, 192, 193
film (as genre), 1, 2, 52, 65, 175, 176
film/new media studies, 4
First Seminole War, 219, 222n14, 223n17
Fischer-Lichte, Erika, 101, 108
folklore, 11, 20, 52, 91, 218
Four Mothers Society, 188

Freud, Sigmund, 32, 34n1, 101, 181, 201, 210, 210n8
Frogs (1972), 134
Frost, Robert, 161, 163; "Directive," 163–66, 167–68, 169, 171
funeral rituals, 3, 188, 192

G. I. Combat, 57
Galbraith, J. K., 150
Galloway, Patricia, 198n4
Gardner, Alexander, 36, 37, 41, 42, 43, 44–46, 50, 50n3
gay culture, 145, 254
Gein, Ed, 158
gender and sexuality studies, 4
gendered bodies, 40
genealogies, 3, 4, 79, 84, 91, 95, 201
ghosts, 1, 3–4, 8, 14, 26, 49, 66, 75n10, 88, 112, 121, 136, 182, 199, 210n2, 210n5, 213, 263–64; in Cable's fiction, 77, 80, 82–83; in Caldwell's fiction, 113, 122; in Chesnutt's fiction, 23, 28, 34; Confederate incarnations, 52, 53–60, 62–63; in Faulkner's fiction, 90–91, 97, 98, 113, 122; in Harris's fiction, 18, 19, 20; in Howe's fiction, 197, 200–202, 205, 207, 208–9, 210; in Kenan's fiction, 236, 238, 239; in Lumbee tradition, 33, 34; in Mootoo's fiction, 230, 234; in Poe's fiction, 23, 34; in Tretheway's poetry, 38, 39, 40, 41; and victims of racial violence, 145, 146, 147
Gilmore, James, 152, 158
Glasgow, Ellen, 116, 117, 176, 177
Gleason, William, 27
Glissant, Édouard, 16
Global South (Gloso) mode, 61
Goddard, Henry Herbert, 152
Goddu, Teresa, 26, 264
Godelier, Maurice, 261
Gone with the Wind (1939 film), 40, 117, 124, 133, 252, 260n4
Goon, The, 3, 248, 256–59

INDEX

Gordon, Avery, 81, 147, 230, 234, 263
gothicism, 174, 176–77, 178, 181–82, 199, 200–201, 261–64. See also Cable, George Washington: gothicism; Caldwell, Erskine: gothicism; Chesnutt, Charles W.: gothicism; discourse: gothicism; Faulkner, William: gothicism; Kenan, Randall: gothicism; Mootoo, Shani: gothicism; Poe, Edgar Allan: gothicism
Gouge, Earnest, 15
Granik, Debra, 174, 177, 178, 184, 185
Grateful Dead, 22
Greeson, Jennifer Rae, 77, 85, 87n2, 126, 128
Grimsley, Jim, 145
grotesque, 5, 23, 48, 60, 83, 91, 100, 108, 111, 119, 134, 186n5, 219, 261, 263
Guattari, Félix, 89
Gulf Wars, 58

Haiti, 2, 71, 72, 73, 75n9, 128; in Faulkner's fiction, 90, 91, 92, 103; revolution, 72, 74, 75n6, 226; United States's military occupation, 64, 75n6, 125–26, 129–31; *White Zombie*, 89, 126–33; zombie mythology, 3, 64–65, 68, 71, 72, 74, 75n12, 135n4
Haitian-American Sugar Company, 64, 135n4
Halberstam, Judith, 238, 242
Halperin, Victor, 125
Hannah, Barry, 60
Harjo, Joy, 15, 16
Harrington, Michael, 157
Harris, Charlaine, 248, 251, 252, 253, 254, 256, 259, 260n5. See also *True Blood*
Harris, Joel Chandler, 14, 25n5
Harris, Wilson: *Jonestown*, 3, 18, 19, 20
Hawthorne, Nathanial, 213
Hayne, Paul Hamilton, 47
Hearn, Lafcadio, 85
Hegel, Georg Wilhelm Friedrich, 66, 67, 70, 75n5, 75n6
Henninger, Katherine, 38
Hentz, Caroline Lee, 117

hillbillies, 3, 173, 175, 178, 258
hillbilly horror films, 3
Hills Have Eyes, The (1977), 173
hippikat poetics, 11
historical amnesia, 39, 147
HIV/AIDS, 7
Hobson, Fred, 257
Hoefer, Anthony, 244, 246n5
Hogan, Linda, 15
Holloway, Karla, 137
Holocaust, 137
Homer, 15, 16
homosexuality, 237, 238, 240. See also gay culture
Horowitz, Tony, 254
Howe, LeAnne, 187, 197–98, 214, 254; *Miko Kings: An Indian Baseball Story*, 188, 189–91, 197, 200–201, 205–6, 208, 209–10; *Shell Shaker*, 15, 188–89, 191–97, 200–201, 202–4, 205, 206–9
Hurricane Katrina, 141, 143, 222n9
Hurston, Zora Neale, 14, 15, 71, 263
Hutchinson, Mary, 16
Hutchisson, James, 24

I Eat Your Skin (1964), 134
I Walked with a Zombie (1943), 90, 124, 130
imperialism (U.S.), 126, 127, 132, 133–34, 226
inanimacy, 5–6, 29, 31–32
Indian removal, 32, 195–96, 198n2, 200, 205–6, 213
Indigenous culture, 13, 19, 27, 204, 205, 218. See also Bayou: Indigenous space/time concepts; Chesnutt, Charles W.: Indigenous peoples absence; Choctaws; colonialism: Indigenous peoples; Faulkner, William: Native Americans; Indian removal; Howe, LeAnne; Indigenous uncanny; Native American ghosts; Native American Studies; University of North Carolina (Pembroke); Native Souths; Poe, Edgar Allan: Indigenous peoples absence

Indigenous uncanny, 201, 202
infection, 7, 55, 72, 91, 92, 95–96, 97–98. *See also* contagion; disease
infestation, 7, 92, 113, 117
Ingle, Sarah, 24, 28

Jackson, Andrew, 81
Jackson, Thomas "Stonewall," 56
James, C. L. R., 64
Janney, Caroline, 63n6
Jenkins, David B., 161
Jews, 137
Jezebel (1938), 124
Jim Crow South, 2, 9n4, 33, 126, 134, 140, 144, 145, 214
Johnson, Gerald, 116, 123n1
Johnson, James Weldon, 14
Johnson, Lyndon B., 154
Jones, Anne Goodwyn, 261
Jonestown. See Harris, Wilson
Josephs, Allen, 161
Jung, Carl, 171

Kakutani, Michiko, 138
Kammen, Michael, 138
Keeney, Bradford, 13
Kenan, Randall: gothicism, 237, 238, 239; *Let the Dead Bury Their Dead*, 136–37, 144–45, 236–38, 239–44, 245–46; "Tell Me, Tell Me," 144–45, 146, 147; *A Visitation of Spirits*, 236, 237, 238
King, Stephen, 213
Kingston, Maxine Hong, 138
Kirkman, Robert, 254–55, 256, 258. See also *Walking Dead, The* (comic); *Walking Dead, The* (television show)
Kite, Elizabeth, 152
Kordas, Ann, 64, 132
Kreyling, Michael, 54, 143–44, 146, 249, 250
Kristeva, Julia, 116, 231, 232, 235n7, 259
Kushner, Tony, 136
Kwantan, Ryan, 253

Kyuk, Betty M., 103
Kyuk, Dirk, Jr., 103

labor exploitation, 64–65, 66–67, 69, 92
Lacan, Jacques, 258
LaCapra, Dominick, 262
LaFitte, Jean, 81
LaFitte, Pierre, 81
Latour, Bruno, 249, 250, 251
Lauro, Sarah Juliet, 72
Lee, Robert E., 55
León, Ponce de, 22
Lestel, Dominique, 236, 246
Lewis, Herschel Gordon, 59, 173. See also *Two Thousand Maniacs!*
Lewis, Matthew, 227
Lewis, Pierce, 85
Liénard, Marie, 112
liminality, 127, 208, 216
Lincoln, Abraham, 63n4, 138
Lindberg, Stanley B., 117
literary exhumation, 136–37, 138–39, 141, 143, 145, 146, 147, 215
Lost Cause ethos/mythology, 2, 17–18, 54, 55–56, 58, 59, 60, 61, 63, 63n3, 63n6, 113
Louisiana Native Guard, 38
Love, Jeremy, 212, 214, 218, 221. See also *Bayou*
Lowe, John, 138
Lowell, Robert, 50
Lowenstein, Adam, 185
Lowery, Melinda Maynor, 32
Luce, Dianne, 158, 160n10
Lugosi, Bela, 89, 129, 135n6
Lumbees, 32, 33–34
lynching, 54, 105, 112, 114, 118, 136–39, 141, 146, 215, 217
Lytle, Andrew, 10, 11, 13

Mackenthun, Gesa, 70, 75n10
Mann, Sally, 36, 37, 41, 42, 43, 45, 49, 50
Marcuse, Herbert, 150, 151, 157
Martin, Trayvon, 147

INDEX

Marx, Karl, 156, 181, 182
materiality, 6, 76, 113, 116, 122, 123, 229, 237, 241
Mbembe, Achille, 197
McAlister, Elizabeth, 89, 91
McCarthy, Cormac, 2, 156, 158, 161; *Blood Meridian*, 162, 171; Border Trilogy novels, 169, 170; *Child of God*, 149–50, 153–54, 156, 159, 160n11, 162; *The Road*, 161–62, 163–70, 171; *Suttree*, 161, 162, 169
McCloud, Scott, 258
McCullers, Carson, 263
McCurry, Stephanie, 54
McFadden, Bernice, 136, 141–43, 144
McGowan, Kay Givens, 196
McGuire, Hunter, 56
McKee, Kathryn, 135n7
McPherson, Tara, 62, 253
melodrama, 77, 82, 86, 176
Melville, Herman, 3, 25, 65, 71; "Bartleby, the Scrivener: A Story of Wall Street," 71, 72; "Benito Cereno," 72–73, 74, 75n13; living dead figures, 64, 66, 68, 70–71, 72, 73; *Mardi*, 66–67, 69, 71; *Moby-Dick*, 66, 67–69, 70–71, 73, 75n10; slavery depictions, 65, 66, 68, 69
memory, 14, 22, 50n1, 83, 90, 93, 97, 143, 165, 167, 169, 231, 232, 245, 250; Confederate, 2, 36, 49, 50, 53, 112; land, 212, 214, 216, 217, 218; public, 37, 38, 48; race, 140, 141, 145, 203, 212, 215, 217; slavery, 28, 70; tribal, 95, 201, 206, 218, 221. *See also* rememory
middle class, 155, 156
Miller, James A., 103
Mitchell, Koritha, 139
Mitchell, Margaret, 117, 133. See also *Gone with the Wind*
mixed-race people, 79, 99n8, 245
mixed-race, 27
Momaday, N. Scott, 203, 210
Monster and the Girl, The (1941), 124
Monteiro, George, 166
Moonshine Mountain, 173

Mootoo, Shani: *Cereus Blooms at Night*, 224–25, 227–34, 234n1; gothicism, 225, 226, 228–29, 230, 232–33; slavery portrayal, 225–26, 227, 230
Mordden, Ethan, 145
Morgan, Patrick, 212
Morrison, Toni, 13, 25, 26, 75n10, 136, 145, 217, 235n5, 264
Moten, Fred, 137, 146, 148n10
Moyer, Stephen, 253
multiculturalism, 13, 19, 192
Mulvey, Laura, 180

Naked Jungle, The (1954), 124, 127
Narváez, Pánfilo de, 22
nationalism, 48
Native American ghosts, 32, 33
Native American studies, 4, 213, 264
Native American University of North Carolina (Pembroke), 32
Native South, 2, 8, 198, 200, 222n12
Neale, Steve, 185
necromanticism, 61
New Agriculture theories, 128
New Left, 150, 151, 152, 157, 158, 262
New Orleans, 3, 16, 76–78, 79–80, 81–86, 251
New Southern Studies, 8, 11, 88
Nordan, Lewis, 243
Norman, Brian, 136, 139, 140, 244–45, 247n6

O'Connor, Flannery, 2, 8, 99n2, 119–20, 263
Oak Ridge nuclear facility, 154
Oates, Joyce Carol, 113
Obama, Barack, 183
Oblong Box, The (1969), 134
Okri, Ben, 14

Packard, Vance, 150, 151, 157
Page, Thomas Nelson, 34–35n3, 117
Paine, Thomas, 138
Palmer, Louis, 118, 119
Paquin, Anna, 253

305

paraleptical doubling, 53
Paravisini-Gebert, Lizabeth, 227
Parchman prison, 94
Pareja, Francisco, 22
pastoralism, 39, 43, 45, 54, 145, 162–63, 168, 215, 216
patriotism, 138
Patterson, Orlando, 2, 8n1
Peeples, Scott, 24, 25, 34–35n3
performance, 11, 100, 101, 102, 104, 107
periodical print culture, 36
personal recollection, 38
perversion, 89, 91, 93, 125
Phillips, Gyllian, 129
photographs, 2, 36–38, 41–45, 50, 50n3, 140, 162, 174, 178, 179–81, 252, 257
physical deformity, 112, 114, 173
plantation horror genre, 3, 125, 127, 128, 129, 131, 134
Poe, Edgar Allan, 32, 261, 262; arabesque, 23; "The Fall of the House of Usher," 23, 27, 28–29, 30–34, 136, 201; "The Gold Bug," 24; gothicism, 2, 26; grotesque, 23; haunted houses, 27; Indigenous peoples absence, 32, 33; "The Man Who Was Used Up," 14; Old South representations, 24; race representations, 24, 25–26; Southern-ness, 25, 34–35n3; storytelling impulse, 31
pole pulling, 192, 195, 198n6
Polk, Noel, 99n7, 104
Pollard, E. A., 56
poor whites, 113, 118, 149–50, 151–59
possession/dispossession, 27
posthumanist thought, 6, 62
postmodernism, 138, 159, 257
postsouthernness, 54, 55, 57, 59, 248, 249, 259
poststructuralism, 249
Pound, Ezra, 16, 18
Powell, Eric, 248, 257, 258. See also *Goon, The*
Powell, Tim, 258
Pratt, David, 177
Presley, Elvis, 258, 260n5
Psycho (1960), 158

Rabbit pedagogy, 13
race relations, 9n4, 74–75n3, 91, 138, 143, 216, 227, 254; capitalism, 89, 91; class, 118, 184, 262, 263; in Faulkner's fiction, 89, 99n8, 106, 111; gender, 199, 236, 262, 263; oppression, 101, 105; racial ambiguity, 129, 134; racial anxiety, 19, 144, 212; racial identity, 23, 27, 28, 55, 62, 131, 151; racial memory, 203, 212; tensions, 52, 112, 122; trauma, 199, 214, 217; violence, 26, 54, 118. *See also* African Americans; color line; lynching
rape complex, 261
rape, 130, 131, 137, 142, 158, 192, 193, 194, 228, 232
Rash, Ron, 60, 61
reanimation, 15, 24, 30, 31–32, 34, 39, 40, 74–75n3, 89
Reconstruction, 25, 124
Reding, Nick, 184
Reed, Ishmael, 136, 137–38, 139, 142, 147n3
reemplacement, 11
reenactment, 144
rememory, 11, 217, 231, 235n6, 264
Renda, Mary, 126
repressed urges, 119, 122
Reynolds, Burt, 173
Rhys, Jean, 14, 128
Rice, Anne, 251
Roach, Joseph, 76, 101
Roche, Katherine, 220
Rolling Stones, 22
romanticized South, 113, 117, 124
Romero, Channette, 191
Romine, Scott, 5, 54, 237, 243, 246, 249, 255
Roosevelt, Franklin D., 127
Rosenberg, Ethel, 136
Rushdy, Ashraf, 146, 147

Sansay, Leonara, 226
Satterwhite, Emily, 176
Saunders, George, 59, 60
Schantz, Mark S., 50

INDEX

Schechner, Richard, 101
Schwarz-Bart, Simone, 14
Scott, Joan W., 261
Scottsboro Boys trial, 131
Seabrook, William, 64, 74
segregation, 15, 27, 112, 135, 139, 215
Selznick, David O., 133
Sepich, John, 171
serial killers, 154, 157–58
sexism, 91
sexuality, 111, 129, 130, 146, 181, 182, 145, 261
Shakespeare, William, 15
shape-shifting, 13, 14, 15, 134, 201, 207
Shaw, Robert Gould, 48
Siebert, Monika, 192
silences/silencing, 117, 122, 146
Simms, William Gilmore, 13, 50–51n5; "Morris Island," 37, 47, 48–49, 50, 51n6; *War Poetry of the South*, 36, 47
Simpson, Lewis, 177
Sitting Bull, 138
Slavery Abolition Act (1834), 227
slavery, 2, 3, 8n1, 32, 35n5, 54, 55, 63, 226, 227, 241, 242, 245, 260n2; ghosts, 199; horrors, 226, 243, 246; literary representations, 24, 28, 30, 65–66, 264. *See also* Melville, Herman: slavery depictions; memory: slavery; Mootoo, Shani: slavery portrayals
Smith, Henry Nash, 261
Smith, Jon, 11, 256
Smith, Paul Chaat, 98
So Red the Rose (1935), 124
Son of Dracula (1943), 125
Soto, Hernando de, 16, 193, 194, 198n4
Southern exceptionalism, 3, 8, 59, 62, 89, 200
Southern foodways, 203
Southern Literary Messenger, 24
Southern Literary Renaissance, 90
southern studies, 4, 8
southernness: authenticity, 54–55, 250–51, 252, 255–56, 258, 259; enforcement, 2, 3, 5; performativeness, 253, 254, 256, 257; reimaginings, 2, 3–4

Spooner, Catherine, 175
Squint, Kirstin, 214
Stallybrass, Peter, 263
stench/odor, 116, 230, 233
sterilization, 152
Stoker, Bram, 130, 133
storytelling impulse, 31–32, 241, 243, 244
Strangers and Kin: A History of the Appalachian Image, 177, 186n1
Straw Dogs (1971), 176
Strong, Jonathan, 145
Stuart, J. E. B., 55, 56, 57, 58
Suarez, Juan, 17
Sweet Honey in the Rock, 12
Sweet, Timothy, 36

Talking Dead, The, 250
Tate, Allen, 50
Taussig, Michael, 89
Taylor, Bayard, 152
Taylor, Franklin, 67
Taylor, L. B., 55, 56
Taylor, Melanie Benson, 196, 221, 222n4
Tennessee Valley Authority, 154, 162, 186n1
Tettenborn, Éva, 239
Texas Chain Saw Massacre, The (1974), 173, 176
Till, Emmett, 3, 136–38, 139–47, 215
Timucuan, 22
Tiresias figure, 16, 17
Todorov, Tzvetan, 180
Toffler, Alvin: *Future Shock*, 151, 157
Trail of Tears, 195
Trefzer, Annette, 197, 213
Tretheway, Natasha, 3, 43; *Native Guard*, 36, 37, 50; "Pilgrimage," 38, 39, 40, 41, 48
tribalography, 214
tricksters, 13
True Blood, 3, 4, 7, 62, 248, 251–52, 253–54, 256, 259
Tucker and Dale vs. Evil (2010), 177
Turner, Darwin, 140
Turtle's tales, 15, 22
Tutuola, Amos, 14

INDEX

Twain, Mark, 14, 18, 74–75n3, 81
Two Thousand Maniacs!, 3, 173

undeadness, 1–8, 12, 14, 18, 19, 23–34, 37, 42, 49, 50, 52–55, 56, 57, 61, 62–63, 64, 65, 67, 69, 70, 71, 72, 74, 77, 82, 89, 95, 97, 104, 107, 109, 111, 146, 163, 164, 174, 175, 178, 208, 229, 233, 234, 238, 243, 248–51, 252, 254, 255–56, 257, 259–60, 261, 264–65
University of Tennessee, 154
Upton, Florence Kate, 219, 222n10

Vaca, Cabeza de, 21
Vampire's Ghost, The (1945), 124
vampires, 1, 5, 7, 62, 122, 134, 251–52, 253–54, 259, 260n5, 261. See also *Dracula*; Harris, Charlaine; Stoker, Bram; *True Blood*; *The Vampire's Ghost* (1945)
Vidler, Anthony, 27, 34n2
Vietnam War, 57
Virgil, 16
Vizenor, Gerald, 138, 198n7
vodou/voodoo, 103, 104, 107, 252
Voight, Jon, 173

Wald, Priscilla, 7
Walker, Alice, 261, 263
Walker, David, 65
Walking Dead The (comic), 248, 254–55, 258
Walking Dead, The (television show), 3, 4, 7, 248, 250, 254–55, 256, 258
Wallace, Michele, 138
Waller, Gregory A., 255
Walpole, Horace, 227
waste/wastefulness, 151, 153, 154–57, 158, 159
Watson, Jay, 17
Weaver, Richard, 249

Weinstock, Jeffrey, 205
Weiser, Kimberly (Roppolo), 212
Wells, Jeremy, 126
Welty, Eudora, 230, 235n5, 261, 263
Wester, Maisha, 237, 247n7
white supremacy narrative, 9n4, 143, 152
White Zombie, 3, 65, 74, 89, 125–34
White, Allon, 263
Whitman, Walt, 167
Whitted, Qiana, 215, 216, 217, 218, 260n2
Williams, Linda Ruth, 173
Williams, Tennessee, 177
Winter's Bone (2010 film), 174, 177, 181–84, 186n7
Wooden, Kenneth, 158
Woodrell, Daniel, 174–75, 177, 187n6. See also *Winter's Bone* (2010 film)
World War II, 57, 183
Wray, Matt, 152
Wright, Richard, 145
Wright, Sarah E., 263

Yaeger, Patricia, 10, 11, 156, 199–200, 262–263, 264, 265

Zeitlin, Behn, 211
Žižek, Slavoj, 52
zombies, 1, 5, 13, 53, 72, 88, 89, 90–92, 93, 97–98, 99n5, 161, 236, 138, 245, 260n2, 261; apocalyptic ends, 240, 243, 244; cultural zombieism, 5, 6, 16–17; mass media portrayals, 7, 64, 65, 89–90, 99n2, 124–34, 136, 255–59; plantations, 14, 89, 99n4; zombification, 1, 67. See also Haiti: *White Zombie*; Haiti: zombie mythology; *I Walked With a Zombie* (1943); *Walking Dead, The* (comic); *Walking Dead, The* (television show)